QUESTIONS AND
INFORMATION SYSTEMS

QUESTIONS
AND
INFORMATION SYSTEMS

Edited by

Thomas W. Lauer
Eileen Peacock
Oakland University

Arthur C. Graesser
Memphis State University

Psychology Press
Taylor & Francis Group

New York London

First Published by
Lawrence Erlbaum Associates, Inc., Publishers
365 Broadway
Hillsdale, New Jersey 07642

Transferred to Digital Printing 2009 by Psychology Press
270 Madison Ave, New York NY 10016
27 Church Road, Hove, East Sussex, BN3 2FA

Library of Congress Cataloging-in-Publication Data

Questions and information systems / edited by Thomas W. Lauer, Eileen
Peacock, Arthur C. Graesser.
  p.   cm.
  Includes bibliographical references and index.
  ISBN 0-8058-1018-8. — ISBN 0-8058-1019-6 (pbk.)
  1. Human information processing.   2. Question-answering systems.
3. Questioning.   4. Artificial intelligence.   I. Lauer, Thomas
Wesley, 1944-   . II. Peacock, Eileen.   III. Graesser, Arthur C.
BF444.Q84   1992
006.3—dc20   91-19599
                                                                       CIP

Publisher's Note
The publisher has gone to great lengths to ensure the quality of this reprint
but points out that some imperfections in the original may be apparent.

Contents

Acknowledgments

In June 1990 a multidisciplinary conference on questioning and information systems was held at Oakland University in Rochester, Michigan. Most of the chapters in this book are substantially revised versions of papers presented at that conference.

Because the conference was the genesis of this book, we would like to acknowledge the groups and individuals that contributed to its success. Support was provided by: an Oakland University Meadowbrook Conference Grant, Digital Equipment Corporation, the Memphis State University Fogleman College of Business and Economics School of Accountancy, the Memphis State University Department of Psychology and the Center for Applied Psychological Research (a Center of Excellence in the state of Tennessee), Meadowbrook Hall, Oakland University School of Business Administration, and the Pontiac Division of General Motors. Special thanks go to the following individuals: Ronald M. Horwitz, Daniel N. Braunstein, Constantine Konstans, Len Zera, Georgina Peacock, Rita B. Lauer, J. Brian Peacock, and Virginia Bennett.

QUESTIONS AND
INFORMATION SYSTEMS

1 Introduction

Thomas W. Lauer
Oakland University

Arthur C. Graesser
Memphis State University

As conveyed in the title of this volume, we believe there is an intimate relationship between questions and information systems. An information system is not merely a repository of static code, which gets transformed by diverse mechanical and symbolic operations. An information system also is in the business of asking questions and answering questions. Yet questions are frequently taken for granted when information systems are studied in academic settings and built by applications developers. By making the relationship between questions and information systems more explicit, we hope to show the value of directly considering the role that questions can play in the analysis, design, and use of diverse information systems.

Information systems have proliferated in business and educational settings during the last 40 years. The utility of these systems critically depends on the adequacy of the question facilities. For example, many information systems store a staggering volume of information. An individual cannot handle all of the information that is available in the system, so the individual asks specific questions that access a very small subset of the database. The information that gets retrieved hopefully is accurate, complete, and relevant. Individuals become frustrated when they receive irrelevant information and fail to receive important information. Modern information systems have sophisticated and intelligent processing mechanisms, such as intelligent tutoring systems, expert systems, and decision support systems. The processing mechanisms are so complex that it is beyond the capacity of humans to keep track of the exact procedures that underlie decision making, reasoning, planning, and information retrieval. Individuals ask questions in order to trace the results of these processing mechanisms and to evaluate the quality of the output.

It is important to identify the conditions in which questions are relevant to the design and use of information systems. We believe that it is best to begin from the perspective of the *user* (Norman & Draper, 1986). That is, users generate questions when they interact with computer systems. For example, "help" functions, queries to large databases, and explanations generated by an expert system all involve user questions. Questions are also generated during the process of system *design*. System analysts use questioning as one method of determining the information requirements of systems. Knowledge engineers ask questions when they elicit knowledge from topic experts during the design of expert systems. When software designers build interfaces that emphasize person-computer dialogue, the designers develop a model of the users' knowledge and questions. Given that questions are essential to building high-quality information systems, it is amazing that the relationship is largely unexplored.

INFORMATION, INFORMATION SYSTEMS, AND QUESTIONS

"Information" has never been an easy construct to define. Shannon and Weaver (1962) attempted to develop a precise measure of information in terms of the selection and reduction of alternatives. Given a set of possible alternatives, the amount of information in a message is the amount of uncertainty that is removed by virtue of the message. For example, if there are 10 possible alternatives, a message that narrows the set to 2 has more information than a message that narrows the set to 5. This definition of information can be applied to questions in a straightforward manner. That is, an informative question or answer would dramatically narrow down the space of possible alternatives. Unfortunately, this definition of information has had limited value when applied to the study of cognition, perception, and information systems in the real world (Gregory, 1981; Neisser, 1967, 1976). In order to measure the amount of information in a message, it is necessary to know the number of alternatives and the likelihood that each alternative would occur. In practice, it is usually a futile exercise to compute the number of alternatives because the number is either indeterminate or delimited along arbitrary criteria.

MacKay (1969) defined information in terms of the operations that are applied to representations. He had a broad definition of representation. Representations included computer memories, properties of the physical world, and cognitive states of organisms. Information consists of any event or message that establishes or alters a representation. According to MacKay, there are three ways that information may affect representations. First, as previously discussed, information may involve the selection of an alternative from a set of alternatives. Second, information may involve construction by adding elements, dimensions, and values to a representation. Third, information may modify that validity of a representation by corroborating part of an existing representation and by refuting another part. Once again, it is easy to see the role that questions play in Mac-Kay's definition of information. Individuals ask questions when they need to augment their knowledge base and build representations. Individuals ask questions when they need to verify whether particular "facts" are true.

Information is meaningful and useful when it addresses the goals of an organism (Davis & Olson, 1985). Individuals constantly need to acquire information in order to support goal-directed behavior, problem solving, and decision making (Miller, Galanter, & Pribram, 1960). Once again, these goals and information needs are reflected in the questions that individuals ask as they complete tasks. Such questions may either be asked explicitly or be manifested implicitly by hand gestures and facial expressions. Conversely, the goals and information needs of a person are central to any mechanism that explains question generation. For example, individuals ask a comparatively large number of questions when they encounter obstacles to their goals and when they have problems explaining anomalous events in the world (Schank, 1986). One productive direction for research is to clarify how our goals and plans constrain the questions that we ask when completing tasks.

It is interesting to note that the Chinese language emphasizes the importance of questions when the concept of knowledge is expressed. The concept of knowledge is expressed as an amalgamation of learning and questioning. Specifically, the concept of knowledge has two component ideographs, as shown in Fig. 1.1. The ideograph for learning pictorially depicts a child at the steps of a temple. In ancient China, temples were used as schools. The ideograph for questioning shows an open mouth, presumably in the midst of evoking a question. The Chinese language therefore explicitly manifests the central role that questions have in the development of knowledge. Rather than being the passive accumulation of facts, knowledge comes about from actively questioning during the learning process.

An information system consists of an arrangement of technical and social elements that form a single entity. (Bostrom & Heinen, 1977) and that achieves the goals of creating, transforming, and disseminating information. It can refer to

學　**Learning**

問　**Question**

FIG. 1.1.   Chinese character for knowledge.

transaction-based reporting systems, decision support systems, database management systems, office automation systems, expert systems, as well as other types of information delivery systems. Hardware and software operate in a context that is defined within a social system. Therefore, the designers of information systems must have both organizational and technical responsibilities. They must consider the decision making and information flow within an organization. They must understand the context and goals in which the organization, groups, and individuals work. There are idiosyncratic constraints imposed by the goals and social context in an organization, so it is not feasible to design generic information systems that end up being useful (Suchman, 1987; Winograd & Flores, 1986). An organization's goals and contextual properties are reflected in the questions that get asked.

A key component in any information system lies in cooperative *dialogue* (Robertson, Zachary, & Black, 1990). The dialogue may occur between two users of a system. Alternatively, the dialogue may be between the computer and a user. Questions and answers form the heart of such dialogues. In *mixed initiative* dialogue systems, the computer both asks and answers questions; similarly, the user both asks and answers questions. In the best of all possible worlds, the participants of the dialogue would engage in a natural conversation that includes questions, answers, commands, requests, and many other types of speech acts.

We have identified many of the functions of questions in the design and use of information systems. The following functions have already been identified in this chapter.

1. To select an alternative among a set of alternatives.
2. To construct or embellish a representation.
3. To verify a fact or claim.
4. To acquire information that is needed to achieve a goal.
5. To explain an anomalous event.
6. To monitor dialogue and information exchange.
7. To extract knowledge from a topic expert.
8. To understand a complex processing mechanism.
9. To improve the design of computer software.
10. To get people to do things.

These functions underscore the pervasive role of questions in information systems.

There are yet other functions of questions. Questions can provide an alternative perspective by directing attention to different information or by reinterpreting available information. For example, a software designer might ask "How would managers as opposed to programmers react to this help facility?" instead of the typical question "How would a generic user react to this help facility?" The process of transforming a question can be illuminating. Central assumptions are re-examined, if not challenged. The questioner considers situations that deviate from normalcy. For example, if a company has enjoyed a stable economic environment for a number of years, a new perspective might emerge by asking what would happen if the economy became turbulent. A change in perspective normally triggers additional questions and insights. As a consequence, questions frequently play a critical role in complex learning (Collins, 1988).

Questions help heal physical, social, and cognitive mechanisms that break down. When such obstacles and malfunctions occur, individuals ask questions throughout the course of troubleshooting the mechanism and identifying the source of the problems. For example, when a mechanic tries to fix an automobile that will not start, the mechanic asks such questions as: "Is the battery alive?" "Does the car have gas?" "Is a fuel line clogged?"; and so forth. The selection and ordering of these questions influences the speed and likelihood of fixing the automobile.

Questions are asked when individuals evaluate information systems along different criteria. For example, a computer program can be evaluated on processing speed, ease of use, the extent to which the program meets its objectives, and so on. These questions may be articulated in an open-ended form (e.g., "What happens when the program crashes?"), the form of a quantitative scale (e.g., "How frequently does the program crash?"), or the form of a checklist. The effectiveness of software design is evaluated by asking dozens of questions that reflect design criteria.

CONTRIBUTIONS IN THIS VOLUME

The contributors to this book come from different fields. The fields represented include cognitive psychology, social psychology, psycholinguistics, artificial intelligence, engineering, management of information systems, and accounting. Some are researchers in academia whereas others are in industry. In spite of our varied backgrounds, we all share a belief in the value of studying information systems from the perspective of questions. The chapters are grouped into four general areas: (a) question generation and the analysis of information systems, (b) the use of questions in the design of computer interfaces and software, (c) answering questions in the context of large databases, and (d) the analysis of questions as a means of understanding complex decision processes.

Determining the Information Requirements of a System

Chapters 2–5 address questioning in the context of determining the information requirements of a system. There are different methods of eliciting information, both in the development of traditional information systems and in the development of expert systems. A popular method for both types of systems is a direct interview conducted by a systems analyst or a knowledge engineer. Until recently, however, the role that questioning plays in this process has not been investigated systematically.

Chapter 2.   LaFrance proposes six principles of using questioning for knowledge acquisition in expert systems. She points out that asking questions is the primary means that knowledge engineers use for extracting the knowledge of topic experts. However, this process is often complicated by a number of factors, such as the fact that the questioner (knowledge engineer) has much less knowledge about the topic than the answerer (topic expert), and the fact that knowledge engineers seriously underestimate the difficulty of knowledge elicitation. The six principles provide a new perspective about the process of eliciting knowledge from experts.

Chapter 3.   Gordon and Gill describe a general knowledge acquisition method for expert system development. The method combines a systematic querying technique with a graphical representation of the topic knowledge (called a *conceptual graph structure*). The content and gaps in the conceptual graph structure determine which questions to ask when knowledge is elicited from topic experts.

Chapter 4.   Lauer, Peacock, and Jacobs examine the relationship between analysts' questions and their ability to represent the information flows in an office system. The results of a study showed a general relationship between the number of questions asked and the correctness of the representation. Further analysis examined the relationship between the questions asked and the specific parts of the representation. Individuals ask a large number of closed-class questions (i.e., questions that produce short answers) to confirm their understanding of the features of the system. This chapter proposes a questioning strategy for use with data-flow diagrams.

Chapter 5.   Lipp, Nourse, Bostrom, and Watson describe a series of knowledge acquisition sessions that were used to develop an expert system for commercial real estate disposition. They contrast the questions asked by their experts for typical versus troublesome cases. They incorporated many of the questions in the expert system. Questions in earlier versions of the system were almost exclusively multiple choice questions. Successive versions of the expert system accommodated increasing numbers of open-class questions.

The Design of Computer Interfaces and Software

Chapters 6–9 examine the use of questions in the design of computer interfaces and software. Questions may be used as part of a design technique. For example, questions can be posed to identify potential usability problems and to provide a means of understanding user needs. The designer of the computer system frequently needs to design questioning facilities. For example, expert systems, intelligent tutoring systems, and "help" systems directly incorporate questions into the user/system dialogue. For these systems, the design of the question-asking and question-answering component of the system is a critical determinant of system quality.

Chapter 6.   Carroll and Rosson explore the relationship between questions and scenario-driven design in the context of designing a Smalltalk inspector. The authors generated questions by observing programmers performing inspection tasks with a Smalltalk inspector. They contrasted the set of questions with usability specifications to show that the specifications could not address the issues raised by the questions. Elaboration on the questions yielded a set of scenarios. These scenarios were subsequently used to guide the design process.

Chapter 7.   Mack's chapter also discusses the use of questions as part of a design methodology. One goal of the design methodology is to anticipate usability problems by raising pertinent questions. Questions are posed by the different members of the design team, each of whom will have a different point of view. For example, one may be concerned with software design whereas another may focus on implementation. Design proceeds by resolving contradictory issues raised by the questions. Mack suggests some research directions that are based on his "design as inquiry" framework.

Chapter 8.   The chapter by Lang, Graesser, Dumais, and Kilman reviews question-asking and question-answering facilities in current computer systems. Each facility and query technique is with a particular type of database. The chapter introduces a P&Q (point and query) interface that enables users to ask questions very quickly (within 2 seconds) and to receive an answer from the computer very quickly (within 2 seconds). The P&Q interface supports a mixed initiative dialogue; questions are initiated both by the user and by the computer system.

Chapter 9.   Graesser, Person, and Huber identify a set of cognitive mechanisms that generate questions. There are four major groups of mechanisms: (a) correction of knowledge deficits, (b) monitoring common ground, (c) social coordination of action, and (d) control of conversation and attention. When question generation has been studied in educational settings, researchers have surprisingly found that spontaneous question generation by students is infrequent. This presents a challenge to designers of information systems that rely on user questions. The authors discuss how their question generation mechanisms have implications for information system design.

Question Answering Applied to Large Databases

Chapters 10–12 present models of question answering that are applied to large databases. The existence of larger data stores and powerful database languages does not necessarily enable users to access precisely and conveniently the information that they desire. For example key-word searches of bibliographic databases typically yield 10% wheat and 90% chaff.The problem of retrieving the correct information exists in intelligent tutoring systems, videotex, and executive information systems as well as bibliographic databases. These chapters discuss intelligent question-answering strategies that focus the search for information when questions are answered.

Chapter 10.   Dahlgren describes a text retrieval system called Interpretext. The goal of the system is to improve text retrieval facilities in applications that include text selection, text routing, and text querying. Interpretext uses several levels of linguistic analysis to interpret and provide answers to natural language queries. The computer system adopts a cognitive model based on naive semantics.

Chapter 11.   Golding, Magliano, and Hemphill present a model of questioning about temporal information. There are few discussions in the literature regarding "when" questions. Answers to "when" questions should address the goals and plans of the questioner. Good answers may vary in grain size and accuracy depending on the context. Their WHEN model could be implemented in information systems whose subject matter includes dates, times, and appointment schedules.

Chapter 12.   Graesser, Byrne, and Behrens discuss question-answering strategies for accessing information from knowledge bases. The chapter presents a model of human question answering called QUEST. QUEST consists of four components: (a) the assignment of the question to a question category, (b) the identification of information sources relevant to the question, (c) convergence mechanisms, which identify a subset of the information in each information source as relevant answers to a question, and (d) the pragmatic features of the question (i.e., goals and common ground of the speech participants). QUEST would be implemented within information systems that produce human-like answers to questions, such as expert systems, decision support systems, and intelligent tutoring systems.

Understanding Complex Decision Processes

Chapters 13–16 explore questioning as a means of understanding complex decision processes. The majority of research on behavioral decision making has concentrated on the decision maker's evaluation of information and the subsequent judgment or choice. The importance of the initial acquisition of information has generally been understated. These chapters show that analysis of questions yields valuable insights about problem formulation, creative processes, and involvement in the solution of problems.

Chapter 13.   Lauer and Peacock examine the questions that auditors ask during the planning stage of an audit. Auditors' questions during audit diagnosis provide a means of contrasting audit diagnosis and diagnosis in other fields. Particular question types and question groupings are associated with different stages of the diagnostic process. The process recommends ways to improve knowledge acquisition for audit expert systems.

Chapter 14.   Steinbart examines whether asking users questions about the advice given by a decision aid affects the user's ability to learn from that advice. He reports two studies that explore this issue. The first examined the effects of system-generated questions on users' understanding of the explanations provided by an expert system. The second investigated the effects of alternative question types on user learning.

Chapter 15.   Paradice explores the relationship between question asking and problem formulation. He analyzed protocols of television shows that discussed some formidable problems and found that few questions are asked to help structure the problem. He offers some suggestions for computer-based support of the problem-formulation process.

Chapter 16.   Kass examines the relationship between questioning and creativity. He claims that the ability to pose useful questions is the key to creativity. Two computer systems illustrate the relationship between questioning and creativity. The ABE system (Adaptation-Based Explainer) develops hypotheses to explain novel situations by accessing and modifying previously stored explanations. The stored explanations are adjusted when the system poses hypothesis-adaptation questions. The Sounding Board system attempts to make the user more creative by asking the user questions.

ACKNOWLEDGMENT

Thanks to Wei-Hwa Chao for the calligraphy in Fig. 1.1. She was also the source of information about the significance of those ideographs.

REFERENCES

Bostrom, R. P., & Heinen, J. S. (1977). MIS problems and failures: A socio-technical perspective, *MIS Quarterly, 1,* 17–32.
Collins, A. (1988). Different goals of inquiry teaching, *Questioning Exchange, 2,* 39–46.

Davis, G. B., & Olson, M. H. (1985). *Management information systems: Conceptual foundations, structure, and development.* New York: McGraw-Hill.

Gregory, R. L. (1981). Questions of pattern and object perception in man and computer. In J. Long & A. Baddeley (Eds.), *Attention and performance* (vol. 9, pp. 97–116). Hillsdale, NJ: Lawrence Erlbaum Associates.

MacKay, D. M. (1969). *Information mechanism and meaning.* Cambridge, MA: MIT Press.

Miller, G. A., Galanter, E., & Pribram, K. H. (1960). *Plans and the structure of behavior.* New York: Holt, Rinehart, &Winston.

Neisser, U. (1967). *Cognitive psychology.* New York: Appleton-Century-Crofts.

Neisser, U. (1976). *Cognition and reality.* San Francisco: Freeman.

Norman, D. A., & Draper, S. W. (Eds.). (1986). *User centered system design: New perspectives on human-computer interaction.* Hillsdale, NJ: Lawrence Erlbaum Associates.

Robertson, S., Zachary, W., & Black, J. (Eds.). (1990). *Cognition, computing, and cooperation.* Norwood, NJ: Ablex.

Schank, R. C. (1986). *Explanation patterns: Understanding mechanically and creatively.* Hillsdale, NJ: Lawrence Erlbaum Associates.

Shannon, C., & Weaver, W. (1962). *The mathematical theory of communication.* Urbana, IL: University of Illinois Press.

Suchman, L. A. (1987). *Plans and situated actions: The problem of human/machine communication.* New York: Cambridge University Press.

Winograd, T., & Flores, F. (1986). *Understanding computers and cognition.* Reading, MA: Addison-Wesley.

2 Questioning Knowledge Acquisition

Marianne LaFrance
Boston College

Among the stories associated with the writer Gertrude Stein, there is one that is particularly apropos to a book devoted to questioning. On her deathbed, she asked, "What is the answer?" When there was no reply, she asked instead, "In that case what is the question?" This story has a number of implications for those who study the nature of questioning, including the arresting idea that questions themselves are informative, often more so than the answers supplied to them. But the story insinuates something else, namely that questions are somehow easier to formulate than answers. As it turns out, nothing could be further from the truth.

In this chapter, I focus on questioning in the context of knowledge acquisition for computer programs called expert systems. I argue first that the questions that knowledge engineers ask of experts are critical to the realization of theses systems. If the expert's domain knowledge is insufficiently explored by program developers, then the resulting knowledge-based system will be inadequate to the task of providing good advice or making informed decisions. But I also want to make the case as have others recently (Riesbeck, 1988) that question generation in artificial intelligence has been critically neglected. The stance toward questioning affects not only the usefulness of a particular expert system but also bears on whether these artificially intelligent systems might be described as "intelligent." Intelligence is signaled not only by the capacity to provide answers and solve problems but also the ability to generate, formulate, and pose questions, as well as knowing all the reasons why someone might be asked a question.

KNOWLEDGE ACQUISITION AND EXPERT SYSTEMS

Expert systems have been devised as one very good answer to the recognized limits of pure reason. During the early stages of work in artificial intelligence, many of the programs depended heavily on methods of formal reasoning to solve difficult intellectual problems. Indeed, there was some success. When a task is well-defined in a highly constrained domain, formal methods can provide powerful means for providing answers. For example, we no longer need to waste time searching for a way to trisect an angle or seeking the best method of calculating the motion of a projectile, because well-established theorems and algorithms have settled those questions once and for all.

Many interesting problems however cannot be solved by relying on formal reasoning alone. The power of logical methods lies in their representation of the world in symbolic and well-understood ways. That power is also their greatest failing. Many types of knowledge, including the equivocal and incomplete knowledge characteristic of real-world problems, do not lend themselves to representation through precise logical formalisms. Moreover, programs that draw exclusively on logic capture only part of the understanding an intelligent person would normally bring to bear in dealing with a difficult situation. Experience provides people with practical intelligence, that is, the kind that derives from familiarity and is encoded into a myriad number of tacit yet useful rules of thumb (Sternberg & Wagner, 1985). Expert systems were devised to capture this latter kind of comprehension, that is, the kind that comes with lots of hands-on practice with domain-specific problems. In other words, expert systems were formulated as a way to capture human reasoning as it is actually accomplished by people in the context of real and particular problems and its power comes not so much from formal reasoning but from acquired expertise.

Expert Systems

Expert systems now number in the thousands and are hard at work on difficult problems in fields as diverse as aircraft design, medical treatment, computer configuration, and equipment repair. The architecture of an expert system has two components that enable it to perform its task: a *knowledge base,* which contains knowledge relevant to a particular task, and an *inference engine* or control strategy, which provides the control mechanisms for applying this knowledge. The inference engine directs the operation of the expert system, deciding which rules to fire, how they will be applied, when the process is complete, and when a solution can be suggested.

The primary source of power in these systems is informal thought based on extensive knowledge painstakingly culled from human experts much of which is then encoded into the knowledge base in the form of hundreds of if–then rules.

The rules constrain search by guiding the program's attention toward the most likely solutions rather than by considering all possible alternatives.

Consider the expert system called MYCIN, which was designed to diagnose infectious blood diseases and to recommend appropriate treatments (Shortliffe, 1976). What MYCIN "knows" is a set of approximately 500 if–then rules of the following form:

> IF: 1.the stain of the organism is grampos, and
> 2.the morphology of the organism is coccus, and
> 3.the growth formation of the organism is chains
>
> THEN: There is suggestive evidence (0.7) that the identity of the organism is streptococcus.

The if–then form of the rules in MYCIN's knowledge base renders individual rules understandable even out of context unlike a traditional program code, which usually makes little sense when approached a few lines at a time. In addition, rules in an expert system are not always absolutes; rather they may be associated with degrees of uncertainty. In the aforementioned example, this uncertainty is made explicit by the attachment of the *certainty factor* of 0.7 to that particular conclusion. MYCIN's inference engine, provided with the name of a suspect symptom or organism, locates and extracts from the knowledge base all of the rules that make conclusions about that particular identity. The inference engine then works through all of these rules at which point it directs a question to the user at which point the process cycles-through again on that matter until the answer is generated.

Finally, the *user interface* in some expert systems enables it to answer some questions asked by users. For example, in MYCIN, a user might ask why a particular conclusion has been reached or why a course of treatment has been recommended. To answer the question, the system backtracks through the sequence of rules it used in arriving at the decision. The explanations are composed from the English text that is held in the machine in conjunction with each rule. Although limited in their ability to answer questions, the answers are nevertheless useful because they are based on credible rules-of-thumb elicited from human experts rather than on the abstract principles of formal logic.

The core ingredient of an expert system is the knowledge base. This is not the same thing as the more commonplace notion of a data base. Although storage and retrieval of information in a particular domain are implicit in each, the knowledge in a data base is only factual or declarative knowledge whereas "a knowledge base contains both declarative knowledge (facts about objects, events, and situations) and procedural knowledge (information about courses of action)" (Mishkoff, 1985, p. 54).

Given the importance of the knowledge base in an expert system, it follows that acquiring that knowledge constitutes a core prerequisite to their development. Knowledge acquisition is the process whereby the problem-solving expertise is transferred from the expert (although other knowledge sources are also used) to a program typically through the efforts of one or more knowledge engineers (Buchanan et al., 1983). It is not a simple undertaking. In fact, many concur that knowledge acquisition is *the* bottleneck in development of intelligent programs (Feigenbaum, 1984). Although the difficulty has long been recognized it has only been recently that there have been concerted efforts to investigate how knowledge can be communicated from those who have it to those who need it. The last 5 years have seen a virtual explosion of efforts in devising means to do this more effectively. (Gaines & Boose, 1988).

Expert system developers have utilized three methods for extracting knowledge from an expert. In the first, the knowledge engineer engages in intense, generally unstructured interviewing of the expert. For example, the knowledge engineer might ask something like, "How do you know that?" when the expert seems to be making some kind of assumption or "What happened then?" when the expert appears to be asserting some kind of causal connection. In the second method, the expert becomes a knowledge engineer and then relies on a combination of introspection and knowledge of expert system architecture to convert knowhow to the knowledge base. In the third method, often referred to as automated knowledge acquisition, the expert is "interviewed" on line, that is the expert interacts directly with the computer, which elicits particular kinds of inputs and translates them directly into the knowledge base of the system.

For a number of reasons, the first of these methods, namely the unstructured interview in which questions are put to the expert by the knowledge engineer constitutes the most common method. Indeed some developers have taken it for granted that the unstructured interview is essentially the only generally useful way to acquire expert knowledge (Weiss & Kulikowski, 1984). Although it may be the most generally useful method, unstructured interviewing of experts is frequently limited and flawed. Part of the reason stems from the fact that expertise is difficult to articulate (LaFrance, 1990) and part of the reason is that the usual interviewing mode is inadequate to the task. Questioning an expert is more complex and involved than typically recognized by knowledge engineers.

In what follows, I describe our efforts to enhance the interviewing of experts. Our aims are twofold; First, we are working toward a conceptual model that elucidates the processes that are involved when one person, initially naive or uninformed about an area, seeks to acquire the expertise another person already possesses about that area (LaFrance, 1989). Second, we are concerned with developing more sophisticated methods of conducting knowledge acquisition that draws inspiration from this model (LaFrance, 1987). Questions are the primary tools for knowledge acquisition. Although they are commonplace, questions are complicated and sensitive tools whose use requires considerable forethought and practice if they are not to alter or erode the very process that they are designed to uncover. Furthermore, they are tools that require at least two cooperating people to make them work, a fact that is downplayed in most accounts of how knowledge engineers go about seeking information from experts.

Efforts to do knowledge acquisition have been one recent and potent reminder of the importance of good questions. Despite recognition that questions are pivotal, computer scientists have been stymied as to how to go about asking the right ones. More specifically, I contend that existing work in knowledge acquisition has seriously underestimated the complexity of the questioning process. One noted developer of these systems has gone so far as to suggest that knowledge acquisition is really no more complicated than having the time and the patience to ask "why?" of an expert 400 times in a row. Even supposing that an expert would have the requisite time and the required patience to sit through such a siege, the resulting output is likely to be significantly less than what an "intelligent" program needs. The central point of this chapter is that questioning in general, and knowledge acquisition in particular, is a social and pragmatic process as well as a cognitive one. The body of this chapter is devoted to articulating what that means.

THE NATURE OF QUESTIONING

It is conventional to define knowledge acquisition as the process by which expert system developers question experts to discover the knowledge that they use to perform a task of interest (Prerau, 1987). This definition, simple and sound as it appears to be, masks the complexity that is involved when one person seeks to understand another person's "compiled hindsight" (Lenat, 1984). In fact, acquisition of knowhow from an expert is one variation on the venerable question of how any person manages to transfer hard-won personal proficiency to someone who is less skilled. We have here then a situation in which the answerer (expert) is clearly more knowledgeable than the questioner (knowledge engineer). It is the latter's task to acquire what the more knowledgeable person knows. This kind of questioning situation represents, however, only one of several kinds of contexts in which questions get asked. Harrah (in press) labels this one as "Make It the Case That I Know." In contrast, in another questioning mode labeled "Make Me Know That You Know," the questioner is more knowledgeable than the answerer and asks questions so that the answerer can demonstrate that the answerer knows the information such as typically occurs in classroom settings (Harrah, in press).

Although scholars have begun to tackle various aspects of questioning, there are many gaps in our understanding of the antecedents and consequences of question asking (Dillon, 1982; Graesser, Lang, & Horgan, 1988; Riesbeck, 1988). Within cognitive psychology, the preponderance of this work has been concerned with developing cognitive models of question *answering* (Graesser &

Black, 1985; Lehnert, 1978). My tack, however, is to stress the process of question *asking*. In the service of this, I propose a number of axioms. Although deriving from efforts to apply artificial intelligence, these six principles are assumed to have relevance whenever questioning is undertaken to facilitate the exchange of expertise between people. Moreover, they are deliberately stated here in a rather doctrinaire fashion in order to highlight issues frequently overlooked when experts are questioned during the building of expert systems.

The six axioms are as follows:

1. Information is *not* extracted by questioning.
2. Questions require common ground.
3. All questions are leading questions.
4. Questions derive from knowledge rather than ignorance.
5. Questions occasion the telling of stories rather than the furnishing of answers.
6. Good answers ring true rather than are true.

Information is Not Extracted by Questioning

The prevailing metaphor in knowledge acquisition is clearly one of information *extraction*. Expertise is described as being extracted from experts by questions put to them by knowledge engineers (Hayes-Roth, Waterman, & Lenat, 1983). The resulting information is then said to be transferred from the expert to the knowledge engineer who transforms the provided information into the knowledge base of the system. The implicit premise underlying the notion of knowledge extraction is that questions are nonreactive tools that pinpoint and transfer existing knowhow. The counterargument presented here is that although questioning can be said to cause the questioner to acquire information, it does not so much extract it as it generates it through the question and in the resulting conversation.

According to the usual extraction conception of knowledge acquisition, expertise exists in a relatively static state in the head of the expert. It is the knowledge engineer's job to find it and transfer it to the system. In other words, knowhow can be discovered through questioning; it exists independently of the expert who accumulated it and the knowledge engineer who acquired it. It can be measured, sectioned, and distributed without disturbance or alteration. In short, it is a material resource. In keeping with this thinking, a number of organizations today actually talk about managing their *knowledge assets*.

The problem is that this rather neat conception, although metaphorically instructive, is literally inaccurate. Although the concept of extraction emphasizes the transmission of information, it misses something that lies at the heart of knowledge acquisition, namely the *creation* of meaning in both expert and knowledge engineer through the process of questioning (Delia, 1970). As a number of organizational theorists have pointed out, the emphasis on extraction and transmission can be a blind spot (Axley, 1984). When information moves among people it is not only lost or gained "it is also qualitatively changed, made more or less meaningful. A small amount of information may generate thousands of reverberating inferences. . ." (Bowers & Bradac, 1982, p. 2). In other words, the knowledge base resulting from interactions between expert and knowledge engineer is not a replica of what the expert knew prior to being questioned about his or her knowhow. It is instead a current construction consisting of a network of inferences that arises in the dialogue between expert and knowledge engineer.

The notion that questions extract information misses a critical facet, namely that knowledge acquisition is less a process of procuring the goods than it is often an occasion for composing them. In their recent book *Understanding Computers and Cognition,* Winograd and Flores (1986) argued that experts do not have nor do they need formal representations of their domains in order to act. Hence "it is fruitless to search for a full formalization of the pre-understanding that underlies all thought and action" (Winograd & Flores, 1986, p. 99). In other words, seeing questioning as information extraction leads us to assume that the knowledge needed for the knowledge base of an expert system already exists in the expert's head fully formulated *and* in the configuration in which it is to be used in the system. On this latter issue, it may be that the preoccupation with ways to represent knowledge in the system has led knowledge engineers to incorrectly assume that their formulation of the knowledge base as rules or frames actually mirrors the structure of experts' knowhow.

In sum, questioning does not extract existing, fully formed knowledge. Rather it generates an explicit invention of it, which is subsequently transformed into the rules comprising the knowledge base. Questions are thus the occasion for experts and knowledge engineers to contrive a useful fabrication.

Questions Require Common Ground

The literature surrounding knowledge acquisition gives rather short shrift to the fact that questioning typically occurs in interaction between people. Questioning like any conversational exchange is a collective act (Clark & Schaefer, 1989). Coordination is a precondition to a successful interchange.

Consider what happens when one person thinks about putting a fairly simple question to another person. In the first place, it is apparent that some common ground is mandatory before any question can be broached let alone answered. The participants have to share a common language and the rudiments of a joint perspective. Otherwise, the question seems to come out of nowhere and the recipient is lost as to where to begin. Question asking presumes intersubjectivity, that is, shared understanding based on a common focus of attention and some shared presuppositions (Riegel, 1979; Trevarthen, 1980). According to Clark and

Schaefer (1989), participants in an exchange attempt to establish a mutual belief that what a questioner meant has been understood by the answerer well enough in order to proceed with an answer. They have to start with some degree of mutual knowledge.

Secondly, it is apparent that any theory of questioning has to specify why recipients consent to be questioned at all. That is, whenever questioning takes place, we need to know about the social contract that allows questions to be asked and creates the conditions that make legitimate the expectation of a reply. Some knowledge engineers implicitly recognize that this expectation is occasionally in doubt. For example, when given the opportunity to indicate issues that they would like to see addressed during knowledge acquisition training, novice developers often present the following questions:

- What are some methods for getting an unwilling expert to speak freely?
- How do you gather knowledge from an uncooperative expert?
- How do we go about making the expert comfortable, so he or she will *want* to work with us?
- How do you handle a reluctant expert—that is, one who does not see the value in sharing his or her knowledge?

In articulating such concerns, knowledge engineers implicitly acknowledge that experts are not neutral about being questioned and that question answering requires cooperation. In the absence of such cooperation, questions are more likely to elicit adverse reactions than full replies. Knowledge engineers know that they need the expert's cooperation but tend not to see it as a relationship issue but rather view it as a matter of individual orientation. In other words, they fail to acknowledge that question asking requires cooperation. Hence they underestimate the fact that answers are made possible or prevented by the nature of the bond between experts and themselves.

The importance of this dynamic becomes more evident when interactants come from different cultures. There are indications that knowledge acquisition across national boundaries is even more problematic because of differences in how groups define which contexts and which relationships permit which types of questions. Members from several countries, including Japan, Germany, and Switzerland report that a person has to earn the right to ask someone else a question. It is not given by the fact that one has a question that needs answering.

The implication of this is that the relationship between knowledge engineer and expert constitutes the ongoing medium through which questions are raised and answers extended. Not only does some kind of relationship have to be in place before one can ask something of someone else but also that subsequent questions modify the nature of that relationship. Relationships are not static and hence the same question asked at different points in a relationship is likely to elicit different interpretations of what is being sought.

Moreover, questions admit of multiple interpretations depending on how they are asked. Just as every communication has a content aspect and a relationship aspect so does every question (Watzlawick, Beavin, & Jackson, 1967). The content aspect conveys *what* is needed; the relationship aspect contains the instructions about *how* the request is to be interpreted. This latter aspect is tacit but very much present. Questioners are often surprised with the answers they get in part because they are insufficiently attentive to the fact that a question can be taken in a number of ways even if they did not intend to convey the meaning that was grasped. Astute questioners take note of how recipients react to questions in order to know what question is in fact being answered. In addition, good questioners are aware that questions are never definitive and hence previously unknown interpretations can become apparent to the questioner when he or she sees how the receiver responds to a particular query. Information exchange is a dynamic process that is affected by the common ground between participants and in turn affects the nature of that common ground.

We can state this axiom quite strongly. It is the composition of the common ground between questioner and answerer and not merely asking questions that makes it possible for knowledge to be shared. A question directed to someone implies the existence of a relationship, which then sets normative standards for what can transpire in a questioning situation. This includes a whole pattern of rights, privileges, and obligations for all parties. This pattern makes questioning possible, structures how it is to be done, and dictates in good measure why some questions never get asked, or if asked, why some answers are not forthcoming.

All Questions Are Leading Questions

Leading questions are not allowed in legal proceedings and are seriously frowned upon in most other kinds of questioning contexts. A leading question, of course, is one framed so as to guide the person being questioned to make a particular kind of reply. Leading questions are said to be improper because questioners ought not put words into recipients' mouths but should instead allow them to voice their views uncontaminated by the prior leanings of the person who is doing the questioning.

Misleading questions can significantly alter what people know or remember (Lehnert, Robertson, & Black, 1983; Robertson, Black, & Lehnert, 1985). An example of this research is the classic experiment by Loftus and Palmer (1974). Subjects viewed a film of a traffic accident. Then they answered questions, including the following: "About how fast were the cars going when they *hit* each other?" Other subjects received the same question, except the verb *hit* was replaced by either *smashed, collided, bumped,* or *contacted.* Even though all subjects saw the same accident, the wording of the question affected their reports. Subjects given the "smashed" question estimated the highest average speed; those responding to the "contacted" question estimated the lowest. But there's more. One week after the experiment, subjects were called back for additional probing. It appeared that the wording of the questions caused subjects to reconstruct their memories of the accident. When asked whether they had seen broken glass at the accident site where none was actually present, more subjects in the "smashed" condition said they did than those in the "hit" condition. The reply made use of two sources of information: the event itself and the content of the question.

The implication of this research is that it is possible to ask questions that do not lead the responder in a particular direction, that is, that there are questions devoid of predisposition. This, however, is in doubt. Research on how individuals answer questions shows that when people encounter a question they need first to understand what is being asked. But the question wording is not inert. The text in the query is added to the recipient's memory representation, which changes the recipient's representation in ways that depend partly on the prior state of the representation and partly on the nature of the question. As Galambos and Black put it, "it is important to notice that the question–answer process involves more than merely surgically probing the representation for the answer but leaving no trace of the question information. Rather, the question adds information to the memory representation" (Galambos & Black, 1985, p. 159). Survey researchers have long recognized that questions can be reactive agents, that is, they can cause the recipient to generate a reply on the spot where none existed previously.

By claiming that all questions are leading questions, I am arguing that it is not possible to ask a question that does not in some way influence the reply. In other words, even the most open-ended and no-holds-barred kind of question contains material that at the very least directs attention away from what might have been asked. But more is involved than opting for one path over another. There is no such thing as a leadingless question because there is no such thing as a contextless question. Novice knowledge engineers tend to assume that just as long as the question itself is clear, it does not much matter who asks the expert the question or whether it is presented on or off the domain site, or what discourse has preceded it. Recent reviews of the survey literature (Bradburn, 1982) provide ample evidence that the process of answering attitude questions can be strongly affected by such weak and momentary influences as question wording or the order in which the items are presented.

One kind of order effect, namely the *carryover effect* (Tourangeau & Rasinski, 1988) was revealed in a recent national survey. Asked whether the Japanese government should be allowed to set limits on how much American industry can sell in Japan, most Americans answered no. Simultaneously, two-thirds of an equivalent sample of Americans answered yes to the same question—because they were *first* asked whether the American government should be allowed to set limits on how much Japanese industry can sell in the United States (Schuman & Ludwig, 1983).

Another kind of context order effect has been termed a *backfire effect* (Tourangeau & Rasinski, 1988). Bradburn (1982) reported that an attitude item that asked respondents to evaluate their overall happiness yielded fewer "very happy" responses when this general question followed a more specific one on marital happiness. The result was interpreted as reflecting the tendency of answerers to exclude marital happiness when the general item came second because they felt that they had already covered their marriage in their earlier answers. It is as if respondents interpreted the general question to mean, "Aside from your marriage, how happy are you?" when the general question came after the marital question.

Again it is important to reiterate that recipients of questions have several tasks before them when presented with a question (Tourangeau & Rasinski, 1988). The first critical task involves deciphering what the question means and what the questioner has in mind. The formation of the answer depends on this assessment. What the question means is inextricably tied up with who is asking it, where it is being asked, how it is being asked, and when it is asked in relation to other queries and replies. In short, where is it leading?

Finally, it is worth noting that in attempting to frame a question, the mental representations of the questioners themselves undergo alteration. Novice knowledge engineers frequently put forth one then another reformulation of the self-same question as their own conceptions change. In other words, alternative versions lead the questioner to reconsider whether that question or an alternative one is preferable.

Questions Derive From Knowledge Rather Than Ignorance

An unresolved issue in knowledge acquisition concerns whether questioning of the expert should be done by a person who is naive or sophisticated with respect to the domain under scrutiny. On the one hand, there are those who argue for naiveté on the grounds that such a person would not start knowledge acquisition with a ready-made conception of the area. They would be more open to what the expert had to say about it. The fear is that a more informed person might actually compete with the authority rather than be curious about what he or she knew. On the other hand, an argument can be raised in support of the position that the questioner should come already equipped with substantial knowledge of the domain. The basic thesis here is that one has to know a great deal about an area even to know what questions to ask about it.

Based on existing work in cognitive psychology, the latter position appears more tenable. Miyake and Norman's (1979) findings led them to title their paper, "To Ask a Question, One Must Know Enough to Know What Is Not Known." It appears that good interviewers tend to know a great deal about an area prior to asking questions. Their questions tend to be more salient, germane, and consequential. It also appears that the ability to ask questions hinges on the degree to which the issue being discussed already makes sense to the questioner. We have found, for example, that the number of questions a person asks is positively correlated with the degree to which the questioner finds the current answer to be plausible. Finally, domain-knowledgeable questioners know how to interpret the answers. Knowledgeable questioners already possess *schemas*, that is mental representations of domain categories that can be extended and elaborated as a function of the replies (Anderson, 1983). Lacking well-developed schemas, a questioner may ask a question that activates a full and thoughtful response from an expert, but may not be able to handle the substantive complexity of the response.

The effect of prior knowledge also means that good interviewers do not possess a standard set of general purpose questions. Instead, their questions tend to be domain specific, that is, the questions spring from an evolving familiarity with an area rather than from a static state of ignorance. General purpose questions may be useful to the extent that one is interested in comparing answers across people. However, such questions are less serviceable when the goal is to understand in depth how people conceptualize problems in their domain and how they go about dealing with them.

This point has rather serious implications for those engaged in efforts to build automated knowledge acquisition tools. Recognizing that knowledge acquisition can be a very time consuming and labor intensive process, a number of researchers have developed programs that elicit domain knowledge from the expert on-line at a computer terminal (Boose, 1986; Davis, 1977; Kahn, Nowlan, & McDermott, 1985). In fact, Buchanan et al. (1983) have suggested that automated knowledge acquisition may actually be preferable to manual knowledge acquisition because automated tools might prove to be more competent than humans in acquiring or refining specific types of knowledge. If so, they can significantly reduce the costs of human resources involved in expert system development. Having said this, they then point out that having the domain expert transfer his or her knowledge directly to the expert system knowledge base via an intelligent program "replaces one set of communications problems with another" (Buchanan et al., 1983, p. 130). In other words, automated knowledge acquisition tools do not circumvent the questioning process. Quite the contrary. All the questions that one might want to put to an expert have to established *a priori* just as do all the categories into which the responses need to be placed.

In stating that questions derive from knowledge rather than ignorance, I am also suggesting that questions emanate from existing dispositions toward cognitive simplicity or complexity. Questions are informative about how questioners deal with information. If so, it seems that there is merit in having some degree of equivalence between expert and questioner in cognitive style. With respect to the ability of a person to comprehend accurately what another person is like, Allport made the following assertion, "as a rule people cannot comprehend others who are more complex and subtle than they" (Allport, 1961, p. 508). Questioning improves to the extent that there is a cognitive match between questioner and expert. The questioner must possess a substantial grasp of the domain and must possess a level cognitive complexity comparable to that of the expert.

Questions Occasion the Telling of Stories Rather Than the Furnishing of Answers

Knowledge engineers worry about two kinds of experts: those who tend to be very tight-lipped and respond to questions with single word answers or those who use the opportunity of a question to tell drawn-out and convoluted stories. The latter group seem particularly troublesome because it is difficult to know what to do with what they provide. Stories do not readily lend themselves to easy classi-fication. More specifically, stories often obscure what question is being an-swered. But despite the difficulty in distilling stories, they are ignored at our risk. For stories constitute the essence of expertise gained through experience.

In his new book entitled, *Tell Me a Story: A New Look at Real and Artificial Memory*, Schank (1990) asserts that human memory is like a collection of stories waiting to be told. In other words, the knowledge that people have about the world is really no more than the set of experiences that they have had and the stories that commit these experiences to memory. Expert system developers acknowledge that there is an important difference between textbook knowledge and actual experience. It is the latter that makes these systems valuable. But having conceded the value of experience, they tend to be impatient with experts who volunteer stories when questioned about the domain of interest, hoping instead to capture a knowledge structure that more closely resembles the require-ments of the system's knowledge base.

Within cognitive psychology there is a rich tradition of research on com-prehension of stories represented in text (Brewer & Lichtenstein, 1981; Mandel, Stein, & Trabasso, 1984; Mandler, 1984; Rumelhart, 1975; Schank & Abelson, 1977; Wilensky, 1983). Relatively less is known about how people encode their personal experiences into stories (Kolodner, 1983) or how information about an event gets translated and stored as a narrative account. For example, Pennington and Hastie (1986) have recently indicated that jurors' explanations of causality in complex criminal trials take the form of coherent narratives in which intentional and causal interrelationships among the various presented incidents are prominent.

When experts are asked questions that take the standard form of who, what, when, where, why, and how, it is likely that they attempt to retrieve a prior case from memory and then proceed to determine its relevance to the current question. They do this because some explanation, conclusion, point, or *index* has been presented in the question that triggers a story. An index is a feature that distinguishes a particular experience or exemplar from other experiences in the same class. At the same time, in making sense of an expert's story, knowledge engineers are assisted by the fact that they already possess a general representation of what a story consists (Rumelhart, 1975; Stein & Glenn, 1979). This provides a structure for understanding the presented story as well as providing the basis from which questions about the story can be generated (Trabasso, van den Broek, & Liu, 1988).

The relation of storytelling to question asking suggests a number of implications for knowledge acquisition. It means that good questioning may be less a process of interrogation than it is one of *reminding*. It means that because stories can be indexed in multiple ways, the challenge for knowledge engineers is to use questioning as a way to register and enumerate what these indices are. It means that stories may be more natural cognitive representations than are rule-based systems for representing expertise in a knowledge base. And finally it means that understanding an expert's story means connecting it to stories that knowledge engineers may already have heard about the domain. Kolodner (1983) has suggested, for example, that similar episodes are organized in memory into generalized episodes termed E-MOPs (Episodic Memory Organization Packets).

Good Answers Ring True Rather Than Are True

One of the more intriguing problems for questioners concerns how to know when one has gotten the answer. The answer, disconcerting although it may be, is that "it depends." It depends in part on the perspective of the questioner. From the literature in social cognition, there is indication that questions about why something happened cease when the questioner gets an answer that is personally convincing. So the criterion of whether a question has been answered has less to do with veracity than it does with perceived credibility. Although some answers can be checked for verification against an independent and impartial standard, many times during knowledge acquisition it comes down to whether the knowledge engineer is comfortable with the answer. Sometimes that means that questioners who desire definite answers will find any answer superior to confusion and ambiguity. Kruglanski (1989) has argued that where there is need for closure, question asking is brought to a halt once some plausible conjecture has been posed.

This need for closure doubtless varies across people and situations (Kruglanski, 1989). With respect to individual differences there is support for the idea that individuals differ in the degree to which they can deal with uncertainty (Hofstede, 1980; Rokeach, 1969). With respect to situational variability, research shows that factors such as time pressure can reduce the motivation to question further.

In another context, the sociologist Erving Goffman has written that "the goodness or badness of an account must, of course, be distinguished from its trueness or falseness. True accounts are often good, but false accounts are sometimes better" (Goffman, 1971, p. 112). This is not to suggest that that falseness is the rule in answering questions. Instead whether an answer stands is less a function of its objective correctness than it is a matter of a negotiated settlement between questioner and respondent. For their part, questioners have tacit "stopping rules" that indicate that a particular question has been satisfactorily answered. For their own part, respondents look to the questioner for signs about whether something more or something different is expected.

CONCLUSIONS

This chapter has identified a number of principles that characterize questioning in the realm of knowledge acquisition for expert systems. The six axioms are not designed to exhaust the domain of questioning but rather to highlight a number of issues that tend to be overlooked when artificial intelligence practitioners fashion methods for eliciting expertise.

Moreover these six axioms combine to suggest alternative ways of thinking about and developing expert systems. For example, in arguing that information is not extracted by questioning, I am proposing that system developers revise their conception from one in which previously established information is transferred from one person to another to a conception in which relevant expertise is crafted and formulated during knowledge acquisition. In suggesting that questions require common ground, I am arguing that the knowledge in the system's knowledge base is not a replica of the domain expert's expertise; it is an explicit contract reflecting a negotiated agreement between expert and knowledge engineer as to what is important and useful and what is not. In stating that all questions are leading questions, I am calling attention to the fact that the process of knowledge acquisition will inevitably alter not only how various people think about the domain in question and report their knowledge of it but will likely alter how work in that domain will subsequently be performed regardless of whether the system is ever implemented.

With respect to the assertion that questions derive from knowledge rather than ignorance, I am claiming that good questions are more likely to come from those who are knowledgeable. By possessing some knowledge about a domain a questioner can make sense of new information by connecting it with prior information. In that sense, information is a prerequisite to good questions. However, an attitude of deliberate inconclusiveness is also necessary for without it an informed questioner can easily turn into an inflexible contender with the expert for the "truth." In hypothesizing that questions occasion the telling of stories rather than the furnishing of answers, the argument is that practical experience in a domain gets cognitively encoded as coherent causal scenarios (Read, 1987) rather than as a set of abstract rules. Replies to questions that take the form of stories (and knowledge bases that can handle story representations) are more likely to contain more valid and useful information than that which seems more abstract and simple. Lastly, in contending that good answers ring true rather than are true, I emphasize the important role that assessment of the answer by the questioner plays in the knowledge-acquisition process.

Although the six principles emerged from work in knowledge acquisition for expert systems, they are proposed as tenable hypotheses concerning question asking more generally. I am currently conducting research that tests the conditions and limits of their applicability.

At an applied level, these six axioms constitute the core precepts of a training program in knowledge acquisition that has been conducted for several years as part of a corporate-sponsored Intelligent Systems Training Program. Novice knowledge engineers come from all over the world assuming that the really hard part in building an expert system is the design and implementation of the computer program. What I hope they discover is that the knowledge-elicitation process warrants as much thought and attention as the blueprint for the inference engine. By building the training on these premises, my aim is to assist knowledge engineers in the complex task of working with an expert to create a viable knowledge base. I also have another goal in mind, namely to provide a solid rationale for asking good questions not only of experts but of the systems themselves. In so doing, the resulting programs may be able to deal with the really important questions that people need to have answered.

ACKNOWLEDGMENT

Preparation of this chapter was supported by National Science Foundation Grant BNS 87-21882 to Marianne LaFrance.

REFERENCES

Allport, G. W. (1961). *Pattern and growth in personality.* New York: Holt, Rinehart & Winston.

Anderson, J. R. (1983). *The architecture of cognition.* Cambridge, MA: Harvard University Press.

Axley, S. R. (1984). Managerial and organizational communication in terms of the conduit metaphor. *Academy of Management Review, 9,* 428–437.

Boose, J. (1986). *Expertise transfer for expert system design.* New York: Elsevier.

Bowers, J. W., & Bradac, J. J. (1982). Issues in communication theory: A metatheoretical analysis. In M. Burgoon (Ed.), *Communication yearbook,* (vol. 5, pp. 1–27). Beverly Hills, CA: Sage.

Bradburn, N. (1982). Question-wording effects in surveys. In R. Hogarth (Ed.), *Question framing and response consistency.* San Francisco: Jossey-Bass.

Brewer, W. P., & Lichtenstein, E. H. (1981). Event schemas, story schemas, and story grammars. In A. D. Baddeley & J. D. Long (Eds.), *Attention and performance* (vol. 9, pp. 363–379). Hillsdale, NJ: Lawrence Erlbaum Associates.

Buchanan, B., Barstow, D., Bechtal, R., Bennett, J., Clancey, W., Kulikowski, C. Mitchell, T., & Waterman, D. (1983). Constructing an expert system. In F. Hayes-Roth, D. Waterman, & D. Lenat (Eds.), *Building expert systems* (pp. 127–168). Reading, MA: Addison-Wesley.

Clark, H. H., & Schaefer, E. F. (1989). Contributing to discourse. *Cognitive Science, 13,* 259–294.

Davis, R. (1977). Interactive transfer of expertise: Acquisition of new inference rules. *Proceedings of the Fifth International Joint Conference on Artificial Intelligence* (pp. 321–328). Los Altos, CA: Morgan Kaufman.

Delia, J. G. (1970). The logic fallacy, cognitive theory, and the enthymeme: A search for the foundations of reasoned discourse. *Quarterly Journal of Speech, 56,* 140–148.

Dillon, J. T. (1982). The multidisciplinary study of questioning. *Journal of Educational Psychology, 74,* 147–165.

Feigenbaum, E. (1984). Knowledge engineering: The applied side of artificial intelligence. *Annals of the New York Academy of Sciences, 426,* 91–107.

Gaines, B., & Boose, J. (Eds.). (1988). *Knowledge acquisition for knowledge-based systems* (vol. 1). New York: Academic Press.

Galambos, J. A., & Black, J. B. (1985). Using knowledge of activities to understand and answer questions. In A. C. Graesser & J. B. Black (Eds.), *The psychology of questions* (pp. 157–190). Hillsdale, NJ: Lawrence Erlbaum Associates.

Goffman, E. (1971). *Relations in public.* New York: Basic.

Graesser, A. C., & Black, J. B. (Eds.). (1985). *The psychology of questions.* Hillsdale, NJ: Lawrence Erlbaum Associates.

Graesser, A. C., Lang, K., & Horgan, D. (1988). A taxonomy for question generation. *Questioning Exchange, 2,* 3–15.

Harrah, D. (in press). The logic of questions. In F. Guenthner & D. Gabbay (Eds.), *Handbook of philosophical logic* (vol. 2). Boston: Reidel.

Hayes-Roth, F., Waterman, D. A., & Lenat, D. B. (Eds.). (1983). *Building expert systems.* Reading, MA: Addison-Wesley.

Hofstede, G. (1980). *Culture's consequences: International differences in work-related values.* Beverly Hills, CA: Sage.

Kahn, G. S., Nowlan, S., & McDermott, J. (1985). MORE: An intelligent knowledge acquisition tool. *Proceedings of the American Association of Artificial Intelligence* (pp. 581–584). Seattle, WA.

Kolodner, J. L. (1983). Towards an understanding of the role of experience in the evolution from novice to expert. *International Journal of Man-Machine Studies, 19,* 497–518.

Kruglanski, A. W. (1989). *Lay epistemics and human knowledge.* New York: Plenum.

LaFrance, M. (1987). The knowledge acquisition grid: A method for training knowledge engineers. *International Journal of Man-Machine Studies, 26,* 245–256.

LaFrance, M. (1989). The quality of expertise: Understanding the differences between experts and novices. *Special Issue of ACM SIGART Newsletter on Knowledge Acquisition, 108,* 6–14.

LaFrance, M. (1990). The special structure of expertise. In K. L. McGraw & C. R. Westphal (Eds.), *Readings in knowledge acquisition: Current practices and trends* (pp. 55–70). New York: Ellis Horwood.

Lehnert, W. G. (1978). *The process of question answering: A computer simulation of cognition.* Hillsdale, NJ: Lawrence Erlbaum Associates.

Lehnert, W. G., Robertson, S. P., & Black, J. B. (1983). Memory interactions during question answering. In H. Mandel, N. L. Stein, & T. Trabasso (Eds.), *Learning from text.* Hillsdale, NJ: Lawrence Erlbaum Associates.

Lenat, D. B. (1984). Computer software for intelligent systems. *Science, 251,* 204–213.

Loftus, E. F., & Palmer, J. C. (1974). Reconstruction of automobile destruction: An example of the interaction between language and memory. *Journal of Verbal Learning and Verbal Behavior, 13,* 585–589.

Mandel, H., Stein, N. L., & Trabasso, T. (Eds.). (1984). *Learning and comprehension of text.* Hillsdale, NJ: Lawrence Erlbaum Associates.

Mandler, J. M. (1984). What a story is. *Behavioral and Brain Sciences, 6,* 603–604.

Mishkoff, H. C. (1985). *Understanding artificial language.* Dallas, TX: Instruments Information Publishing Center.

Miyake, N., & Norman, D. A. (1979). To ask a question, one must know enough to know what is not known. *Journal of Verbal Learning and Verbal Behavior, 18,* 357–364.

Pennington, N., & Hastie, R. (1986). Evidence evaluation in complex decision making. *Journal of Personality and Social Psychology, 51,* 242–258.

Prerau, D. S. (1987, Summer). Knowledge acquisition in the development of a large expert system. *AI Magazine,* pp. 43–51.

Read, S. J. (1987). Constructing causal scenarios: A knowledge structure approach to causal reasoning. *Journal of Personality and Social Psychology, 45,* 323–334.

Riegel, K. F. (1979). *Foundations of dialectical psychology.* New York: Academic Press.

Reisbeck, C. K. (1988). Are questions just function calls? *Questioning Exchange, 2,* 17–24.

Robertson, S. P., Black, J. B., & Lehnert, W. G. (1985). Misleading question effects as evidence for integrated question understanding and memory search. In A. C. Graesser & J. B. Black (Eds.), *The psychology of questions* (pp. 191–218). Hillsdale, NJ: Lawrence Erlbaum Associates.

Rokeach, M. (1960). *The open and closed mind: Investigations into the nature of belief systems and personality systems.* New York: Basic.

Rumelhart, D. E. (1975). Notes on a schema for stories. In D. G. Bobrow & A. M. Collins (Eds.), *Representation and understanding: Studies in cognitive science.* New York: Academic Press.

Schank, R. (1990). *Tell me a story: A new look at real and artificial memory.* New York: Scribner.

Schank, R., & Abelson, R. (1977). *Scripts, plans, goals, and understanding.* Hillsdale, NJ: Lawrence Erlbaum Associates.

Schuman, H., & Ludwig, J. (1983). The norm of even-handedness in surveys as in life. *American Sociological Review, 48,* 112–120.

Shortliffe, E. H. (1976). *Computer-based medical consultations: MYCIN.* New York: Elsevier.

Stein, N. L., & Glenn, C. G. (1979). An analysis of story comprehension in elementary school children. In R. O. Freedle (Ed.), *New directions in discourse processing.* Norwood, NJ: Ablex.

Sternberg, R., & Wagner, R. K. (Eds.). (1985). *Practical intelligence: Origins of competence in the everyday world.* New York: Cambridge University Press.

Tourangeau, R., & Rasinski, K. A. (1988). Cognitive processes underlying context effects in attitude measurement. *Psychological Bulletin, 103,* 299–314.

Trabasso, R., van den Broek, P. W., Liu, L. (1988). A model for generating questions that assess and promote comprehension. *Questioning Exchange, 2,* 25–38.

Trevarthen, C. (1980). Instincts for human understanding and for cultural cooperation: Their development in infancy. In M. von Cranach, K. Foppa, W. Lepenies, & D. Ploog (Eds.), *Human ethology: Claims and limits of a new discipline* (pp. 530–571). Cambridge, England: Cambridge University Press.

Watzlawick, P., Beavin, J. H., & Jackson, D. D. (1967). *The pragmatics of human communication.* New York: Norton.

Weiss, S. M., & Kulikowski, C. (1984). *A practical guide to designing expert systems.* Totowa, NJ: Rowman and Allanheld.

Wilensky, R. (1983). Story grammars versus story points. *Behavioral and Brain Sciences, 6,* 579–623.

Winograd, T., & Flores, F. (1986). *Understanding computers and cognition: A new foundation for design.* Norwood, NJ: Ablex.

3 Knowledge Acquisition with Question Probes and Conceptual Graph Structures

Sallie E. Gordon
Richard T. Gill
University of Idaho

Technological advances have provided a broad base for developing a wide variety of information systems. Such systems currently range from relatively simple and straightforward information reporting systems to complex, high-level advisory structures, such as expert systems, decision support systems, hypertext documents, and interactive tutorials. The common factor among all such systems is that they are structured around large, complex databases that provide support for the performance of human cognitive activities. When designers develop any of these complex information systems, they must identify (a) the information content of the system, (b) the representational format of the information within the system, and (c) the means by which the user will access the information.

In this chapter, we present a general knowledge acquisition method that supports the designer in the first process, that of identifying and systematically organizing the information content of the system. By general, we mean that it can be used to identify the knowledge base for many types of complex information systems, including linear instructional documents, hypertext, computer-based tutorials, and expert systems. It combines the use of a systematic querying technique (called *question probes*) with a graphical notation system (called *conceptual graph structures*). Although the details of the procedure are described mostly within the context of eliciting knowledge from experts through structured interviews, it can be applied to document-based knowledge acquisition with very little modification.

KNOWLEDGE ACQUISITION

Knowledge acquisition is crucial to any sophisticated, complex information system to which humans must have access. The information base must be well-organized, complete, and accurately represent the current state of knowledge as it exists in human and archival form. Creating such a complete and coherent information base is necessary for expert systems to run without error. However, other types of information systems, such as training manuals or computerized tutorials, would also be enhanced to the extent that they shared these characteristics. Thus, the process of knowledge acquisition is critical for all such systems, and effective methods of knowledge acquisition are still needed (Gordon, 1989, in press; Gordon & Lewis, 1990).

We believe that a knowledge-acquisition method should have the following characteristics:

1. It is relatively simple, straightforward, and easy to use, both for the knowledge engineer and for experts who are being asked to share their knowledge.
2. It is efficient, resulting in a large ratio of knowledge acquired relative to the time to acquire it.
3. It optimizes the process in terms of increasing the completeness and consistency of the information.
4. It is soundly rooted in psychological theory and research, which will increase the likelihood that the knowledge acquired with the method is valid and reliable.
5. It can be used to acquire a wide variety of *types* of knowledge so that the final system representational format is not overly constrained.
6. It results in information that is represented in such a way that it translates easily into the various common representational formats (e.g., semantic networks, rules, object-oriented languages, etc.).

In developing our method for knowledge acquisition, we were aware of the fact that many people who develop expert systems (who may or may not have training as "knowledge engineers") tend to use relatively quick and unstructured methods, such as open interviews. The use of unstructured interviews is seemingly straightforward and easy to implement; it requires little or no training, and seems efficient to the novice knowledge engineer. Even in circumstances where documents do exist, the content of those documents is often informally evaluated and combined with information obtained through interviews.

The use of unstructured interviews and informal evaluation of documents has many drawbacks from the standpoint of the previous list of criteria. For example, these methods are, in actuality, neither simple and straightforward nor efficient, because the knowledge engineer has no way of knowing what questions to ask, how to structure the information that has been acquired, how to know when the knowledge base is complete, and so forth.

Given that most people are comfortable with the idea of using interviews and documents for knowledge acquisition, we developed a method to structure those processes in a way that met the aforementioned criteria. The method is comprised of two complementary components. The first is the use of a representational format to record and organize the knowledge as it is acquired, regardless of the source (e.g., expert, documents, etc.). The format is that of *conceptual graph structures* (CGSs), a graph syntax developed by Graesser and colleagues (Graesser, Byrne, & Behrens, chap. 12 in this volume; Graesser & Clark, 1985; Graesser & Franklin, 1990; Graesser & Gordon, 1991; Graesser, Gordon, & Brainerd, in press). From the very start of the knowledge acquisition process, CGSs are used to represent the information. This is critical because it is a notational system that captures not only the content of the knowledge, but also the relationship between the various components of the knowledge base.

The second component of our approach is a method for querying the source (i.e., human expert or document) and obtaining additional information. The querying method is that of *question probes*, a systematic technique for generating questions. These questions are then answered either by the expert or by the knowledge engineer looking up the answers in documents. The answers produced by the questions include new information that is added to the CGS.

In summary, the knowledge acquisition method consists of using CGSs to *represent* the information as it is acquired, and question probes to structure the *process* of acquiring information. Each of these two components is elaborated in the following sections.

CONCEPTUAL GRAPH STRUCTURES

CGSs were originally developed within a research context different from the use of knowledge acquisition techniques to develop information systems. Because we wished to use CGSs as a knowledge acquisition tool, we were forced to modify Graesser's syntax slightly. In this section, we briefly describe the syntax as developed by Graesser and presented in Graesser and Gordon (1991). We then describe the modified graph syntax that we use in conjunction with question probes for knowledge engineering.

CGSs consist of nodes that are linked by labeled directional arcs. Figure 3.1 shows an example of a very small CGS for information relevant to a video recorder (VCR). Each node in the CGS contains specific information in the form of a concept or statement (e.g., "VCR," or "VCR reads signals on tape") and

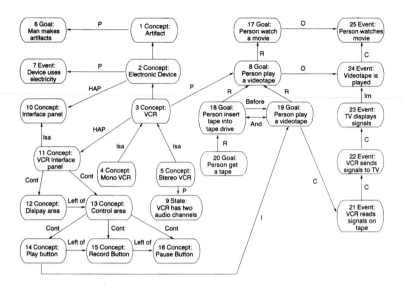

FIG. 3.1.   Conceptual graph structure for knowledge about VCRs. The abbreviations for the arc categories are: C = Consequence, Cont = Contains, HAP = Has Part, I = Initiate, Im = Implies, O = Outcome, P = Property, R = Reason.

the category of that information (e.g., concept or event). The node categories include concept, state, event, style, and goal.[1] The arcs are both labeled and directional, specifying the nature and direction of the relationship between two nodes.

CGSs frequently vary in the types of information that they contain. These types of information can be categorized as different types of substructures. For example, a structure that represents the procedures for some activity would consist predominantly of hierarchically organized goal nodes that are interconnected by Reason arcs. This type of structure is termed a *goal* hierarchy. Within the graph shown in Fig. 3.1, Nodes 8, 17, 18, 19, and 20 comprise a goal hierarchy for watching a movie on a VCR. There are three other common types of structures: (a) *Taxonomic* hierarchies capture the definitional and descriptive properties of concepts (e.g., Nodes 1–7 and 9–11 in Fig. 3.1); (b) *Spatial* region hierarchies represent the spatial layout of objects and regions (e.g., Nodes 11–16 of Fig. 3.1); and (c) *Causal* networks contain information relevant to the event chains in domains such as physical, biological, and technical systems (e.g., Nodes 19 and 21–25 in Fig. 3.1). CGSs can consist of only one type of substructure, or an amalgamation of several types. The reader is referred to more detailed

---

[1]Nodes can also be static or dynamic images. For the sake of simplicity we will restrict our discussion to graphs of verbal material. However, the extrapolation to include imagery is very direct.

discussions in previously published research (Graesser & Clark, 1985; Graesser & Gordon, 1991).

In knowledge acquisition, the substructures may either be developed independently of one another or be developed in a composite fashion. The goals and specific content area of a project will determine which is most appropriate (e.g., Gordon & Gill, 1991). As an example, consider a scenario in which a hypertext help network is being developed to augment a word processing software system. The designers might determine that, of the various substructure types, a goal hierarchy would support users most effectively. Although abundant taxonomic and spatial "system information" is available (e.g., key layout, function, etc.), this information might be packaged in the hypertext network separately from the task-oriented goal hierarchy. In this case, the knowledge engineers would develop a separate goal hierarchy graph.

For the purposes of knowledge engineering, we have slightly expanded Graesser's syntax. This was necessary to develop the question probes to be described shortly. In particular, we have specified goal nodes as being one of two types: goal/action versus goal. *Goal/action* denotes a combined goal (or desire to perform an action) with the performance of the action by an agent. *Goal* denotes a state or event desired by the agent; it may or may not end up being achieved. The graph type known as a goal hierarchy has been expanded into a goal/action hierarchy. This term indicates that the knowledge of how to perform some procedure includes the knowledge of goals and specific actions performed to achieve those goals (such as digging the ground to plant a rose bush, in order to have roses). Goals and goal/actions can be related within a goal/action hierarchy via *either* upwardly directed Reason arcs or downwardly directed Means arcs. Finally, we expanded "Is-a" arcs into "Is-a," "Equivalent-to," and "Instance-of" arcs.

Other than the points just listed, we essentially follow Graesser's constraints in defining the types of structure, and the "legal" combinations of nodes and arcs within the structures. Table 3.1 lists the node and arc combinations that we use for knowledge engineering projects. The table is organized around the arc categories listed down the center. For each arc, a row indicates the legal source nodes on the left and the legal terminal nodes on the right. For example, a Property arc can only emanate from a concept; as an example, in Fig. 3.1, "Concept: Electronic device" has the property of "Event: Device uses electricity." Notice that this particular property is a dynamic event. As shown on the right side of Table 3.1, the Property arc can point to events, states, goals, and goal/actions. As another example, if you ask someone for a property of a telephone, they might tell you that you use them to call people.

The set of nodes and arcs listed in Table 3.1 acts as a base syntax for any knowledge engineering domain. It is only a base because for some domains, it is convenient to use additional arc types that are more specific to the particular domain. These are usually more specific types of Property arcs. For example, in

TABLE 3.1
Node Categories and Arc Labels for Four Types of Information Structures*

Source Node	Arc	Terminal Node	Arc Definition
Goal Hierarchy			
Goal, Goal/Action	Reason	Goal, Goal/Action	Terminal node is reason, motive, or superordinate node for source node
Goal, Goal/Action	Means	Goal/Action	
Event, State, Style	Initiate	Goal, Goal/Action	Source node initiates or triggers the terminal node
Goal, Goal/Action	Before/After/During	Goal, Goal/Action	Specifies the temporal relation between source and terminal nodes
Goal, Goal/Action	Refers to	Concept	Source node has a component that refers to the terminal node concept`
Goal/Action	Manner	Goal/Action, Style	Terminal node specifies the manner in which the source node occurs
Goal/Action	Consequence	Event, State, Style	Source node causes or enables terminal node or precedes terminal node
Goal	Outcome	Event, State	Terminal node specifies whether source node (goal) is achieved
Goal, Goal/Action	and/or	[similar node type]	Both source and terminal nodes exist Either source or terminal nodes exist
Taxonomic Structure			
Concept	Is-A	Concept	Source node is a kind or type of terminal node
Concept, Event, State	Equivalent-to	[similar node type]	Source is similar to terminal node, differences are inconsequential
Concept, Event, State	Instance-of	[similar node type]	Source node is a specific instance of the terminal node

mathematics or engineering, a concept may be related to an equation by a Has-Equation arc. The use of domain-specific arcs is warranted when an arc type is common and it is difficult or awkward to represent the relation with the basic syntax.

Some additional points should be noted that pertain to the use of CGSs for knowledge acquisition and knowledge engineering. First, semantic nets or con-

Concept	Property	Event, State, Goal, Goal/Action	Source node concept has the property of the terminal node
Concept	Has Part	Concept	Source node has as a part, the terminal node
Concept	Refers-to	Concept	Complex source node has a component that refers to the terminal node concept
Concept, Event, State, Style	And/Or	[similar node type]	Both source and terminal nodes exist Either source or terminal nodes exist

Spatial Structure

Concept	Spatial Relation**	Concept	Specifies spatial relationship between source and terminal nodes

Causal Structure

Event, State, Style	Implies	Event, State, Style	Source node implies existence of terminal node, overlap in time
Event, State Style	Consequence	Event, State Style	Source node causes or enables terminal node
Event	Manner	Event, Style	Terminal node specifies the manner in which the source event occurs
Style	Manner	Style	Terminal node specifies the manner in which the style node occurs
Event, State, Style	And/Or	Event, State, Style	Both source and terminal nodes exist Either source or terminal nodes exist
Event, State	Before/After/During	Event, State	Specifies the temporal relation between source and terminal node Event, State, Style
Event, State, Style	Refers-To	Concept	Source node has a component that refers to the terminal concept

*Each row specifies the legal source nodes and terminal nodes for a given arc category.
**For example, Contains, Left-of, North-of, and so on.

ceptual graphs are becoming common as a representational format in artificial intelligence (AI), including part or all of the knowledge base underlying expert systems (cf. Amir, 1989; Hillman, 1988; Sowa, 1984). Thus, their use for knowledge acquisition is becoming increasingly justified. Second, there are now programs available for developing conceptual graphs directly on computers (e.g., Fisher, 1990; Fisher et al., 1990; Woodward, 1990).

KNOWLEDGE ACQUISITION WITH QUESTION PROBES

The knowledge acquisition process consists of developing an initial CGS and then expanding the graph using question probes until the graph is complete. Completion is achieved when the information being acquired is either (a) already contained within the graph or (b) outside of the domain as it has been defined. These criteria will be elaborated later in the chapter.

The knowledge acquisition process has four steps. The designer proceeds through all four steps and then iterates Steps 2 through 4 until the knowledge base is complete.

Step 1: Initiate a CGS.

Step 2: Develop question probes.

Step 3: Use graph and probes to acquire new information (through interviews, behavioral observation, or document analysis).

Step 4: Add information to the graph.

The four-step procedure will be described in the following sections and illustrated with a simple knowledge acquisition scenario for the domain of *residential landscape design*.

Step 1: Initiate the CGS

The knowledge acquisition process begins by developing a small graph. This is often most easily accomplished via an unstructured interview with a subject matter expert. This interview can be very short; the expert is asked to provide a simple overview of the domain or task that is the central focus of the knowledge base.

One advantage of the four-step approach is that, to a great extent, it does not matter what the expert says in the first session. If the expert gets off on a tangent, it will usually not have an impact on the final representation. However, the process will be most efficient if the knowledge engineer keeps the discussion at a rather general level.

The initial interview lasts as little as 10–15 minutes and is tape-recorded. In order to keep the expert focused, we also sketch a CGS as the expert is talking. If the expert gets off on a tangent, we can look at the graph, find nodes higher up on the hierarchy that are more general, and ask the expert to focus on those concepts or statements.

As an example, we asked a local residential landscape architect (initials DB) to act as our expert for the topic of "selecting plants for a residence." We first asked DB to give a basic overview of his job, including basic concepts and procedures. This provided a necessary *context* for the body of knowledge to be elicited. He spoke for 4 minutes on that topic. During that time we sketched a graph with about 15 nodes, one of which was " residential landscape design."

We then asked DB to discuss/elaborate "residential landscape design." He spoke 4 minutes on that concept, which resulted in a sketched graph containing about 25 nodes. One of the nodes was "selecting plant materials," the topic that we had originally designated as being the focal point for the knowledge base. The previously elicited information does not specifically contribute to knowledge regarding how to select planting materials. However, it is initially included in the graph to provide a context, and may also be necessary information in the final information system.

Figure 3.2 shows a subset of the CGS from the interview that contains the node "select plant materials." We asked the expert to describe briefly the basic concepts and procedures involved in selecting plant materials. He discussed this for about 3 minutes and we concluded the interview.

After the initial interview (or document analysis), the knowledge engineer translates the information in the interview tapes into one or more CGSs. Although these structures may be developed as separate subtypes (e.g., spatial, causal, etc.), we have typically found that the knowledge engineering process proceeds more smoothly if all knowledge types are combined into one network. However, to keep the project manageable, we often physically divide the graph into separate subsections. For example, the node "select plant materials" in Fig. 3.2 would be the starting node of a separate graph, adding all of the nodes that are subordinate to it.

Based on the transcripts of the initial interview with DB, we developed the CGS in three subgraphs. The first subgraph covered his basic job and contained 40 nodes, including "residential landscape design." The second subgraph was on "residential landscape design" (one of the nodes in Fig. 3.2), and contained

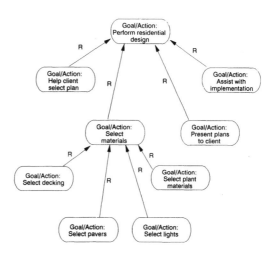

FIG. 3.2. Part of conceptual graph structure for residential landscape design. R denotes a Reason arc.

about 50 nodes including "selecting plant materials." The third subgraph, centered around "selecting plant materials," contained about 45 nodes.

Step 2: Developing Question Probes

The goal of the second step is to expand the graph(s) by at least one layer. That means adding a set of arcs and nodes to every existing node that is considered relevant to the knowledge base being developed. In our example, we would expand all of the nodes contained in the third subgraph, but not in the other two subgraphs. In expanding the graph, questions are used to generate new information which is then added to the graph. Thus, our method is to systematically generate explicit questions for each node; the questions elicit information to be attached to each of those nodes.

Generic Question Probes. One way that the knowledge engineer could expand the graph would simply be to ask: What other information is relevant to this concept (or event, goal, etc.)? This question could be given to the expert or used to evaluate existing documentation. This would certainly be a legitimate method for expanding the knowledge base. However, this type of question could be too vague for the experts. It certainly does not guarantee that the knowledge engineer would elicit important and/or relevant information.

As an alternative, we ask a specific set of questions that are designed to elicit the entire array of information that might be associated with a given node. The development of such a set of questions was possible because there is a theory that underlies the CGSs, a theory supported by empirical research (see, Graesser & Clark, 1985; Graesser & Gordon, 1991). With this method, our objective is to pursue the types of arcs that are likely to emanate from and lead to each node in the CGS. For any given type of node, the theory specifies a particular subset of arcs that will potentially emanate from the node or terminate at the node (see Table 3.1). Therefore, only particular types of information are relevant to or associated with any given node, and only certain types of questions are appropriate to elicit such information.

For example, a concept node would not have a Reason arc emanating away from it (e.g., the concept of bird does not have a "reason"). Therefore, one would not ask "Why?" with respect to a concept, because there is no Reason-related node to elicit. Similarly, a Goal/Action node does not have properties, so one would not ask for the properties of such a node. However, a Goal/Action can legally have Reason arcs emanating from it, so we would want to ask a question that would elicit the information at the other end of the Reason arc(s). Such a question would be "Why do you (Goal/Action)?" If a Goal/Action node has a Means arc emanating from it, an appropriate question to elicit the information at the other end of the arc would be "How do you (Goal/Action)?"

We used the set of constraints on node/arc combinations to determine the generic questions that one could legitimately ask about any given *type* of node. That is, each node has a subset of arc types that may point to or away from the node. For each of these arc types, we identified a question that would be most likely to elicit that particular type of information. Thus, for a Consequence arc we ask "What is the consequence?" for a Manner arc we ask "How?" and so forth. Table 3.2 lists the node categories and their associated set of generic question probes. It can be seen that there is some partial overlap among the sets of questions for the different types of nodes. However, for the purposes of

TABLE 3.2
Generic Question Probes for Six Node Types

Node	Question Probes
Concept:	What is____?
	What are the types of ____?
	What are specific instances or examples of ___?
	What are the properties of ___?
	OR
	What are the properties of ____ that distinguish it from ___?
	What are the parts of ___?
	(any other more domain-specific questions such as, what is left of, What is the equation for, etc.)
Event:	What happens before ____?
	What happens after ____?
	What are the consequences of ____ occurring?
	Why does ____ occur? (Optional because it covers the same information as previous two)
State:	What happens before ____?
	What happens after ____?
	What is the consequences of ____ occurring?
	What causes or enables ____?
	Why is ____? (Optional because it covers the same information as previous two)
Style:	What are the consequences of ___?
	What causes or enables ___?
	How ____?
	What happens if not ____?
Goal:	What happens before having the goal of ___?
	What happens after having the goal of ___?
	How is the goal of ____ attained?
	What state or event initiates the goal of ___?
	What is the outcome of ____?
	Why is the goal ____? (Optional because it covers the same information as previous two)
Goal/Action:	How do you (how does a person) ____?
	What do you (what does a person) do before ____?
	What prevents you from being able to ____?
	What do you (what does a person) do after ____?
	What states or events cause or enable you (a person) to ___?
	Why do you (why does a person) ___?
	What are the consequences of ___?
	What happens if you do not ____?

knowledge engineering, it is most efficient to organize the sets according to node type.

One of the questions listed in Table 3.2 needs some explanation. "Why" questions are listed as optional because they tend to elicit more than one type of information. For example, asking a "Why (State)?" question may elicit (a) a Goal/Action, Event, State, or Style that resulted in that state (obtained by traveling backward through a Consequence arc) or (b) the Events, State, or Style that are a result or consequence of the node (traveling forward through Consequence arcs). For knowledge acquisition, we want to ensure that we elicit *both* types of information. As an example, suppose we ask a person "Why is this pen red?" We might be told, "Because someone made it red." That person might also think it is red because the consequence of being red is that you will see it easily on your desk. If that belief is held, we might not elicit it unless we specifically ask for the consequences of the pen being red.

To address these needs, we developed more specific questions than simply asking "why" questions. In Table 3.2, for the Event, State, and Goal question probes, we included the "why" question. However, the question is noted as optional because it elicits the same types of information as the more specific questions listed above it. It should also be noted that "why" questions for Goal/Action nodes are not of this general nature; they are used specifically as a means of eliciting information associated with Reason and Means arcs.

Developing the Domain-Specific Question Probes.   At this point, the knowledge engineer develops a set of domain-specific question probes for structuring knowledge acquisition. This is accomplished by combining each node on the initial graph (e.g., Fig. 3.2) with the set of generic question probes appropriate for that node type (as specified in Table 3.2). For example, one of the nodes in our third subgraph was "plants." Obviously, this is a concept node, and would be combined with all of the questions in Table 3.2 associated with the category of "Concept." This results in a set of six questions about plants:

1. What is a plant?
2. What are the types of plants?
3. What are specific instances or examples of plants?
4. What are the properties of plants?
5. What are the properties of plants that distinguish them from other living organisms?
6. What are the parts of a plant?

Step 3: Acquire New Information

The set of question probes developed in Step 2 is used to query the expert in a structured interview. Alternatively, the set of questions can be used as a guide to search for specific information in documents.

In using the question probes to structure an interview, the knowledge engineer has two alternatives. First, the question probes can be written as a list and simply read to the expert, with the answers tape-recorded. Or second, the questions can be noted on the CGS next to the relevant nodes; during the interview the questions are read by the knowledge engineer directly from the graph. Both of these methods have worked for our knowledge engineering projects. Although question probe lists tend to be easier to use as the graphs become larger, having the graph present during knowledge elicitation proves useful. In particular, when the new information is inconsistent or different from information on the graph, this is readily apparent and can be addressed immediately. In addition, the graph provides a good medium for externalizing the knowledge in a form that the expert and knowledge engineer can use to communicate about the topic. In our work, we have found that the experts enjoy being able to see the graph notation. They use it as a record of previous sessions and make additions and changes directly to the information on the graph. For these reasons, we generally prefer to work directly from the graph if possible.

The expert is asked to answer the question probes as directly as possible and to keep answers relatively brief. This keeps the expert focused on the portion of the graph being expanded. The order of question presentation is relatively unimportant, although the most natural order is descending through the hierarchy of the graph, moving from questions about the more abstract, top-level nodes to questions regarding more specific, lower-level nodes. If possible, it is advantageous to write the answers as new nodes on the graph as they are verbalized.

An important point the knowledge engineer must keep in mind during the process is that a question may often need to be repeated. For example, if we ask the expert to tell us the properties of plants, the expert may say that they all perform photosynthesis. We should continue to elicit properties until the expert cannot state any new ones. For example, our expert ended up stating that there were no other properties that distinguished plants from other living things; most people think that plants have the property of being non locomotive, but that is actually not the case. Although the repetition of questions may seem tedious and unnecessary, it is extremely important in assuring completeness of the structure. This is another advantage of having the graph at the interview. As the expert verbalizes various answers to the same question, the graph acts as a reminder. The expert looks at previous answers and tells the knowledge engineer when there are no *new* pieces of information that come to mind. This eliminates much of the repetition that characterizes unstructured interviews.

The interviews are tape-recorded, whether question probe lists or the graph are used to structure the interview. Since the interviews are recorded, any information that the expert verbalizes beyond the immediate answer to the question can simply be added to the graph at a later time. However, with the question probe method, it is soon very obvious to the expert that the material will be covered in depth. As a result, the experts tend to keep their answers relatively short and to the point.

It is often the case that not all of the questions can be covered within one session. The process of querying an expert is somewhat wearing on both sides, even when highly structured. The questions can be spread over a series of interview sessions without any negative consequences.

Although question probes were designed to structure expert interviews, they can be used in conjunction with actual problem solving scenarios as well. For example, if experts cannot passively articulate how they perform some activity (in an interview), it is possible to have them perform the activity and present them with question probes either during the process or retrospectively. The question probes provide a way to structure questions about the actions performed and CGSs provide a means to represent the activities as well as expert explanations.

Step 4: Adding Answers to the Graph

The answers to the question probes provide information that is added to the initial graph. The information is translated into nodes and links in the same manner as the initial information. The answers may consist of long chains of thought or they may be short and simple. An example of the former occurred when DB was asked why trees are good for reducing global warming. He started by stating a property of trees; they are larger than other plants. As a consequence of this state, they have more leaf surface. The state of having more leaf surface has the consequence of the leaves having more area for photosynthesis. This results in the leaves releasing large amounts of oxygen and so on. In the CGS, these states and events are represented as a causal chain of nodes that are connected by Consequence arcs.

Steps 2 through 4 are iterated until the graph is complete. There are currently no methods for objectively determining the completeness of any complex knowledge base. However, with question probes, the method has a built-in indicator that the *verbalizable* knowledge base has been thoroughly covered (see Gordon, in press, for a discussion of eliciting nonverbalizable knowledge). The graph is complete when the questioning process elicits only two kinds of answers: (a) information that is already on the graph, and (b) information that is judged by the expert (usually in conjunction with the knowledge engineer) to be outside of the domain boundaries. This judgment depends on the expert's ability to determine what information belongs in the knowledge base. In our example, DB verbalized "concrete" as one of the concepts (referenced by the Concept node, "concrete buildings"). He considered the concept of concrete to be a boundary term; specifying the properties of concrete was not relevant to selecting residential plants.

It is clear that choice of the boundaries of the knowledge base, as well as the level of necessary detail, will depend on the specific application for the information system. It will also depend on the knowledge, skills, and goals of the system users. The process of identifying the appropriate boundaries, system representation, and other factors are not covered here. However, we have addressed these issues for the design of hypertext systems in other papers (Gordon & Gill, 1991; Gordon & Lewis, 1990).

SUMMARY AND CONCLUSIONS

To summarize, knowledge engineering is an important part of any complex information system. Many of the knowledge acquisition methods developed for expert system design are appropriate for a much wider set of information system applications. Our particular approach to knowledge engineering combines two methodologies: the representation of the knowledge base with conceptual graph structures and structuring the process of knowledge acquisition with question probes.

There are several advantages of using graph structures as a representational medium during the knowledge acquisition process:

1. It is a general syntax that is applicable to a wide variety of domains. Much of the generality derives from the various types of substructures. For example, causal networks can be used to represent structural and causal relationships in a complex physical system, whereas a goal hierarchy can be used to represent a complex set of activities. Thus, it can be used to represent explicitly both declarative and procedural information.

2. CGSs provide a useful shorthand notation for communication with the expert. The graph makes the concepts represented in the knowledge base explicit, but more importantly, it makes the relations between the concepts explicit as well. This makes it easy for the expert and knowledge engineer to see where information is missing or inconsistent.

3. Because the graph acts as a reminder for the knowledge engineer (and sometimes for the expert), it reduces question and answer redundancy. It provides a well-organized basis for the knowledge engineer to generate questions.

4. The graphs tend to be self-organizing. This property is difficult to describe in the abstract, but by translating information into graphs, the graphs become organized and cohesive by virtue of the type of structure being imposed on the information. For example, because of the nature of the graph syntax, all of the properties specific to a hi-fi VCR must be linked directly to that node, rather than being scattered throughout an information data base.

5. Graphs represent information in a form that is easily translated into a wide variety of applications, including linear documents, expert systems, tutorials, and hypertext.

The use of question probes to guide the knowledge acquisition process also has several advantages.

1. Most importantly, the probes provide a structure for knowledge engineers in facing the enormous task of acquiring a complex body of knowledge. Currently, most knowledge engineers use educated guesswork in determining what questions to ask during interviews. They place themselves in the role of student; they intuitively try to determine what they still have not heard or understood, and they use these intuitions to generate questions. This process is clearly not an optimal one.

2. Question probes place the burden of determining the direction of knowledge acquisition on the shoulders of the knowledge engineer rather than on the expert.

3. Question probes function as a *press*, moving the questioning into areas of knowledge that might otherwise not be explored. This significantly increases the chances of eliciting the entire body of knowledge.

We have used the methods outlined in this chapter in a variety of field projects, ranging from expert systems in forestry and education to instructional design in physics and engineering mechanics. Knowledge engineers working on the projects have felt that the method improved their ability to interact with experts and elicit relevant knowledge.

Obviously, empirical research is needed to evaluate the use of CGSs and question probes for knowledge engineering. However, some relevant findings already exist. For example, we used question probes to elicit student's knowledge about engineering statics or about using VCRs (Gordon & Gill, 1989). We found that the elicited information predicted 90% of subjects' problem-solving behavior. In a separate study, information elicited with question probes was highly correlated with the content and structure of the same person's free recall verbalizations. However, the number of propositions in the question probe data strongly outnumbered those in free recall data; means were 223 versus 40, respectively (Gordon & Gill, 1989). This provides evidence that the cuing function of question probes will elicit more information than would be obtained by asking experts more general questions (e.g., tell me about X).

We have recently evaluated the extent to which question probes can elicit information that is not normally verbalized by an expert. We asked an instructor of engineering mechanics to describe the factual and procedural knowledge necessary to solve three types of simple statics problems. This information was translated into three separate CGSs and question probes were used to elicit further information. As a result, the graphs were expanded by over 200%. All of the new information was judged by the expert to be relevant to the problem-solving tasks, and over one-third was judged to be critically relevant. This suggests that question probes do increase the likelihood of eliciting important information, even when the expert is someone whose profession entails the verbalization of knowledge.

One component of the method presented in this chapter consists of the use of

CGSs for knowledge representation. Given that one of our criteria at the outset was that the method be soundly rooted in psychological theory and research, we can question the extent to which CGSs adequately capture knowledge held by experts. Graesser and colleagues have developed a model of question answering (called QUEST) that is based on CGSs (Graesser & Franklin, 1990; Graesser & Gordon, 1991; Graesser et al., in press; Graesser, Hemphill, & Brainerd, 1989). This research has not specifically addressed the issue of expertise. However, the model has been able to account for a large proportion of answers that adults give to questions about a variety of topics such as physical systems, spatial structures, and goal-related activities (Graesser & Franklin, 1990; Graesser et al., 1989; Graesser & Murachver, 1985).

Even with the findings described, several questions still remain. First, how effective are question probes and CGSs relative to other knowledge engineering methods (other than free verbalization)? To answer this question directly, one would have to perform knowledge engineering with question probes as well as with alternative methods. The results could then be compared in terms of accuracy, completeness, or other criteria. The possibility of such an evaluation brings us to a second, more difficult question. How does one evaluate whether a knowledge base is complete? If we define *complete* as containing all of the knowledge that the user will need, it is clear that there will be situations where we do not have any way to determine the completeness of the knowledge base. There really are no algorithms to verify that a knowledge base is complete in the sense of meeting all the potential needs of the user.

Although we do not have any ultimate answer to the question of determining completeness, we have developed one approach that has worked for evaluating procedural goal/action hierarchies. We simply ask a novice to read the graph and perform the activities represented there. A novice is defined as someone who has the necessary background or prerequisite knowledge to understand the information contained in the graph, but does not directly know the information itself. For example, in reading a graph for operating a VCR, background knowledge would include how to push buttons, insert objects into slots, turn on a TV, and so forth. Clearly most adults would have such background knowledge. If the graph is complete, all knowledge needed to perform the tasks will be available, even if the person must delve into several layers of nodes to understand the procedures and concepts. Although this method of evaluation appears to work well with goal/action hierarchies, we desire a more systematic and reliable method that could be applied to all types of structures.

In the meantime, we have obtained a reasonable amount of evidence that question probes elicit significantly more information than less structured verbalization methods. Combined with the fact that the technique supports the knowledge engineer by specifying the questions to be presented, we feel that the approach constitutes a substantial enhancement to current knowledge acquisition practices.

ACKNOWLEDGMENTS

This research was supported in part by a grant awarded to the authors by the Air Force Office of Scientific Research (88-0063). We are grateful to Arthur Graesser for his helpful insights as we refined the question probe methodology.

REFERENCES

Amir, S. (1989). Building integrated expert systems. *AI Expert, 4*, 26–37.

Fisher, K. N. (1990). Semantic networking: The new kid on the block. *Journal of Research and Science Teaching, 27*, 1001–1018.

Fisher, K. N., Saletti, J., Patterson, H., Thornton, R., Lipson, J., & Spring, C. (1990). Computer-based concept mapping. *Journal of College Science Teaching, 19*, 347–352.

Gordon, S. E. (1989). Theory and methods for knowledge acquisition. *AI Applications in Natural Resource Management, 3*, 19–30.

Gordon, S. E. (in press). Implications of cognitive theory for knowledge acquisition. In R. Hoffman (Ed.), *The cognition of experts: Psychological research and empirical AI*. New York: Springer-Verlag.

Gordon, S. E., & Gill, R. T. (1989). *The formation and use of conceptual structures in problem-solving domains* (Tech. Rep. for AFOSR grant No. 88-0063). Moscow, ID: University of Idaho.

Gordon, S. E., & Gill, R. T. (1991). *Knowledge engineering for hypertext documents*. Unpublished manuscript, University of Idaho, Psychology Department, Moscow, ID.

Gordon, S. E., & Lewis, V. (1990). Knowledge engineering for hypertext instructional systems. *Proceedings of the Human Factors Society 34th Annual Meeting* (pp. 1412–1416). Santa Monica, CA: Human Factors Society.

Graesser, A. C., & Clark, L. F. (1985). *Structures and procedures of implicit knowledge*. Norwood, NJ: Ablex.

Graesser, A. C., & Franklin, S. P. (1990). QUEST: A cognitive model of question answering. *Discourse Processes, 13*, 279–304.

Graesser, A. C., & Gordon, S. E. (1991). Question answering and the organization of world knowledge. In G. Craik, A. Ortony, & W. Kessen (Eds.), *Essays in honor of George Mandler* (pp. 227–243). Hillsdale, NJ: Lawrence Erlbaum Associates.

Graesser, A. C., Gordon, S. E., & Brainerd, L. E. (in press). QUEST: A model of question answering. *Computers and Mathematics with Applications*.

Graesser, A. C., Hemphill, D. H., & Brainerd, L. E. (1989). Question answering in the context of causal mechanisms. *Proceedings of the 11th Annual Conference of the Cognitive Science Society* (pp. 621–626). Hillsdale, NJ: Lawrence Erlbaum Associates.

Graesser, A. C., & Murachver, T. (1985). Symbolic procedures of question answering. In A. C. Graesser & J. B. Black (Eds.), *The psychology of questions* (pp. 15–88). Hillsdale, NJ: Lawrence Erlbaum Associates.

Hillman, D. (1988). Bridging acquisition and representation. *AI Expert, 3*, 38–46.

Sowa, J. F. (1984). *Conceptual structures: Information processing in mind and machine*. Reading, MA: Addison-Wesley.

Woodward, B. (1990). Knowledge acquisition at the front end: Defining the domain. *Knowledge Acquisition, 2*, 73–94.

4 Question Generation and the Systems Analysis Process

Thomas W. Lauer
Eileen Peacock
Sheila M. Jacobs
Oakland University

Soaring software costs make the economic consequences of even minor productivity improvements in the process of software development substantial. Estimates in 1985 place U.S. software costs at $70 billion, worldwide software costs at $140 billion, and the growth rate at 12% (Boehm, 1987). It is also well-known that a large percentage of custom-developed systems are unsuccessful because they are late, over budget, or fail to meet specifications. Maintenance costs that run from two to four times the original development cost of a system are partially a byproduct of this failure (Shemer, 1987). Nevertheless, most informed information systems (IS) researchers and practitioners have recognized that there is no panacea for the problem of software productivity. This is a multifaceted problem that must be attacked on various fronts.

From the standpoint of error frequency and error cost, the determination of information requirements is a most crucial stage. It is during this stage that the systems analyst must have the greatest interaction with the user. The direct interview of the user is still a primary means of obtaining the information necessary to begin building a system (Awad, 1985). Some practitioners identify this process indirectly as a source of "software gaps" (Barnes, 1989) or directly as a "communication bottleneck" (Hurd, 1989). By and large, very little is known about the role of questioning in the process of information requirements determination. The body of knowledge in IS has little to offer in this area other than platitudes and naive theory.

The objective of this study is to explore the role that questioning plays in the information requirements determination process. This chapter reports on an exploratory study that examined the relationship between questioning processes and the subsequent representation of a system in the form of a data-flow diagram

(DFD). We take the general approach of mapping question types onto an ideal representation. We then compare the questions that subjects ask to this mapping. This chapter is organized in three parts. First, we examine relevant literature on systems analysis. Second, we briefly describe a theory of questioning from cognitive psychology. Third, we report a study and some conclusions we could induce from the data analysis.

BACKGROUND FOR PROJECT

Errors are pervasive during the early analysis and conceptual design of an information system. For example, one large study showed that the information requirements determination phase had to be repeated in over 50% of the systems studied because important requirements were missed (Jenkins, Naumann, & Wetherbe, 1984). There are positive relationships between time spent during the early logical design stage of the life cycle and both budget compliance and user satisfaction (McKeen, 1983). There are serious economic repercussions of errors occurring early in the life cycle and discovered when the system becomes operative (Boehm, 1973).

This research calls attention to the importance of errors in analysis and design by emphasizing outcomes. Both the error itself and its economic consequence are important outcomes. It is now necessary to extend this research by examining the processes that lead to these errors. A number of researchers have stressed the importance of understanding the process by which the analyst identifies the user's information requirements. Unfortunately, there is inadequate knowledge regarding the processes of analysis and design (Banbury, 1987; Turner, 1987), particularly the interaction between the analyst and the user.

Note that many software development methodologies emphasize product rather than process. There are various deliverables associated with each step of the life cycle. For example, there is an information requirements specification document that represents the agreement between the user and the analyst. However, methodologies offer little guidance about the process of information exchange between the analyst and the user that leads to the creation of this document.

As mentioned earlier, the interview is still a common means of information gathering for the analyst. A number of authors underscore the importance of interviewing and communication skill to the analysis and design process (Barnes, 1989; Malhotra, Thomas, Carroll, & Miller, 1980; Gould & Lewis, 1985; Hurd, 1989; Shemer, 1987). Malhotra et al. (1980) claimed that communication problems between users and analyst/designers constitute the greatest cause of software problems. They suggest that improvements in communication methods could have a major impact on software cost. Unfortunately, there is not a solid theoretical and conceptual foundation that dictates optimal interviewing and questioning techniques.

In conclusion, the IS field is in need of research that examines the process of analyst/user question-and-answer dialogues. Research of this type should investigate the analyst's evolving understanding of the user's problem. It should also examine the relationship between that understanding and the means by which the analyst gains information, namely through a question-and-answer dialogue.

PSYCHOLOGICAL RESEARCH ON QUESTIONING

Recent psychological research on questioning seeks to discover the relationship between a person's questions and that person's cognitive representations and processes. These studies have spanned several social and communication activities. Some of this research specifically investigated the relationship between question answering and knowledge structures (Collins, Warnock, Aiello, & Miller, 1975; Lehnert, 1978; Lehnert, Dyer, Johnson, Young, & Harley, 1983; Norman, 1973; Singer, 1990; Souther, Acker, Lester, & Porter, 1989). The work of Graesser and colleagues (Graesser & Clark, 1985; Graesser & Franklin, 1990; Graesser & Goodman, 1985) has mapped different semantic categories of questions with different knowledge structures. For example, goal hierarchies are structures that represent goals, plans, and intentional actions. Goal orientation questions and instrumental/procedural questions are appropriate for extracting information from goal hierarchies.

In their scheme, the knowledge structures are represented by means of a conceptual graph that shows nodes (roughly equal to propositions) and arcs showing the relationship between nodes. The nodes which represent concepts, states, events, or goals are connected by directional and categorized arcs. The categories of arcs include property, consequence, implies, and reason (see Fig. 4.1). For example, the state (S) "company has a credit clerk" is implied (Im) by the event (E), "credit clerk checks customer credit."

A few studies have developed taxonomies for classifying questions. For example, Lehnert (1978) developed an artificial intelligence model that specified question answering procedures for 13 semantic categories of questions. Graesser, Lang, and Horgan (1988) extended that research by refining the semantic categories and by adding pragmatic and communication dimensions. These two additional dimensions explicitly consider the context of the question. For example, the pragmatic dimension addresses the questioner's motives for asking a question. Some examples of pragmatic categories are information acquisition and assertions. Questions in the information acquisition category are prototypical questions in that the questioner genuinely seeks the information. In contrast, assertions include rhetorical questions in which the questioner expresses a point of view.

The pragmatic category that characterizes the most common motivation for the systems analyst's questioning is information acquisition. The objective of the analyst/user interview is to develop a common understanding of the user's infor-

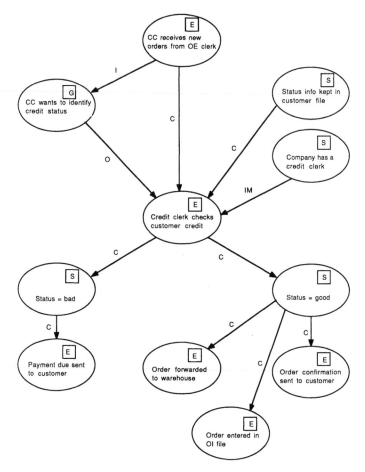

FIG. 4.1. Partial conceptual graph for the credit clerk's role. C = Consequence; I = Initiate; Im = Implies; O = Outcome; G = Goal; S = State; and E = Event.

mation processing activities. Many questions are directed toward determining the common ground between the analyst and the user. Other questions seek to confirm the analyst's speculations about roles and procedures in the user's department.

The semantic categorization scheme makes most sense when considering bona fide questions asked for the purpose of acquiring information. We used the semantic categories from the Lehnert (1978) taxonomy as modified by Graesser et al. (1988) to classify the analyst's questions. The majority of the questions fell within the five categories shown in Table 4.1.

Research Issues

The research described in this chapter is exploratory. We were interested in understanding how systems analysts use questioning to gain an understanding of the information flows in a business system. More generally, we were interested in discovering how systems analysts develop a conceptual understanding of an information system. There are two categories of data models, physical models, and logical models. Physical models describe the physical storage of data. They represent the physical characteristics of the storage media. Logical models represent the user's conceptualization of the data (Davis & Olson, 1985).

One criticism of traditional data models (hierarchical, network, and relational) has been their relative closeness to physical data models (Hull & King, 1990). Traditional models do not support conceptual modeling adequately. One result of this has been that users typically have difficulty understanding the traditional data model. A goal of semantic data modeling has been to counteract this difficulty by developing a formalism for the clear representation of the semantic structure of the application (Hammer & McLeod, 1990). The process of database development includes the development of a logical representation, translation of the logical representation into a physical representation, and implementation of the physical representation. This research aims at clarifying the process by which the analyst develops a logical model, in this case, a data-flow diagram (DFD).

TABLE 4.1
Semantic Categories Frequently Found in the User/Analyst Interviews

Category	Description and Example
Verification	Inquires whether a proposition is true. "Does the order entry clerk contact accounts receivable?"
Disjunctive	Inquires about which of a set of alternatives is the case. "Do all the orders go to the credit clerk or the warehouse?"
Concept completion	Requests further clarification (who, what, when, where) regarding states, actions, or events. "Who takes telephone orders?"
Causal consequent	Inquires about the effects of some event. "What happens if the customer is late paying their bill?"
Instrumental/Procedural	Inquires about what plans or procedures are used by an agent to carry out some intentional act. "How does the credit clerk check a customer's credit?"

Mapping questions onto a logical model provides a basis for examining the questions that analysts actually ask.

Specifically, the research determined what information, elicited through question-answer dialogues, is useful for representing an information system in the form of a DFD. A DFD is drawn using four basic symbols. The data-flow symbol is an arrow showing the flow of data. The process symbol is a rounded box depicting processes that transform the data. The data store symbol is an open rectangle showing where the data is stored. The external entity symbol is a rectangle that indicates the sources or destinations of the data.

The analysis explored the relationship between questions asked and an overall evaluation of the DFD that was produced. Inasmuch as we were able to represent the description of the business system in the form of a conceptual graph, we were able to make some predictions about what questions the analyst would need to ask to discover the missing information in specific parts of the DFD. This enabled us to associate individual questions with specific parts of the DFD during the iterative process of converging on its correct representation.

Experimental Procedure

Twenty-two information systems majors, who were enrolled in an undergraduate systems analysis class, participated in the experiment for class credit. They had studied the process of information requirements determination and the development of DFDs. In addition, they had all worked on a systems analysis case and completed exercises in which they prepared DFDs based on text descriptions of business situations.

Subjects were given the incomplete description of a business system shown in Table 4.2. They were told that their task was to develop a thorough understanding of the system by means of the interview process and then to represent the system in a DFD. They were told to read the written description of the system and to think about what additional information they would need to acquire before drawing a DFD.

TABLE 4.2
Incomplete Description of Music-By-Mail Business System

The Music-by-Mail Record Club advertises record and record albums in a variety of magazines. The club's receptionist handles the incoming mail and distributes it to the appropriate departments. The order-entry clerk in the sales department does the initial work on the mail-in orders and also handles phone orders. Pertinent information is then sent to the credit clerk.

The order-entry clerk also handles order cancellations, including communication with the customer and the warehouse.

The credit clerk handles customer credit status procedures, including dealings with the customer and and warehouse. The warehouse is responsible for order-filling procedures and also interfaces with the accounts receivable department.

The accounts receivable department handles customer bills and payments and maintains files.

Adapted from Whitten, Bentley, and Ho (1986).

TABLE 4.3
Complete Description of Music-By-Mail Business System

The Music-by-Mail Record Club advertises records and albums in a variety of magazines. Most orders are submitted by magazine subscribers who complete and send coupons to the mail order company. All mail arrives at the receptionist's desk. The receptionist sorts and distributes the mail to the appropriate departments. Mail orders and letters requesting order cancellations are forwarded to an order-entry clerk in the sales department.

The order-entry clerk initially checks the availability and the price of the ordered items, possible mailing a bac-order notice to the customer. This clerk also takes orders from customers directly by phone and forwards all fillable orders to the credit clark.

When the order-entry clerk receives a letter requesting an order cancellation (or a cancellation by telephone), the status of the order is first determined. If the customer order has not been invoiced, the order-entry clerk informs the warehouse that the order should not be canceled and then informs the customer that the cancellation has been completed.

When fillable orders are received by the credit clark, the customer's credit status is checked. Orders are approved and an order-confirmation letter is sent to those customers with good credit standing. Customers with bad credit standing are sent a payment-overdue notice requesting prepayment. The credit clark forwards approved orders to the warehouse.

The warehouse fills the approved order and updates the inventory availability. A packing slip is sent with the packaged order to the customer, and a shipping notice is sent to the accounts receivable department.

Accounts receivable bills the customer for the products shipped. This department also maintains the invoice data files, updating them to reflect charges or payments received. Payments are received in the mail and delivered to accounts Receivable by the receptionist. A payment is sent to the customer.

Adapted from Whitten, Bentley, and Ho (1986).

After studying the written description, each subject was ushered into an office in order to interview an "employee" of the company. One of the researchers, who had thoroughly studied the complete system description found in Table 4.3, played the role of the employee throughout the experiment. The subject was provided with paper and pencil to take notes during the interview. The interview was recorded on audio tape. There was no time limit for the interview. After the interview, the subject was escorted to another office and was told to draw a DFD of the system. There was no time limit for this part of the experimental task.

Analysis

The initial analysis of the experimental results consisted of classifying the questions in the transcribed interviews into the semantic categories of the Graesser et al. taxonomy and grading the DFDs. Two of the authors classified the questions into the semantic categories independently of each other. Any disagreements that they had in the classification of a particular question were resolved through discussion. We tabulated the number of questions asked by each subject and the frequencies for the different question categories. Each question was also given a topical classification using the same procedure. This classification identified the specific flow or element of the DFD that the question addressed. Some questions asked about specific flows that were possible but did not actually exist. For example, there was no data flow between the receptionist and the warehouse.

Such questions were classified as associated with the theoretical flow. The other questions were not analyzed further.

An important issue that can influence the validity of the results is interrater reliability. Huck, Cormier, & Bounds (1974) suggested the use of percent agreement calculations as a measure of interrater reliability for categorical classification. For a sample of 363 questions, the two judges agreed on 321 of them ($\hat{p} =$ .88 for the entire corpus of questions). The resulting 99% confidence interval for the reliability score indicates that initial agreement for the entire corpus of questions in the experiment was between .85 and .92.

The DFDs were graded by one of the researchers. The correct DFD is shown in Fig. 4.2. It consists of 9 elements and 19 flows. We calculated a DFD quality score by awarding 2 points credit for each correct component of the DFD making a total of 56 possible points. For some of the flows, there were two items of data transferred. If the subject correctly identified only one of these, 1 point was given.

It is possible that the subjects did not actually gain any useful information from their interviews. In order to test this, the abridged problem description shown in Table 4.2 was given to another group of 20 IS majors taking the same undergraduate systems analysis class in a different semester. This second class was taught by the same instructor using the same material and teaching methods. This control group of subjects was told that there was missing information in the description but that they would not be permitted to ask any questions. After studying Table 4.2, they were asked to represent the system as a DFD.

Results

The DFD quality scores were significantly higher in the experimental group than in the control group. The mean score for the experimental group was 39.4, whereas the mean score for the control group was 32.8. A t-test was run to assess whether the means were significantly different and was found to be significant ($t = 4.213$, $p < .005$). The fact that the DFD quality scores were higher for the experimental group suggests that the process of question asking improves performance of the task.

Subsequent analysis concentrated on the relationships between actual question generation and the correctness of the DFD. To test the association between the total number of questions asked by a subject and the DFD results, the Pearson correlation coefficient was calculated. There was a significant relationship between the number of questions a subject asked and the DFD score ($r = .54$, $p <$ .01). One striking result is the large number of verification questions (57% of the total). The second most common question type was the concept completion question (21% of the total). Instrumental/procedural questions made up 9% of the total.

Although the semantic categories were adequate for classifying the questions, in many cases the subjects used a conditional type of construction to pose a question. These questions were in the form: IF condition X, THEN question, as shown in the following: (a) "If a customer has good credit, how does the process continue?" and (b) "If it is not available, then does he or she communicate with the customer?" The first example is an instrumental/procedure question. The subject is asking what the procedure is for handling a customer with good credit after the credit check is completed. The second question is a verification question.

A further analysis of the verification questions revealed that a significant number of the verification questions were forms of confirmation. That is, the questioner proposed a hypothesis and followed it with a verification question. The questioners used this type of question to validate their understanding of some part of the system. Of all verification questions, 43.3% were forms of confirmation. Examples are provided in the following: (a) "When it is sent to the credit clerk, all orders are sent to the credit clerk, correct?" and (b) "Is it the case that the inventory file is checked to make sure things are in when he or she does the initial work on the mail in and phone orders?"

There was enough information in the abridged description of the business situation to enable the subject to discern all of the process elements in the DFD. In total, 14 of the subjects made no mistakes on these elements and only 2 had more than one error on the process elements. The information gained during the interviews concerned the data flows. It is for this reason that the more finely grained analysis that follows concentrated on the data flows.

We developed a conceptual graph for the part of the DFD that shows the flows that concern the credit clerk. This conceptual graph is shown in Fig. 4.2. Based on the conceptual graph structure, we predicted that the following questions would elicit the information necessary to represent the flows relating to the credit clerk.

1. What causes the credit clerk to check the credit status?
2. How does the credit clerk check the credit status?
3. What happens if the credit status is good?
4. What happens if the credit status is bad?
5. What does the credit clerk do after checking credit status?

There was a systematic relationship between the predicted question and the probability of correctly representing the DFD flow ($X^2 = 12.28, p < .005$). For 75% of the cases when the DFD flow was incorrect, a predicted question was not asked. For 77% of the cases when the predicted question was asked, the flow was correctly represented. A further analysis of the cases where the subject asked questions but still misrepresented the flows showed one subject who accounted for 4 out of 10 such errors. This individual misunderstood DFDs or data flows in

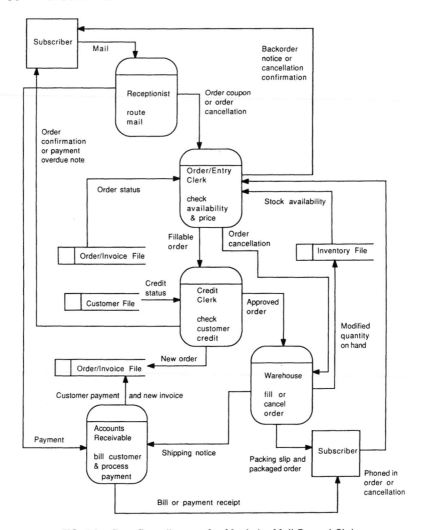

FIG. 4.2. Data-flow diagram for Music-by-Mail Record Club.

general. His DFD showed flows from the credit clerk to the customer passing through computer files.

For 33% of the cases, the subject was able to represent correctly the data flow without asking the relevant question. In these cases, the subject may have already had insight into the problem that stemmed from previously asked questions and from a general insight into business systems.

A similar analysis was carried out for those flows that are theoretically possible but are not actually present in the business situation. For example, there is no data flow between the credit clerk and the receptionist. In this case, an error is made by including a flow where none should be. If the flow is feasible, it may be necessary to ask a question in order to determine that it does not exist.

There was a significant relationship between asking a question and correctly representing these nonexistent flows ($X^2 = 6.84, p < .01$). For 87% of the cases when an erroneous flow was included, no question was asked. For 68% of the cases when a question was asked, the subject correctly omitted the erroneous flow.

DISCUSSION

A major result of this study is the finding that there is a positive relationship between the number of questions asked and the DFD score. On the surface this appears to be obvious. One might conclude that the best advice to give an analyst is to ask a lot of questions. However, in order to ask a question, a person must have a certain level of knowledge. Complete novices have so little knowledge that they cannot formulate useful questions for problem solving. One study (Miyake & Norman, 1979) manipulated learners' background knowledge and the difficulty of the material to be learned. Those with greater background knowledge asked many more questions about the more difficult material. They also asked many fewer questions about the simpler material presumably because they already knew the answers.

The analysis of the direct relationship between the questions asked and the correct representation of the specific parts of the DFD is complicated by the general knowledge possessed by the individual subjects. Individual subjects were sometimes able to get many parts of the DFD correct without asking a specific question about that part. In these cases, subjects were apparently able to understand the data flow based on other information they had gained from the interview. It should be noted that the subjects did not ask questions about the vast majority of the theoretically possible flows. One wonders how they were able to economize their search by eliminating nonexistent flows from consideration and concentrating their efforts on the other flows.

The QUEST model of question answering (Graesser & Franklin, 1990) is based on the assumption that there are two types of information sources when answering a question. Episodic knowledge structures (EKS) are representations of knowledge gained from specific experiences. For example, a systems analyst may have studied the office procedures for some particular department with an organization or may have had a conversation about the office procedures in another company. Generic knowledge structures (GKS) are more abstract representations that summarize the properties that characterize the object, activity, or other type of concept. For example, a systems analyst would have a GKS for a computer that would include the features and properties of a generic computer.

In QUEST, it is assumed that a person's cognitive system contains a large number of GKSs and EKSs and that these serve as the information sources for questions. This conceptualization is useful for theorizing about the analyst's process of understanding a business situation through a question-and-answer dialogue. The analyst brings a complex knowledge structure consisting of several GKSs and EKSs and maps of these structures to a skeletal description of a business situation. The resulting knowledge structure allows the analyst to identify gaps that must be filled prior to representing the business situation in some form such as a DFD. The richness of the knowledge will determine the number of significant gaps that the analyst can identify.

The preceding account is consistent with current views concerning the nature of expertise. Expertise is defined as operative knowledge that manifests itself in the active solution of problems (Johnson, 1984; Johnson, Zualkernon, & Garber, 1987). The expert is able to process information more quickly and efficiently than the novice. Experts apparently have access not only to greater amounts of knowledge but also have a more efficient organization of that knowledge (Chi, Glaser, & Rees, 1981). Experts have a greater understanding of the implications of different events or facts.

The skilled analyst is better able to identify the information needed to represent a business situation correctly. This manifests itself through the asking of more and better-targeted questions. Furthermore, research on expertise indicates that this is a skill that can be learned. Rather than being an art that is manifested more or less randomly in the population, skill in the analytical process can be studied and then taught.

Part of the folklore of interviewing for systems analysts is that they should avoid closed questions (Semprevivo, 1982). The results of our study show that the preponderance of the questions asked by the subjects were verification questions. These are closed questions that can be answered with a yes or no response. There is an issue as to whether these questions are less desirable in that they will normally elicit less information.

The pragmatics of a question concern the goals of the speech participants. For much discourse, both participants share responsibility for the exchange of information. Pragmatically cooperative answers to imperfectly phrased questions may correct misconceptions rather than directly answer the question (Kaplan, 1983). The person supplying a pragmatically cooperative answer attempts to understand and answer the intended question rather than answering the question literally. What this means in terms of verification questions is that the pragmatically cooperative answer may be more than yes or no. For example:

Q: Are there any other documents that the warehouse deals with (when they send the goods out)?
A: Yes, they notify accounts/receivable.

For this question, the answer *yes* is technically correct but not pragmatically cooperative by itself.

Verification questions may not elicit less information except when the situation is uncooperative. An example of this type of setting would be an attorney interviewing a hostile witness. For most common analyst-user interviews, the situation should be sufficiently cooperative that verification questions will not have an adverse effect.

CONCLUSION

Improvement in the process of information requirements determination could be leveraged to yield large productivity gains in the development of applications software. This research has aimed at understanding the effects of questions posed by analysts on the subsequent representation of a system in the form of a DFD. The results of this exploratory research lead to the conclusion that the analysis of questions can give insight into the analyst's cognitive representations.

Although this research is exploratory it enables us to speculate about a general strategy of questioning that can be used in conjunction with DFDs. The DFDs representing business systems consist of process elements, data flows, data stores, and external entities. The process elements are persons whose roles are defined by the tasks they perform and computer processes. The data flows carry the inputs and outputs of each process element. Inputs to and outputs from the business system originate or terminate in external entities. A data store is used to store internally the output from a process.

An appropriate first set of questions should be directed toward identifying the process elements of the DFD. These questions inquire about the people (with job roles) or the computer processes that make up the department. The subsequent questions identify specific tasks relevant to each process element previously identified. Additional follow-up questions further decompose the tasks into subtasks. This decomposition would ask about: (a) what causes the person (or process) to perform the task, (b) how the person carries out the task, (c) what different contingencies are related to the task, (d) what the consequences are for each contingency, and (e) what happens after the task is carried out. The following example dialogue illustrates these types of questions.

Q: What does the credit clerk do?
A: Checks credit.
Q: What causes the credit clerk to check credit?
A: The credit clerk receives a new order from the order entry clerk.
Q: How does the credit clerk check credit?
A: The credit clerk checks the customer's credit status in the customer file.
Q: What different kinds of credit status can there be?

A: Good and bad.

Q: What if credit is good?

And so on.

One premise of this study has been that the development of process skills can provide qualitative improvements in the products of development methodologies. Our results show a significant relationship between the analyst's questions and the correct representation of the data flows. These results illustrate the value of mapping questions to logical models. This approach is a practical method for learning how analysts develop an understanding of a business system. It was not necessary for the subjects in our study to ask questions about every possible data flow. A model of the analyst's inquiry process would have to account for questions that are omitted as well as those generally asked.

Our research approach should also be useful for determining effective question asking strategies for developing other logical models such as entity relationship diagrams or semantic data models. Logical models are important products of systems development methodologies. They may serve as an objective focus for analyst-user communications. In addition, they are used as the input for the physical design of the system.

This research has implications for both the practice of systems development and the training of systems analysts. Improving the process and products of systems development depends in part on the development of effective inquiry strategies. Inquiry strategies can be incorporated into system development methodologies.

REFERENCES

Awad, E. M. (1985). *Systems analysis and design.* Homewood, IL: Irwin.

Banbury, J. (1987). Towards a framework for systems analysis practice. In R. J. Boland & R. A, Hirscheim (Eds.), *Critical issues in information systems research* (pp. 79–96). Chichester: Wiley.

Barnes, J. (1989). Trapping those computer gaps. *Computerworld, 23,* 21.

Boehm, B. W. (1973). Software and its impact: A quantitative assessment, *Datamation, 19, 5,* 48–59.

Boehm, B. W. (1987). Improving software productivity. *Computer, 20, 9,* 43–57.

Chi, M. T. H., Glaser, R., & Rees, E. (1981). Expertise in problem solving. In R. J. Sternberg (Ed.), *Advances in the psychology of human intelligence* (Vol. 1, pp. 7–75). Hillsdale, NJ: Lawrence Erlbaum Associates.

Collins, A., Warnock, E. H., Aiello, N., & Miller, M. L. (1975). Reasoning from incomplete knowledge. In D. G. Bobrow & A. Collins (Eds.), *Representation and understanding* (pp. 383–414). New York: Academic Press.

Davis, G. B., & Olson, M. H. (1985). *Management information systems: Conceptual foundations, structure, and development.* New York: McGraw-Hill.

Gould, J. D., & Lewis, C. (1985). Designing for usability: Key principles and what designers think. *Communications of the ACM 28, 3,* 300–311.

Graesser, A. C., & Clark, L. F. (1985). *Structures and procedures of implicit knowledge.* Norwood, NJ: Ablex.

Graesser, A. C., & Franklin, S. P. (1990). QUEST: A cognitive model of question answering. *Discourse Processes, 13,* 279–303.

Graesser, A. C., & Goodman, S. M. (1985). How to construct conceptual graph structures. In B. K. Britton & J. B. Black (Eds.), *Understanding expository text.* Hillsdale, NJ: Lawrence Erlbaum Associates.

Graesser, A. C., Lang, K., & Horgan, D. (1988). A taxonomy for question generation. *Questioning Exchange, 2,* 3–15.

Hammer, M., & McLeod, D. (1990). Database description with SDM: A semantic database model. In A. F. Cardenas & D. McLeod (Eds.), *Research foundations in object-oriented and semantic database systems* (pp. 34–69). Englewood Cliffs, NJ: Prentice-Hall.

Huck, S. W., Cormier, W. H., & Bounds, W. G., Jr. (1974). *Reading statistics and research.* New York: Harper & Row.

Hull, R., & King, R. (1990). A tutorial on semantic database modeling. In A. F. Cardenas & D. McLeod (Eds.), *Research foundations in object-oriented and semantic database systems* (pp. 1–33). Englewood Cliffs, NJ: Prentice-Hall.

Hurd, A. (1989). Systems analysts for the 90's. *Computerworld, 23,* 69–73.

Jenkins, A. M., Naumann, J. D., & Wetherbe, J. (1984). Empirical investigation of systems development practices and results. *Information and Management, 1,* 73–82.

Johnson, P. E. (1984). The expert mind: A new challenge for the information scientist. In Th. M. A. Bemelmans (Ed.), *Beyond productivity: Information systems development for organizational effectiveness* (pp. 367–386). Amsterdam: Elsevier Science.

Johnson, P. E., Zualkernon, I., & Garber, S. (1987). Specifications of expertise. *International Journal of Man-Machine Studies, 26,* 161–181.

Kaplan, J. (1983). Cooperative responses from a portable natural language query system. In M. Brady & R. C. Berwick (Eds.), *Computational models of discourse* (pp. 167–208). Cambridge, MA: MIT Press.

Lehnert, W. G. (1978). *The process of question answering.* Hillsdale, NJ: Lawrence Erlbaum Associates.

Lehnert, W. G., Dyer, M. G., Johnson, P. N., Young, C. J., & Harley, S. (1983). BORIS—An experiment in understanding in-depth narratives. *Artificial Intelligence, 20,* 15–62.

Malhotra, A., Thomas, J. M., Carroll, J. M., & Miller, L. A. (1980). Cognitive processes in design. *International Journal of Man-Machine Studies, 12,* 119–140.

McKeen, J. D. (1983). Successful development strategies for business application systems, *MIS Quarterly, 7,* 47–65.

Miyake, N., & Norman, D. A. (1979). To ask a question, one must know enough to know what is not known. *Journal of Verbal Learning and Verbal Behavior, 18,* 357–364.

Norman, D. A. (1973). Memory, knowledge, and the answering of questions. In R. Solso (Ed.), *Contemporary issues in cognitive psychology* (pp. 135–166). Washington, DC: Winston.

Semprevivo, P. C. (1982). *Systems analysis: Definition, process, and design.* Chicago: Science Research Associates.

Shemer, I. (1987). Systems analysis: A systemic analysis of a conceptual model. *Communications of the ACM, 30,* 506–512.

Singer, M. (1990). Answering questions about discourse. *Discourse Processes, 13,* 261–277.

Souther, A., Acker, L., Lester, J., & Porter, B. (1989). Using types to generate explanations in intelligent tutoring systems. In *Proceedings of the Eleventh Annual Conference of the Cognitive Society* (pp. 123–130). Hillsdale, NJ: Lawrence Erlbaum Associates.

Turner, J. A. (1987). Understanding the elements of system design. In R. J. Boland & R. A. Hirscheim (Eds.), *Critical issues in information systems research* (pp. 97–112). New York: Wiley.

Whitten, J. L., Bentley, L. D., & Ho, T. I. M. (1986). *Systems analysis and design methods.* St. Louis: Times Mirror/Mosby College Publishers.

5
The Evolution of Questions in Successive Versions of an Expert System for Real Estate Disposition

Astrid Lipp
Clemson University

Hugh O. Nourse
Robert P. Bostrom
Hugh J. Watson
The University of Georgia

There are two major categories of research that address the role of questions during knowledge acquisition when expert systems are developed. The first category focuses on the questions that a knowledge engineer should ask an expert to best elicit the expert's knowledge. The second examines the questions that experts ask. LaFrance (1988) has enumerated the types of questions that knowledge engineers should ask experts. Lauer and Peacock (chap. 13 in this volume) have examined the questions that individual auditors asked about three scenarios and have compared the profiles of questions asked by different experts. We adopted an approach similar to that of Lauer and Peacock. That is, we analyzed the questions asked by experts. However, instead of comparing profiles of questions asked by individual experts, we compared the profiles of questions experts asked about typical versus troublesome cases. We also compared the questions experts asked with the profiles of questions in successive prototype programs.

Six experts in real estate disposition agreed to participate in four knowledge acquisition sessions. These sessions were intended to elicit the questions that experts actually asked about properties requiring disposition. Our original objective was to incorporate these questions into a knowledge-based system. The research originally assessed the usefulness of the collaborative work support software called PLEXSYS (now called GroupSystems) in supporting the process of simultaneous knowledge acquisition from multiple experts. However, as the experts examined the questions in prototype knowledge-based systems, they realized that in order for the knowledge-based system to be useful to less experienced real estate managers, the questions used by the system would have to be phrased differently than the questions they actually asked. This motivated us to analyze the questions asked by the experts and the questions in successive versions of the system we were developing.

In the first section of this chapter we discuss what motivated us to undertake the study and to use particular research methods. An analysis of the questions asked by experts and the questions that occurred in successive versions of the program follows in the second section. The results of our study and a summary of the conclusions appear in the final section.

THE MOTIVATION FOR THE RESEARCH

The real estate needs of organizations change. Leased space may no longer be needed. Expansion or modification of existing buildings may not be possible or economically feasible. Retailers must abandon outlets in declining retail districts and move closer to thriving new shopping centers. A corporate real estate manager tries to dispose of the property, if no one else in the organization can use it. Nourse and Kingery (1987) surveyed corporate real estate managers and found that only a small percentage of these managers treat the disposal of surplus real estate as an opportunity for their companies to realize a significant profit. Inasmuch as expertise in disposition is scarce, we felt that a knowledge-based system could help disseminate knowledge about real estate disposition among industry personnel, as well as among college students taking real estate courses.

Experts in disposition use heuristics they have developed as a result of years of experience in the disposal of properties. Inasmuch as every property is unique, and conditions for disposition vary from one place to another, as well as over time, an algorithmic approach to selecting a disposition strategy appeared to be inappropriate. The proposed application met Waterman's (1986, pp. 129–132) criteria for determining whether expert system development is possible, justified, and appropriate. Therefore, we undertook an exploratory study to determine whether some of the experts' heuristics could be incorporated into a rule-based system and whether such a system would be useful to their less experienced colleagues.

Surplus properties vary greatly in several characteristics, such as their size, their location, the current real estate market, and the needs of the company that wishes to dispose of the property. Also, disposition is a time-consuming process that may stretch over months or even years. As a result, each individual expert has been involved in the disposition of a relatively small number of properties, and the experiences of individual experts vary considerably. Consequently, the authors felt that a knowledge-based system that contained the knowledge of multiple experts would be more useful than a program based on the knowledge of a single expert.

McGraw and Harbison-Briggs (1989) identified two general methods for knowledge acquisition from multiple experts: *individual* and *group* consultation of multiple experts. A knowledge engineer who interviews experts individually must identify inconsistencies in the knowledge contributed and then either ask the experts to resolve inconsistencies or include multiple lines of reasoning in a single program. Alternatively, a knowledge engineer may build a program based on the knowledge contributed by one expert and then ask other experts to react to the program. In this case, participating experts identify areas of disagreement, but the knowledge engineer may meet repeatedly with experts to resolve conflicts. Although it is more difficult to schedule interviews with groups of experts, such groups can quickly identify and reconcile differences in the knowledge contributed. The knowledge represented in the resulting expert system represents the group consensus. Trice (1988), Ostrovsky (1987), and Plaza, de Mantaras, Aguilar, and Agusti (1987) have described methods for identifying and reconciling inconsistencies in the knowledge contributed by experts who are interviewed individually. McGraw and Harbison-Briggs (1989) have reviewed the results of research involving knowledge acquisition from multiple experts.

The authors felt that group consultation with experts (i.e., simultaneous rather than sequential knowledge acquisition) was best suited for this application. Interaction among experts in disposition might help experts to articulate their knowledge. We expected this to be useful because of the differences in the experiences of our group of experts. The builders of the expert system called ExperTAX^{sm} had found that using two experts for knowledge acquisition was better than using only one because there was a synergistic effect when two experts worked together. Experts in disposition often work alone and do not regularly communicate the details of their thought processes to others. As a result, their initial attempts at verbalizing what they did might not be accurate and complete. We felt that an expert's peers would be best able to detect inaccurate or incomplete formulations of heuristics. Other experts would also be able to identify those terms and procedures that are peculiar to a particular company or industry, as opposed to those that are widely used.

The use of simultaneous knowledge acquisition to build a knowledge-based system would require some means for managing the conflict that was expected to arise among experts. O'Bannon (1988) asked experts, whom he was teaching to write knowledge bases, to work on the same application. The arguments among the experts became so heated that O'Bannon had to "separate them from one another's throats." Texas Instruments knowledge engineers avoid working with multiple experts because of high levels of conflict among the experts. Knowledge-acquisition efforts are sometimes abandoned when more than three experts are involved because of the resulting conflicts. We hoped that computer-based support would minimize the problems associated with simultaneous knowledge acquisition from multiple experts.

Researchers at the University of Arizona developed a set of software tools called PLEXSYS to support collaborative work (Applegate, Chen, Konsynski, &

Nunamaker, 1987; George, Nunamaker, & Vogel, 1988; Heltne, Vinze, Konsynski, & Nunamaker, 1988; Nunamaker, Applegate, & Konsynski, 1987). Although PLEXSYS was originally designed to support group decision making, Bostrom and Anson (1988a, 1988b) have used it to support long-range planning and logical systems design. For this reason, they refer to Collaborative Work Support Software (CWSS) to describe electronic support for activities that include, but are not limited to, decision-making tasks. Most CWSS provide computer-based support for one or more group processes, such as idea generation, issue analysis, and voting (Gray, 1988). PLEXSYS can be used to support all of these group processes.

According to Vogel, Nunamaker, Applegate, and Konsynski (1987), the use of PLEXSYS reduced meeting time for groups of eight or more and improved the quality of decisions made by groups of six or more. The use of PLEXSYS also prevented large groups from becoming bogged down or dominated by a few strong personalities. Because participants in meetings contributed their ideas simultaneously, rather than sequentially, the contributors of comments could not be identified.

Connolly, Jessup, and Valacich (1990) conducted an experiment to investigate the effect of anonymity and evaluative tone on the quantity and quality of ideas generated. Exploratory research at Arizona revealed that users of PLEXSYS thought anonymity of input to PLEXSYS helped a group focus on ideas rather than personalities. They found that experimental subjects made more negative comments when they could enter their comments anonymously. Nevertheless, the negative comments made via PLEXSYS were not taken personally. The system appeared to serve as a buffer between participants in PLEXSYS sessions.

The researchers at the University of Arizona had recognized that PLEXSYS could also be used to support simultaneous knowledge acquisition from multiple experts. Nunamaker et al. (1988) had successfully used PLEXSYS to elicit knowledge from IBM Information Center personnel. The knowledge was represented in the knowledge-based system called ICE-H, which was designed to help users identify and correct software problems. If the program is unable to help a user, an E-mail message is automatically sent to a Help Desk staffer. We concluded that additional investigation was needed to assess the usefulness of PLEXSYS in supporting knowledge acquisition.

To elicit knowledge and to help experts reach a consensus about the knowledge that ICE-H should contain, Nunamaker et al. (1988) used the same PLEXSYS tools in exactly the same sequence as they had been used to support groups engaged in planning. We felt that other PLEXSYS tools and combinations of tools could be used to support knowledge acquisition. Presumably, it would be informative to investigate the matching of tools with the tasks to be supported.

The experts who participated in the development of ICE-H all worked for the same company. Therefore, they had a shared vocabulary and similar experiences in advising clients of the Information Center. They were proficient in the use of computers and had good keyboarding skills. In addition, the problems they were asked to solve occurred frequently and could usually be resolved quickly. In contrast, our group of experts in real estate disposition worked for different companies and had been involved in disposing of different properties. Most characterized themselves as hunt-and-peck typists who use computer terminals or personal computers more than twice a week to work with spreadsheets and corporate systems. We hoped that the use of PLEXSYS would make knowledge acquisition efficient and effective and that it would minimize acrimony among experts.

When we planned the agenda for the first knowledge acquisition session, we focused on: (a) formulating the questions that PLEXSYS would ask the experts carefully and (b) capturing the questions that individual experts keyed into PLEXSYS. This permitted us to determine how much the sequence and wording of questions overlapped among experts. We expected to capture the questions experts asked one another about specific properties, so that we could incorporate both the exact wording and the correct sequence of questions in the program. However, as the experts discussed specific properties, it became apparent that many questions they asked one another could not be included in a program unless the program also had access to detailed information about specific real estate markets and the real estate needs of specific industries; such information would have to be updated regularly. Because it was not feasible to incorporate detailed information about specific markets and industry needs into the program, our experts decided to modify the questions in the program so that it would be generally useful. As they ran prototype programs, our experts also realized that the program would not be able to process natural-language answers to most questions.

This chapter examines the questions asked by the experts while they were discussing specific surplus properties. We also analyze the questions that the experts felt that the knowledge-based system should contain. Once we realized that experts' questions would have to be altered for our program to be useful, we wanted to explore the differences between experts' questions and those they determined should be included in successive versions of the program.

RESEARCH METHODOLOGY

The Experts

Before any experts in disposition were identified, an expert was defined as someone who: (a) has 8 or more years of experience in the disposition of surplus corporate real estate, (b) is highly regarded by his or her peers, and (c) is involved in professional organizations. An alternative definition of an expert was someone who is considered an expert in the disposition of surplus corporate real estate by a person who meets the first three criteria.

Once these criteria had been formulated, 24 corporate real estate managers or independent consultants who met the first three criteria were identified and invited to participate. These experts suggested that we invite 13 other real estate professionals, whom they considered to be experts in disposition. Of the 37 people contacted, 6 experts agreed to participate in four knowledge-acquisition sessions.

Although the titles of participating experts varied, all were or had recently been managers of corporate real estate units. The experts' ages ranged from 43 to 63, with an average age of 54.3. All experts had completed some college courses. Two had bachelor's degrees, and three had master's degrees. Not all of these experts' work experience had involved corporate real estate or even disposition. Although they had been employed full-time an average of 29 years (with a range of 18 to 36 years), the average number of years of experience in corporate real estate was 21.2 (with a range of 6 to 31 years), and the average number of years of experience in disposition was 18.2 years (with a range of 5 to 25 years).

The Knowledge-Acquisition Process

Agendas for the four knowledge-acquisition sessions called for experts to discuss those properties with which they had direct experience. Experts would also react to prototype knowledge-based systems during the second, third, and fourth sessions.

Initially, the research design encouraged PLEXSYS support whenever possible during the first, second, and fourth knowledge-acquisition sessions, but not during the third knowledge-acquisition session. Presumably, we would be in a better position to assess the usefulness of PLEXSYS support if it was not available during one session. A single process facilitator and two technical facilitators provided support during all four sessions. The public screen was used throughout the knowledge-acquisition process. The arrangement of people and equipment during the first knowledge-acquisition session is illustrated in Fig. 5.1. Although another room was used for subsequent sessions, room arrangements were similar, except that experts were seated at a U-shaped table.

Existing research and anecdotal observation have emphasized the difficulties associated with eliciting knowledge (Hart, 1986; Hoffman, 1987; Johnson, 1983; McGraw & Harbison-Briggs, 1989; O'Bannon, 1988). We rejected the possibility of having a faculty member in real estate studies generate case descriptions that experts would discuss. Experts might not be able to access their knowledge as readily if they were asked to discuss cases that were very different from those with which they were familiar. Moreover, the selection of the cases could bias the input we got from the experts. Instead, we asked experts to prepare for the first session by thinking about dispositions in which they had been directly involved.

One method for eliciting knowledge is to observe an expert work. However,

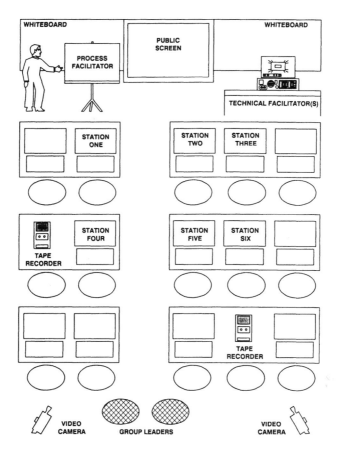

FIG. 5.1. The arrangement of people and equipment during the first knowledge-acquisition session.

this was not practical, because it can take months or even years until the disposition of a property is completed. Although it was not possible to watch these experts work in their normal settings, we wanted to create a setting that would allow them to apply their expertise in a way that could be observed and recorded. By asking experts to discuss cases, we tried to simulate the exchanges that real estate personnel engage in while working on an actual disposition. Such exchanges may involve junior real estate managers working on a disposition who come to experts in disposition for advice, top management of the organization, and lower-level personnel familiar with the property requiring disposition.

Our original intent was to capture the exact wording of the experts' questions and answers while solving these problems, so that these could be incorporated in the knowledge-based system. We did not want to build a program that contained only what experts reported that they did because retrospective reports of behavior are known to be unreliable indicators of actual behavior (Ericsson & Simon, 1980). For example, O'Bannon (1988) cited the case of cardiologists whose observed behavior in treating patients did not coincide with descriptions in their book. Similarly, Johnson (1983) observed a discrepancy between how a colleague taught his medical students diagnosis and how he did it.

During the first two sessions, experts discussed properties and recommended disposition strategies. The prototype knowledge-based systems prepared after each knowledge-acquisition session were based on transcripts of experts' discussions. The questions the experts asked about specific properties were incorporated verbatim whenever experts felt that the answers to these questions were important in selecting a disposition strategy. During the last two knowledge-acquisition sessions, experts modified the wording and sequence of questions in the KBS without discussing any additional cases. The following questions were collected:

1. *Inputs to the PLEXSYS system.* Protocols of all questions asked about specific properties as well as the answers provided by the experts who contributed the descriptions were displayed on the public screen and saved. Similarly, experts' revisions of the structure of the program and the wording of questions the program should ask were entered into PLEXSYS's word processor and displayed.

2. *Audiotapes and videotapes of all formal sessions.* All interactions were recorded on two tape recorders and two video cameras, one positioned on each side of the room.

3. *Successive versions of the knowledge-based system.* A prototype program was demonstrated at the beginning of the second, third, and fourth knowledge-acquisition sessions. Feedback provided at the last session was incorporated into the fourth version of the program. The current version of the program reflects changes requested by the experts during telephone conversations.

Description of the Knowledge-Acquisition Sessions

At the beginning of the first knowledge-acquisition session, the experts established their objective for the program, namely "to build a knowledge-based system to help less experienced corporate real estate managers in the disposition or redeployment of surplus corporate real estate." After consolidating the list of types of properties and the list of strategies, they decided the order in which they would discuss cases. Those cases classified as *occur most frequently/day-to-day/typical* would be discussed first, followed by cases in other categories: *most troublesome, learned the most from, most costly, most lucrative, corporate urgency, memorable cases, and straightforward cases.*

Eight "Folders" of the Topic Commenter tool in PLEXSYS were given the titles just listed. The experts were asked to select the appropriate category and then to key in a description of each case they wished to contribute. They entered 19 descriptions of properties into PLEXSYS. The description of the first property discussed appears in Table 5.1.

Discussion of each case occurred in several steps. The description of the property was first displayed on the public screen. The process facilitator asked the contributing expert only to fill in details missing in the description. For example, one expert had given the important parameters, but not their values. A technical facilitator entered the additional details into the description of the case. Experts were then asked to use the Alternative Evaluator tool of PLEXSYS to evaluate the appropriateness of using each disposition strategy in the list of strategies created earlier. They used a scale of 0 to 10, with 0 meaning "I would not consider using this disposition strategy for this property" and 10 meaning "This is my preferred choice of disposition strategy for this property, given what I know about the property." PLEXSYS automatically tabulated the results of voting and provided a tabular display of results, a rank ordering, and a bar chart that graphically represented the results. After every vote, results were displayed on the public screen. Results of the initial vote always showed a diversity of views about which strategies were appropriate.

Experts were asked to simultaneously enter one question about the property into the Topic Commenter tool of PLEXSYS. These questions were displayed on the public screen. As the contributor of the case answered each question, a technical facilitator keyed in the expert's answer, which then also appeared on the screen. Experts continued to key in questions until every expert had all the information he needed to recommend a disposition strategy. At this point, experts were again asked to vote using the Alternative Evaluator. The results of the second vote still showed some divergent thinking, although there was a greater level of consensus. Experts were asked to explain under what circumstances each alternative would be most appropriate. Finally, the process facilitator asked the experts to tell him what factors associated with the property were most important in making a disposition decision. Table 5.2 shows a transcript of the questions

TABLE 5.1
Description of the First Property Discussed

(Expert's name), Warehouse (Distribution Ctre.), City of Commerce, CA
Critical Factors:

- Location - LA market area
- Size: 118,000 SF [sq. ft.]
- Environmental condition - good
- Clearance hght [height] - 22 ft.
- Physical Condition - excellent
- Zoning classification - industrial
- Availability (V & C)[Vacant & Clear] - immediate

TABLE 5.2

Questions Experts Asked About the First Property Discussed, Together With the Answers of the Expert Who Contributed the Description of the Property

Q:	What was the property purchased and improved and for how much [sic]?
A:	Built to suit for (company name) about 20 years ago.
	First cost @ $300,000 (land only).
	Book value currently insignificant (building is almost fully depreciated).
Q:	Does the building need any renovation at all? Is it ready to move into?
A:	Depending upon use, some code changes may be necessary (handicapped facilities).
Q:	Tell us about the immediate neighbors? I ask that question because there is an area in Commerce City that is completing changing to offices.
A:	Typical distribution warehouse area.
Q:	Why did you move?
A:	Restructured the lamp distribution system and replaced that warehouse with a 270,000 sq. ft. facility right near the airport, leased a new facility in Ontario, CA.
Q:	Size of parcel?
A:	5 acres.
Q:	Location with reference to L.A. city limit.
A:	Outskirts of L.A.
Q:	Are there any changing land use patterns occurring immediately surrounding the property?
A:	No.
Q:	Is there any surplus land adjacent to the building?
A:	No, due to land requirements for truck loading/unloading.
	Could expand if one went to local distribution.
Q:	Did you receive any offers for the property when it became public knowledge that you were moving?
A:	Yes, we sold it direct.
Q:	Is this a soft or strong sellers [sic] market?
A:	Absolutely (very strong seller's market).
Q:	What is the access to public transportation?
A:	Not significant, no rail access. (We always used trucks.)
Q:	Was there fuel storage on the site (above or underground)?
A:	Only for heating, no gasoline (underground).

the experts asked about the first property and the answers of the expert who contributed the first property description.

During the discussion of the first property, the process facilitator observed that many experts felt inhibited by having to key in text. For this reason, questions about all subsequent cases discussed were asked verbally. The expert who contributed the case responded immediately to each question.

Three typical cases were discussed during the first knowledge-acquisition session. One typical case was discussed during the second knowledge-acquisition session. Because this exhausted the list of typical cases that had been contributed, the remainder of the second session was spent in discussing the first three cases categorized as most troublesome. Experts also dictated the wording of questions needed in the environments in which they worked. Such questions included information needed to uniquely identify a property. The second version of the program was prepared after the second knowledge-acquisition session.

Although the agendas for the third and fourth knowledge-acquisition sessions included a provision for the discussion of additional cases, this did not occur. The process facilitator allowed the discussion of the structure of the knowledge-based system to continue for the entire time allotted for the third session, because experts were providing knowledge that could be included in the program as they discussed its structure. During the fourth knowledge-acquisition session, discussions associated with revising the wording of questions in the program consumed the entire allotted time.

RESULTS

Analysis of Questions

With the exception of a few jokes, our corpus of questions consists of bona fide requests for information, as opposed to requests phrased as questions. For this reason, the Graesser, Lang, and Horgan (1988) taxonomy appeared to be most appropriate for categorizing both the questions experts asked one another and the questions in successive versions of the program. A similar taxonomy, which includes all Graesser, Lang, and Horgan (GLH) categories as well as a few additional categories, appears in Table 9.1 in Graesser, Person, and Huber (chap. 9 in this volume).

We also categorized inquiries that were not interrogatives (i.e., with question marks) but were classified as assertions or indirect requests (D'Andrade & Wish, 1985). For definitions of categories in the Graesser et al. (1988) taxonomy see Graesser, Person, and Huber (chap. 9 in this volume). All of the GLH categories, except for causal antecedent questions, were represented by at least one question in our corpus. Examples of each GLH category of question follow. The information in parentheses indicates whether a question was asked by an expert, whether it appeared in one or more versions of the program, or both.

1. Verification.
    Is it in the suburbs? (Expert)
    Does that $100,000 mean that you could sell it for $100,000 now? (Expert)
    Did you receive any offers for the property when it became public knowledge that you were moving? (Expert & program)
2. Disjunctive.
    Is it a big space or small? (Expert)

Were these occupants of these homes year-round, or were they visiting? (Expert)

Is this Class A, Class B, or Class C office space? (Program)

3. Concept Completion.

Where did they relocate? (Expert)

Please enter a description of the property that uniquely identifies it. Call it whatever you would normally call it. You could use the address, the city, the township, the property I.D. number, or any combination of these. (Program)

4. Feature Specification.

Exact location? (Expert)

What was the attitude of the community? (Expert)

What type of property is involved? (Program)

5. Quantification.

What's your book value? (Expert)

What is the tax value of the property? (Program)

6. Causal Consequence.

Which best describes the effect of the topography on the market for the property? (Program)

7. Goal Orientation.

Why did you move? (Expert and program)

8. Enablement.

How could you [raise the asking price] on 99-year leases? (Expert)

9. Instrumental/Procedural.

How do you protect your noncompete restriction? (Expert)

On what basis was the potentiality valued? (Expert)

10. Expectational.

Why can't you abandon it? (Expert)

11. Judgmental.

So there's no sense in taking the building down? (Expert)

Is subdivision of the land feasible? (Program)

Both the questions asked by experts and the questions asked by all versions of the program were categorized independently by the first two authors. Raters agreed on categorizations of 85.1% of questions asked by experts and 97.4% of the questions in the five versions of the knowledge-based system. After consulting with Graesser and Lang, the raters were able to agree on the categorization of all items.

Analysis of Questions Asked by the Experts

Experts asked one another a total of 183 questions about individual properties. Of these, 56.8% were verification questions, 35.0% were short-answer open-class questions (6.0% were disjunctive, 5.5% concept completion, 8.2% feature specification, and 15.3% quantification questions), and 8.2% were long-answer open-class questions (1.6% were goal orientation, 0.6% enablement, 2.2% instrumental/procedural, 0.6% expectational, and 3.3% judgmental questions). Our experts asked verification questions significantly more often than they asked short-answer open-class questions, the second most frequent category, X^2 (1) = 9.52, $p < .01$. Short-answer open-class questions occurred significantly more frequently than long-answer open-class questions, X^2 (1) = 30.39, $p < .001$. Clearly, our experts tended to generate questions that required short answers and rarely asked questions that required long answers.

We directed the experts to ask all the questions they needed answered about individual properties before they could recommend disposition strategies. Experts were not asked to adjust the wording of their questions to accommodate the needs of a computer. However, the process facilitator did ask the experts who had contributed troublesome cases to provide only the information specifically requested, when they began to volunteer information about properties. By volunteering information they knew their colleagues would want to know, our experts were being cooperative. That is, they were responding to the pragmatic as well as the syntactic and semantic content of the questions others asked (Kaplan, 1983). When the experts who were familiar with properties stopped volunteering information, their colleagues were forced to ask more questions.

Profiles of questions experts asked about typical cases and the most troublesome cases appear in Table 5.3. The profile of questions asked about troublesome cases was significantly different from the profile for typical cases, X^2 (2) = 23.18, $p < .001$. Verification questions predominated among the questions experts asked about troublesome cases, whereas verification questions and short-answer open-class questions occurred with equal frequency when typical cases were discussed. Because the expected frequency of occurrence of many catego-

TABLE 5.3
Questions Experts Asked One Another About Typical and Most Troublesome Cases

Category	Typical Cases (1-4) %	Most Troublesome Cases (5-7) %	All Cases (1-7) %
Verification	44.4	68.8	56.8
Disjunctive	11.1	1.1	6.0
Concept Completion	5.6	5.4	5.5
Feature Specification	11.1	5.4	8.2
Quantification	18.9	11.8	15.3
Goal Orientation	3.3		1.6
Enablement		1.1	0.6
Instrumental/ Procedural	2.2	2.2	2.2
Expectational	1.1		0.6
Judgmental	2.2	4.3	3.3
Total number of Questions	90	93	183

TABLE 5.4
Categorization of Questions That Experts Asked During the First Two Knowledge Acquisition
Sessions

Category	Session 1 in Percentages	Session 2 in Percentages	Both Sessions in Percentages
Verification	38.8	63.4	56.8
Disjunctive	18.4	1.5	6.0
Concept Completion	8.2	4.5	5.5
Feature Specification	14.3	6.0	8.2
Quantification	14.3	15.7	15.3
Goal Orientation	4.1	0.8	1.6
Enablement		0.8	0.6
Instrumental/ Procedural	2.0	2.2	2.2
Expectational		0.8	0.6
Judgmental		4.5	3.3
Total Number of Questions	49	134	183

ries was below five, categories were pooled, as recommended by Siegel and Castellan (1988). Here, as for all other statistical tests in this chapter, the numbers of questions in three categories were compared: verification questions, short-answer open-class questions, and long-answer open-class questions.

Table 5.4 presents profiles of questions that experts asked during the two knowledge-acquisition sessions in which properties were discussed. The profile of questions asked during the second knowledge-acquisition session differed significantly from the profile of questions asked during the first session, $X^2 (2) = 41.14$, $p < .001$. Specifically, there were more verification questions in the second session than the first. Only one typical case was discussed during the second knowledge-acquisition session. The comments of the other experts indicated that they did not routinely dispose of special-purpose facilities designed to house telecommunications equipment. Thus, experts' questions about this property resembled those they asked about troublesome cases rather than typical cases.

As Table 5.3 and the preceding analysis revealed, experts asked more verification questions about troublesome cases than about typical cases. Verification questions are apparently more prevalent when there is less common ground among speech participants. There were also differences in the content of verification questions in troublesome versus typical cases. When experts asked verification questions about typical cases, they wanted information to determine whether specific strategies were feasible and to identify shortcomings of the properties that could interfere with their disposition. Examples of such questions are: "Is there any surplus land adjacent to the building?" and "Was there fuel storage on the site (above or underground)?" Some of the verification questions that experts asked about troublesome cases resembled the preceding examples, but the experts also asked: (a) questions to determine whether potential interested parties had been identified and contacted, (b) questions to determine whether various disposition strategies had been attempted, (c) questions about the circumstances of the company trying to dispose of the property, and (d) questions designed to test the accuracy of inferences they had made about the property. Examples of these four types of questions include: "Did you have an appraisal of the highest and best use?"; "Has it been promoted?"; "Were there discussions regarding the joint venture of this property with anyone?"; "Is the company motivated to sell and get rid of it for some reason other than finance?"; "Did the company have a negative cash flow?"; "So there's no market?"; and "This $40,000 represents interest?" The experts asked one or two judgmental questions about every case (including the last typical case) during the second knowledge-acquisition session, but they did not ask any judgmental questions during the first knowledge-acquisition session.

Comparison of Experts' Questions With Those in the Program

Profiles of the questions in successive versions of the program appear in Table 5.5. The profile of questions in the first version of the program did not differ significantly from the profile of questions asked by experts during the first session, $X^2 (2) = 0.53$, $p > .10$. In contrast, the profile of questions in the

TABLE 5.5
Categorization of Questions in Successive Versions of the Program*

Category	Program Version 1 %	Program Version 2 %	Program Version 3 %	Program Version 4 %	Program Version 5 %
Verification	36.4	36.8	35.7	36.6	36.7
Disjunctive	21.2	18.4	22.2	15.9	13.9
Concept completion			.8	1.4	1.3
Feature				1	
specification	27.3	15.8	15.1	12.4	12.7
Quantification	6.1	21.1	17.5	16.6	17.7
Causal consequence			1.6	8.3	8.9
Goal orientation	3.0	2.6	.8		
Judgmental	6.1	5.3	6.3	9.0	8.9
Total Number of Questions	33	38	126	145	158

*User interface questions are not shown, since this category of question does not involve disposition.

second version of the program was significantly different from the profile of all experts' questions, X^2 (2) $= 7.15, p < .05$. This significant difference between the profile of questions in the second version of the program and the profile of all experts' questions can be attributed to the fact that most of the verification questions experts asked about troublesome cases were so specific that they could not be incorporated into the program. However, most of the quantification questions that experts asked about troublesome cases were sufficiently general to be included in the program. Such an interpretation is supported by the fact that the questions in the second version of the program were not significantly different from those asked by the experts during the first knowledge-acquisition session, X^2 (2) $= 0.23, p > .10$.

Like the questions in the second version of the program, the questions in the third version were significantly different from all questions asked by the experts (X^2 (2) $= 25.20, p < .001$), but they were not significantly different from the questions experts asked during the first knowledge-acquisition session, X^2 (2) $= 1.71, p > .10$. However, changes experts made to the wording of questions in the program during the last knowledge-acquisition session were so extensive that the profile of questions in the fourth version of the program is significantly different from both the entire body of questions experts asked (X^2 (2) $= 30.14, p < .001$) and the questions experts asked during the first knowledge-acquisition session (X^2 (2) $= 31.60, p < .001$). Changes made to the program after the fourth knowledge-acquisition session are relatively minor, with the result that the profile of questions in the fifth and final version of the program is also significantly different from both the entire corpus of experts' questions (X^2 (2) $= 33.75, p < .001$) and the questions our experts asked during the first knowledge-acquisition session (X^2 (2) $= 37.53, p < .001$).

Analysis of Questions in Successive Versions of the Program

As Table 5.5 shows, the first version of the program consisted almost entirely of verification, disjunctive, and feature specification questions. It should be noted that the multiple-choice questions were not always categorized as disjunctive questions. Categorization of questions was based on the question alone and not on the possible answers the program permitted. All but 10 of the questions in the first version of the program had a multiple-choice format. The percentage of quantification questions appeared to increase in the second version of the program; experts decided that the program should ask the user basic quantitative information about a property before it determined which disposition strategies should be considered. However, the profile of questions in the second version of the program was not significantly different from the questions in Version 1, X^2 (2) $= 0.07, p > .10$. Similarly, Version 3 was not significantly different from Version 2, X^2 (2) $= 0.15, p > .10$. However, Version 4 was significantly different from Version 3, $X^2 (2) = 14.47, p < .001$. This change in the profile of questions reflects the experts' decision during the last knowledge-acquisition session to replace many short-answer questions and groups of short-answer questions with causal consequence questions. The experts also introduced additional judgmental questions. Although experts requested some additional changes after reviewing the fourth version of the program, these changes did not significantly alter the composition of questions in the final version of the program, $X^2 (2) = 0.04, p > .10$.

Inasmuch as major changes in the profile of questions occurred in Version 4, we will examine the relative proportions of various types of questions as well as specific questions in the two significantly different versions of the program. During the fourth knowledge-acquisition session, our experts realized that a program would not be able to assess the significance of various detailed information. As a result, some short-answer open-class questions (disjunctive, feature specification, and quantification questions) were either dropped or reworded as long-answer open-class questions (causal consequence and judgmental questions), while new long-answer open-class questions were added.

During the last knowledge-acquisition session, our experts realized that their questions reflected their knowledge of what types of industries and businesses prefer what type of property. Because all this knowledge could not be included in the program in the limited time available, experts noted that they hoped that the program could eventually be connected to a database that would contain property characteristics required or desired by each industry. The experts also recognized that the significance of a user's answers would vary from one region to another (a 2,500 square foot space located in Manhattan would not be considered small) and over time. For this reason, they decided that many questions should be rephrased as causal consequence or judgmental questions, to make the program more generally useful. For example, Version 3 of the program contained two multiple-choice questions about the roof of each building ("Which best describes the roof's design?" and "Of what material is the roof constructed?") as well as a quantification question ("How old is the roof of the building?"). In Version 4, these three questions were replaced by the single multiple-choice, causal consequence question "How does the condition of the roof affect the marketing of the property?" Questions requesting details were replaced with causal consequence questions that address how the available public transportation, the existing access, the frontage, the number of levels, the adjacent zoning, the topography, and the traffic environment affect the marketability of the property. Similarly, the quantification questions "What is the width of the building (in feet)?" and "What is the depth of the building (in feet)?" were replaced by the judgmental question "Does the building configuration contribute positively to its value?" As a result of these changes in the questions asked by the program, more knowledge of real estate is required on the part of the user of the program.

Comparisons of question profiles required a monothetic categorization of questions. For this reason, only the wording of questions determined how questions were categorized. As a result, the limitations on how questions in various versions of the program could be answered were not reflected in comparisons of question profiles. A polythetic categorization of questions (Graesser et al., 1988) also allowed questions to be categorized on the basis of how they could be answered. Questions that had a multiple-choice format could be categorized as disjunctive, even if the wording of the question itself was not disjunctive. A polythetic categorization of the questions in the final version of the program revealed that 19 of the 22 questions categorized as feature-specification questions had a multiple-choice format, 1 quantification question required the user to choose from a menu of ranges, and 10 causal consequence questions and 6 judgmental questions required the user to choose from a menu of options. Similarly, 7 judgmental questions required a yes or no answer.

A comparison of the disjunctive questions the experts asked one another with the disjunctive questions contained in various versions of the program revealed still another difference. Most of the disjunctive questions posed by experts mentioned only two choices. Examples of experts' disjunctive questions include the following: "Is this a soft or strong sellers [sic] market?" and "I would like to know if the lease is at the market or below." In contrast, only a few disjunctive questions and multiple-choice questions in the final version of the program included only two alternatives. The question "Which of the following best describes the environmental condition of the property?" was followed by three choices. Similarly, the user was given a choice of four policies toward committing resources for cleanup of environmental problems. Obviously, it would be unnatural for experts to list all possible choices when they ask a disjunctive question. On the other hand, providing a list of all possible choices to the user of the program eliminates the problems associated with having a user enter a detailed answer, as opposed to selecting from a finite list of alternatives. It would be more difficult for the program to interpret free-form input, because there would be wide variations in spelling and phrasing. The list of alternatives in the program is intended to make the less experienced user aware of alternatives that he or she might not know exist.

Another difference between the questions experts asked and the questions contained in the last version of the program is that many questions in the program include more than a request for information. Our experts felt that inexperienced real estate managers would not be able to answer some questions correctly without additional guidance. For this reason, definitions of terms, advice on how to obtain the answer to the question, and examples of phenomena are displayed together with some questions. For example, the possible answers to the question "Which of the following best describes the environmental condition of the property?" are defined. Similarly, the question "Is subdivision of the land feasible?" is followed by the following guidelines for answering the question: "Determining feasibility requires considering local laws, serviceability, and marketability.

Physical, economic, and legal factors must be considered. Subdivision can include selling air rights."

Problems in Categorizing Questions

A few problems arose in categorizing the occurrence of various types of questions. When an expert had not heard the answer to a question when it was first asked or had forgotten the answer and asked it again, the second occurrence of a question for a particular case was not counted. However, the same expert who asked the question "Is there an Indian reservation nearby?" and was told "No." later asked "There are no Indian reservations around?"; the second version of the question was interpreted as "Are you sure that there are no Indian reservations around?" In this case, the second occurrence of the question was counted. Generally, there is no clear-cut way to decide whether a pair of similar questions should be counted once or twice in the analyses.

Many questions were not phrased in standard question format. Some experts made statements whose intonation alone indicated that they should be interpreted as questions. Other statements were normal statements of fact. Only the context indicated that the questioner expected the contributor of the case to either confirm or deny that the assumption being expressed was correct. Although they are not interrogatives, such items were considered "assertion/questions" (D'Andrade & Wish, 1985) and were categorized as questions. In still other cases, the question consisted of a single word or a sentence fragment. In such cases, the implicit question was categorized. The discussion following the utterance indicated whether or a not a question had been correctly interpreted. In our analyses, a question was not counted if (a) a question was not fully expressed and (b) the expert who contributed the case could not understand the question.

ADDITIONAL OBSERVATIONS

Lauer and Peacock (chap. 13 in this volume) found significant differences among experienced auditors in general scanning and diagnostic activity. We assume that similar differences exist among experts in disposition. Questions generated during the brief period in which experts simultaneously entered their questions suggest variation among disposition experts in both the questions asked and in the sequence of questions asked. Questions that experts simultaneously entered about the first property suggest that experts do not ask the same questions in the same order. Because our experts only asked questions simultaneously about the first case, we do not have enough data to draw firm conclusions about differences among experts in disposition.

Discussions of cases also revealed that experts had dealt with different types of cases. For example, disposing of special-purpose buildings was a typical problem for only one of the assembled experts. Lauer and Peacock's findings as well as our own findings suggest that our decision to use multiple experts to build this knowledge-based system was appropriate. During the last knowledge-acquisition session, our experts stated that they came up with more questions as a group than any single individual would have asked. These questions were important in understanding the marketability of each property and in determining the appropriateness of individual disposition strategies. Experts stated during the last knowledge-acquisition session that they would not have come up with the same knowledge if they had been interviewed separately. The interaction among them helped each expert to tap his knowledge.

Independently, the experts participating in this project decided that the program should ask basic questions about each property before considering which disposition strategies were appropriate. The current version of the program contains basic questions covering all major characteristics of a property. This is similar to the use of checklists of questions by auditors. Follow-up questions are triggered if answers to general questions suggest that a problem may exist.

For a disposition expert system to give good advice, any information about market conditions that it draws on would have to be updated regularly. There was no database of regional market conditions and the real estate needs of various industries that the program could tap. Also, our experts felt that the program should not require regular updating to reflect changing market conditions. To make the program more generally useful and stable, our experts decided to reword many questions in the program, so that the user would have to make some judgments.

In problem domains in which experts spend months solving individual problems and therefore deal with a limited number of cases, it is appropriate to incorporate the knowledge of multiple experts into a program. Experts can access their experience more easily when they interact with one another as a group and discuss specific cases with which they are familiar. Using a public screen, a process facilitator, and a technical facilitator can facilitate communication among experts and between the experts and the knowledge engineer. When the experts' ideas are displayed on a public screen, all participants can direct their criticism at the screen and not at the person who contributed an idea. As a result, conflict among experts can be minimized.

The major findings of this research can be summarized as follows:

1. The questions that experts in real estate disposition ask about troublesome cases are very different from those they ask about typical cases.

2. Many questions that experts ask about typical cases can be incorporated into a knowledge-based system. In contrast, most questions experts ask about troublesome cases are too specific to be included in a general-purpose program.

3. Although the principles that guide real estate disposition are relatively stable, the effect of various details on the marketability of a property varies from

one real estate market to another and over time. A knowledge-based system for disposition can be made more generally useful and stable by replacing some of the short-answer open-class questions that experts ask with causal consequence and judgmental questions.

ACKNOWLEDGMENTS

This research was supported in part by a grant from the Homer Hoyt Institute. Additional research support was provided by the End User Computing Research Center, Department of Management, College of Business Administration, University of Georgia, Athens, Georgia.

The authors would like to thank Mr. Charles K. Greenwald of Premark International, Inc., Mr. Edmond P. Rondeau of the Contel Corporation, Mr. James T. Schaefer, and independent consultant, Mr. Harvey Shupe, formerly Real Estate Manager for Republic and LTV Steel, Mr. Wilburn Sutherland of the McDonald's Corporation, and Mr. Stephen T. Wahn of the General Electric Company for sharing their knowledge of real estate disposition. The authors are also indebted to Mr. Abhijit Gopal and Mr. Barry P. Robichaux, who served as technical facilitators during knowledge acquisition sessions.

REFERENCES

Applegate, L. M., Chen, T. T., Konsynski, B. R., & Nunamaker, J. F., Jr. (1987). Knowledge management in organizational planning. *Journal of Management Information Systems, 3*, 20–38.

Bostrom, R. P., & Anson, R. (1988a). *A case for collaborative work support systems in a meeting environment.* Unpublished manuscript, University of Georgia, Department of Management, Athens, GA.

Bostrom, R. P., & Anson, R. (1988b). *Using computerized collaborative work support systems to improve the logical systems design process* Unpublished manuscript, University of Georgia, Department of Management, Athens, GA.

Connolly, T., Jessup, L. M., & Valacich, J. S. (1990). Effects of anonymity and evaluative tone on idea generation in computer-mediated groups. *Management Science, 36*, 689–703.

D'Andrade, R. G., & Wish, M. (1985). Speech act theory in quantitative research on interpersonal behavior. *Discourse Processes, 8*, 229–259.

Ericsson, K. A., & Simon, H. A. (1980). Verbal reports as data. *Psychological Review, 87*, 215–251.

George, J. F., Nunamaker, J. F., Jr., & Vogel, D. R. (1988). Group decision support systems and their implications for designers and managers: The Arizona experience. In E. S. Weber (Ed.), *DSS-88 transactions: Eighth International Conference on Decision Support Systems* (pp. 13–25). Providence, RI: Institute of Management Sciences.

Graesser, A. C., Lang, K., & Horgan, D. (1988). A taxonomy for question generation. *Questioning Exchange, 2*, 3–15.

Gray, P. (1988). The user interface in group decision support systems. In E. S. Weber (Ed.), *DSS-88 transactions: Eighth International Conference on Decision Support Systems* (pp. 203–25). Providence, RI: Institute of Management Sciences.

Hart, A. (1986). *Knowledge acquisition for expert systems.* New York: McGraw-Hill.

Heltne, M. M., Vinze, A. S., Konsynski, B. R., & Nunamaker, J. F., Jr. (1988). ICE: Information Center Expert: A consultation system for resource allocation. *Data Base, 19,* 1–15.

Hoffman, R. R. (1987). The problem of extracting the knowledge of experts from the perspective of experimental psychology. *AI Magazine, 8,* 53–67.

Johnson, P. (1983). What kind of expert should a system be? *Journal of Medicine and Philosophy, 8,* 79–97.

Kaplan, S. J. (1983). Cooperative responses from a portable natural language database query system. In M. Brady & R. C. Berwick (Eds.), *Computational models of discourse* (pp. 167–208). Cambridge, MA: MIT Press.

LaFrance, M. (1988). The knowledge acquisition grid: a method for training knowledge engineers. In B. R. Gaines & J. H. Boose (Eds.), *Knowledge-based systems: Vol. 1. Knowledge acquisition for knowledge-based systems* (pp. 81–91). London: Academic Press.

McGraw, K. L., & Harbison-Briggs, K. (1989). *Knowledge acquisition: Principles and guidelines.* Englewood Cliffs, NJ: Prentice-Hall.

Nourse, H. O., & Kingery, D. (1987). Marketing idle corporate real estate. *Real Estate Issues, 12,* 21–25.

Nunamaker, J. R., Jr., Applegate, L. M., & Konsynski, B. R. (1987). Facilitating group creativity: Experience with a group decision support system. *Journal of Management Information Systems, 3,* 5–19.

Nunamaker, J. F., Jr., Konsynski, B. R., Chen, M., Vinze, A. S., Chen, Y. I. L., & Heltne, M. M. (1988). Knowledge-based systems support for information centers. *Journal of Management Information Systems, 5,* 6–24.

O'Bannon, R. M. (1988, August). *The characteristics of knowledge engineering.* Presentation to the Atlanta AI Users Group, Atlanta, GA.

Ostrovsky, R. (1987). HOLMES-I, a prolog-based reason maintenance system for collecting information from multiple experts. In B. Bouchon & R. R. Yager (Eds.), *Uncertainty in knowledge-based systems* (pp. 329–336). Berlin: Springer.

Plaza, E. C. A., de Mantaras, R. L., Aguilar, J., & Agusti, J. (1987). Consensus and knowledge acquisition. In B. Bouchon & R. R. Yager (Eds.), *Uncertainty in knowledge-based systems* (pp. 294–306). Berlin: Springer.

Siegel, S., & Castellan, N. J., Jr. (1988). *Nonparametric statistics for the behavioral sciences* (2nd ed.). New York: McGraw-Hill.

Trice, A. (1988). *Facilitating consensus knowledge acquisition.* Unpublished manuscript, MIT School of Management, Information Technologies Group, Cambridge, MA.

Vogel, D., Nunamaker, J., Applegate, L., & Konsynski, B. (1987). Group decision support systems: Determinants of success. In O. A. El Sawy (Ed.), *DSS-87 transactions: Seventh international conference on decision support systems* (pp. 118–128). Providence, RI: Institute of Management Sciences.

Waterman, D. A. (1986). *A guide to expert systems.* Reading, MA: Addison-Wesley.

6

Design by Question: Developing User Questions Into Scenario Representations for Design

John M. Carroll
Mary Beth Rosson
IBM Thomas J. Watson Research Center
Yorktown Heights, NY

Research on user interface design during the 1980s focused concertedly on developing empirical methods for determining *user requirements,* properties that systems need to embody in order to be experienced as useful, learnable, pleasant, and so on by the people interacting with them. Wixon, Whiteside, Good, and Jones (1983) demonstrated how user errors with an early prototype could be used to iteratively define a more usable command language. Gould and Boies (1983) designed a series of voice messaging applications, and Carroll (1990a) designed a variety of user training materials, using a similar empirical methodology.

In general, this work incorporated the proposal, often quite explicitly, that usability requirements can be managed in the design process in the same way as traditional functional requirements (Bennett, 1984; Carroll & Rosson, 1985). Thus, as a system might be functionally specified by a set of command definitions for developers to implement, its usability might be specified by a set of precise usability goals: for example, "90% of a secretarial sample with no prior word processing experience, using only the training materials provided, will be able to create and print a memo in 30 minutes."

This approach is very pragmatic. It takes for granted a system design process in which the external view of the system is initially planned through the development of *functional specifications* (systematic, decompositional specifications of the functions the system being designed will provide; an example is given in Fig. 6.1). It enhances this established practice without fundamentally questioning it. Usability specifications, like the word processing skill acquisition specification just illustrated, can be planned, managed, and ultimately assured just as a command language can be designed, tracked through the development process, and finally verified. One of most important consequences of this approach is that it

The Inspector is a low-level debugging aid used to examine and edit objects in the system.
Inspector objects: The objects that are part of the Inspector are the "instance variable list"
and the "instance variable contents."
The instance variable list appears in a list pane that appears in the left pane of the Inspector. The
first instance variable in the list is Self, the object of being inspected.
The instance variable contents appears in a text pane that appears in the right pane of the
Inspector. It displays the contents of the currently selected instance variable.
There is a special Inspector for Dictionary objects: The instance variable list pane lists Dictionary
keys, rather than instance variable names and indices. The special variable self is not displayed in
the instance variable list of a Dictionary Inspector.
There is also a special "method" Inspector for the system debugger (see below).

Inspector properties:

Browsing the instance variable list: Instance variables (including Self) can be selected in the
instance variable list pane and their contents will be displayed in the instance variable contents
pane.
Evaluation in the instance variable contents pane: Expressions typed in the instance variable
contents pane can be evaluated.
Evaluations under the scope of self: All of an inspected object's instance variables can be used
in expressions to be evaluated in the instance variable contents pane.
Save and update: Expressions created in the instance variable contents pane can be saved, and
will replace the previous values of the selected instance variable in the instance variable list pane.

Interface with other system tools: A "method" Inspector is incorporated into the
system debugger. The object inspected is the receiver of the currently selected method in the
method walkback list. However, the instance variable list pane of the Inspector displays only the
receiver (self), the method arguments, and the method's temporary variables (i.e., the receiver's
instance variables are *not* displayed).

Inspector functions:

Inspect: Inspection is initiated by sending the **Inspect** message to an object (e.g., via typed
command in a Workspace). Subsequently, inspections can be initiated from the Inspector by
menu selection. The pane menu for the instance variable list pane has the single function,
Inspect. The currently selected instance variable is inspected.
Text pane functions: The pane menu for the instance variable contents pane is the standard
Smalltalk Text pane menu. It includes the eight functions: Restore, Copy, Cut, Paste, Show It, Do
It, Save, and Next Menu.
Window pane functions: The window menu for the Inspector window is the standard Smalltalk
window menu. It includes the seven functions: Color, Label, Collapse, Cycle, Frame, Move, and
Close.

FIG. 6.1.   Illustrative functional specification for a Smalltalk inspector.

incorporates usability considerations throughout the entire design process. Particularly in the early 1980s, this was seen as a crucial need in user interface design (e.g., Gould & Lewis, 1983; Hammond, Jorgensen, MacLean, Barnard, & Long, 1983).

However, a significant weakness of the usability specifications approach is that it focuses on relatively superficial aspects of usability. The emphasis on assurability entails a heavy bias for simple, quantitative task time and error rate measures of usability. Unfortunately, this bias tends to force consideration of usability toward later portions of the design process. For example, finding out that 70% and not 90% of test secretaries can create and print a memo in 30 minutes probably will not mean very much until a fairly robust prototype is available. Ironically, this severely undermines the original objective of usability specifications, namely, to incorporate usability considerations with functionality considerations throughout the design process.

The design process seems to trade in qualitative requirements, at least until very late in its cycle. Only near the end would the 90% or the 70% mean much, and at that point the only decision may be whether to go or not to go. Through the balance of the design process, and particularly through the early stages—the stages through which coordinating design for functionality and usability may matter most—we need design solutions or specific task-oriented constraints. Merely giving performance numbers alienates usability evaluators from designers and provides little real guidance for design *ab initio*. (See Scriven's, 1967, distinction between *formative* and *summative* evaluation logic.)

Several lines of research have attempted to address this need by representing user requirements in user task descriptions. One approach analyzes the nature of specific subskills users must attain and perform to interact successfully with a system (Carroll & Rosson, 1985). For example, Furnas, Landauer, Gomez, and Dumais (1983) characterized the need for rich aliasing in the subskill of referring to things by name. Such qualitative subskill analysis can be useful in guiding early stages of user interface design. Another approach seeks to anticipate aspects of user performance with new interface technologies by studying simulations, for example, of speech recognition (Gould, Conti, & Hovanyecz, 1983) or intelligent help (Carroll & Aaronson, 1988) *before* actual applications employing these technologies are developed.

One might go so far as to suggest that the usability specification given earlier for creating and printing a memo might be as useful without the 90% and 30-minute parameters specified as it is with them. Indeed, this is the basic proposal that we wish to explore in this chapter. We propose that instead of including usability specifications with function specifications that we combine both in a more comprehensive user-oriented design representation. Specifically, we propose that end-user applications be represented and developed in the design process as a set of typical and/or critical user-interaction scenarios.

In next section, we illustrate some of the recent history and typical practice of user interface design. We exemplify traditional functional specifications as a design representation, suggesting how they can fail to reveal important usability considerations. We show how scenarios, concrete descriptions of typical and/or critical user interaction patterns, have emerged increasingly as an ancillary design aid to address limitations of functional requirements. We propose that end-user applications be represented in the design process as a set of such scenarios (independently, Wexelblat, 1987, developed a similar proposal that stressed scenarios as an informal medium for customer/designer interaction). We develop an example of this approach applied to the design of a new inspector for the Smalltalk programming environment.

A disclaimer: Clearly, one cannot make a demonstrative argument about what in essence are problem-solving heuristics. Our intention is to give voice to what we see as an on-going process of evolution in the representations employed in current user interface design, and perhaps to focus and hasten what we see as a salutary technical development.

FUNCTIONAL SPECIFICATIONS AND
INTERACTION SCENARIOS

Th functional specification in Fig. 6.1 provides a logical description of the Inspector, a tool incorporated in the Smalltalk programming language/ environment (we are working with *Smalltalk/V 286;* Digitalk, Inc., 1988). Smalltalk is an object-oriented programming language and environment in which programming tasks are accomplished by creating computational objects (encapsulated bundles of data and algorithm) and defining message-passing protocols among these objects. The Inspector is a browser for objects, providing access to an object's internal data (instance variables). It is used as a debugging aid.

The functional specification in Fig. 6.1 systematically decomposes the Inspector into components and functions. Thus, an Inspector consists of two objects, the instance variable list and the instance variable contents. These appear as two panes in the Inspector window: The user can select a variable in the instance variable list pane and see its value in the instance variable contents pane. Smalltalk Inspectors have been specially adapted for the inspection of dictionaries and for use with the system debugger.

In addition to browsing the instance variable list pane, the user can evaluate and alter instance variable contents. Expressions created in the Inspector can be saved to update the value of the instance variable currently selected in the instance variable list pane. The Inspector window has the seven standard functions of a Smalltalk window; the instance variable contents pane has the eight standard functions of a Smalltalk text pane. The instance variable list pane has only the single function inspect.

The functional specification for the Smalltalk Inspector comprehensively defines the Inspector: its underlying objects, appearance, functionality, and specializations (for dictionaries and the debugger). However, such a description abstracts away from what programmers might want to *do* with an Inspector, and the contexts within which they might want to do it. That is to say, the specification in Fig. 6.1 is systematically structured, but not task-oriented. Thus, a design process guided by working representations like the one in Fig. 6.1 might tend to produce artifacts that are formally coherent, but not necessarily well-engineered for users.

Consider a simple inspection episode in which a user is trying to understand an application by examining its principal objects. The user is exploring a Blackjack (card game) application, and opens an Inspector on an instance of PlayerHand (i.e., a collection of cards "dealt" to the player). The user sees in the

Inspector that the PlayerHand object has an instance variable named My-Game; this variable currently points to an instance of BlackJack. In fact, the variable points back to the BlackJack game to which the PlayerHand belongs. When the user opens a second Inspector on the MyGame, variable, the instance variables defined for the BlackJack instance is accessed. One of these is the Player variable, which contains the instance of PlayerHand from which the inspection process initiated!

A third Inspector opened on the Player variable will be identical to the first one (opened on the instance of PlayerHand). This "circular" inspection could go on forever, and for someone just learning how an application works it can be hard to diagnose. Smalltalk's window management scheme overlaps successive Inspector windows, so that each new Inspector occludes most of the previous ones, making it difficult to recognize the circularity in the episode.

The possibility for circular inspections is inherent in the structure of Smalltalk objects (they need to point to one another in order to have two-way communication), and in the functional specification of the Smalltalk Inspector in Fig. 6.1. However, because the functional specification only implicitly considers what users need to do in typical inspection episodes, circular inspection per se is not treated as a design issue.

A second example is an episode in which a user is interacting with an application that malfunctions in some way. For example, in playing the Blackjack game the user is dealt a deuce and a four. The user takes a hit and is dealt a nine. The user requests another hit, but sees no consequence of this latest request in the game's graphic interface. The user wants to inspect the PlayerHand to see if a third card was ever dealt. But there is no way to do this directly in the game's interface. The user must move to a Workspace and type PlayerHand AllInstances Inspect, which opens an Inspector on an array including all current instances of the PlayerHand class. By examining the fist two cards of each instance, the use can find (and inspect) PlayerHand in use by the current game.

This episode shows how the design of the Inspector presumes initiating inspections from a Workspace with a typed command. This in turn entails that one must already know how to refer to an object in order to inspect it. In this example, the user knew that the object was an instance of PlayerHand, but in many cases the user might only know where on the display the graphics for an object appear. In such a case, the user must find a way to break into the running application, and then use debugger facilities to track down the object of interest.

As a third example, suppose that a programmer is enhancing an application. Through the course of work, some of an object's instance variables are obviated, that is, in the enhanced code they are pointing to nothing (the Nil object), and are never used. In the Smalltalk Inspector, it is quite difficult to recognize this situation: As specified in Fig. 6.1, the instance variable contents pane displays only the contents of the currently selected instance variable. An instance variable that is never used is very unlikely to be selected in the course of work, and thus its constant `Nil` value may never be detected. Again, these difficulties are inherent in the functional specification for the Inspector, but they are not evident in that specification because it does not explicitly represent the user's likely inspection tasks.

The need for more explicit consideration of user tasks in design has become well-recognized in recent years. It is increasingly the case that scenario descriptions of user tasks are included as supplementary material in functional specification documents. Specific scenarios are often used to describe usability problems with systems and applications (Carroll & Mazur, 1986), and sets of standard scenarios can serve as the foundation for empirical evaluation techniques (Roberts & Moran, 1983). Scenarios have been used to evaluate the applicability of psychological theories to usability analyses (Young & Barnard, 1987; Young, Barnard, Simon, & Whittington, 1989). Indeed, designers routinely use scenarios to understand user requirements, to test and extend their understanding of requirements, and to discover new requirements and partial solutions (Carroll, Thomas, & Malhotra, 1979; Guindon, 1990a, 1990b; Rosson, Maass, & Kellogg, 1988).

We see these developments as salutary with respect to the need to inject more planning that is more explicitly task-oriented into the design process. We propose to push the current role of scenarios in user interface design a step further by considering scenarios of use as a *representation* of the design. In the next section we illustrate a user interface design methodology in which the design is codified by the set of user scenarios it affords. The design process is the successively more specific reexpression of this set of scenarios.

AN EXAMPLE: DESIGNING A SMALLTALK INSPECTOR

The design of user scenarios begins with the identification of critical user task goals. These goals might be critical for a number of reasons—for example, they may be goals frequently encountered, they may be goals whose satisfaction is a key component of the overall task, or they may be goals whose satisfaction is expected to test the boundaries of system functionality. In our example, the general activity being supported is the design and implementation of Smalltalk applications, more specifically the design and implementation of objects that accomplish things by sending, receiving, and evaluating messages. An Inspector contributes to this activity by allowing the user to examine and modify the objects used by the application; thus inspection tasks typically involve questions or concerns a user has about one or more of these objects.

The concerns that programmers pursue with the Inspector can be reified as questions, for example, "Why did this object change like that?" A programmer who has such a concern or question in mind may undertake a series of actions to address the concern, to answer the question. A description of such an action sequence is what we refer to as a *scenario*. We use the questions that evoke these episodes of programmer behavior as names for the scenarios. The questions in Fig. 6.2 were generated from an empirical analysis of Smalltalk Inspector usage, from inspection tasks we either observed or performed ourselves.

The questions in Fig. 6.2 reflect inspection scenarios at different levels of abstraction. So, for example, the first three questions concern an instantiated object. They represent the situation in which a user is debugging an application and wants to understand or experiment with the internal state or visual representation of a specific object at some point in time. The fourth and fifth scenario represent a higher level of interaction with an object, where the user is considering more general ramifications of an object's characteristics—the questions involve the *structure* of an object rather than the value of a particular attribute. The final scenario represents an even higher level of concern, where the user does not have a running application, but is trying to determine if an object of some sort might be useful (an important characteristic of programming in languages like Smalltalk is the reuse and specialization of existing object definitions).

In our empirical task analysis, the questions in Fig. 6.2 were used to label specific scenarios, that is, descriptions of actual programming episodes. However, these same questions can also play a role in generating and codifying the design of alternate Smalltalk Inspectors. We can imagine programming episodes through which Smalltalk programmers would pursue these object inspection concerns, episodes whose descriptions convey the design of a new Inspector.

The questions in Fig. 6.2 provide little detail about how the programmer's concerns might be pursued. However, even at this early point, the basic contrast between a representation based on programmer concerns and a functional specification is obvious. It is impossible to determine if the questions in Fig. 6.2 are addressed by the system whose functional specification appears in Fig. 6.1. Although designers developing that sort of specification may in fact believe that such goals should be satisfied, the goals are not explicitly part of the representation, and as a result there is no direct way to tell if they are addressed by the design.

Why did this object change like that?
Something changed in an application that you don't understand.
What will happen if I change this object?
You're thinking of changing something inside an object.
Why does this object look like that?
You don't like the appearance of something in an application.
What depends on the type of this object?
You're thinking of changing a class definition.
How does this object get used?
You're trying to understand the relationship of an object to other objects in the application.
Is this the right type of object to use?
You're trying to decide whether to use a particular class in your program design.

FIG. 6.2.   Initial scenario specification for a Smalltalk inspector.

The process of *scenario-based design* involves taking user concerns like those in Fig. 6.2, and projecting them into arbitrarily detailed descriptions of scenarios that would satisfy the concerns. For example, a concern with understanding a change in an instantiated object is elaborated by the scenario designer into a hypothetical programming episode where such a concern might arise and be resolved. This enables the key contribution of the scenario representation: Design details are developed *in the context* of likely usage situations. Instead of looking across a set of user concerns for abstractions (e.g., deciding that all of the tasks will require access to an object's instance variables), extracting these requirements from the context that generated them, and then separately elaborating them, the design characteristics are elaborated by elaborating the scenarios of use.

The elaboration of an individual scenario takes place in concert with all other scenarios in the set. Working within such a set provides mutual constraint: The imagined alternate Smalltalk Inspector that satisfies one user question may not satisfy others. In designing our alternate Smalltalk Inspector, we worked with the entire set of questions in Fig. 6.2.

The usage context for scenarios is an interaction of many factors—psychological structures and propensities, social organization and dynamics, and technological possibilities and constraints. For example, fluent and reliable human activity requires a simple and direct mapping between goals and actions (Norman, 1986). This suggests that the elaboration of the "What will happen if I change this object?" scenario should involve direct access to and editing of the object. Analogously, the constructs and interaction conventions of Smalltalk both suggest and limit the elaboration of the scenarios (e.g., how windows are structured, how instance variables are understood).

In Fig. 6.3 we elaborate the initial Inspector questions of Fig. 6.2. For purposes of the example, we provide only a single hypothetical situation for each. In an actual design process, the elaboration would be more comprehensive and would often involve the development of multiple usage situations for each initial-concern scenario. It might also involve discarding or radically transforming the initial usage goals, as well as recognizing new ones (Carroll & Rosson, 1985).

The intermediate scenarios (in Fig. 6.3) assume little about the details of presentation or of interaction techniques. Their role is to specify possible instantiations of the initial task goals, as well as how these goals are achieved. At this stage, the scenario representation pushes beyond the general observation that users might want to examine the values of a particular object's instance variables; the representation seeks to provide an example situation in which that concern makes sense (e.g., noticing that a pane is displaying something unexpected), so that design details can emerge in support of realistic task goals.

Note that key design concepts evolve through and pervade the scenarios—Inspectors can be opened "on" a pane in a window; inspectors can provide

Why did this object change like that?
You are puzzled by the contents of one of the panes in your interactive application. You have just selected a menu option to begin entering a client list, but the new list has written over the list title. You open an inspector on the client list pane, and check the pane contents method. You immediately see that you have included the list title only in the case when the list is empty. You correct the problem and test the result.

What will happen if I change this object?
You want to get rid of the menu to a pane and you're wondering if you can just set it to Nil. You open an inspector one the pane and find an instance variable whose value is the menu yuou want to get rid of. You change its value to Nil, then request the pane menu. The default menu for this type of pane appears. Apparently, you will need to use a pane type that has no default menu.

Why does this object look like that?
You open your e-mail application for the first time, and see that the pane you are using to list incoming notes is much too small. You open an inspector on the incoming notes pane, and examine the information on the relative sizes of the panes in the window. You adjust some sizes and return to your application to view the result.

What depends on the type of this object?
You have decided to change the object you're using to keep track of the game score from an Array to a Dictionary, so that you can identify the scores by player name. You open an inspector on an instance of the game, then check to see what methods refer to the score object. You see that several score reporting methods use the access protocols for Arrays rather an Dictionaries, so you modify them appropriately before making your change.

How does this object get used?
You are enhancing a note editor. In trying to understand the code, you open an inspector on a note pane and explore the values of the note's instance variables. You then add a name to the distribution list and inspect it again, noting that the Recipient variable has a new element. But you also notice that the Address variable is NIL, as it was in the previous state. You wonder what that variable contributes, and continue to use the application and inspect the note, looking for a change in Address. It never changes, and you suspect that it is an unused variable left over from earlier versions of the system. You ask to see the "users" of this variable and confirm that no method ever refers to it, so you remove it from the class definition.

Is this the right type of object to use?
You are trying to decide whether to use a TextPane or a ListPane to display the contents of your grocery bag; you know that both types of panes can be used to format a list of strings. You select a line in a TextPane and then open an inspector on it. You browse the instance variables, find Selection and inspect it, discovering that it refers to the *position* of the text selected. You do the same for ListPane and discover that the analogous variable refers to the *index* of the string in the list. Because you want to be able to tell directly which item has been selected, you decide to use ListPane.

FIG. 6.3.   Intermediate scenario specification for a Smalltalk inspector.

information about where a variable is used. But these characteristics are not separated out as generic functionality that is feasible or that seems like a good idea; they are embedded as necessary components of accomplishing particular goals. The process of elaborating scenarios is one in which the situations of use and the needs, preferences, and goals of the projected users are imagined in increasing detail and vividness.

Elaboration of scenarios requires consideration of cross-scenario constraints: What is being elaborated finally is a *set* of scenarios. Our initial scenarios, for example, have the built-in assumption that inspection can distinguish among instances of an object class and the class specification itself. This distinction is inherent in the architecture of the Smalltalk environment and thus constrains the types of tasks that are meaningful within it. Other constraining factors may devolve from preexisting artifacts used in the same programming context as the Inspector (e.g., the System Debugger), or from generic interaction techniques (e.g., the use of right-button pop-up menus to provide context-specific function). The important point is that the implications of these factors are not articulated in a generic way; they are realized in the context of meaningful tasks.

In Fig. 6.4 we have provided detailed specifications for three of the original scenarios. They are mutually consistent with respect to various interface characteristics (e.g., the way menus are requested, the use and appearance of "method browsers," and the general appearance of the inspector when opened on a user interface object). This is desirable: we would not want scenario-based design to introduce gratuitous differences in the look and feel of a system. However, because the interface characteristics were developed with these particular tasks in mind, we can be more confident that they will enhance system usability.

Our earlier discussion of the Inspector functional specification pointed to problems that occur when the design representation abstracts away from the tasks people will actually be doing with a system. To some extent, such problems are

---

Why did this object change like that?
You are puzzled by the contents of one of the panes in your interactive application. You have just selected a menu option to begin entering a client list, but the pane has lost the list's title. Moving the mouse to the client list pane, you press the Inspect function key. A graphic inspector open—the user interface graph is in the upper pane, with the client pane node already selected, and the pane's instance variables and their values are listed in the lower two panes. You select "update contents" from the pane inspect menu, and a method browser appears, containing the method used in updating the pane's contents; the method name and location appears in the upper pane, and its method text below. You immediately see that you have included the list title only in the case when the list is empty. You make the appropriate change to the method text, save it, and test the result by adding another client.

What will happen if I change this object?
You want to get rid of the menu to a text pane and you're wondering if you can just change it to Nil. Moving the mouse to the text pane, you press the Inspect function key. A graphic inspector open—the user interface graph is in the upper pane, with the text pane node already selected, and the pane's instance variables and their values are listed in the lower two panes. You examine the instance variable values and discover that paneMenuSelector has been set to the name of the text pane's menu. You select the menu name and replace it with Nil, selecting "save" from the variable edit menu. You then test your change, selecting your application, and clicking the right mouse button in the text pane: a default text-editing menu appears. Apparently, panes of this class retrieve a default menu if no special menu is provided; you will need to specialize the TextPane class to override this default behavior.

What depends on the type of this object?
You have decided to change the object you're using to keep tract of the fame score from an Array to a Dictionary, so that you can identify the scores by player name. You move the mouse to the title bar of the application and press the Inspect function key. A graphic inspector opens—the user interface graph is in the upper pane, with the model node already selected, and the model's instance variables and their values are listed in the lower two panes. Selecting the Score instance variable, you request the instance variable inspect menu and select "users." A method browser appears, containing all methods that refer to score; the upper pane lists the methods by name and location, the lower text pane provides the method text for any method selected in the upper pane. You select each method in turn, modifying it as needed to use Dictionary rather than Array accessing protocol.

FIG. 6.4.   Detailed scenario specification for a Smalltalk inspector.

inevitable in designing for human use: People do surprising things. However, many user tasks can be anticipated. For example, we can anticipate that users will wonder "Is this the right object?" (Figs. 6.2 and 6.3). Such a concern is likely to induce inspection at deeper and deeper levels of an object and hence could entrain the circular inspection problem we described earlier. But building this concern into the foundation of a design representation makes it a central issue and not an untoward side-effect of the select and display protocol for reiterative inspections. Were we to expand the "Is this the right object?" scenario, a better capability for reiterative inspection would emerge.

The two other problematic examples we discussed with respect to the functional specification are also addressed by our scenario representation. Inspection by direct pointing emerges in elaboration of the "Why did this object change like that?" scenario (see Fig. 6.4). The user's concern with recognizing unused or obviated instance variables is captured in the "How does this get used?" scenario and could be addressed by displaying all variable contents by default.

Note that the scenario representation incorporates a task focus while still providing the information captured by functional specifications. System entities are enumerated and defined (e.g., the objects of the user interface making up the graph, the instance variables, and their contents), as are system functions (e.g., a user can access the contents of a pane). But instead of gathering the individual objects and functions together in a list, their roles in the design as a whole are emphasized by embedding them in user scenarios; perhaps more importantly from the standpoint of the design process, their role in the design emerges from a process of considering contexts of use.

The Inspector scenarios described here served as the design specification for a prototype Graphic Inspector for Smalltalk/V 286. It was possible to implement most of the scenarios as described; in a few cases, minor changes were made to better reflect details of the Smalltalk environment (e.g., to acknowledge that there are two methods that provide the contents for a pane—one when the window is first opened and another when something changes). As one would expect, the development of the prototype also suggested new user questions (e.g., "Why does this object look like that?"), which were elaborated and integrated into our original set of scenarios.

DISCUSSION

An exciting fallout of scenario-based design is that the design documents themselves (in this case, the scenarios) can have many further uses in the overall design process. For example, a set of scenarios is a critical requirement for the design of task-oriented user instruction and other documentation (e.g., Carroll, 1990a). We know of one case in which a scenario, originally added to a functional specification document purely as an illustration, later became the basis of the user tutorial for the system (needless to say, nothing else in the specification document had any useful life after the implementation).

A second arena of further use for scenario design representations is in evaluation. Any thorough usability evaluation must begin from a set of user interaction scenarios. Typically these are produced very late in the design process, or perhaps produced generically for a class of applications (e.g., Roberts & Moran, 1983). However, if a system has been functionally specified by a set of user interaction scenarios, these are clearly the most appropriate possible scenarios from which to develop usability evaluations. Wexelblat (1987) suggested other potential application of scenarios, as analytic walk-through evaluations, orientations for maintenance programming, and scripts for product demonstrations.

We have already observed that scenarios are playing an increased and diverse role in user interface design—as brainstorming tools, evaluation tools, and illustrations in functional specification documents. We urge that they be considered for further roles, namely as design representations. User interface work in the 1980s focused on developing methods for empirically determining user requirements and for incorporating the consideration of user requirements in the design process, for example, as usability specifications defining target performance times and error rates for standard user tasks. We see scenarios as an important possibility for integrating the roles of traditional functional specifications with the most important aspect of usability specifications, namely the enumeration of the key user tasks.

This can only be a suggestion on the strength of our brief example. But it suggests a variety of questions and issues for further research, which we are pursuing in our own current prototyping work. What exactly *is* a scenario from the perspective of scenario-based design? Wexelblat (1987) provided a structural schema including change history, background context, assumptions, and issues, along with the "core" narrative. Our recent work has tried to integrate the implicit psychological design rationale of artifacts with scenario-based representations of their use. For example, a programming environment like Smalltalk can be seen as embodying a range of claims about what programmers know, what they want to do and can do, what they experience, the nature of programming tasks and the contexts within which these tasks are carried out, and so on. These claims inhere in, and to that extent define, the scenarios that the artifact enables (Carroll, 1990b; Carroll, Kellogg, & Rosson, 1991).

What are the differences among the purely textual scenarios that we used here, storyboard scenarios, and video scenarios, as described by Vertelney (1989)? Should the characteristic needs and activities of different categories of users be represented in distinct categories of user scenarios, and if so, how fine a taxonomy of user categories will be worthwhile?

Where do scenarios come from, and where *should* they come from? We used task analysis, direct empirical observations, and psychological theory in designing and developing our Inspector scenarios. As we prototyped our new Smalltalk Inspector, we further modified and extended the set of scenarios. Of course, combining different types of constraints and iteratively enhancing a representation are typical design activities. How might these be rendered in a formal methodology for scenario-based design? As part of developing a course on design, we have developed a "typology" of user concerns, which might optimistically be seen as a theory of scenarios, but which we offer to students as a generation aid for developing rich sets of scenarios to seed the scenario-based design process.

Finally, can a development team implement a system from scenario representations? What kinds of coverage problems will this method incur relative to traditional kinds of functional specifications (Wexelblat, 1987, sketched some possibilities for managing known gaps in scenario set)? How many scenarios are required? The small set of scenarios in the figures of this chapter was used to design a new Inspector for Smalltalk/V 286. Elsewhere we have documented our use of scenario-based design in the development of two powerful Smalltalk environments (Carroll & Rosson, 1991).

Many researchers and practitioners in user interface design have hailed the emergence of better prototyping tools and the greatly increased flexibility these afford in user interface design (and other arenas of system development). From the standpoint of design representation, design documents, and design planning generally, there is also a dark side to *rapid prototyping* (the programming paradigm in which powerful tools and environments allow running systems to be roughed out and implemented faster than they can be systematically planned): Why agonize over design activities that are largely procedural obstacles and whose chief raison d'être is bureaucratic? Design representations in the age of rapid prototyping must offer rapid leverage: leverage rapid enough or great enough to offset the option of merely hacking it out straight-off.

Taking scenarios of human-computer interaction seriously as design representation makes a particularly strong case on these pragmatic grounds. User scenarios allow preliminary usability analysis to guide design: Rapid prototyping requires such guidance to avoid degenerating into design by trial and error. User scenarios are concrete and easily produced; and they may have uses *after* initial design that can lend a coherence and efficiency to the design process that rapid prototyping itself cannot (in guiding formal usability evaluation, in producing user documentation, etc.). This may be a good enough bargain that they will actually be used.

ACKNOWLEDGMENT

We are grateful to our colleagues Jerry Archibald, Mona El-Gayar, and Janice Singer for discussion and collaboration on the design of Inspectors for Smalltalk/V 286. The Graphic Inspector prototype was developed by Mona El-Gayar and Janice Singer.

This chapter revises and extends an earlier paper: Carroll, J. M., and Rosson,

M. B. Human-computer interaction scenarios as a design representation. In B. D. Shriver (Ed.), *Proceedings Volume II of HICSS-23: 23rd Hawaii International Conference on System Sciences, Software Track.* (2–6 January 1990; Kona, HI). Los Alamitos, CA: IEEE Computer Society Press, pp. 555–561.

REFERENCES

Bennett, J. L. (1984). Managing to meet usability requirements: Establishing and meeting software development goals. In J. Bennett, J. Sandelin, & M. Smith (Eds.), *Visual display terminals* (pp. 161–184). Englewood Cliffs, NJ: Prentice-Hall.

Carroll, J. M. (1990a). *The Nurnberg Funnel: Designing minimalist instruction for practical computer skill.* Cambridge, MA: MIT Press.

Carroll, J. M. (1990b). Infinite detail and emulation in an ontologically minimized HCI. In J. C. Chew & J. Whiteside (Eds.), *Proceedings of CHI'90: Human factors in computing systems* (pp. 321–327). New York: Association for Computing Machinery.

Carroll, J. M., & Aaronson, A. P. (1988). Learning by doing with simulated intelligent help. *Communications of the ACM, 31,* 1064–1079.

Carroll, J. M., Kellogg, W. A., & Rosson, M. B. (1991). The task-artifact cycle. In J. M. Carroll (Ed.), *Designing interaction: Psychology at the human-computer interface* (pp. 74–102). New York: Cambridge University Press.

Carroll, J. M., & Mazur, S. A. (1986). LisaLearning. *IEEE Computer, 19*(11), 35–49.

Carroll, J. M., & Rosson, M. B. (1985). Usability specification as a tool in interactive development. In H. Hartson (Ed.), *Advances in human-computer interaction* (vol. 1, pp. 1–28). Norwood, NJ: Ablex.

Carroll, J. M., & Rosson, M. B. (1991). Deliberated evolution: Stalking the View Matcher in design space. *Human-Computer Interaction, 6.*

Carroll, J. M., Thomas, J.C., & Malhotra, A. (1979). A clinical-experimental analysis of design problem solving. *Design Studies, 1,* 84–92. [Reprinted in B. Curtis (Ed.), 1985, *Human factors in software development* (pp. 243–251). Washington, DC: IEEE Computer Society Press.]

Digitalk, Inc. (1988). *Smalltalk/V 286: Object-oriented programming system.*

Furnas, G. W., Landauer, T. K., Gomez, L. M., & Dumais, S. T. (1983). Statistical semantics: Analysis of the potential performance of key-word information systems. *Bell System Technical Journal, 62,* 1753–1806.

Gould, J. D., & Boies, S. J. (1983). Human factors challenges in creating a principal support office system—The Speech Filing System approach. *ACM Transaction on Office Information Systems, 1,* 273–298.

Gould, J. D., Conti, J., & Hovanyecz, T. (1983). Composing letters with a simulated listening typewriter. *Communications of the ACM, 26/4,* 295–308.

Gould, J. D., & Lewis, C. H. (1983). Designing for usability: Key principles and what designers think. In A Janda (Ed.), *Proceedings of CHI'83 Human Factors in Computing Systems* (pp. 50–53). New York: Association for Computing Machinery.

Guindon, R. (1990a). Designing the design process: Exploiting opportunistic thoughts. *Human-Computer Interaction, 5,* 305–344.

Guindon, R. (1990b). Knowledge exploited by experts during software system design. *International Journal of Man-Machine Studies, 33,* 279–304.

Hammond, N., Jorgensen, A., MacLean, A., Barnard, P., & Long, J. (1983). *Design practice and interface usability: Evidence from interviews and designers* (Report No. HF082). IBM Hursley Human Factors Laboratory, Hursley Park, U.K.

Norman, D. A. (1986). Cognitive engineering. In D. A. Norman & S. W. Draper (Eds.), *User *centered system design: New perspectives on human-computer interaction* (pp. 31–65). Hillsdale, NJ: Lawrence Erlbaum Associates.

Roberts, T. L., & Moran, T. P. (1983). The evaluation of text editors: Methodology and empirical results. *Communications of the ACM, 26,* 265–283.

Rosson, M. B., Maass, S., & Kellogg, W. A. (1988). The designer as user: Building requirements for design tools from design practice. *Communications of the ACM, 31,* 1288–1298.

Scriven, M. (1967). The methodology of evaluation. In R. Tyler, R. Gagne, & M. Scriven (Eds.), *Perspectives of curriculum evaluation* (pp. 39–83). Chicago: Rand McNally.

Vertelney, L. (1989). Panel abstract for "Drama and personality in user interface design." In K. Bice & C. Lewis (Eds.), *Proceedings of CHI'89: Conference on Human Factors in Computing Systems* (pp. 107–108). New York: Association for Computing Machinery.

Wexelblat, A. (1987, May). *Report on Scenario Technology* (Tech. Rep. No. STP-139-87). MCC.

Wixon, D., Whiteside, J., Good, M., & Jones, S. (1983). Building a user-defined interface. In A. Janda (Ed.), *Proceedings of CHI'83 Human Factors in Computing Systems* (pp. 24–27). New York: ACM.

Young, R. M., & Barnard, P. B. (1987). The use of scenarios in human-computer interaction research: Turbocharging the tortoise of cumulative science. In J. M. Carroll & P. P. Tanner (Eds.), *Proceedings of CHI+GI'87: Conference on human factors in computing systems and graphics interface* (pp. 291–296). New York: Association for Computing Machinery.

Young, R. M., Barnard, P. B., Simon, T. & Whittington, J. (1989). How would your favourite user model cope with these scenarios? *SIGCHI Bulletin, 20,* 51–55.

7 Questioning Design: Toward Methods for Supporting User-Centered Software Engineering

Robert Mack
IBM Thomas J. Watson Research Center
Yorktown Heights, NY

This chapter explores the role that questions can play in the design of computer systems. There are two senses of questions in this design context. The first pertains to questions that arise in concrete software design activities aimed at developing software that meets multiple design and development objectives. I am especially interested in bringing to the design process questions that encourage user-centered perspectives on design. The latter include traditional usability concerns such as how quickly users can learn to use software, how productive they can be in accomplishing tasks of interest using the software, how satisfied users are using the software, and so on. These perspectives are as important for design as traditional software engineering objectives such as providing a certain range of functions within limited development time and resources. This chapter demonstrates how these perspectives can be expressed in questions about how users interact with software, and how software functions support tasks that users want to accomplish.

In addition to the role of concrete questions about design, questioning is meant in the broader metaphorical sense of design as a process of inquiry and invention. Designing software that really meets users' needs increasingly requires early and continuing involvement with users, and implies a process of iterative refinement of design and implementation throughout the development cycle. This process can be managed (see Gould, 1987; Whiteside, Bennett, & Holtzblatt, 1987) but it can be more open-ended than that implied by traditional models of software development (e.g., Brooks, 1987; Gilb, 1990).

The chapter has five sections. The first briefly focuses on, by way of background, the goals and methods of the field of human-computer interaction. The next three sections show the role of questions in various phases of design and development. The main focus is on design and implementation. The discussion is largely based on a specific design collaboration that is described later in more detail. I will also draw on experiences of colleagues working on other design projects. My goal is to develop a more general framework of questions out of these design experiences. A final section outlines possible research directions that are based on this framework.

HUMAN-COMPUTER INTERACTION

Understanding and improving how people use computer technology has become an important field of research investigation and practical action called human-computer interaction (HCI). The practical goals of HCI professionals are to understand and improve the use of computers as tools for supporting individuals and groups in their work (e.g., business professionals). The research goals of HCI professionals are to develop and refine methodologies for accomplishing these practical goals and to discover general principles of human-computer interaction. HCI professionals apply empirical methods and conceptual frameworks that have been successful in other disciplines, most notably basic and applied psychology (see, e.g., Card, Moran, & Newell, 1983), software human factors and ergonomics (see, e.g., Rubenstein & Hersh, 1984), computer science and artificial intelligence, and even anthropology, among other disciplines (see, Suchman, 1987 for a multidisciplinary perspective). In addition to Card et al. (1983) and Suchman (1987), just cited, the interested reader can find additional general discussions of the HCI domain from varied methodological and meta-theoretical perspectives in Newell and Card (1985), Carroll and Campbell (1989), Landauer (1986), Whiteside and Wixon (1986), Gould (1987), Norman (1986), Whiteside, Bennett, and Holtzblatt (1987), and Winograd and Flores (1986).

Guiding Design: Usability Engineering

A relatively standard albeit quite broad and eclectic framework has emerged in HCI for guiding the user-centered design of software systems. The framework has been described in various ways including user-centered system design (Norman & Draper, 1986), empirical and iterative design (Gould, 1987; Gould & Lewis, 1985), and usability engineering (e.g., Bennett, 1984; Whiteside, Bennett, & Holtzblatt, 1987). Each description emphasizes different aspects of a common framework of goals and methods. I prefer the term *usability engineering* because it emphasizes the process of transforming broad usability considerations pertaining to the quality of people's interaction with computers into methods that are rigorous, focused, and grounded in engineering.

Figure 7.1 shows a standard representation of usability engineering. The

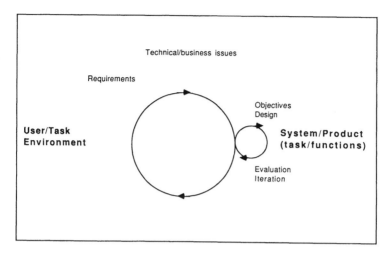

FIG. 7.1. How to guide design. Usability Engineering.

major cycle (the larger circle) begins with an understanding of users and their tasks. This understanding can be used to motivate and guide a design and development cycle (the smaller circle) that creates a new or improved "tool" (e.g., product or system) whose functions are intended to make it easier to perform some or all of those users' tasks. The cycle returns to the user and task environment with a product in the marketplace. Users' (customers') experience provides a basis for future iterations (e.g., product releases) of that tool.

The essence of usability engineering consists of methods for (a) understanding user tasks and requirements in the existing work environment, (b) representing those tasks and requirements within the design cycle (as product objectives), and (c) providing a process for guiding design to meet these objectives. Empirical evaluation and measurement of user performance is a typical way to provide guidance, by providing user feedback for assessing design and providing feedback for improving it. Increasingly, evaluation drives design modification in an iterative cycle until objectives are met. Usability engineering is a framework that has evolved through practice (e.g., as described in Gould, 1987; Whiteside, Bennett, & Holtzblatt, 1987) and through research (e.g., as represented in Carroll and Rosson's work, chap. 6 in this volume; see also Carroll & Kellogg, 1989; Carroll, Rosson, & Kellogg, 1991; Kellogg, 1989; see also Wixon, Holtzblatt, & Knox, 1990).

Empirical and iterative design can be contrasted with an alternative model of software development that is sometimes caricatured as the "Waterfall Model" of software development (Gilb, 1988, 1990; Goldberg, 1986). According to this contrasting view, design and development follows a predictable and roughly linear set of stages, including (a) specifying general requirements, (b) coding components of the software system, (c) integrating these components into a system, (d) code testing, (e) evaluation in the "laboratory" and in the field, (f) release, and so on. (I will use "design and development" as shorthand for the range of design and development activities including task analysis, code generation, empirical and analytical evaluation of evolving programs, and so on.) All these components of design are real but they do not unfold in this predictable, linear chain of activities (for a discussion of these development models from a software engineering perspective, see Brooks, 1987; Gilb, 1990). Instead, all these components are present and interact throughout design. A more fitting metaphor, articulated by Brooks (1987) is that of incremental growth of systems driven iteratively through diverse design, implementation, and user experiences. The iterative, empirical user-driven character of software development represents an important (and still emerging) shift in thinking within software engineering. For a theoretical analysis of this process, with implications for how it might be grounded in general principles, the reader should consult Carroll and Rosson (chap. 6 in this volume; see also Carroll & Rosson, 1990), as well as Carroll, Rosson, and Kellogg (1991).

Design as Bounded Inquiry

In the context of an iterative, open-ended design process, design is usefully characterized in two complementary ways. First, it is a process of engineering aimed at developing software that satisfies multiple, typically competing objectives and constraints. Second, it is a process of inquiry in the sense that developing a solution to these multiple constraints involves iteration and discovery. Typical constraints, which are expressed as development objectives, include developing functions that meet user's needs, and doing so within the limits of a development schedule, and resources (including funding and personnel). Increasingly important are additional objectives that express levels of usability to be achieved along with these traditional "function, schedule, and cost" objectives. All these objectives need to be managed together to achieve a system that really meets users' (customers') needs. Interaction among multiple perspectives and iteration are essential attributes of this process because of the complexity of the design task. It is virtually impossible to anticipate how people will ultimately interact with a complex software system and what impact these user experiences (notably problems) will in turn have on the implementation as we try to meet usability objectives.

The design process, however, is bounded in that it aims to achieve a practical result, namely a system or product. To say that the design of real software systems is a process of inquiry is not necessarily to characterize it as research or to claim that managing the process is not possible. Rather, the claim is that much of design cannot be specified at the outset and is discovered through a design process that must be iterative and open-ended. We need techniques for *satisficing*

(Simon, 1981), that is, converging on a result that meets multiple objectives that may require trade-offs and compromises (Bennett, 1984; Gilb, 1988). Questions help to develop specifications of design elements and issues; integrate these elements into a working whole; and uncover problems and identify solutions.

As researchers in HCI, we are interested in improving the practice of design by reflecting on and refining methods that contribute to successful design (a goal shared with Carroll and Rosson, chap. 6 in this volume). Questioning within the process of design analysis and review represents a methodology with this potential, but one which is not yet well-articulated, -understood, or -applied.

In order to illustrate how questions and question-asking can be integrated with design, I make use of examples and analyses of design activities in which my colleagues and I have been involved. These colleagues include John Karat and John Bennett, both of whom I collaborate with on design issues in an applied setting, and Joan Roemer, who led usability activities for a specific prototype project that I will refer to frequently in this chapter (see also Acknowledgments). Most of the design experiences I focus on derive from collaboration with an advanced technology group within IBM. That group prototyped a computer system aimed at supporting the work of "high end" business professionals, namely executives. Executives are a specialized group of professionals. Unfortunately, many of the standard office or decision support applications do not really meet their needs. However, so-called executive support systems (ESS) are having some impact on executives. The ESS prototype eventually became a product, but in this chapter I focus on early prototyping with which Joan and I were involved.

UNDERSTANDING USERS AND THEIR TASKS

This section sets the stage by discussing briefly the first arena for design and development: understanding users and their tasks. The overriding objective for the design team for developing a computer system is to enable people (users) to carry out tasks more quickly and easily with the technology than without it. There are two key questions. First, what user tasks does the computer tool need to support. (What goals are users trying to accomplish? With what methods?) Second, what quality of user experience does the prototyping team want to achieve? (What is an acceptable effort to learn our tool? Or what level of productivity do users need and expect)?

With respect to the first question, the objective may be to substitute more efficient methods for accomplishing the tasks that users want to perform. This may involve identifying and solving problems with existing computer tools or a manual process. The software should enable users to do new, more powerful things that could not be done easily or at all with existing tools. Indeed, we may want to provide a computer tool where formerly there was none. With respect to the second question, we want people to learn to use this tool with acceptable effort. We want the tool to enable experienced users to be more productive, beyond initial learning, compared to existing methods of performing tasks. There are yet other goals that pertain to users' satisfaction with the tools.

There are empirical methods for discovering what people do in the workplace, how they perform tasks with existing tools and technology, what problems they have, what expectations they have about the domain, and how their task performance might be improved. These methods certainly represent a form of inquiry in HCI. Indeed, these methods are one of the main contributions of behaviorally oriented HCI professionals. Understanding users and their tasks involves gathering and interpreting empirical information of diverse sorts and scales. It ranges from observations and interviews in the field to highly focused, controlled observations in the laboratory that are aimed at resolving specific questions about user problems, or user facility with specific techniques. Many of these methods are well-understood, and standard textbook treatments exist (see, e.g., Gould, 1987; Karat, 1987; Landauer, 1987; Rubenstein & Hersh, 1984). However, new approaches are emerging out of anthropological studies and hermeneutic interpretations of human-computer interaction (see Tetzlaff & Mack, in press, for additional discussion; see also Whiteside et al., 1987; Winograd & Flores, 1986).

In the context of this chapter, a key question is how empirical information about users and their tasks can be represented and analyzed in order to contribute to design in a concrete way. Concrete representations are needed of what people do and of psychological attributes expressing the quality of people' interaction with software. What people do can be expressed in task scenarios, that is, descriptions of user goals and the actions involved in accomplishing them. Qualitative descriptions can be developed of psychological attributes of usability, such as ease of learning, ease of using (following learning), overall satisfaction, and so on. Scenarios and attributes can frame empirical evaluations of developing systems and can guide design in ways that will be discussed further. For example, scenarios of use can be used to identify functions needed to support user tasks. Attributes of usability can be turned into a framework of quantitative (measurable) objectives that can be used to measure and track progress in achieving acceptable levels of performance and user satisfaction. For example, the objective "easy to learn" can be defined as the ability to carry out a subset of basic, high frequency tasks without error following completion of some specified level of training (Carroll & Rosson, 1985; Gould, 1987; Whiteside, Bennett, & Holtzblatt, 1987).

Understanding Executives and Their Tasks

I can illustrate the methodology just alluded to by describing the gathering of initial requirements for the executive support project. The prototyping team began by asking several questions. What do executives do such that a computer might help them? What expectations do they have about usability? The team examined past experiences (some internal, unpublished corporate attempts to implement so-called decision support systems for corporate executives) and published research (most notably, Rockart & De Long, 1988; see also Rockart & Bullen, 1986). We collected interview data. We developed a description of executive tasks and computer use, most notably that most executives do not find computers useful. The reasons for this became clear when we considered key tasks characteristic of executives' work. Executives need selective access to information critical to managing their business. Executives spend much of their time gathering information, including participating in formal scheduled face-to-face meetings that are highly interactive. Executives also need to manage a high volume of communication including hardcopy and electronic mail. Much of the background to this activity, such as scheduling events, preparing reports and presentations, traveling, and handling relevant correspondence is supported by technical and administrative staff. Computers play an indirect, background role from the executive's perspective. Clearly, finding a meaningful role for computers in the support of executive tasks poses a challenge.

Nonetheless, the prototyping team had reason to believe that for some executives in some business situations, computers could play a useful albeit limited role. Rockart and De Long (1988) cited cases where executives have been able to make quicker decisions that were beneficial to the business—decisions based on faster, more focused access to critical information (e.g., tracking and responding to oil prices on the spot market). We also had reason to believe that direct access by executives to key business data could stimulate longer-term improvements in how critical business information is tracked and reported from development labs or marketing organizations to executive decision makers. Finally, it was clear that for executives who used computers, ease of learning and use were essential attributes. Executives have no time or tolerance for struggling with poorly implemented software.

These general task descriptions and considerations of usability need to give way to a still more concrete level of representation of users' tasks and expectations. This can be achieved in scenarios that describe specifically what executives do and how they do it. Table 7.1 summarizes a scenario of use that I focus on for purposes of discussion. The scenario involves the handling of electronic mail. Its content is based on interviews we conducted in the field.

One executive, for example, set aside his first half hour in the morning to review mail. His administrative assistant printed each electronic mail item and sorted these items, along with hardcopy mail, into folders color-coded by importance (e.g., "eyes only" vs. "informational"). The assistant was authorized to handle some items; the executive simply checked a handwritten annotation describing what was done. For other items the executive would make his own handwritten instructions. Executives sometimes have more than one secretary, specializing in various administrative activities, like handling mail or managing time. Nonetheless, we had reason to believe that computers could play a more direct role for some executives. For example, executives not only deal with mail

TABLE 7.1
Scenario: Handling Mail

Scenario

- Secretary uses host-based office system to print all notes, one note per page
-Secretary sorts notes into color-coded folders by category of importance
--Executive reviews notes in folders on desktop, verifying delegated handling notes and
  annotating with handwritten handling instructions
-Secretary carries out handling requests and tracks any follow-up needed

Problems

--Labor intensive
--Ties executive to office
--Depends on secretary setup
--Mail review regimented

Possible benefits of direct mail access by executive

--Executive can do some or all of own mail handling
--Executive can work with mail when and where executive wants to

during dedicated time periods in the office, but they also handle mail at home, in remote temporary offices while traveling, and during brief moments of free time between appointments. Quick, *ad hoc* access to mail in all these situations would be desirable. Computers are available in all these situations. Therefore direct access to electronic communication seemed a desirable possibility.

Out of these kinds of empirical observations, the prototyping team constructed both key scenarios and objectives that we wanted the prototype to achieve. In the case of our prototype, two objectives are shown in Table 7.2. A key requirement for the basic mail function was the ability to access and scan mail quickly and the ability to specify quickly short handling instructions. The team suspected that sorting mail was an important requirement. To some extent these are standard electronic mail functions. However, based on interviews (and other sources of information on executives) it was clear that these functions would have to be implemented in ways that were uncompromisingly easy to learn. Executives indicated no tolerance for software that is difficult to learn or use. Their "mental model" for executing tasks was to "push one button." Moreover, executive users would have to experience clear benefits over current methods for accomplishing mail-handling tasks. The usability objectives shown in Table 7.2 describe these objectives in qualitative terms.

Design-Relevant Representations: Scenarios and Objectives

The scenario in Table 7.1 and the objectives in Table 7.2, describing what mail tasks (functions) the software needed to support, represent two related and complementary types of representations for guiding design. Scenarios capture what users do concretely, first in some existing domain of methods and later in the domain of new methods available with the new tools being developed. Scenarios can be described at different levels of specification that range from high-level goals, independent of how the goals are accomplished, to descriptions that refer to specific methods, objects, and actions. The general design objectives cover both function (what we want users to be able to do with the system) and usability (characterizing the quality of the user's interaction that we want to achieve). The functional objectives in Table 7.2 describe the objects a user must deal with (e.g., mail notes) and actions carried out on them (e.g., viewing, scanning, sorting, and specifying handling instructions). Functional objectives represent a level of abstraction and generalization across scenarios that is needed to extract an underlying set of system-related methods through which task goals can be achieved. The design of a mail handling system should accommodate the scenario in Table 7.1, for example, as well as mail handling scenarios of other executives.

Finally, design and development objectives typically include other business and technical considerations.For example, the prototyping team was committed to exploring the potential of graphical user interface techniques and standards under development within the corporation (IBM Corporation, 1989). There were also competitive product offerings whose capabilities needed to be accounted for, to the extent that the prototype could provide direction for possible future prod-

TABLE 7.2
Executive Mail Support: Illustrative Functional and Usability Objectives

---

Functional Objectives

---

1. Basic mail handling:
   —scan notes
   —preview part content or view full content
   —sort notes by sender

2. Mail handling instructions:
   —forward/reply
   —standard "canned" instructions
   —free-form text entry

Usability Objectives

All functions provide acceptable and efficient ("quick") alternative (or complement) to current practice

1. Functions can be learned with brief training (reference card)

2. Finding and handling mail can be accomplished quickly relatively to current (paper) methods

3. Mail facility can be accessed and set aside quickly and unobtrusively

---

ucts. The team wanted to produce a useful prototype within a certain schedule, given limited personnel and funding. All these considerations impose interacting constraints on design and implementation.

DESIGN AND IMPLEMENTATION

A key challenge for HCI professionals lies in translating broad, empirically informed understanding of users' tasks and expectations into concrete design and implementation guidance. That is, the goal is to develop useful design specifications and an effective design process on the basis of general objectives and scenarios. Developing methodologies to accomplish this represents an important research focus for HCI professionals (see Carroll, 1991, for comprehensive discussion of this HCI research focus).

Techniques for Supporting Design

The central design problem is to create a design that meets both user objectives and development objectives. I share the view of Karat & Bennett (in press) that the design process is analogous to a complex problem-solving task because it involves generating design possibilities and "testing" design possibilities against multiple technical and user objectives of the sort we have been describing. No one set of considerations or perspectives is sufficient to drive design.

In the ESS prototype, for example, the prototyping team based their initial design on new graphical interface techniques, hypothesizing that these techniques would enable the development of a mail application that was considerably easier to use than available host-based interface technology. Corporate standards (IBM Corporation, 1989) called for using specific interface techniques such as pull-down menus, windows, an object-action form of interaction, and so on. The underlying operating environment provided certain programming possibilities that contributed to this interface style (e.g., ready-made programming modules). However, it was necessary to shape these design building blocks into a software environment that met the objectives we illustrated in the previous section.

The team hypothesized that specific design techniques (e.g., cascading card file model, windows, pull-down menus) would satisfy the general functional and usability objectives that were extracted from initial observations and interviews with executives. We evaluated these design possibilities against the objectives for ESS by asking how these specific design elements worked, both technically and from the user's perspectives. We did this by laying out possible designs and conducting walk-throughs that explored specific steps users might experience. We asked how this effort might be perceived by users and where they might have problems.

Two features of this design approach are of special interest. The first is a framework of questions that my colleagues and I have found useful in facilitating the process of design analysis and review (see especially Bennett 1983, 1984). The second is a group design situation in which design questions can be posed and influence design and implementation. Questions and group design are not the only activities relevant to software and usability engineering, but they are key activities where user-relevant design considerations can influence design. Design questions and group design are discussed in the next two sections.

Framework of Questions

Table 7.3 summarizes a framework of questions that are aimed at identifying a set of functions that meet users' needs. The first three questions in Table 7.3 pertain to translating general objectives and task scenarios into specific design possibilities: (a) Can a set of functions be designed that enable key user tasks to be accomplished?; (b) Do proposed functions meet users' task requirements and expectations about the usability of functions?; and (c) Can functions be implemented within development constraints and resources?

These questions are not independent, but they play off each other. A proposed implementation may initially emphasize mainly technical considerations (Ques-

TABLE 7.3
Summary of User-Centered Design Questions for Design Analysis

1. Can a set of function be designed that enable key user tasks to be accomplished?
2. Do proposed functions meet users' task requirements and expectations about the usability of functions?
3. Can functions be implemented within anticipated development resources and constraints?

Questions about usability of software functions. Given a task and a design proposal:

4. What would a user see?
   What interface objects (e.g., screens) and actions?

5. What would users have to know?
   Are there preconditions for actions? Side-effects?
   Are interaction techniques consistent (for the user) across components of the system?

6. What would user do?
   What steps?

5. What would users have to know?
   Are there preconditions for actions? Side-effects?
   Are interaction techniques consistent (for the user) across components of the system?

7. What if users carried out a wrong action?
   How would users know? How would they recover?

Questions about how well functions enable users to accomplish key tasks.

8. How complete is the functionality (with respect to what users want/need to do)?

9. Are new tasks created by the design?
   Do the tasks enhance or conflict with users' goals?

10. What are possible boundary conditions for a design?
    Are there limits in a design element?

tion 1), such as the availability of tools, or a code that can be easily adopted. Such an implementation may satisfy the development objective of achieving a working system quickly and cost effectively. However, the implementation may not satisfy the objective of enabling users to accomplish target tasks easily, as Question 2 tries to capture. Conversely, a set of usability considerations may indicate the need to implement function in a certain way. However, as captured in Question 3, we need to assess whether this implementation can be carried out given available implementation tools and resources.

For example, when the prototyping team considered possible design alternatives, we asked implementation questions such as what effort, time, and cost would be needed to implement some function, and what resources (e.g., existing code) existed to facilitate implementation. The team had to evaluate trade-offs in the scope and the depth of function that could be implemented, based on these considerations. Some innovative technical possibilities were not seriously considered, such as voice recognition or automatic or "intelligent" mail filtering because we knew they were not possible given the resources available. It seemed more useful to pursue other alternatives such as the graphical direct manipulation techniques alluded to earlier. Some possibilities, such as touch and gesture interface techniques were explored in the prototype, because they seemed more feasible.

These general questions can be broken down into more specific questions that can be used to probe aspects of design. Question 2, in particular, can be elaborated into the remaining Questions 4 through 10 in Table 7.3. Consider specific questions about implementing the basic mail facility. A direct mapping of mail organizing and reviewing tasks into software analogues of manipulating color-coded folders and their contents required abstraction from physical details and an initial mapping into available application and interface techniques. The prototyping team assumed, for example, that visual attributes of folder shape and color were less important than the ability to rapidly scan and assign handling instructions to mail items. Accordingly, the initial design adapted a structured cascading card file model whose "cards" corresponded to mail notes that could be quickly "flipped through." Selecting a note brought it to the front of the stack where more detailed review could take place and actions relating to mail handling could be performed. The design enabled several lines of each note to be viewed in the cascaded set, whether or not the note had been selected (and hence was the first mail item).

The basic design seemed reasonable in broad outline and much supported by software tools. The design was prototyped, enabling key interaction details to be examined with respect to known scenarios of use and with respect to various design objectives. Specifically, the prototype implementation for mail was evaluated analytically via scenario-driven walk-throughs. The team asked what a user would do to accomplish various mail-related tasks, and probed that experience with respect to expectations developed out of interviews and observations. In effect, we tried to simulate users' interaction through the questions, beginning with Question 4 in Table 7.3.

What Do Users See?   Given a user task, Question 4 asks what a user would see in terms of user interface objects, for example, screens and screen flows. In this context, it is possible to ask what users need to do to accomplish a task (captured in Question 6, to follow) in terms of the proposed design and in terms of the actions associated with each step of the task scenario. We ask where the focus of a user's attention is likely to be at each step. Visual information also includes terminology of menu items, screen button labels and application titles, and the form and content of visual, pictorial symbols (icons) characteristic of graphical interface styles. We need to know what visual indications exist for conveying to the user the outcome of a step and what indications exist for suggesting or prompting the next step. These indications are typically text descriptions, but increasingly make use of nontextual graphical symbols. Considerable time was spent, for example, designing menu and screen button labels that avoided computer jargon, yet conveyed relevant actions.

What Do Users Need To Know?   How users interpret what they see, and plan what to do depends largely, of course, on what they know. It can be useful at each step of a task scenario to ask, as Question 5 does, what a user would need to know to carry out that step. Further questions could ask how the user would interpret visual prompts for what to do, or interpret visual indications relating to the outcome of an action. It can be useful to question where users will acquire the necessary knowledge for how to use the software. Where training or help are invoked, it is useful to ask how realistic it is to rely on these methods of learning, in light of expectations on the part of users about how much training or help they are likely to tolerate. Past experience can also influence how users interact with computer software. It is useful to ask what analogies users might make between the interface objects and actions provided and other tools and methods for accomplishing tasks (Carroll, Mack, & Kellogg, 1987). Along similar lines, it can be useful to ask whether experience with one application area of a system transfers to another, that is, assess the consistency of basic user interface interaction methods across different components of the system. In the ESS prototype, the team was especially interested in the pervasiveness and consistency of interaction techniques from one application area to another, for example mail handling as compared to working with on-line reports of business data.

What Do Users Need To Do?   Given a layout of user interface objects, it is possible to ask what users need to do to accomplish a task in terms of the system methods provided. That is, given a goal and a user-task scenario, it is useful to walk through the steps required by a design proposal for accomplishing that task, in relation to specific screens, screen flows, and actions. Crude assessments of effort can be made by counting steps. The number of steps in a design proposal can be compared to those required by competitive products, or predecessor systems that provide similar function, or across different interaction techniques under consideration.

In the case of the ESS prototype, for example, corporate standards called for the use of a menu bar and pull-down menu style of selecting actions, instead of entering typed commands or pressing function keys on the keyboard. The menu implementation of mail actions seemed to provide clearer descriptions of available actions, compared to highly abbreviated function key labels in a host-based predecessor system. Despite these guidelines, the prototyping team was quickly led to consider a pervasive role for screen buttons over pull-down menus (i.e., display representations of buttons that could be clicked with a mouse pointing device). A quick walk-through of the menu pull-down implementation suggested that pull-down menus required too many steps for executives. Although they did not like working with keyboards and jargon-labeled function keys, they did want "push-button"-like directness for executing functions. This "push-button" rationale was reinforced by a technical objective, which was to explore the effectiveness of a touch interface for the prototype. Users could select mail items and perform actions on them by touching graphical objects on the screen (rather than using a mouse pointing device).

What if Users Did the Wrong Thing at This Point?   It is useful not only to walk through "correct" sequences of steps, but also to try to anticipate and evaluate "incorrect" interpretations and actions based on them. That is, it can be useful to conduct an "error analysis" of users' interactions, as captured in Question 7. This involves asking what errors a user might make in carrying out an action or interpreting some system feedback. How would users know that they had made an error (what feedback was available?) What consequences might an error have and how readily a user might recover? For example, in our case we had learned that an internal predecessor ESS prototype developed elsewhere in the company had been criticized for an action that dropped a user into a user shell quite different in character from the initial ESS system. This outcome was perceived as an intolerable error. The design team concluded that it was essential to avoid this possibility. This led to questioning whether the prototype was prone to this error. Needless to say, a desirable outcome of error analysis is to conclude that errors are in the design and to generate alternative designs that prevent or reduce the likelihood of users' making this particular error.

A third set of questions (captured in Questions 8–10 in Table 7.3) again probe the functionality of the system with respect to users' goals. The initial implementation is driven by an understanding of users' goals and tasks (see Questions 1, 2, and 3 in Table 7.3). However, in the context of a concrete design (or a running prototype) and concrete scenarios, it is possible to discover missing functions, or to reconsider functions that designers might have originally decided not to implement. Designers might also decide that certain aspects of the implementation are system overhead—a distraction from the user's task of interest.

How Complete Is the Functionality?   A first-order question, captured in Question 8, is whether functions support users' tasks. It may be discovered that certain user requirements or concerns are not represented in a design, and this may motivate design change. In our case, for example, the card-file model seemed to enable most of the basic mail handling tasks we thought executives needed. However, as the prototyping team analyzed the prototype design, we revisited some scenarios that went beyond handling individual mail items. One example is the availability of single letter mail handling commands that could be entered in a single character command line for each mail item. This enabled users to specify at one time actions for multiple mail items, and different actions if desired. This was possible with a predecessor host-implementation. However, the structure of the mail folder did not readily lend itself to entering single letter commands from the keyboard.

Another example pertains to implementing handling instructions for notes. Executives could not make handwritten annotations to notes presented on the screen, whereas they could do so for printed copies of notes. They could type messages on the screen in text entry fields made available for this purpose. But executives do not like to use keyboards or to type. Moreover, many of their handling instructions are stereotyped and short. So the team hypothesized that a menu of standard handling instructions might work. The team explored possible boundary conditions for providing a standard set of handling instructions. In fact, standard handling options do accommodate some but not all handling instructions. Executives needed to be able to customize their own set of standard instructions. So this led into questions about the extent to which the user interface could be customized.

Are New Tasks Created by the Design? Do These Tasks Enhance or Conflict With Users' Goals?   In analyzing what users need to do to accomplish tasks and whether these software-implemented tasks really accomplish users' goals, we can also ask if a design creates new subtasks that are not directly related to users' goals. This is reflected in Question 9. These new subtasks may be perceived as *system tasks* that are a distraction for users (for discussion, see Nielsen, Mack, Bergendorff, and Grischkowsky, 1986; Mack & Nielsen, 1988). They may not represent an acceptable trade-off in effort compared to what the user can accomplish with the function. On the other hand, these subtasks may actually represent new capabilities for users. For example, the executive support system made use of an overlapping window environment. On the plus side, windows enabled executive users to work with more than one application, for example, mail and briefings, or mail and calendar. This was clearly an improvement over a predecessor facility that some executives had used prior to our prototype. On the negative side, windows entail window management actions. The prototyping team considered such actions too effortful for executives. Ultimately the ESS system made cautious use of multiple windows, providing default window arrangements that minimized the need to manage multiple windows.

What Are Possible Boundary Conditions for a Design?   Sometimes a design works for some sets of conditions but not for others. Some sequences of steps may be judged acceptable when carried out occasionally, but not repetitively. This raises new considerations expressed in Question 10. The ESS prototype used screen buttons arrayed along the bottom of an application to enable user actions. The decision to use screen buttons rather than provide actions only in pull-down menus was driven in part by the effort required to carry out frequent actions by opening up and selecting from pull-down menus. On the other hand, the number of buttons that could be arrayed in a single line across the bottom of a window was more limited than the number of menu items that could be displayed in a pull-down. This seemed reasonable given the limited number of actions that executives wanted. However, the prototyping team asked what boundary conditions might exist for the number and layout of screen buttons. For example, what if executives wanted to do more with mail than the subset we anticipated? What if an executive wanted to use mail with another application, requiring more than one window to be displayed (reducing the window area for screen buttons)? Could the design accommodate these new situations? This was a new consideration to apply to the scenarios and the design, namely whether the set of actions required for the set of scenarios could be mapped into a single line of screen buttons. Perhaps two lines of screen buttons are needed? Would such a design be permissible by corporate user interface standards?

I believe that questions like those in Table 7.3, asked in the context of scenario-driven walk-throughs of design layouts (screens and screen flows), help to specify designs to levels that enable designers to probe how these designs can meet objectives. Questions draw out possibilities and assumptions about design by simulating users' interactions. Of course, questions cannot always be answered immediately or unequivocally. And the ultimate test of usefulness and usability is the user's actual experience and satisfaction with the system, neither of which can be predicted in detail with analytical evaluation. However, questioning designs analytically can increase the likelihood of uncovering design decisions that past experience suggests are likely to result in user difficulty (the so-called "howlers" in design). Questions and design assessments stimulated by them can also frame follow-up design, implementation, or empirical evaluation activities.

I have not said much about the dynamics of questioning or the contexts in which questions are asked and answers explored. The next two sections discuss these issues at greater length. However, the questions discussed in this section represent a degree of idealization and abstraction of the actual design activities to which we contributed. The questions summarized were not necessarily applied in a mechanical way and in well-defined design situations. I believe these analyses can be applied more systematically, in a way more integrated with the fuller design team, as I discuss in the next section. However, many of the user-related analyses discussed earlier were done informally and communicated informally to designers and implementers.

Moreover, it should be understood that in actual design situations, the questions summarized in Table 7.3 provide only starting points for design analysis. General questions quickly lead to more specific questions whose form and content depend on context, timing, and opportunism. In reality, one question can lead to another. Questions can overlap, and in answering one question a design team may discover that it is addressing or needs to address other questions as well. For example, asking what users need to do to accomplish a task and what visual information is available to prompt users for this action inevitably leads to asking what a user would need to know in order to interpret visual indicators in the appropriate ways. What users know can suggest what errors a user might make, and how easily he or she could recover from them (see Mack, 1990, for examples in text editing domain). There are well-known trade-offs in user interface design that can be applied in considering answers to questions. For example, one might conclude that new or casual users may be unlikely to easily learn (or remember) some sequence of steps. One might consider modifying the procedure to make it easier. Or a decision may be made, pending later user testing, to retain the implementation because one believes that users can recover easily enough from the consequences of making a wrong action, and development resources need to be devoted to other aspects of design. It may be decided that novice users will not likely know what menu option labels mean and that the system needs to be prompted. However, this may need to be balanced against the visual clutter of a heavily prompted interface and the constraints that being prompted might impose on users as they become more experienced.

Group Design: Four Walls Techniques

In the experience of my colleagues and myself, design activities and design questions occur in many settings, formal and informal, throughout design and implementation. Questions, in particular, arise in designers' and implementers' individual problem solving, in *ad hoc* design meetings (e.g., in the hallway or over lunch), as well as in more formal, group design situations. However, we have been especially interested in what happens in group design situations. We would like to develop methods for guiding and facilitating design in these situations. John Karat and John Bennett, in particular, have begun to codify these techniques and to analyze how they contribute to effective design. In this section, I highlight some of their major interpretations, which are summarized in Table 7.4, and the key techniques of which are schematized in Figure 7.2. A fuller

TABLE 7.4
Group Design: The Four Walls Technique, Goals and Approach

Goals

1. Discover and help solve design problems that involve multiple perspectives and sources of expertise.

2. Create common picture of larger shared design among team members.

Approach

1. Lay out different components of design space on walls

    a. Design objectives (function, schedule, usability)
        i. express implementation targets

    b. Concrete design (screens and screen flows)
        i. context for scenario-driven walk-throughs

    c. Design abstractions
        i. actions arrayed across objects

    d. Implementation means and mechanisms
        i. tools and resources

2. Scenario and question-driven analysis of design issues and assumptions

---

treatment, based on a wider set of design experiences than have been described in this chapter, can be found in Karat and Bennett (1991) and Bennett and Karat (1991).

The starting point is to lay out a *design space* consisting of the general considerations we have already referred to: namely, design objectives, the concrete design expressed in screens and screen flows, and relevant implementation tools and resources. This design space can be complicated. It can be useful to lay out these specific considerations on walls in the room where the group can work as a team. Figure 7.2 schematizes key design representations and techniques and illustrates some of the design questions we discussed in the last section. Figure 7.2 also schematizes abstractions of system structure and function, which can stimulate questions or help answer them. An example are tables that compare application objects to the actions that apply to them. These are intended to uncover possible commonalities in actions that can influence how functions are named, among other things.

In this design setting, design teams can work through these sets of design considerations, asking the kinds of questions I have already illustrated, in relation to the kinds of representations sketched in Fig. 7.2. Questions are a key vehicle for developing design representations and for constructively analyzing design issues. By posing questions, design problems can be identified and steps can be taken toward their resolution. Connections and interactions among design elements can be developed. Implementers are exposed to possible implications for user performance of their design decisions. HCI professionals, in turn, are made aware of possible implementation difficulties associated with design changes motivated by usability problems. The design team can work through the trade-offs, facing the constraints of development schedules and resources.

An example from the ESS design can illustrate these dynamics. An implementer had prototyped a text comment entry area in the same way for both reply and forwarding notes. The entry area was a single line typing field. Working through reply and forwarding scenarios suggested that this field was not enough, particularly for forwarding notes in which the reasons for forwarding were usually longer than replies (which usually are "yes" or "no"). Initially, an additional step was needed to open up a more extensive text entry area. The question was whether this more extensive text area should be the default, or the single line

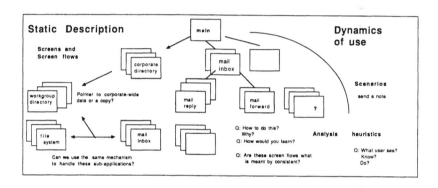

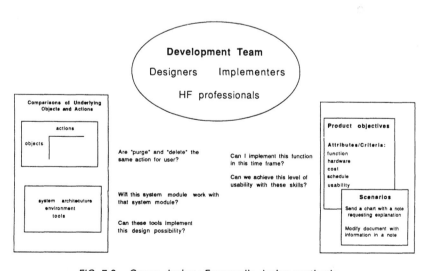

FIG. 7.2.   Group design: Four walls design methods.

entry area, with an option to invoke a larger text entry area. The simpler design was easier to implement and it did not require redesigning other elements of the reply or forward screen. The design also seemed to achieve one level of consistency (physical identity). The implementer correctly believed that consistency was important. However, the issue was not simply visual consistency but consistency of how the functions operated with respect to what users expect to do in order to carry out their tasks. In working through the scenario the prototyping team made these assumptions explicit and posed alternative assumptions about consistency (from the user's perspective). This led to a different implementation for reply and forward.

Group meetings are obviously not the only way that design analysis can take place. Other mechanisms include more narrowly focused design reviews that seek to assess the compliance of a design to explicit functional specifications. When prototypes or early systems are available to pilot users, specialized electronic mail bulletin board systems provide another mechanism for communicating problems to developers. These activities and facilities also play a role in design and design iteration. Moreover, the outcomes of group design are not the only analyses or representations of design. Design continues individually when implementers return to their offices. We have anecdotal evidence that individual design activities share similarities to processes observed in group design. For example, unpublished studies of initial "paper" designs suggest that designers working alone generate their own *ad hoc* mini-scenarios, and use them to evaluate function and interface possibilities (Tetzlaff & Schwartz, 1991; also personal communication). However, group design can be an important part of the overall design processes: What individuals do ultimately becomes part of a whole, and interactions among individuals are important for communication and coordination.

General Characteristics of Design Inquiry

Let me highlight two characteristics of the design and implementation activities that have been discussed. First, the process of asking and answering questions is complex from both cognitive and group dynamic perspectives. As a cognitive task, the design process is an interplay between multiple considerations, both general and specific. In order to write software, a team needs to work down to specific design considerations. It needs scenarios, screens, and concrete steps. Yet, it may be necessary to capture aspects of design that cut across scenarios and implementation components. It is necessary to bring out similarities and differences from a user's perspective (e.g., Are these actions really different?) or an implementation perspective (e.g., Can one use the same underlying programming mechanism for multiple components of the application?). The process of asking questions is heuristic and opportunistic across these levels of considerations, as I indicated earlier. Asking questions about one design issue can lead to questions about other design issues. Multiple questioning paths may result in similar conclusions. Questioning does not unfold in an algorithmic way, but involves interaction and iteration. This dialectic seems to be an important characteristic of the dynamics of design as a whole. Managing it is cognitively challenging in any setting, but especially in a group design situation.

Second, from the perspective of group dynamics, group design requires skill to manage this question-driven dialectic toward results. Questions range over levels of technical design considerations, and involve contributions from different individuals. Skill is needed to balance depth of questioning and analysis against the breadth of design issues that may need to be analyzed. And skill is needed to create a supportive environment to encourage questioning people's assumptions and decisions. Questions can make people uncomfortable. They can challenge management practices and assumptions, especially in design groups where there might be contention or uncertainty about objectives and responsibilities. This was not the case for our prototype involvement, but it is often characteristic of development teams. Management practices of the last few decades have led to a compartmentalization of work (e.g., Reich, 1983), which in a software engineering context may make it difficult to manage aspects of design that involve the integration and interaction of components.

Questions can also be challenging to team members who may not immediately appreciate the connection between what they do and aspects of the overall system, particularly those involving usability. For example, asking questions about how users might experience an aspect of a system may seem outside an implementer's responsibility. Such questions may seem to conflict with other assumptions about how usability considerations are incorporated into systems; for example, that usability problems are local and transient or that problems can be dealt with through help and training. HCI professionals need to question these assumptions; noting, for example, that problems accumulate and neither on-line help nor training are adequate solutions to software problems. Although these kinds of perspectives do not necessarily require invoking deep cognitive analysis, they can have a constructive impact on designers when applied in concrete ways in a supportive environment.

To summarize, the four walls approach to group design is an arena in which design questions can be posed and answers explored. The approach is intended to encourage and support problem solving by a group, where problems and solutions typically transcend the scope of an individual's expertise or initial responsibility. Questions provide methods for facilitating design problem solving. Putting design analyses on walls, for example, is intended to provide a means for capturing and representing in a highly visible and cumulative way the key results of this shared problem solving. Separating design objectives from concrete design layouts and implementation is intended to emphasize an important distinction between the goals (objectives) of the development effort and the means and mechanisms the team believes can achieve these goals (John Bennett, personal communication). From the perspective of group dynamics, group design attempts to create a common understanding of the emerging design, thereby contributing to team building.

EVALUATION AND ITERATION

Our characterization of design is not sufficient. Design takes place in a larger context that includes empirical evaluations with users. Behavioral evaluations provide useful feedback that can guide and iteratively refine design. Behavioral evaluations are a mainstay of software human factors and the HCI profession. How are behavioral evaluation and design connected? Why not rely solely on behavioral evaluation? The short answer to both questions is that design and evaluation are complementary activities, each necessary and neither sufficient to guide design alone.

Empirical evaluation is the ultimate test of whether a software system has indeed met its objectives and for providing insights into user problems that can drive iterative improvement. As noted earlier, the same objectives and scenarios that drive the initial design can be adapted as a framework for evaluation. General objectives and scenarios can be used to develop testable objectives that provide operational definitions of usability attributes like ease of learning, user satisfaction, and so on. Measurements of system use against objectives provides indicators of system quality that can be tracked and compared across system iterations (see Whiteside, Bennett, & Holtzblatt, 1987). Empirical evaluation also provides qualitative feedback on problems from which designers can infer possible design improvements (see, e.g., Lewis, Henry, & Mack, 1990). In many cases, users themselves can suggest specific design recommendations that may not have occurred to developers.

However, empirical evaluation is not sufficient in itself. Empirical evaluation depends on design analysis and prototyping, both of which are as much in the domain of conceptual analysis as driven by user feedback. Behavioral evaluation, even when informal, is relatively time-consuming and limited in scope. Usability evaluators cannot test everything, at least not in a timely way. And it may not be necessary to test everything to the extent that it is possible to apply strong intuitions to design analysis, based on past experience or applications of relevant general guidelines. Testing involves decisions about what to test and where to focus limited testing resources. Empirical results often need to be interpreted with respect to some conceptual framework and in the context of other design considerations (e.g., trade-offs with development schedule or cost). All these considerations underscore the importance of conceptual and analytical evaluation in addition to empirical evaluation.

DESIGN AS INQUIRY: RESEARCH DIRECTIONS

The contribution of HCI professionals to design represents a conscious shift from a traditional evaluative role to a creative design role. HCI researchers want to understand and improve design and development practices (see also Carroll & Rosson, chap. 6 in this volume). I believe that question-asking methods, and the group design situation described provide effective methodologies for guiding design. However, informal methods of question asking and answering in a group situation need to be turned into a methodology whose procedures can be taught, and whose utility, scope, and boundary conditions are established. Systematizing and grounding question-driven design activities in guidelines, if not in theory, is a desirable goal, indeed one that motivated this chapter. There is much more work to do to fulfill this goal. In the remainder of this chapter, I sketch research directions that should contribute to this goal.

User-Centered Design Methods

The first research direction is to establish how the design approaches described in this chapter relate to other design approaches existing or emerging in HCI practice. Our experiences seem to be consistent with emerging studies of the psychology of software development (Olson, Sheppard, & Soloway, 1987; Rosson, Maass, & Kellogg, 1988). These studies analyze software design and development as a complex problem-solving task, in which analyzing and managing subtasks can be problematic. Multiple perspectives on the design task are important, but difficult to expose, maintain, and coordinate.

Existing software engineering techniques, embodied in programming environments, claim to support aspects of the user-centered design considerations discussed here. Computer-assisted software engineering (e.g., or CASE) tools, for example, claim to represent task requirements (e.g., work flows), aid the translation of requirements into software design specifications, and provide programming tools for implementation (Goldberg, 1986). What is less clear is how deeply they represent user-centered perspectives and how well they support iteration and interaction among different levels of, and perspectives on, design. These techniques may complement user-centered design techniques we have discussed, but more is needed.

Early research strategies in HCI attempted to apply cognitive theory to model and predict aspects of users' performance with computers. The goal was to provide usability assessments of user interface designs to the development process. These attempts began most notably with Card, Moran, and Newell (1983). They have been elaborated into production system modeling approaches (Kieras & Polson, 1985; Polson, 1988). These approaches have proven to be of limited applicability, at least for the kind of software design and development described in this chapter (but see Olson & Olson, 1990 for a lengthier review and more positive assessment). More informal and qualitative applications of these cognitive analyses have been proposed for design analysis and review (Karat, 1988; Kieras, 1987). Lewis, Polson, Wharton, and Rieman (1990) have recently found that questions asked analytically about an interface during scenario-driven walk-throughs provide some basis for anticipating problems that real novices have with the software.

More recently, alternative research strategies have emerged that focus less on applying cognitive theory to model and predict human performance. Instead, these strategies aim to develop comprehensive, qualitative, psychological descriptions of user interface design features. The aim is to extract and assess the psychological claims made (explicitly or not) about how user interface techniques support user actions and goals (see most notably the forthcoming Carroll, 1991; also Carroll & Kellogg, 1989; Kellogg, 1989; MacLean, Young, & Moran, 1989).The aim is to use these analyses not only to evaluate designs, but also to guide design and provide a framework for accumulating expertise about effective interface techniques beyond specific software systems. Related research projects aim to exploit hypermedia software technology in order to provide electronic tools for representing and tracking design decisions and design rationale. Examples include project NICK (Cook, Ellis, Graf, Rein, & Smith, 1987) and the issue-based information system gIBIS (Conklin & Begeman, 1989). Even more ambitious projects attempt to automate or support certain kinds of analyses of an evolving design, such as uncovering possible inconsistencies or conflicts among design components, by applying knowledge-based systems (Neches, 1988). Finally, new programming technologies may also contribute to developing more effective user-centered design analyses. Rosson and Alpert (1990), for example, have recently provided a cognitive analysis of object-oriented programming methods. Their analysis reinforces the long-standing claim that such programming environments encourage software design that better exploits concepts and methods of real-world tasks, which the software is intended to support.

These more recent approaches could complement, if not provide a more theoretical foundation for, the design analysis techniques we have been discussing. Questioning design rationale and design claims, and simulating user's interaction through walk-throughs of design, share a similar goal with the techniques discussed in this chapter: namely, the goal of developing methods for systematically and thoroughly articulating the relationship between the technical attributes of the user interface and the psychological attributes and processes underlying people's use of the interface to accomplish tasks.Moreover, the opportunistic and context-sensitive character of design questions should not obscure the fact that question-driven analysis, especially in a group design setting, requires preparation and representations. We have discussed representations including scenarios, statements of objectives, and screen layouts tied to scenario walk-throughs. Formal, systematic design analysis schemes can contribute to the development of these representations. They may provide guidelines or methods for capturing and tracking the results of design analyses throughout design and development.

Nonetheless, our application of questions in design walk-throughs has been driven, to date, by considerations other than producing complete analyses of user interactions and, in particular, predicting user's interaction with software. It is not clear how the systematicity and rigor of these methods trades off against the scope and breadth of the design analysis that is possible in the larger design situations we have described. It is not yet clear whether these techniques can be scaled up in a timely way to complex design problems. We believe it is useful to engage the design team directly in analysis and review of designs, in addition to developing stand-alone cognitive analyses. Often it is sufficient simply to ask a question in a design setting to elicit useful analyses that can constructively influence a design or implementation. It is not always easy to find potential problems with seemingly mundane design elements with which one is intimately familiar.

The Basis for User-Centered Design Questions

The second research direction is to understand better the basis for effective user-centered design questions. A particular challenge is to develop a better understanding of how people's goals and tasks are related to the objects and actions provided by software functions. The goal is not only to evaluate how well proposed functions support users' tasks. The goal ultimately is to help generate useful functions in the first place. To be more specific, Questions 1 and 2 in Table 7.3 are deceptively simple to pose, but very difficult to answer.

Currently, all the questions in Table 7.3, and the design analyses driven by them, are best regarded as based on practical experience. This includes experience based on observing or working with users. It includes intuitions based on our own use of software. These intuitions in turn are clearly informed by concepts and principles from cognitive psychology, applied to problems of human-computer interaction (e.g., Norman, 1986). Usability guidelines are loosely based on psychological principles (e.g., Rubenstein & Hersh, 1984), although skill and experience is needed to apply them usefully in specific design situations. Examples of relevant psychological theory include findings and concepts relating to problem solving and learning. An example of the former is the analysis of direct manipulation user interface techniques by Hutchins, Hollan, and Norman (1986). An example of the latter is the analysis by Carroll, Mack, and Kellogg (1987) of how prior knowledge, characterized in metaphors, can influence how people learn and use computers. The challenge is to make these analyses relevant in a concrete and specific way to design analysis methods. The Lewis, Polson, Wharton and Rieman (1990) research on cognitive walk-throughs is an example of how a theory of novice learning might be used to drive the analysis of computer interfaces.

From a practical perspective, I believe we are in the domain of bounded rationality (Simon, 1981), where "folk psychology," informed by qualitative psychological principles, has considerable face validity. That is, the manifest content of user goals and expectations can provide a basis for generating useful user-centered questions about design. Where intuitive considerations fall short, of course, we must appeal to empirical evaluation to inform and correct our intuitions.

Finally, in the context of empirical evaluation it should be noted that there are connections between the questions in Table 7.3 and actual user concerns. The possible connections between actual user questions and the questions raised in design analysis are promising and deserve closer examination. For example, asking users to learn and to use a system by asking an expert questions in place of (or in addition to) using documentation or help turns out to be a useful qualitative method for eliciting user needs and problems (Kato, 1986). The questions that users ask are similar to those that can be asked analytically in scenario-driven walk-throughs. Conversely, asking users questions about their experience working with a computer can be useful for probing their expectations and assumptions about how to do things with computers (Graesser & Murray, 1990; Mack, 1990). Mack and Burdett (in press) review the use of question asking by users as a qualitative method in HCI design and evaluation, noting the similarities and differences compared to traditional thinking-aloud protocols. In some design contexts, user questions can provide quite direct design input. For example, in our laboratory we have used question asking to help design the content of on-line assistance (Campbell, 1990; Campbell & DiBello, 1988).

Group Dynamics

The final research direction is to understand how to involve more effectively designers and developers in analysis and review of designs (in contrast to doing stand-alone cognitive analyses). As suggested earlier, software design may be too complex and shifting to rely only on unidimensional analysis tools or frameworks. There is an important role for the kinds of interactive design conversations that we have found useful. The representation of user perspectives requires probing that is difficult to mechanize or capture in formal tools. We need to articulate better the various skills discussed earlier as needed to manage effective group design processes. In particular, we must be able to teach these techniques.

Group design and problem solving is important in our emerging framework. However, it is not always accorded as much legitimacy as formal analysis that is motivated by theory. It is easy to focus on analytical techniques, and give much less legitimacy to the contexts in which the techniques are applied to achieve results. Complex problems are often not solved by straightforward unidimensional application of research, but through more pluralistic and participatory problem solving. The participatory character of software design and development, involving HCI professionals, software engineers, and even users (as workers or customers) has emerged as an important theme in HCI research and practice (Bodker, 1989). Solving practical problems as the ultimate test of formal research has also been a theme in metadiscussions of research strategy in social science (Lindbloom & Cohen, 1976) and in cognitive science (Anderson, 1987).

CONCLUSIONS

Asking questions about software design and implementation provides the basis for a useful methodological contribution in the HCI practice. In this chapter, I have identified a set of user-centered design questions based on concrete design experiences (Table 7.3). We understand to some level how these questions relate to the larger usability engineering context that includes empirical evaluation and the dynamics of working within a development team. Considerable work is needed to achieve our objective of turning the techniques discussed here into an effective, teachable methodology. However, we certainly have a basis for practical action (see also Bennett & Karat, 1991), as well as a research agenda for progressing toward a better user-centered design methodology.

ACKNOWLEDGMENTS

I would like to thank Art Graesser, Thomas Lauer, John Bennett, Dick Dewid, Joan Roemer, and John Karat for their careful reviews of this chapter. The chapter is much improved for their suggestions. I also thank John Bennett for inviting me to participate in group design opportunities over several years and for conversations that pointed the way toward turning useful human factors "consulting" into a potential methodology research focus for HCI. I would like to thank Robert Rauf, prototype project leader in IBM's Application Solutions Division, for the opportunity to work on the executive support project, aspects of which are discussed here. Finally, I would like to thank Joan Roemer and Dick Dewid for inviting me to participate in various usability-related activities related to the prototyping. The ideas developed in this chapter, although benefiting from all these people, are not necessarily shared by them.

REFERENCES

Anderson, J. (1987). Methodologies for studying human knowledge. *Behavioral and Brain Sciences, 10,* 467–505.

Bennett, J. (1983). Analysis and design of the user interface for decision support systems. In J. Bennett (Ed.), *Building decision support systems* (pp. 41–64.). Reading, MA: Addison-Wesley.

Bennett, J. (1984). Managing to meet usability requirements: Establishing and meeting software development goals. In J. Bennett, D. Case, J. Sandelin, & M. Smith (Eds.), *Visual display terminals* (pp. 161–184). Englewood Cliffs, NJ: Prentice-Hall.

Bennett, J., & Karat, J. (1991). *Facilitating a user-centered perspective in design meetings.* Unpublished manuscript.

Bodker, S. (1989). A human activity approach to user interfaces. *Human-Computer Interaction, 4,* 171–195.

Brooks, F. (1987, April). No silver bullet: Essence and accidents in software engineering. *Computer,* pp. 10–19.

Campbell, R. (1990). *On-line help: A conceptual analysis* (Research Rep. No. RC 15407). IBM Thomas J. Watson Research Center, Hawthorne, NY.

Campbell, R., & DiBello, L. (1988). *The usability of hypertextual on-line help: A laboratory study.* Unpublished manuscript.

Card, S., Moran, T., & Newell, A. (1983). *The psychology of human-computer interaction.* Hillsdale, NJ: Lawrence Erlbaum Associates.

Carroll, J. (Ed.). (1991). *Designing interaction: Psychology at the human-computer interface.* Cambridge, MA: Cambridge University Press.

Carroll, J., & Campbell, R. (1989). Artifacts as psychological theories: The case of human-computer interaction. *Behavior and Information Technology, 8,* 247–256.

Carroll, J., & Kellogg, W. (1989). Artifact as theory-nexus: Hermeneutics meets theory-based design. In K. Bice & C. Lewis (Eds.), *Proceedings of CHI"89: Conference on Human Factors in Computing Systems* (pp. 7–14). New York: Association for Computing Machinery.

Carroll, J., Mack, R., & Kellogg, W. (1987). Interface metaphors and user interface design. In M. Helander (Ed.), *Handbook of human-computer interaction* (pp. 67–85). New York: Springer-Verlag.

Carroll, J., & Rosson, M. B. (1985). Usability specifications as a tool in iterative development. In R. Hartson (Ed.), *Advances in Human-Computer Interaction* (pp. 1–28). Norwood, NJ: Ablex.

Carroll, J., & Rosson, M. B. (1990). Human computer interaction scenarios as a design representation. *Proceedings of HICSS-23: Hawaii International Conference on System Sciences* (pp. 555–561). Los Alamitos, CA: IEEE Computer Society Press.

Carroll, J., Rosson, M. B., & Kellogg, W. (1991). The task-artifact cycle. In J. Carroll (Ed.), *Designing interaction: Psychology at the human-computer interface* (pp. 74–102). Cambridge, MA: Cambridge University Press.

Conklin, J., & Begeman, M. (1989). gIBIS: A hypertext tool for exploratory policy discussion. *ACM Transactions on Office Information Systems, 6,* 303–331.

Cook, P., Ellis, C., Graf, M., Rein, G., & Smith, T. (1987). Project Nick: Meetings augmentation and analysis. *ACM Transactions on Office Information Systems, 5,* 132–146.

Gilb, T. (1988). *Principles of software engineering management.* New York: Addison-Wesley.

Gilb, T. (1990). *The evolutionary delivery model for analysis, design and test of human-machine systems.* Plenary address presented at Interact '90, Third IFIP Conference on Human-Computer Interaction, Cambridge, England.

Goldberg, R. (1986). Software engineering: An emerging discipline. *IBM Systems Journal, 25,* 334–353.

Gould, J. (1987). How to design usable systems. In M. Helander (Ed.), *Handbook of human-computer interaction* (pp. 757–790). Netherlands, Amsterdam: Elsevier Science.

Gould, J., & Lewis, C. (1985). Designing for usability: Key principles and what designers think. *Communications of the ACM, 28,* 300–311.

Graesser, A., & Murray, K. (1990). A question-answering methodology for exploring a user's acquisition and knowledge of a computer environment. In S. Robertson, J. Black, & W. Zachery (Eds.), *Cognition, cooperation and computing* (pp. 237–267). Norwood, NJ: Ablex.

Hutchins, E., Hollan, J., & Norman, D. (1986). Direct manipulation interfaces. In D. Norman & S.

Draper (Eds.), *User centered system design: New perspectives on human-computer interaction* (pp. 87–124). Hillsdale, NJ: Lawrence Erlbaum Associates.

IBM Corporation. (1989). *Systems application architecture, Common user access: Advanced interface design guide.* Boca Raton, FL: IBM Corporation.

Karat, J. (1987). Software evaluation methodologies. In M. Helander (Ed.), *Handbook of human-computer interaction* (pp. 891–903). North-Holland: Elsevier Science.

Karat, J. (1988). Approximate modeling as an aid to software design. *Human Factors Society Bulletin, 31,* 1–3.

Karat, J., & Bennett, J. (1991). Working within the design process: Taking design seriously. In J. Carroll (Ed.), *Interfacing thought: Cognitive aspects of human-computer interaction* (pp. 269–285). Cambridge, MA: MIT Press.

Kato, T. (1986). What "question asking protocols" can say about the user interface. *International Journal of Man-Machine Studies, 25,* 659–673.

Kellogg, W. (1989). *Extracting psychological claims from artifacts in use* (Research Rep. No. RC 15511). IBM Thomas J. Watson Research Center, Yorktown Heights, NY.

Kieras, D. (1987). Towards a practical GOMS model methodology for user interface design. In M. Helander (Ed.), *Handbook of human-computer interaction* (pp. 135–158). North-Holland: Elsevier Science.

Kieras, D., & Polson, P. (1985). An approach to the formal analysis of user complexity. *International Journal of Man-Machine Studies, 22,* 365–394.

Landauer, T. (1987). Research methods in human-computer interaction. In M. Helander (Ed.), *Handbook of human-computer interaction* (pp. 905–928). North-Holland: Elsevier Science.

Landauer, T. (1986). Relations between cognitive psychology and computer system design. In J. Carroll (Ed.), *Interfacing thought: Cognitive aspects of human-computer interaction.* Cambridge, MA: MIT Press.

Lewis, C., Polson, P., Wharton, C., & Rieman, J. (1990). Testing a walk-through methodology for theory-based design of walk-through design of walk-up-and-use interfaces. In J. Chew & J. Whiteside (Eds.), *Proceedings of CHI 1990* (pp. 235–242). New York: Association for Computing Machinery.

Lewis, J., Henry, S., & Mack, R. (1990). Integrated office benchmarks: A case study. In D. Diaper (Ed.), *Interact '90: The Third IFIP Conference on Human-Computer Interaction* (pp. 337–343). Cambridge, England.

Lindbloom, C., & Cohen, D. (1976). *Usable knowledge: Social science and social problem solving.* New Haven, CT: Yale University Press.

Mack, R. (1990). Understanding and learning text-editing skills: Observations on the role of new user expectations. In S. Robertson, J. Black, & W. Zachery (Eds.), *Cognition, cooperation and computing* (pp. 304–337). Norwood, NJ: Ablex.

Mack, R., & Burdett, J. (in press). When novices elicit knowledge: Question-asking in designing, evaluating and learning to use software. In R. Hoffman (Ed.), *Cognition of experts: Psychological research and empirical AI.* New York: Springer-Verlag.

Mack, R., & Nielsen, J. (1988). *Software integration in the professional work environment: Observations on requirements, usage and interface issues* (Research Rep. No. RC 12677). IBM Thomas J. Watson Research Center, Hawthorne, NY.

MacLean, A., Young, R., & Moran, T. (1989). Design rationale: The argument behind the artifact. In K. Bice & C. Lewis (Eds.), *Proceedings of CHI'89: Conference on Human Factors in Computing Systems* (pp. 247–252). New York: ACM.

Neches, R. (1988). Knowledge-based tools to promote shared goals and terminology between interface designers. *ACM Transactions on Office Information Systems, 6,* 215–231.

Newell, A., & Card, S. (1985). The prospects for psychological science in human-computer interact. *Human-Computer Interaction, 1,* 209–242.

Nielsen, J., Mack, R., Bergendorff, K., & Grischkowsky, N. (1986). Integrated software usage in the professional work environment: Evidence from questionnaires and interviews. In M. Mantei and P. Orbeton (Eds.), *Proceedings of CHI'86 Human Factors in Computing Systems* (pp. 162–167). New York: ACM.

Norman, D. (1986). Cognitive engineering. In D. Norman & S. Draper (Eds.), *User-centered system design* (pp. 31–61). Hillsdale, NJ: Lawrence Erlbaum Associates.

Norman, D., & Draper, S. (Eds.). (1986). *User-centered system design*. Hillsdale, NJ: Lawrence Erlbaum Associates.

Olson, J., & Olson, G. (1990). The growth of cognitive modeling in human-computer interaction since GOMS. *Human-Computer Interaction, 5,* 221–266.

Olson, G., Sheppard, S., & Soloway, E. (Eds.). (1987). *Empirical studies of programmers: Second workshop*. Norwood, NJ: Ablex.

Polson, P. (1988). A quantitative theory of human-computer interaction. In J. Carroll (Ed.), *Interfacing thought: Cognitive aspects of human-computer interaction* (pp. 184–235). Cambridge, MA: MIT Press.

Reich, R. (1983). *The next American frontier*. New York: Penguin.

Rockart, J., & Bullen, C. (Eds.). (1986). *The rise of managerial computing: The best of the Center for Information Systems Research. Sloan School of Management, MIT*. Homewood, IL: Dow Jones-Irwin.

Rockart, J., & De Long, D. (1988). *Executive support systems: The emergence of top management computer use*. Homewood, IL: Dow Jones-Irwin.

Rosson, M. B., & Alpert, S. (1990). The cognitive consequences of object-oriented design. *Human-Computer Interaction, 5,* 345–379.

Rosson, M. B., Maass, S., & Kellogg, W. (1988). The designer as user: Building requirements for design tools from design practice. *Communications of the ACM, 31,* 1288–1298.

Rubenstein, R., & Hersh, H. (1984). *The human factor*. Bedford, MA: Digital Press.

Simon, H. (1981). *The sciences of the artificial* (2nd ed.). Cambridge, MA: MIT Press.

Suchman, L. (1987). *Plans and situated actions: The problem of human-machine communication*. New York: Cambridge University Press.

Tetzlaff, L., & Schwartz, D. (1991). The use of guidelines in interface design. In S. Robertson, G. Olson & J. Olson (Eds.), *Proceedings of CHI'91: Conference on Human Factors in Computing Systems*. (pp. 329–334). New Orleans: Association for Computing Machinery.

Tetzlaff, L., & Mack, R. (1991). Methodological perspectives in Human-Computer Interaction. In J. Carroll (Ed.), *Designing interaction: Psychology at the human-computer interface* (pp. 286–314). Cambridge, MA: Cambridge University Press.

Whiteside, J., Bennett, J., & Holtzblatt, K. (1987). Usability engineering: Our experience and evolution. In M. Helander (Ed.), *Handbook of human-computer interaction* (pp. 791–818). North-Holland: Elsevier Science.

Whiteside, J., & Wixon, D. (1986). Discussion: Improving human-computer interaction—A quest for cognitive science. In J. Carroll (Ed.), *Interfacing thought: Cognitive aspects of human-computer interaction* (pp. 260–293). Cambridge, MA: MIT Press.

Winograd, T., & Flores, F. (1986). *Understanding computers and cognition: A new foundation for design*. Norwood, NJ: Ablex.

Wixon, D., Holtzblatt, K., and Knox, S. (1990). Contextual design: An emergent view of system design. In J. Chew & J. Whiteside (Eds.), *Proceedings of CHI, 1990 (Seattle, Washington, April 1–5, 1990)*. (pp. 329–336). New York: Association for Computing Machinery.

8 Question Asking in Human-Computer Interfaces

Kathy L. Lang
Bellcore, Morristown, NJ

Susan T. Dumais
Belcore, Morristown, NJ

Arthur C. Graesser
Memphis State University

David Kilman
Memphis State University

Question asking in computer use has been a relatively ignored topic of study. The research that has been conducted has been primarily limited to the domain of information retrieval from databases. Limited research on question answering has also been performed in the area of expert systems (Lang, Graesser, & Hemphill, 1990). However, there are many aspects of computer usage in which question asking could play a major role, such as "help" systems, training, and accessing information from large information systems. If users are going to obtain information that is important to them, they must be able to ask the computer questions and receive informative answers to these questions.

The goal of this chapter is to propose an interface that will help users of computer systems to construct questions and receive informative answers. The interface may be applicable to a number of computer domains including information retrieval in large information systems and help systems in software packages such as word processing. The interface is based on a theoretical understanding of the process of question asking and question answering. This theoretical foundation helps identify questions that are relevant to users and guides in the construction of answers that may be more satisfying to users.

In this chapter, we first review some of the question-asking and question-answering facilities in current computer systems. We then review psychological research that has investigated question answering and question asking in the computer domain. We subsequently report on a study that illustrates how and why question asking is studied empirically in the context of human-computer interaction. Finally, we introduce a computer interface that enables users to ask questions quickly and easily. The name of the interface is P&Q, which stands for "point and query."

The concept of querying a computer has often been limited to retrieving information from databases. These databases range from highly structured relational databases to less structured sets of objects. A highly structured relational database may contain inventory information for a company. Queries appropriate to this type of database may ask about the quantity of a particular type of exemplar in the database (e.g., "How many Macintosh computers are stored in managers' offices?"). On the other hand, a less structured database may contain a set of document names, abstracts, or even lengthy documents. For this unstructured database, a user may want to identify all of those documents that are relevant to a particular topic of interest (e.g., lung cancer).

Methods for querying each of these types of databases have been developed. Indeed, the types of questions that can be asked are determined by the structure of the database to a greater extent than the topic or content of the database. Unfortunately, there has been little research on what types of questions are most appropriate for particular knowledge domains. Individuals are undoubtedly inhibited from asking the right kinds of questions because of the constraints in the structure and content of the database.

TECHNIQUES FOR QUERYING SYSTEMS

In the first section of this chapter, we review the different types of query methods that have been developed. At one extreme, there are structured query methods that are strict command sequences in which it is necessary for users to memorize complicated commands and the parameters of each command. At the other end of the continuum, there are natural language methods that accept simple English statements.

Structured Queries

Structured queries are used to elicit information from relational databases. Traditional relational databases consist of objects and specified relations between these objects. For example, users of relational databases may perceive the data as being in tabular form. Users are able to manipulate the data and query the database by using operators that create new tables from the old ones (Date, 1986). One command may be used to pull out a subset of rows from a particular table, whereas another operator may pull out a subset of the columns.

Other types of relational databases have roots in artificial intelligence, such as semantic networks (Collins & Loftus, 1975), scripts (Schank & Abelson, 1977), frames (Minsky, 1975), and conceptual graphs (Sowa, 1984). These databases are structured in a fashion that supports rapid, intelligent, and knowledge-intensive retrieval. Rather than being constructed from a set of rows and columns, these databases are structured according to the types of information they contain. For example, information may include taxonomic, causal, descriptive, or goal-oriented knowledge. Each of these types of knowledge is structured in a different way and does not assume the traditional tabular form.

There have been at least five major methods for querying traditional relational databases. These include (a) rigid query syntax, (b) retrieval by reformulation, (c) menu-driven natural language, (d) natural language, and (e) query using truth-table exemplars.

Rigid Query Languages

Structured Query Language (SQL) and Query By Example (QBE) are two examples of rigid query languages (Date, 1986). The use of rigid query languages requires detailed knowledge of the particular statements used to interrogate the system (Date, 1986). For example, consider an individual who is using SQL and has a database of cooking recipes. If the user wanted to see all of the recipes the user would request this by typing in the following command:

SELECT * FROM RECIPE

Now suppose the user wanted to identify all of the recipes that involve desserts. In this case, the user might type the following:

SELECT * FROM RECIPE WHERE ITEMTYPE = 'DESSERT'

The term *where* in the preceding command restricts the output to those records that satisfied the specified condition (Date, 1983), namely the *dessert* recipe item. Although SQL attempts to make the queries somewhat "English-like," as is clearly shown in the preceding examples, the commands are cryptic, difficult to learn, and awkward for nonprogrammers to use.

With QBE, the user completes a template of the actual database, specifying the fields the user would like to see and the requirements that must be met in the fields (Zloof, 1975). In the case of the recipe database example, a user may complete the following table:

Recipe	Itemtype	Cost
.p Chocolate Cake	dessert	

The idea behind the QBE approach is for the user to supply an example of the type of information for which the user is searching. In response to this example, the computer searches for other items that match the characteristics of the example. In the preceding example, the underlining of *chocolate cake* indicates that the term chocolate cake is an example of the type of item the user is searching for. The ·p represents the command to print.

The advantages and disadvantages of command-based interfaces, have been extensively studied. In general, users of query languages have difficulty with the syntax of the languages. Reisner (1977) found that users had trouble with basic commands, such as selection, assignment, and logical operations (and/or), which resulted in a 10% to 35% error rate for both programmers and non-programmers. More complicated functions, such as grouping, correlation, and computed variables resulted in error rates up to 90%. Reisner (1981) argued that the primary source of errors is the process of translating an English question to a structured query command.

Thomas and Gould (1975) studied the usability of QBE. They found the QBE approach to be a good one with 67% of the queries being correctly specified. Although QBE was found to be a promising approach, a few types of errors were committed frequently. Twenty-five percent of the errors occurred when subjects confused the operators of SUM, COUNT, and COMPACT-COUNT. For another 25% of the total errors, users incorrectly specified universal quantification. That is, subjects had trouble identifying the total set of objects they wanted as output.

Retrieval by Reformulation

One alternative to the query techniques just described has been introduced by Williams (1984). Williams' approach is based on a concept called *retrieval by reformulation*. In retrieval by reformulation the user is constantly reformulating an original question, based on the examples retrieved by previous questions. Retrieval by reformulation is implemented in Williams' RABBIT interface. In the RABBIT interface, the user first identifies a concept or basic category. Based on this concept, the computer constructs an initial query and displays an instance that satisfies the query. Using the returned example, the user subsequently modifies or refines the query. To refine the query the user points to various properties of the instance and "critiques" them.

The query can be refined using six options: (a) require, (b) prohibit, (c) alternatives, (d) describe, (e) specialize, and (f) predicate. When a user selects the "require" option the user wants to add an attribute to the existing query. The "prohibit" option negates an attribute in the query. That is, the user does not want any records that contain the "prohibited" attribute. The "alternatives" option enables the user to select alternative values for the attributes. The "describe" option "allows the recursive specification of an embedded query" (Williams, 1984, p. 336). That is, a user can restrict the selection of information to output from the information that was obtained in the previous query. The "specialize" options enable the user to further refine and limit the query by selecting subconcepts. Finally, the "predicate" option enables the user to apply a predicate to the value of an attribute (e.g., $>$, $<$). The user may select only those refine options that are legal at a particular time. Consider the example of the recipe database and suppose the user was shown output from a query that obtained a listing of all the recipe items. The user may realize that the user really wanted output from the desserts rather than all of the recipes. In order to identify all of the desserts that existed in the database, the user could select the "specialize" option for the Itemtype attribute. The user would then be given a list of Itemtypes (e.g., desserts, main course) to select from. The user would then select desserts and the query is again reformulated. The process of redefining an original query by using the six options is a time-consuming process. It may take a number of iterations before identifying the desired objects.

Menu-Driven

Menu-driven interfaces have been developed in order to eliminate the need for users to memorize complicated commands while maintaining more structure than natural language. In a menu-driven interface, users are presented with a set of options from which they may select. The selection of a particular option typically results in the presentation of another set of options from which the user can choose (Dumais, 1988; Paap & Roske-Hofstrand, 1988). An important feature of menu-driven systems is that they do not require users to generate queries, instead it is only necessary for users to recognize the desired components in the query. In most systems, users are expected to select a large number of different options before completing their goals.

Researchers at Texas Instruments have developed a *menu-driven natural language* interface in order to help users to construct queries (Tennant, 1987). This system was developed in order to minimize the major bottlenecks found in natural language systems. Menu-driven natural language systems enable the user to "construct" a query by selecting options from a series of menus associated with each major word in the query. In this way, the user can select "English-like" words during the process of constructing a query. In addition, only those words that contribute to a legal query can be selected. This results in 100% legal queries. Using our example of the recipe database, the user would first select the word *list* from a command menu. Then the user would select a term that satisfies a condition that the query must satisfy (e.g., all), followed by a selection of the item that the user wishes to list (e.g., recipes). The resulting query may look like the following: "List all recipes." If the user wanted to restrict the query to desserts, the user would select *dessert* instead of *all* when specifying the condition that must be met. The resulting query would be: "List dessert recipes."

Unfortunately, menu-driven natural language interfaces tend to be extremely cumbersome and time-consuming (Scha, 1988). Users also may not know what each of the concepts in the menus mean or how to combine them in order to construct a query that will retrieve the desired information. Finally, menu-driven interfaces often restrict the types of queries that users can ask. Users often settle for a legal query rather than constructing the query they really want to generate, that is the users want something that is not specified on the menu (Dumais, 1988;

Paap & Roske-Hofstrand, 1988). Consequently, they often become frustrated with the restrictiveness of the syntax and the types of queries that can be handled.

Natural Language

Natural language interfaces attempt to take advantage of the communication skills that individuals use in their everyday life (Ogden, 1988). This is in contrast to command-based systems, which demand communication methods that are unnatural to users and difficult to learn. Many researchers investigating the area of natural language are attempting to develop natural language interfaces that would enable the user simply to type in a query in "plain English" (Fitter, 1979). For example, a user who wants to identify recipe items in the recipe database discussed earlier might type in the following command: "What recipes do I have?" If the user wanted to identify all of the available dessert recipes, the user would type: "What dessert recipes do I have?" When using natural language, users are not restricted to the cryptic and awkward query language commands. Instead, it is possible to type the question in the same form that users think about the question.

Natural language would appear to be the most natural and desirable interface. It could be argued, however, that natural language is not the best method for interacting with computers. Natural language contains a great deal of ambiguity, so it is not appropriate in situations where precision is required (Fitter, 1979; Hill, 1972). At the present time this debate can be left unresolved because technology is not at the point where true natural language is available. Winograd and Flores (1986) argued that computers will never reach the point where they will truly be able to understand natural language.

There have been a limited number of laboratory and field studies that have investigated natural language queries in relational databases (see Ogden, 1988, for a review). Research has found that natural language query systems tend to perform well when users are knowledgeable about the domain represented in the database (Hershman, Kelly, & Miller, 1979) or when users are provided information and feedback about the domain (Ogden, 1988). In addition, providing users with training in the natural language helps improve performance. Finally, users tend to perform tasks better when the tasks are generated by experimenters rather than the users. On the other hand, poor performance is obtained when users are not trained and when users have a limited understanding of the database domain (Ogden, 1988).

Jarke et al. (1985) compared subjects using a natural language system (USL) with a formal query system (SQL). Subjects were provided with training on both systems. Unfortunately, task assignment to the different languages was uncontrolled and resulted in some tasks being performed with one language and other tasks performed with the other (Ogden, 1988). However, there were a few tasks that were performed with both systems. Results of this study indicated that users of SQL were able to solve more tasks than users of the natural language system (Ogden, 1988). Analyses indicated that only 23.6% of the fully solvable problems were solved using the natural language system whereas 52.4% were solved using SQL.

There are many reasons why a successful natural language system is difficult to achieve. One reason is that it is necessary for successful natural language systems to be "habitable" (Ogden, 1988). Habitable systems enable users to convey all that is required to perform a task, using those words and sentences that are legal in the system. There are at least four major components that combine in order to insure that a system is habitable. These range from rules concerning query construction to the conceptual meaning of queries. The degree to which a natural language system is habitable helps determine the success of a system.

Another problem that hinders the success of natural language systems concerns the degree of inferencing that must be performed by the system (Scha, 1988). When individuals communicate with each other, they often fail to specify important aspects of the conversation. This does not present much of a problem to humans when they interact because participants in the conversation have an understanding of the speaker's plausible goals and ways to achieve them (Allen, 1983; Sidner, 1985). The listener makes a number of inferences about what the speaker is trying to convey. Unfortunately, this inferencing presents quite a problem in the computer domain. Researchers in artificial intelligence are interested in identifying ways in which computers can use world knowledge about the goals and plans of users in order to infer the meaning of user queries (Lehnert, 1978). A system that truly had a natural language interface would need to consider the user's goals and plans in order to generate an appropriate response. Some of the existing natural language systems have attempted to identify user goals (Allen, 1983; Schank & Abelson, 1977; Wilensky, 1983) but the complexity of these mechanisms make it difficult, if not impossible, to develop commercial systems that can handle any question a user might enter.

In this section, we have discussed natural language query systems in the domain of relational databases. However it is important to point out that natural language is applicable to a number of different types of systems including more unstructured databases.

Query Using Truth-Table Exemplars

The Truth-table Exemplar-Based Interface (TEBI) enables users to construct queries without any logical operators, parentheses, or fixed syntax (Greene, Devlin, Cannata, & Gomez, 1990). In the TEBI interface the user constructs an initial query that only contains attributes and sample values. This initial query contains no formal logic. After the user specifies the initial query, the user further clarifies the desired output by completing a table containing system-generated exemplars. The system uses these exemplars to infer the logical operators that the user desires.

Consider a user who wanted to find all of the items in a recipe database that were low to moderate cost desserts. The user would first specify an initial query by indicating the attributes (e.g., Itemtype) and values (e.g., dessert) that should be returned. The user's initial query could be specified with the following command: "Recipe, Itemtype = Dessert, Cost = moderate." Once this query has been specified, the TEBI system generates a type of "truth table," which contains sample items. This table is used by the subject to select examples of the types of items that should be included in the final output. Each unique attribute from the query represents a column. However, whereas in standard truth tables TRUE and FALSE are entered as values, in the TEBI system true values are represented by the attribute's value from the query and false values are represented by system-generated values (Greene et al., 1990). The user then chooses those examples that represent desired instances. Based on the pattern of examples chosen by the user, the computer infers the meaning of the query without the user specifying the formal logic. Table 8.1 shows a simplified table from which the user may select desired exemplars. The user who wanted to see only low-to-moderate cost desserts would choose the examples "chocolate cake" and "chocolate mousse." The TEBI system would then use these examples to generate an appropriate logical command to obtain the desired items.

The TEBI interface appears to be similar to the QBE interface, however they are different in at least one important way. In the QBE interface, users must specify the logic of the query by generating the values of the attributes in the example table. In the TEBI approach, the examples are generated by the system and users are required only to recognize desired output.

Empirical studies have shown that queries constructed in the TEBI interface are more effective than in SQL. Greene et al. (1990) obtained an average of 94.2% queries correct in the TEBI interface whereas the mean percent of queries correct for SQL was 57.5%. In addition, mean time to construct queries in the TEBI interface was 23.7 seconds whereas the mean time to construct queries in the SQL interface was 82.5 seconds. In addition to these findings, Greene et al.

TABLE 8.1

Recipe	Itemtype	Cost
Chocolate cale	dessert	low
Chocolate mousse	dessert	moderate
Cherries jubilee	dessert	high
Spaghetti	main course	low
Chicken	main course	moderate
Steak	main course	high

(1990) found that TEBI was more resistant to influences of age and cognitive skills than SQL.

More Flexible Query Techniques

The query methods just described are appropriate for structured databases that specify the relationships between objects (e.g., a menu hierarchy) or that contain explicitly specified attributes (e.g., a relational database). Many types of databases, however, are not as highly structured. These types of databases require more flexible techniques for specifying user queries.

Keyword Retrieval

In this approach, each information object has a set of keywords associated with it (Dumais, 1988). Keywords can be assigned by authors or indexers. Alternatively, when textual objects are available, all words within an object can be used as keywords. No *explicit* structuring is required by the author or database creator. In general, keyword-based retrieval works by matching keywords in user queries against the keywords describing each object. No attempt is made to parse the query or objects; both are treated as unordered lists of words. Most library or bibliographic retrieval systems work in this way.

Keyword retrieval systems have been quite popular. However, there are a number of problems associated with their use. Users often retrieve information that they do not want. On the other hand, these systems often fail to provide information that would be relevant to the user (Dumais, 1988). A major reason for these retrieval problems is that a particular word often means different things in different contexts (e.g., *deck* can mean a type of patio in the context of landscape architecture but a punch to the body in the context of fighting). This causes irrelevant information to be retrieved. On the other hand, there may be a number of ways to say approximately the same thing (e.g., deck, patio, porch . . .). This would cause some important information to be overlooked during the search.

Ideally, a retrieval system would return 100% of the relevant information and none of the irrelevant information. These parameters of information retrieval are measured by examining the *recall* and *precision* of systems. Recall refers to the proportion of relevant information retrieved by the system whereas precision measures the probability that a retrieved item is relevant. An ideal system would have both high recall and precision. However, in practice there is a tradeoff between these two parameters, such that higher recall is associated with lower precision. In general, systems often perform with 50% recall and 50% precision. Research has found that users are typically supplied with approximately 50% of the relevant material in the database and only 50% of the supplied material is relevant (Dumais, 1988).

Latent Semantic Indexing

Several methods have been developed in attempts to minimize the problem of variability in human word usage and to improve retrieval performance. These methods have included: (a) restricting the allowable indexing and retrieval vocabulary, and training intermediaries to generate terms for these restricted vocabularies, (b) hand-crafting domain-specific thesauri to provide synonyms for user's search terms, (c) constructing explicit models of domain-relevant knowledge, and (d) automatically clustering terms and documents. The rationale for restricted or controlled vocabularies is that they are by design relatively unambiguous. However, they have high costs in terms of human effort, and agreement about the assignment of index terms is poor (Sievert & Andrews, 1991). In addition there are marginal (if any) retrieval benefits compared with automatic indexing based on the full content of texts (see, e.g., Salton, 1986). The use of a thesaurus is intended to improve retrieval by expanding terms that are too specific. Unfortunately, this also has the unwanted effect of retrieving irrelevant information. Overall, one can expect small retrieval improvements for carefully constructed thesauri in limited domains. More standard AI techniques for knowledge representation are also beginning to be used for information retrieval (see Croft, 1987, for a review). Such methods are currently applicable to small, stable domains and have not been systematically compared with more standard methods.

Automatic methods for analyzing the relationships among words and documents are promising and much more widely applicable. For example, Deerwester, Dumais, Landauer, Furnas, and Harshman (1990) have described an automatic method called Latent Semantic Indexing (LSI) for organizing textual materials into a kind of semantic structure that is useful for many retrieval tasks. The LSI method begins by viewing the words or terms contained in a document as incomplete and unreliable indicators of the content of the document. Automatic statistical methods are used to model the implicit higher-order structure in the association of terms with documents. In this model, the similarity of terms and documents is determined by the overall pattern of word usage in the entire collection, so documents can be similar to each other regardless of the precise words they contain. A description of terms, objects, and user queries based on the underlying latent semantic structure, rather than surface-level word choice, is used for representing and retrieving information. What this means from the user's perspective is that documents can be similar to a query even if they share no terms. LSI has been shown to improve retrieval performance by 20%–30% compared with word-matching.

In summary, we have reviewed query techniques found in two primary types of databases. More structured command language techniques are typically found in structured relational databases. On the other hand, more flexible query styles are implemented in less structured databases. It is important to recognize that the type of query technique selected is dependent on the type of database structure. In this chapter, we propose a new interface and query technique that places the highest priority on the types of questions that users want to ask.

P&Q Interface

We propose a method by which the computer *quickly* helps the user construct an appropriate question. Several types of queries (e.g., "Why?"; "How?"; "What does X mean?") are supported by our technique. In the proposed system, queries are formed by selecting a *concept* and then selecting a particular *question type* from a menu. In the example of the database containing recipes, the user may "point" to the concept "recipe items" and then query the database by pointing to a question type "What X are stored?" If the user wanted only the dessert recipe items, the user would point to the term "dessert" and then point to the query type "What X are stored?" We call this interface a *Point and Query* (P&Q) interface. In the P&Q interface, a user can point to a particular concept on the display with the use of a mouse or touch screen and then point to a question category to be asked about the concept.

We believe that P&Q has two important advantages over structured query methods. First, users do not need to learn specific commands. Second, users are cued with alternative questions. This is important because users do not always know the particular question or set of alternative questions they could ask. By utilizing these two advantages, the P&Q interface encourages active dialogue and inquisitive thought because the act of asking questions is extremely simple. In addition to these features, the P&Q interfaces provides answers to questions that are relevant and informative. The answers to particular questions are based on the type of information that is queried and the type of question that is asked. As a result, the P&Q interface provides answers that are satisfying to users.

Up to this point we have been discussing query options typically found in databases. However, the ability to ask questions is also important in other types of computer systems and for tasks other than direct information retrieval. For example, users often need help when they are learning a computer or using a familiar system. At these troublesome points, users need to query the system in order to access information about how to proceed. At other times, a user may not be stuck, but may be using a less than optimal method for achieving a goal. At these times, it would be appropriate for the computer to prompt the user with a more optimal method and to allow the user to ask questions about the optimal method. In order for the computer to prompt the user with suggestions, it will be necessary for the computer to have knowledge of the user's goals and plans (Robertson & Zachary, 1990). A question-answering dialogue between the user and computer will enable the computer to identify the goals and plans of the user. The P&Q interface incorporates a *mixed initiative dialogue* between the computer and user. In a mixed initiative dialogue, both the computer and user may query the other for information.

Three important sources of information are used in the development of a query-based interface. First, it is important to have an understanding of the existing research on question asking in the context of computers. Second, it is important to examine ways in which question asking could be studied empirically. Finally, it is important to have an underlying theory of questioning that will provide a framework in which to understand the empirical work and provide guidance in design. In this article we address these issues before presenting the details of the P&Q interface.

PAST RESEARCH ON QUESTION-ASKING AND COMPUTER SYSTEMS

A few studies have analyzed the questions that users ask when they interact with computer systems. One issue addressed in the literature is the extent to which question asking affects task performance. That is, does the opportunity to ask questions increase an individual's success on task completion? In a study conducted by Allwood and Eliasson (1988), two groups of subjects were required to learn a text-editing program. Half of the subjects had the opportunity to ask the experimenter questions after reading sections of the manual whereas the other half read the manual without the opportunity to ask the experimenter questions. The results showed no significant difference on task performance between those subjects who were allowed to ask questions and those subjects who did not have the opportunity to ask questions. However, further analyses revealed that particular types of questions were correlated with good task performance. Specifically, individuals who tended to ask more questions about hardware and fewer questions about software performed poorly on both the computer interaction task and on a questionnaire. These results show that it is important to help users ask the right kind of questions. The process of asking questions alone is not sufficient to improve performance; the right questions must be asked.

Miyake and Norman (1979) reported that the tendency for subjects to ask questions depended on a combination of the subjects' level of expertise and the difficulty of the material that the subject was trying to learn. Novices asked more questions when they were trying to understand easy material whereas trained subjects asked more questions while trying to learn hard material. When learning difficult material, novices do not ask many questions. Once again, it is not enough simply to allow users to ask questions. They may not have enough background knowledge to generate questions.

Other studies of question asking have examined in more detail the types of questions users ask when learning a new system. Aaronson and Carroll (1987) examined interactions of users and advisors, and they categorized the types of questions that were asked. Aaronson and Carroll reported that 76% of the questions were *verification* questions in which users asserted an hypothesis about the correct answer and wanted confirmation that this hypothesis was correct. An example verification question is "In order to delete this word, I just press the delete key?" In addition, a majority of questions in the Aaronson and Carroll study involved the negotiation of a solution. That is, subjects did not simply ask one question and accept the first answer, but rather discussed the problem and possible solutions.

Robertson and Swartz (1987) examined question-asking behavior in the context of subjects learning a spreadsheet. They identified four major types of questions: *plan, system operation, task,* and *act* questions. Plan questions were asked when the subject had identified a goal but did not know the correct procedure to perform in order to accomplish the goal. An example of a plan question is "How do I send a note?" When asking this question, users know the goal they want to accomplish (i.e., send a note) but do not know the procedure that will accomplish the goal. Plan questions were the most frequent type of question asked in the Robertson and Swartz study. Plan questions accounted for 30% of the total questions asked on the first trial. The frequency of this type of question increased to 45% by the last trial. System operation questions were the second most frequent type of question asked. System operation questions queried information about the states of the system and how the system worked. An example of a system operation question is "Will the system notify me that the note was sent?" Task questions asked about the particular task the subject was working on. An example task question is "Do you want me to send this note to my mother?" Subjects asked act questions when they were unsure of the actions that brought them to a particular state. For example, a subject might ask "What did I do to get this prompt?" An interesting result of the Robertson and Swartz study was that the proportion of plan questions increased as a function of the expertise of the user.

There have been only a handful of studies that have investigated question asking during use of computer systems. Yet question asking is an extremely important component in the human-computer interaction process both in learning and information retrieval. For example, the primary reason for interacting with a large database is to obtain particular information sought for some purpose. A major way in which individuals acquire information is by asking questions. Therefore, it is important that we develop ways that will facilitate a question-asking process in the computer domain.

COLLECTING INFORMATIVE QUESTION TYPES

In the P&Q interface, subjects query the system by selecting a question from a set of possible questions. In order to display a set of potential questions to the user, the designer must identify the set of important questions associated with each element to which the user points. There are two primary methods through which the designer can identify a set of questions. The first method is an empirical approach, whereby a set of questions is generated by subjects. This approach requires experimenters to test subjects on potential systems and encourage the subjects to ask questions as they use the system. In this way, designers identify the important questions that come to users' minds as they interact with the system.

The second method for identifying the set of questions associated with a display element has a theoretical foundation. Namely, it would be desirable to have a theory that makes predictions about what questions are most appropriate for particular classes of display elements. A theory of question answering could help identify the boundaries of possible question types and help the designer focus on the few important questions. A theory of question answering also provides information concerning the types of answers that are useful to users. In addition to asking the right question, it is important that the computer respond with an appropriate answer. A theory of question answering is needed to identify those answers most appropriate to particular questions. The success of a question-answering system relies on its ability to provide satisfying and informative answers.

In addition to these two approaches, it is important to conduct an in-depth task analysis of the target domain. Task analysis helps designers understand the tasks that users need to perform and the ways in which the system will help users perform these tasks (Rubin, 1988). By examining various aspects of the task, the designer will identify important question types.

To summarize, it is important to adopt all three approaches when constructing a P&Q system. A theoretical approach will help to identify some boundaries for the types and number of questions asked, whereas an empirical approach will help identify those questions that may be idiosyncratic to a particular system and overlooked by theory. A task analysis will help identify critical components of the task and target crucial question-asking situations. In this chapter, we review the empirical and theoretical approaches in detail while acknowledging the importance of a thorough task analysis. First, we review an empirical approach, in which we examine some questions obtained from subjects who were learning a computer network. In the second part of this section, we describe a model of question answering (called QUEST) and discuss the types of questions identified by this model.

Questions That Users Generate When Learning a System

We examined a total of 574 questions that were collected when individuals were learning various computer systems. The goal of this investigation was to identify the types of questions learners ask when learning a new system. This would of course be useful for determining which question types to include in the "question menu" of a help system. One corpus involved students learning how to use a network. These questions were obtained through a face-to-face interaction between a teacher and student. A second corpus of questions was obtained from a system in which individuals send their system questions to a consultant.

The first corpus of questions was collected by Alan Collins at Bolt, Beranek, and Newman. The students were learning how to use the ARPANET system. We analyzed 74 student questions asked in a face-to-face interaction. The second corpus of questions was collected by Alex Hurwitz at IBM. These questions were taken from a collection of questions and comments made by individuals while they used a computer system. The computer users typed their questions and comments into the computer and then sent them to a consultant. Because of this methodology, answers were not given immediately. However, a question would typically be answered in a day or two. There were 500 questions in this corpus.

We categorized each question according to the categorization scheme of Lehnert (1978). Lehnert's classification scheme is based on a theory of question answering that has been implemented in a computer program called QUALM. Table 8.2 displays 12 semantic question categories that are identified in Lehnert's theory. The categories are distinguished by the type of information requested in the question. Table 8.2 also displays an abstract specification and a specific instance of each question category. A similar taxonomy has been used by Graesser, Lang, and Horgan (1988) and by contributors to this volume (Graesser, Person, & Huber, chap. 9 in this volume).

Verification Questions

Verification questions are asked when the questioner wants the answerer to verify that a statement is true or false. Appropriate answers to verification questions include "yes," "no," "maybe," and "I don't know." In the current context, many of the verification questions required the answerer to expand on the literal answer to the question. For example, one subject asked "Can I see the scripted file on the screen?" In this question, the user is not only asking for a "yes" or "no" response. The user is also asking the consultant to provide a procedure that achieves the goal.

Disjunctive Questions

This type of question is asked when the questioner wants to know which member of a set of alternatives is appropriate. An example disjunctive question in the ARPANET context was "Are they scattered all over the U.S. or do they extend to other countries?" In this question, the questioner supplies the answerer with two alternatives and the answerer is expected to supply the correct alternative.

TABLE 8.2
Semantic Categories in Question Taxonomy

Category	General and Specific Examples
Verification	Is X true or false? "Am I notified when I am sent a note?"
Disjunctive	Is X or Y the case? "Are they scattered all over the U.S. or do they extend to other countries?"
Concept completion	Who? What? When? Where? "On what disk do I link the FREEMAP model?"
Feature specification	What is the value on a variable? "What color is the screen?"
Quantification	How much? How many? "How many networks can I connect to?"
Causal antecedent	What caused some event to occur? "Why did the computer crash?"
Causal consequence	What happened as a consequence of X occurring? "What happens after I sent a note?"
Goal orientation	Why did an agent perform some action? "Why would I want to delete a file?"
Enablement	What is needed for an agent to perform some action "What will enable me to see my settings?"
Instrumental/procedural	How did the agent perform an action? "How can I create a file?"
Expectational	Why isn't X occurring? "Why didn't the colors on my terminal change?"
Judgmental	What should an agent do? "What color should I make my screen?"

Concept Completion Questions

This type of question requires the answerer to fill in an argument slot of a proposition. These argument slots may require the specification of people (who), objects (what), times (when) and locations (where) in propositions that describe states, events, and actions. An example of a concept completion question is "Where are the pfkey definitions kept?"

Feature Specification

Feature specification questions are asked when the questioner wants to know the value of an attribute in an object-attribute-value triplet. An example question in this category is "Are there special problems about the use of satellites?" In this example, the object is *satellites,* the attribute is *special problems* and the value of *special problems* is expected to be supplied by the answerer.

Quantification

Quantification questions are asked when the questioner wants to know the magnitude (how much) or the frequency (how many) of an attribute, measured on a quantitative scale. An example quantification question is "How many bytes are there in a megabyte?"

Causal Antecedent Questions

Causal antecedent questions are asked when the questioner wants to know what prior events and states causally led to some particular event. An example causal antecedent question is "Why did my program bomb out?" This question category applies to events that are not intended by an agent. When the event is not intentional, appropriate question stems are "why" and "how."

Causal Consequence Questions

Causal consequence questions are asked when the questioner wants to know the events and states that will unfold causally after a particular event. This question can take a variety of forms: "What are the consequences of pressing the transmit key?"; "What if I send you a note?"; and "What happens after I press the F1 key?" Causal consequence questions trace the causal chain extending into the future, in contrast to causal antecedent questions, which trace occurrences in the past.

Goal Orientation Questions

This type of question is asked when the questioner wants to know an animate agent's goals and motives for performing a particular action. In the computer domain, a questioner may want to know the reasons why a user would want to perform an action. For example a user may ask, "Why would I want to delete a file?"

Enablement Questions

Enablement questions are asked when the questioner wants to know what objects, abilities, states, and resources are required in order for an agent to perform some action. An example enablement question is "What will enable me to be able to see my print settings?"

Instrumental/Procedural Questions

These questions are asked when the questioner wants to know the plan, style, or instruments used when an agent performs some action. When a computer user asks this type of question the user wants to know the procedure to perform in order to attain a specified goal. This type of question is extremely common in the computer domain. An example instrumental/procedural question is "How do I get rid of a file?" The user is asking for the step-by-step procedure that gets rid of a file.

Expectational Questions

Expectational questions are asked when an event or action is expected to occur, but fails to occur. The questioner is confused as to why the expected sequence of actions did not take place and therefore asks a question. An example expectational question is "How come the colors on my terminal did not change?"

Judgmental Questions

These questions are asked when the questioner wants the answerer to provide the questioner with advice about what actions to take. An example judgmental question is "What color do you think I should make the screen?"

We categorized each of the questions according to the categorization scheme of Lehnert (1978). A *polythetic* categorization scheme was used, that is, each question may have been placed in more than one category (Sokal, 1974). Because some of the questions belonged to more than one category, the percentages of answers among the 12 categories would not necessarily add to 100%. This was a very common situation for questions that belonged to the verification category. Many of the verification questions were also instrumental/procedural, causal antecedent, causal consequence, or enablement questions. For example, the following question is both a verification and instrumental/procedural question: "Can I see the SCRIPTed file on the screen?"

Table 8.3 shows the frequency of questions and the proportion of category assignments for the questions generated in the on-line consultant group and the face-to-face ARPANET session. Because more than one question could be placed in more than one category, the proportions represent the proportion of category assignments for each question type. In the on-line consultant corpus, 32 of the verification questions were also placed in one other category and 5 of the concept completion questions were also placed in another category. In the AR-PANET corpus, 4 of the verification questions were also placed in another category. Instrumental/procedural questions were by far the most common questions, with 385 of the questions falling into this category. The second most common types of question were the verification and concept completion questions, with frequencies of 77 and 78, respectively. The judgmental category had no questions.

The vast majority of the questions fell into the instrumental/procedural category. It is interesting, however, that the instrumental/procedural category had the largest frequency in the on-line consultant group but this was not the case for the

TABLE 8.3
Frequency and Proportion Data for Questions Asked in Two Different Computer Tasks

Question Category	On-line Consultant Tasks		Face-to-Face Arpanet Tasks	
	Frequency	Proportion Category Assignments	Frequency	Proportion Category Assignments
Verification	53	.099	24	.308
Disjunctive	3	.006	2	.026
Concept completion	59	.110	19	.244
Feature specification	1	.002	4	.051
Quantification	3	.006	4	.051
Causal antecedent	8	.015	0	.000
Causal consequence	8	.015	1	.013
Goal orientation	11	.020	5	.064
Enablement	12	.022	2	.026
Instrumental/procedural	371	.691	14	.179
Expectational	8	.015	3	.038
Judgmental	0	.000	0	.000

ARPANET group. In the ARPANET group, the three most frequent categories were verification, concept completion, and instrumental/procedural, with instrumental/procedural having the least number of questions of the three categories. One reason for the difference in results between the on-line consultant group and the ARPANET group may be that the users who asked questions to the on-line consultant were relative experts to the computer domain. According to Singley and Anderson (1987–1988), when experts learn new software they are primarily interested in learning procedures for achieving particular goals. Robertson and Swartz (1987) have also found an increase in the number of questions about plans as expertise is increased. Therefore, our finding that so many of the on-line consultant questions were aimed at procedures is consistent with the existing literature. Users who were learning ARPANET were novices with regard to the operation of ARPANET. Therefore, they needed to ask a larger variety of question types, covering more than just the procedures for performing particular tasks. Unfortunately, the corpus of questions was so small that it is hard to make any general conclusions. It would be interesting to examine a larger corpus of novice questions.

The present study confirmed some differences between expert and novice questions. Experts tend to ask more procedure-oriented questions whereas novices ask a greater diversity of question types including concept completion and verification. Because there appear to be differences in the types of questions that novices and experts ask, it is important to study the area in more detail in order to design effective interfaces for both types of users. It may be that the questions and answers appropriate to novices are completely different than those appropriate to experts. An effective interface must be able to handle both expert and novice needs.

By categorizing the questions asked in a particular context, we can begin to understand the types of questions that should be included as options in P&Q's hypertext and help systems. In hypertext systems, users can pursue concepts of interest by pointing to particular objects and words on the display. Hypertext systems enable users to pursue items of interest while not being bombarded with irrelevant information. It is important that the development of a P&Q interface be an iterative process. Usability studies for particular systems must be performed by collecting question-asking data and redesigning displays. It is important to determine the particular questions that are important for individual systems. For example, the present analysis showed a large number of procedural questions. It is essential to understand what questions are asked in order to design systems that will effectively answer questions.

The QUEST Model of Question Answering

In the previous section, we described a large corpus of questions obtained from users learning new systems. That is, subjects are observed interacting with a particular system and are encouraged to ask questions. These questions may then be used to help design a P&Q system, which enables users to select those questions asked by a majority of subjects. In addition to empirically identifying question types, it is also important to identify questions that have been identified as important questions by a theory. We base our proposal for P&Q on the QUEST model of question answering and theories in cognitive science (Graesser, Byrne, & Behrens, chap. 12 in this volume; Graesser & Franklin, 1990). QUEST provides information about important questions for particular types of knowledge structures: taxonomic hierarchies, spatial structures, causal networks, and goal/plan hierarchies. The QUEST model of question answering also explains what information constitutes appropriate answers to these questions. A key to successful retrieval systems lies in the system's delivering relevant and informative answers. Systems that do not give appropriate answers to questions will not be trusted by their users (Lang et al., 1990).

According to the QUEST model (Graesser & Franklin, 1990), approximately 21 different types of questions (e.g., why, how, when, where, what are the consequences of) would be informative to human-computer interaction. That is, there are approximately 21 types of questions that users might generate when interacting with a computer. In addition, there are four major types of knowledge that can be queried. These four types of knowledge include: (a) goal/plan hierarchies, (b) causal networks, (c) taxonomic hierarchies, and (d) spatial region hierarchies. Different questions types are appropriate for different types of knowledge. The combination of question type and knowledge type results in a particular answer. The QUEST model specifies how a particular answer is determined, given particular question and knowledge types (Graesser, Byrne, & Behrens, chap. 12 in this volume; Graesser & Franklin, 1990; Graesser, Lang, & Roberts, in press).

The QUEST model is reviewed in Graesser, Byrne, & Behrens (chap. 12 in this volume). Of particular interest to the P&Q interface are the arc search procedures specified in the model. Arc search procedures specify the particular path of arcs that are traversed in a knowledge structure when a question is asked. The arc search procedures are based on the type of knowledge being queried (e.g., causal vs. goal-oriented) and the type of question asked (e.g., causal antecedent, goal orientation; see Table 8.2). For example, the arc search procedure for a "why" question that is asked about goal-oriented knowledge would pursue forward Reason arcs. On the other hand, answers to "why" questions asked about causal knowledge are obtained by pursuing backward causal arcs. Thus, the same question stem (e.g., why, how, when, etc.) can elicit different answers, depending on the knowledge domain.

Table 8.4 displays the various types of knowledge structures and those questions most suitable to each type of knowledge. Each of these questions produces a particular set of answers, depending on the type of knowledge structure queried

TABLE 8.4
Knowledge Structures and Associated Question Types

Goal Hierarchies

Why <goal G>?
How is <goal G> Achieved?
What are the consequences of <goal G> being achieved?

Causal networks

Why does X occur?
How does X occur?
What are the consequences of X occurring?
When did X occur?

Taxonomic structures

Is an X an F?
Does X have property F ?
What does X mean?
What are the properties of X?
What is an X?
What is an example of X?
How is X similar to Y?
How is X different than Y?

Spatial region hierarchies

Is X in Y?
What <regions> are in X?
Is X above/below/left/right/touching Y?
Where is X?
What is in X?

and the type of question asked. The QUEST model of question answering spec-ifies particular procedures for generating appropriate answers. The P&Q inter-face would incorporate the QUEST model in order to provide users of computers with a selection of good questions and a set of satisfying answers. We now summarize in some detail the four major types of knowledge structures and the types of questions appropriate for each type of knowledge.

Goal Hierarchies

Goal-oriented knowledge embodies goals, plans, and intentional actions that are performed by agents (Lang et al., 1990). The nodes in a goal hierarchy include a set of goal statements. Each goal represents a state or event desired by the agent. Figure 8.1 depicts a simplified goal hierarchy for an individual who would like to obtain a printed copy of a report. Most of the nodes in the goal hierarchy are connected by Reason (R) arcs. Each superordinate goal represents a reason for the subordinate goal (Graesser & Gordon, 1991). For example, one reason for activating the word processor is to type in a report.

The QUEST model accounts for a variety of questions that are asked about goal hierarchies. Question-answering procedures help determine the correct an-swer for different question types. For example, good answers to "why" ques-tions are generated by pursuing (a) superordinate goals on paths of forward

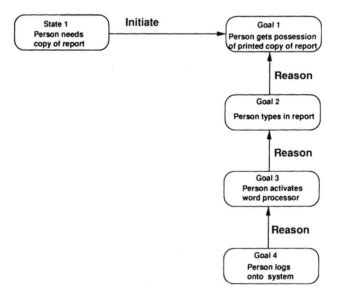

FIG. 8.1. Goal hierarchy for individual who would like to obtain a printed copy of a report.

Reason arcs and (b) sibling nodes that are connected to the queried goal by a forward *before* arc (Graesser & Franklin, 1990; Graesser & Gordon, 1991). Good answers to the question "Why does a person activate the word processor?" would include: "in order for the person to type in the report [Goal 2]" and "in order for the person to obtain a printed version of the report [Goal 1]." A bad answer to this "why" question would be Goal 4 ("in order for the person to log onto the system"). On the other hand, question answering procedures for "how" questions sample subordinate goals (paths of backward Reason arcs). Therefore, Goal 4 ("the person logs onto the system") would represent a good answer to the question "How does the person activate the word processor?" Goals 2 and 1 would represent bad answers to this "how" question. In addition to "why" and "how" questions, consequence (CONS) questions are appropriate for goal hierarchies. In contrast, feature specification and quantification questions are not the most informative questions to ask about goal hierarchies.

Causal Networks

Cause-oriented knowledge contains sequences of events and states that unfold over time in physical, biological, and technological systems (e.g., tornadoes, mitosis, and computers). For example, consider the following event chain on computers.

1. A computer program is entered into the computer.
2. The computer translates the program into bits.
3. The bits are processed.
4. The processed bits are translated into information.
5. The information is presented on the computer's terminal.

The preceding event chain could be represented as a series of event nodes connected by Cause (C) arcs (i.e., [1]—C→[2]—C→[3]—C→[4]—C→[5]).

The QUEST model specifies how answers to particular questions about these causal networks are produced. Answers to "why," "how," and "when" questions are generated by sampling causal antecedents (i.e., backward C-arcs). Answers to "what if" and "CONS" questions are produced by sampling causal consequence (i.e., forward C-arcs). For example, legal answers to the question "What are the consequences of the bits being processed?" include Node 4 ("The processed bits are translated into information") and Node 5 ("The information is presented on the computer's terminal"). When considering a causal network it would be inappropriate to ask definitional and spatial questions such as "What is a bit?" or "Where is the information?" These questions are more suitable for taxonomic and spatial region hierarchies, respectively.

Taxonomic Knowledge Structures

Taxonomic knowledge structures include a set of entities, concepts, and categories that are normally captured by nouns and are arranged in a hierarchy. Each of the concepts in a taxonomic structure is connected by *is-a* arcs (e.g., a Cray *is-a* computer). In addition, each concept in a taxonomic structure has certain distinguishing properties associated with it (Graesser & Franklin, 1990; Graesser & Gordon, 1991). For example, a PC has a property of "has one user," which distinguishes it from a mainframe that can have multiple users. Properties must be distinctive and hold true of the concept in question but not generally be true of sibling nodes.

There are several question categories that are appropriate for taxonomic structures. These are listed in Table 8.3. Two question categories that are not naturally suited to the taxonomic domain include "why" and "where" questions. For example, it would be inappropriate to ask the question "Why are there computers?" when referring to a taxonomic knowledge structure. This question, however, would be appropriate when referring to a goal hierarchy.

Spatial Region Hierarchies

Spatial region hierarchies represent the spatial layout and location of objects and objects within regions (Graesser & Franklin, 1990). Individuals may wish to ask questions concerning the spatial location of objects within a given location. Spatial regions are connected with *is-in* arcs (e.g., Paris *is-in* France). In addition, spatial region hierarchies contain directional arcs that represent the relative spatial relation of the objects. These arcs include directional labels such as *above* (with its inverse *below*) and *left-of* (with its inverse *right-of*). Questions that are appropriate for spatial region hierarchies are listed in Table 8.4. Questions that are inappropriate for spatial region hierarchies include "What is an *X*?" and "What are the consequences of *X*?" For example, a spatial region hierarchy would not be able to generate an answer to the question "What is a computer?" This question would be more suitable to a taxonomic knowledge structure.

As with the taxonomic knowledge structures, there are particular procedures that dictate how answers are produced. For example, an answer to the question "Where is *X*?" is generated by sampling nodes that are (a) superordinate in the region hierarchy, on paths of forward *is-in* arcs, and (b) directional arcs that radiate from *X*. Therefore, an appropriate answer to the question "Where is Newark?" would be "Newark is in New Jersey."

Incorporating Different Question Sources

This section focused on methods for collecting informative question types and described the empirical and theoretical methods that are used to design a P&Q interface. It should be emphasized that development of a P&Q interface is an iterative process. When creating the initial prototype, the interface can be based on: (a) the theoretical questions and corresponding answers and (b) questions generated through empirical studies and task analysis. As user testing is performed on the prototype, more question categories can be discovered and infrequent categories can be discarded.

P&Q INTERFACE

The idea behind P&Q is to help users ask questions and have the computer provide appropriate answers. In the P&Q interface, the user points to a concept or object on the primary display and then selects a particular question category. For example, the user may point to a concept "field definition" in a database management software package and then point to a question category "What does X mean?" In this way the user can obtain a description of the field definition concept. In the P&Q interface, there are a number of question categories and concepts from which the user can choose. The method by which the user asks questions is quick and easy. Therefore, the P&Q interface encourages active information seeking by the user. It should be noted that the P&Q interface is applicable to a diverse set of computer applications. However, it will be illustrated in this chapter in the context of a help system in database management software.

At this point, we have not actually implemented these ideas in a working system. We acknowledge the current limits of system development, but at the same time we are providing a goal for designers. As mentioned, the ideas presented in the P&Q interface are based on theories of question answering and data obtained in the field.

There are two primary ways in which P&Q may be helpful to task performance. First, both novice and expert users may wish to ask questions in order to understand how to use the system. The second way in which P&Q can be helpful is in error recovery and suggesting alternative methods for achieving particular goals. In error recovery, a user may ask the computer questions regarding how to proceed and compensate for the error. At other times, a user may be using a less than optimal method for achieving a goal and a question–answer dialogue may help the user to obtain more optimal methods for achieving the goal in question.

The question-asking facility in the P&Q interface is dynamic with respect to the type of questions that the user can ask. When the user selects a particular concept, a set of questions is displayed that is appropriate to the type of knowledge to which the concept belongs. In many cases, nouns refer to taxonomic knowledge structures; the P&Q interface would display questions appropriate for taxonomic knowledge structures when nouns are selected (i.e., "What does X mean?" "What are the properties of X?"). On the other hand, verbs frequently refer to procedural knowledge; potential questions would be generated from those questions associated with goal-oriented or causal knowledge structures (e.g., *why, how, what-if*).

Figure 8.2 displays a sample interface for a user interacting with a database management package. In Fig. 8.2a, the user is currently at a topic index in a help system. The concepts that the user is allowed to query are shown in uppercase, bold characters. In this example, a user selects the DEFINING A FIELD concept and then is shown the display shown in Fig. 8.2b. This figure displays questions the user may wish to ask about the DEFINING A FIELD command. Figure 8.2c shows the display that the user would see on choosing the "why" question category. Good answers to "why" questions contain the goals and motives associated with a particular concept. On the other hand, good answers to "how" questions contain procedural information that helps the user to perform the concept in question. Although the answer displayed in Fig. 8.2c is satisfactory as an answer to a "why" question, it is definitely unacceptable as an answer to a "how" question.

A hypertext and hypermedia foundation would be extremely valuable parts of the P&Q interface. Hypertext information systems consist of a series of "display" nodes that are connected by links representing user decisions on where to branch (Nielsen, 1990). The nodes represent chunks of information on a single display. Particular objects or words within a display are identified as *hot spots* or areas that, when activated, will display detailed information about the activated concept or objects. In the P&Q system, hypertext links could be used to display relevant answers to particular questions. Certain areas of the display would be identified as hot spots or question points. The user would point to a hot spot and then point to a question type. The combination of hot spot and query type would result in an appropriate answer. In addition, as answers to questions are presented, a user would have the opportunity to "point to" various words or concepts within the answer and ask questions about these concepts. For example, Fig. 8.2c displays the answer to a "why" question asked about the concept "define field." Contained in this answer are a number of concepts that the user may not understand or may want to learn more about (i.e., field, database, object, modify, and delete). Suppose the user wanted to know more about the concept "modify." In the P&Q interface, the user would simply point to the "modify" concept and ask a question about it. The user may want to know "why" someone would want to modify or "how" to perform modify. In this way, question asking can be seen as an iterative process. Subjects have the opportunity to continue to ask different types of questions about the concept about which they read.

In the P&Q approach, each display would have a set of N concepts, each of which could be queried by Q questions. Therefore, there are $N \times Q$ possible queries that can emanate from each display. Similar to other hypertext systems, a history window would display concepts and question-types about which the user had previously asked.

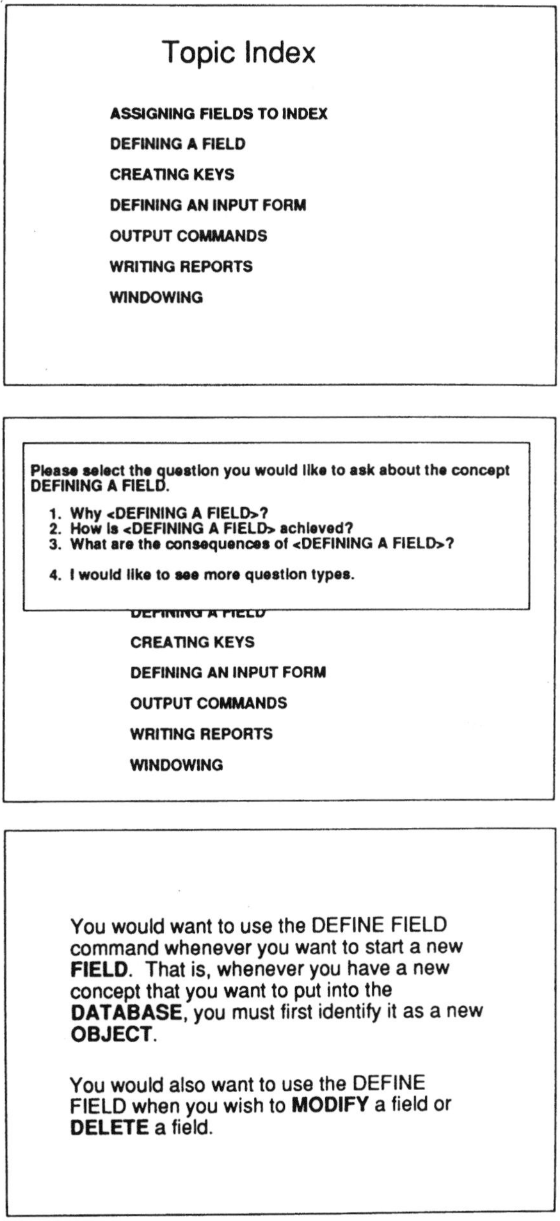

Topic Index

ASSIGNING FIELDS TO INDEX

DEFINING A FIELD

CREATING KEYS

DEFINING AN INPUT FORM

OUTPUT COMMANDS

WRITING REPORTS

WINDOWING

Please select the question you would like to ask about the concept DEFINING A FIELD.

1. Why <DEFINING A FIELD>?
2. How is <DEFINING A FIELD> achieved?
3. What are the consequences of <DEFINING A FIELD>?

4. I would like to see more question types.

DEFINING A FIELD

CREATING KEYS

DEFINING AN INPUT FORM

OUTPUT COMMANDS

WRITING REPORTS

WINDOWING

You would want to use the DEFINE FIELD command whenever you want to start a new **FIELD**. That is, whenever you have a new concept that you want to put into the **DATABASE**, you must first identify it as a new **OBJECT**.

You would also want to use the DEFINE FIELD when you wish to **MODIFY** a field or **DELETE** a field.

FIG. 8.2.   Sample interface for user interacting with a data base management package. (2a) Topic index in a data base management help system. (2b) Possible questions that a user may ask about defining a field. (2c) Answer to a "why" question for defining a field.

P&Q On-Line Help

In the context of help systems, the P&Q interface utilizes both an active and passive help facility (Carroll & Aaronson, 1988). In a passive help system, the user initiates queries to the computer. That is, the computer is passive until the user asks for help. On the other hand, sometimes it is necessary for the computer to initiate help and ask the user questions. This represents an active help system because the computer acts when it discovers the user needs help. Active help is difficult to achieve.

Robertson and Zachary (1990) discuss some of the important components of cooperative systems such as the P&Q interface. Robertson and Zachary (1990) discuss the importance of (a) plan and goal recognition, (b) an awareness of the immediate situation and how it may modify or influence the current plan, and (c) an ability to influence the actions of the other members in the system. The P&Q interface addresses these issues by incorporating a mixed initiative dialogue in a question-asking framework. A user can ask the computer questions. In addition, the computer can also ask the user questions. We cannot expect the computer system to automatically know the goals and motives of each user. Rather, the computer can only identify the user's goals and motives by asking the user questions. We first discuss situations in which user-initiated questions are important. We then discuss some occasions when it would be important to have computer-initiated questions.

User-Initiated Questions

There are at least three major occasions when it is necessary for users to ask the computer a question. The first occasion is when a user has a particular question in mind and would simply like to query the system. A second situation occurs when a user does not have a specific question in mind but has no idea of how to proceed. In this situation, it is necessary for the system to help the user to generate an appropriate question. A third situation in which questioning becomes important is when the user has committed an error or when the system is responding in a way that is unexpected by the user. These three situations are described below.

User-Initiated Specific Queries.   Sometimes users have specific information requests in mind. Previous examples of the P&Q interface have focused on this case. The user may initiate the question-asking process by pointing to a concept on the display and then pointing to a particular question type. The question types displayed in Fig. 8.2 were derived from theories of question asking and question answering in cognitive science. This list of question types is neither exhaustive or fixed. It is possible that different types of software may require different question types. We have used this list as a preliminary step in illustrating how a user might select a particular concept and question type. The type of answer given will depend on the type of question that was asked (e.g., "why" question) and the particular type of knowledge queried (e.g., goal hierarchy).

User Is Unsure of Specific Question.   Research has demonstrated that naive students often do not ask many questions (Miyake & Norman, 1979). This phenomenon is important when considering a help system in which the user may ask questions. Even if it were possible to build a system that understood natural language, the system may not be helpful to the novice who cannot even begin to generate a question. In a study examining student questions, Miyake and Norman (1979) found that people ask more questions about material that is consistent with their level of knowledge. As a result, a system based on natural language input may only be beneficial to those users who know the system and have a particular question in mind. It is important, therefore, to provide the capability for assisting the naive user in generating questions. The computer must somehow help the user identify a question that will help achieve the user's goals. One feature of the P&Q approach is that it enables the user to select options from the display and choose a question suitable to their needs.

Allowing users to select options is a crucial feature in interface design. In a study examining user errors, Lang (1990) found that users committed two basic types of errors: (a) display-driven errors and (b) user-initiated errors. Display driven errors occurred when the user misinterpreted information contained on the display and as a result performed an erroneous action. For example, the user may have misunderstood the meaning of a menu option and therefore performed the wrong action in order to fix the error. User-initiated errors occurred when the user generated an erroneous action based on past experience with another software item. An interesting result of Lang's study was a positive correlation between the occurrence of display-driven errors and the likelihood of users completing their task. That is, systems that tended to elicit display-driven errors were associated with software that had higher likelihoods of task completion and therefore were easier to learn. Lang concluded that this result was due to the fact that the menu-driven interfaces (which tended to have a large proportion of display-driven errors) prompted the users and guided them through the interface. Therefore, information from the display was useful in that it provided the user with options to try. In the P&Q interface, the question menu provides users with a choice of questions to select from. In this way, it is not entirely the user's responsibility to generate questions. Stated differently, P&Q broadens the horizon of questions for users to ask.

In traditional systems, when users are unsure of a particular action to take, they may consult an on-line index or a list of topics in a help menu. Often these topics mean very little to the novice user. With the P&Q approach, we propose an interface in which the user can use the basic query types to ask questions about the topics in the index. Figure 8.2 displays a sample interface for a database management system. The user can select a topic and then ask questions about the topic. For example, the user may wish to know "What does 'field definition' mean?" or "Why would I want to define a field?" (see Fig. 2b and 2c).

Errors and Unplanned Consequences.   Users often plan a sequence of actions in order to achieve a goal, but the actions result in errors. Often these errors are accompanied by cryptic error messages. At these points in the interaction, users should be able to query the system about the particular error. For example, suppose a user tried to enter information into an undefined field and received an error message that said "field not defined." The user may wish to know "What should I do?" as a result of performing this error. In the P&Q approach the user could select the "What should I do?" question on the menu and receive information concerning the appropriate course of action.

Computer-Initiated Questions

An important feature of a help system is the ability of the user to select a help key and get help even when the user does not have a particular question in mind. At these times the computer may have to ask questions concerning the user's goals. Once the system identifies a user's goals, it can then make recommendations concerning future actions. If the user does not understand the suggested actions, the user could then ask questions about the actions. In the P&Q interface, the user can ask questions such as "Why do I do X?," "How do I do X?," "What does X mean?," "What should I do?," "What if X?," and "When do I do X?."

It is also important for the computer to offer help and suggestions at appropriate times. We have identified four occasions when it would be useful for the computer to ask questions and to make suggestions concerning future actions. These situations are described below.

General Help Key.   As mentioned earlier, sometimes users are simply stuck. They do not know the next action to perform and they do not have enough knowledge to form an appropriate question. At these times the user may need a general help key that initiates computer diagnosis of the user's goal and suggests an appropriate action. In the diagnosis process, the computer would ask questions about the user's goals and about the actions that have already been performed. Based on this knowledge, the computer would suggest a plan and accompanying sequence of actions.

Perseveration of Errors.   Users are frequently caught in error loops. Lang (1990) discovered that individuals often perseverate on their errors, that is, they perform the same error many times in succession. At these times it would be important for the computer to jump into the interaction and attempt to diagnose the goals of the user. In order for the computer to diagnose the goals, the computer would need to ask the user questions. Once the computer identified the user's goals, the computer would recommend a particular course of action.

Long Pauses.   When users do not know what the next action should be, they experience long pauses. These pauses may be due to the fact that users are searching through manuals, thinking, or just at a loss concerning what action to perform. When the user experiences long pauses, the computer would prompt the user and ask if the user needs any help. If the user does need help, the computer can initiate an interaction in order to diagnose the user's goals and identify the appropriate course of action.

Suggestions for More Effective Methods.   Often users use inefficient methods for achieving particular goals. At these times, it would be important for the computer to suggest a more appropriate method. For example, many new users of word processors erase an entire sentence and then retype the sentence in a new position because they either (a) do not know they can move the sentence or (b) they do not know the procedure for moving a sentence. When the computer identifies that an inefficient method is being used, it might initiate a dialogue with the user to confirm the user's goals and construct a more appropriate procedure. A feature similar to this has been implemented by Shrager and Finin (1982). In their system, inefficient command sequences are recognized by the computer and more efficient strategies are recommended. This "suggestion" facility is a more difficult feature for P&Q to implement because the computer would need to keep track of the user's actions, goals, and the optimality of methods.

Limits of the P&Q Approach

The ability to ask the computer questions appears to be a necessary component of the human-computer interaction process. However, there are a few limitations or potential problems in asking questions on a computer that may hinder the development of question-asking systems. These limitations are acknowledged in this section.

One of the findings reported in research on question asking and human-computer interaction is that users do not ask many questions. Allwood and Eliasson (1988) found that the ability of some subjects to ask questions did not improve performance over those subjects who were not given the opportunity to ask questions. Further, Miyake and Norman (1979) found that subjects must have some amount of knowledge in order to be able to generate questions. These results illustrate that providing the facility for people to ask questions in the human-computer interaction context may not help user performance. However, the P&Q interface may help to overcome the limitations identified in these studies. In the P&Q interface, the user is provided with a list of alternative question types. Therefore, the user does not have to generate a list of appropriate questions. In addition, the Allwood and Eliasson study indicated that it is important to ask the right kind of question. In the P&Q interface, appropriate questions are identified and are provided as options to the user. A further advantage of the P&Q approach is that questions are answered quickly. Users will be reluctant to ask questions if they cannot receive an answer within a couple of seconds.

A second potential limitation of the P&Q interface involves the fanout problem. That is, the fanout from each display has the potential to increase exponentially and lead to a limitless number of possible questions. The P&Q interface helps to decrease this problem in a number of ways. First, all concepts may not be queried. That is, only some concepts are identified as hypertext hot spots. Secondly, users are notified when all possible questions have been asked about a particular concept. Consequently, users will not continue to ask questions about concepts they have already queried. Finally, the P&Q interface approach utilizes empirical data and iterative design. Successive versions of a P&Q system will include the most frequent questions asked about particular interfaces and will restrict the questions and hot spots according to the empirical data.

FINAL COMMENTS

Computers and electronic information systems are rapidly becoming common in more environments and necessary in more daily activities. One of the main reasons why computers are becoming so critical is their ability to store and provide quick access to a large amount of information. However, accessing information must be made easier for nonprogrammers. Traditionally, people have acquired information by asking other people questions or asking themselves questions as they searched through some type of document. If computers are to become valuable sources of information, they must enable users to ask questions very quickly and supply good answers efficiently. As we have discussed in the introduction, question asking in computer systems is important for such diverse tasks as learning new software, using on-line help, and in information acquisition.

In this chapter, we have proposed a method that helps users to conduct a question dialogue with the computer. The P&Q interface allows the user to ask specific questions in a hypertext environment. The P&Q interface therefore has the potential to have a major impact on interaction styles. At the current time, users are restricted to reading static help screens and searching through manuals. With the P&Q interface, users can actively pursue answers to a variety of questions. This will help them become more inquisitive in their interactions with computers and the topics they are learning. They will also acquire relevant information as answers to their questions. Consequently, they should find their interactions with computers more rewarding and satisfying.

Although we have discussed the P&Q interface in terms of learning a computer system, we believe that questioning must be seriously considered in a variety of large information systems. It is hoped that, in the future, computer applications will enable home users to do grocery shopping, to obtain information on practical topics (e.g., weather, news, and real estate) and to perform a host of other activities. In all of these information systems, the users' queries are the driving force. Clearly then, it is important for developers of these systems to understand how people ask questions and the types of information they expect as answers. As can be seen, we must develop techniques for conducting question-asking dialogues that do not require extensive training and computer knowledge.

ACKNOWLEDGMENTS

This research was funded in part by grants awarded to the second author by the Office of Naval Research (N00014-88-K-0110 and N00014-90-J-1492).

REFERENCES

Aaronson, A. P., & Carroll, J. M. (1987). The answer is in the question: A protocol study of intelligent help. *Behavior and Information Technology, 6*, 393–402.

Allen, J. F. (1983). Recognizing intentions from natural language utterances. In M. Brady & R. C. Berwick (Eds.), *Computational models of discourse*, 107–166. Cambridge, MA: MIT Press.

Allwood, C. M., & Eliasson, M. (1988). Question asking when learning a text-editing system. *International Journal of Man-Machine Studies, 29*, 63–79.

Carroll, J. M., & Aaronson, A. P. (1988). Learning by doing with simulated intelligent help. *Communications of the ACM, 31*, 1064–1079.

Collins, A. M., & Loftus, E. F. (1975). A spreading activation theory of semantic processing. *Psychological Review, 82*, 407–428.

Croft, W. B. (1987). Approaches to intelligent information retrieval. *Information Processing and Management, 23*, 249–254.

Date, C. J. (1983). *Database: A primer*. Menlo Park, CA: Addison-Wesley.

Date, C. J. (1986). *An Introduction to database systems*. Menlo Park, CA: Addison-Wesley.

Deerwester, S., Dumais, S. T., Landauer, T. K., Furnas, G. W., and Harshman, R. A. (1990). Indexing by latent semantic analysis. *Journal of the Society for Information Science, 141*, 391–407.

Dumais, S. T. (1988). Textual information retrieval. In M. Helander (Ed.), *Handbook of human-computer interaction* (pp. 673–700). New York: North-Holland.

Fitter, M. (1979). Towards more "natural" interactive systems. *International Journal of Man-Machine Studies, 11*, 339–350.

Graesser, A. C., & Franklin, S. P. (1990). QUEST: A cognitive model of question answering. *Discourse Processes, 13*, 279–303.

Graesser, A. C., & Gordon, S. E. (1991). Question answering and the organization of world knowledge. In G. Craik, A. Ortony, & W. Kessen (Eds.), *Question-answering and the organization of world knowledge*. Hillsdale, NJ: Lawrence Erlbaum Associates.

Graesser, A. C., Lang, K. L., & Horgan, D. (1988). A taxonomy for question generation. *Questioning Exchange, 2*, 3–15.

Graesser, A. C., Lang, K. L., & Roberts, R. R. (in press). Question answering in the context of stories. *Journal of Experimental Psychology: General.*

Greene, S. L., Devlin, S. J., Cannata, P. E., & Gomez, L. M. (1990). No IFs, ANDs, or ORs: A study of database querying. *International Journal of Man-Machine Studies, 32*, 303–326.

Hershman, R. L., Kelly, R. T., & Miller, H. G. (1979). *User performance with a natural language query system for command control* (Technical Report no. NPRDC-TR-79-7). San Diego, CA: Navy Personnel Research and Development Center.

Hill, I. E. (1972). Wouldn't it be nice if we could write computer programs in ordinary English—or would it? *Computer Bulletin, 16*, 306–312.

Jarke, M., Turner, J. A., Stohr, E. A., Vassiliou, Y., White, N. H., & Michielsen, K. (1985). A field-evaluation of natural-language for data retrieval. *IEEE Transactions on Software Engineering, 11*, 97–114.

Lang, K. L. (1990). *Understanding errors in human-computer interaction.* Unpublished dissertation, Memphis State University, Memphis, TN.

Lang, K. L., Graesser, A. C., & Hemphill, D. D. (1990). The role of questioning in knowledge engineering and the interface of expert systems. *Poetics, 19*(1–2), 143–166.

Lehnert, W. G. (1978). *The process of question answering.* Hillsdale, NJ: Lawrence Erlbaum Associates.

Minsky, M. (1975). A framework for representing knowledge. In P. H. Winston (Ed.), *The psychology of computer vision.* New York: McGraw-Hill.

Miyake, N., & Norman, D. A. (1979). To ask a question one must know enough to know what is not known. *Journal of Verbal Learning and Verbal Behavior, 18*, 357–364.

Nielsen, J. (1990). *Hypertext & hypermedia.* New York: Academic Press.

Ogden, W. C. (1988). Using natural language interfaces. In M. Helander (Ed.), *Handbook of human-computer interaction* (pp. 281–299). New York: North-Holland.

Paap, K. R., & Roske-Hofstrand, R. J. (1988). Design of Menus. In M. Helander (Ed.), *Handbook of human-computer interaction* (pp. 205–235). New York: North-Holland.

Reisner, P. (1977). Use of psychological experimentation as an aid to development of a query language. *IEEE Transactions on Software Engineering, 3*, 218–229.

Reisner, P. (1981). Human factors studies of database query languages: A survey and assessment. *Computing Surveys, 13*, 13–31.

Robertson, S. P., & Swartz, M. (1987). Question asking during procedural learning: Strategies for acquiring knowledge in several domains. *Program of the Ninth Annual Conference of the Cognitive Science Society* (pp. 325–335). Hillsdale, NJ: Lawrence Erlbaum Associates.

Robertson, S. P., & Zachary, W. W. (1990). Conclusion: Outlines of a Field of Cooperative Systems. In S. Robertson, W. Zachary, & J. Black (Eds.), *Cognition, computing, and cooperation.* Norwood, NJ: Ablex.

Rubin, T. (1988). *User interface design for computer systems.* West Sussex, England: Ellis Horwood.

Salton, G. (1986). Another look at automatic text-retrieval systems. *Communications of the ACM, 29*, 648–656.

Scha, R. J. H. (1988). Natural language interface systems. In M. Helander (Ed.), *Handbook of human-computer interaction* (pp. 941–956). New York: North-Holland.

Schank, R., & Abelson, R. P. (1977). *Scripts, plans, goals, and understanding: An inquiry into human knowledge structures.* Hillsdale, NJ: Lawrence Erlbaum Associates.

Shrager, J., & Finin, T. (1982). An expert system that volunteers advice. In *Proceedings of the National Conference on Artificial Intelligence* (pp. 339–340). Pittsburgh, PA: AAAI.

Sidner, C. L. (1985). Plan parsing for intended response recognition in discourse. *Computational Intelligence, 1*, 1–10.

Sievert, M. C., & Andrews, M. J. (1991). Indexing consistency in information science abstracts. *Journal of the American Society for Information Science, 42*, 1–6.

Singley, M. K., & Anderson, J. R. (1987–1988). A keystroke analysis of learning and transfer in text editing. *Human Computer Interaction, 3,* 223–274.

Sokal, R. R. (1974). Classification. *Science, 185,* 1115–1123.

Sowa, J. F. (1984). *Conceptual structures: Information processing in mind and machine.* Menlo Park, CA: Addison-Wesley.

Tennant, H. R. (1987). Menu-based natural language. In S. C. Shapiro & D. Eckroth (Eds.), *Encyclopedia of artificial intelligence* (pp. 594–597). New York: Wiley.

Thomas, J. C., & Gould, J. D. (1975). A psychological study of query by example. *Proceedings of the National Computer Conference, 44,* 439–445, Montvale, NJ: American Federation of Information Processing Societies Press.

Wilensky, R. (1983). *Planning and understanding.* Cambridge, MA: Addison-Wesley.

Williams, M. D. (1984). What makes RABBIT run? *International Journal of Man-Machine Studies, 21,* 333–352.

Winograd, T., & Flores, C. F. (1986). *Understanding computers and cognition.* Norwood, NJ: Ablex.

Zloof, M. M. (1975). Query by example. *Proceedings of the National Computer Conference, 44,* 431–438. Montvale, NJ: American Federation of Information Processing Societies Press.

9 Mechanisms that Generate Questions

Arthur C. Graesser
Natalie Person
John Huber
Memphis State University

Whenever Bert learns about a new topic, he is an active, inquisitive, creative, intellectual "sponge." He energetically asks dozens of questions, impatiently waits for answers, and is not.satisfied until he receives a good answer. When Homer learns about a new topic, however, his style is completely different. He is a passive recipient of knowledge. He assumes that the social and physical world is sufficiently kind to supply him with useful, relevant information. He never imposes himself on anyone with a question.

Researchers and teachers have often discussed the virtues of being an inquisitive learner who actively exerts control over the material to be learned by asking questions. Unfortunately, educational researchers have consistently observed that most learners are like Homer rather than Bert. Student-generated questions are infrequent and unsophisticated (Dillon, 1987, 1988; Flammer, 1981; Kerry, 1987). Student-generated questions constitute approximately 1% of the questions in a classroom, at an average rate of one question per hour. The questions are normally simple questions that involve the recall and interpretation of explicit material rather than higher-level questions that involve inferences, application, synthesis, and evaluation. When teachers attempt to increase the frequency of student-generated questions by positive reinforcement, the outcome has been discouraging because there is only an increase in shallow questions (Neber, 1976). A learner needs to master a significant amount of the material before the learner begins to formulate good questions (Miyake & Norman, 1979).

The fact that there are few student-generated questions is not surprising when the costs of asking a question in a classroom are considered (van der Meij, 1987). These costs include (a) personal failure and public recognition for revealing one's lack of knowledge, (b) an imposition on the instructor, who normally does not want to be bothered with the students' questions, and (c) a lower likelihood of receiving help in the future, when the student critically needs an answer to a question. Instructors often have difficulty understanding a student's question when the student has low domain-specific knowledge (Coombs & Alty, 1980); in these instances, the instructor ends up dismissing the question or answering the wrong question. Regarding the sophistication of questions, instructors are not particularly good role models for students. Less than 4% of the instructor-generated questions are higher-level demanding questions, that is, those that involve inferences, application of an idea to a new domain of knowledge, synthesis of multiple information sources, and informed evaluation (Kerry, 1987). Teachers are rarely sophisticated Socratic tutors who ask carefully planned sequences of thought-provoking questions that expose the students' misconceptions and contradictions.

Given that question generation is a surprisingly rare phenomenon in the educational enterprise, there is a sobering bottleneck in any computerized information system that relies on an inquisitive user. Facilities for user-generated questions are indeed available in many expert systems, decision support systems, and intelligent tutoring systems (Buchanan & Shortliffe, 1984; Sleeman & Brown, 1982; Wenger, 1987). However, most users will probably not benefit from these facilities unless they radically change their styles of learning and thinking. The problem is aggravated by the poor quality of the answers that computers produce when users do manage to ask questions (Lang, Graesser, & Hemphill, 1990). The "help" systems in most computer software are notoriously poor at supplying useful relevant information when a user encounters a barrier and needs critical information. An inept question-answering facility on a computer will rapidly kill any incentive for a user to ask the computer questions.

So far we have sketched a pessimistic picture of question generation in the educational enterprise and in computer technology. However, we have hardly given up hope in the "power of the question." It is quite possible that educators and computer scientists have missed a fundamental insight. Specifically, we need to understand the *mechanisms* that trigger questions when individuals are genuinely seeking information. Once we understand these mechanisms, we can design educational programs and computers that tap into these mechanisms and thereby maximize good questions.

The primary purpose of this chapter is to identify a set of cognitive mechanisms that generate questions. Before we present our catalogue of question-generation mechanisms, however, we need to identify the types of questions that individuals generate. Therefore, the chapter begins with a taxonomy of questions and inquiries. The subsequent section presents a catalogue of question-generation mechanisms. The final section briefly points out some implications of this research for information systems.

A TAXONOMY OF QUESTIONS AND INQUIRIES

There is an important distinction between an *interrogative* expression and an *inquiry*. An interrogative expression would always end syntactically with a question mark (?) if it were captured in print. An inquiry is defined conceptually rather than syntactically (van der Meij, 1987). An inquiry is an expression (i.e., speech act, utterance) in which the speaker is genuinely seeking information from the listener. Before the inquiry, the speaker does not know about X but wants to know about X; by virtue of the inquiry, the speaker is requesting the listener to supply relevant information about X. An inquiry can be captured with different syntactic forms and with different pragmatic categories of speech acts. For example, all of the following expressions constitute inquiries when expressed by a student in a tutoring session.

> What is a factorial design? (interrogative, question)
> Tell me what a factorial design is. (imperative, directive)
> I don't understand what a factorial design is. (declarative, assertion)

Thus, inquiries are sometimes but not always interrogative expressions. In a similar vein, interrogative expressions are not always inquiries. All of the following expressions are interrogatives, but only the first would be an inquiry in the context of a tutoring session.

> Why is this a factorial design? (inquiry)
> Why don't we begin on page 12? (request)
> Why do we have to learn this stuff, anyway? (gripe)

From the standpoint of this chapter, a *question* may either be an inquiry, an interrogative expression, or both.

Questions vary in the degree to which they specify the information being sought. The three questions that follow correspond to a high, medium, versus low degree of specification.

> If you put one zero with tens and two zeros with hundreds, then what do you do with thousands? (high specification)
> Okay, what about the zeros? (medium specification)
> What about these? (low specification)

When there is a low degree of specification, the answerer must rely on the dialogue context and world knowledge to interpret the meaning of the question. Whenever the questioner and answerer have a rich common ground (i.e., mutual knowledge that both participants know they share), then they can tolerate a low degree of specification. When there is minimal common ground, then there should be a higher degree of specification in order to prevent misinterpretations of questions.

In the proposed taxonomy of questions, the categories are distinguished on the basis of semantic, conceptual, and pragmatic criteria rather than syntactic and lexical criteria. We do not have one category for each question stem (e.g., *why, how, when,* etc.) because most of these stems are polysemous lexical items. A "how" stem, for example, would frequently occur in both quantification questions (e.g., "How many countries are in Africa?") and procedural questions (e.g., "How does a person change a flat tire?"). The distinction between quantification and procedural questions is an important conceptual contrast in the proposed taxonomy, whereas the wording of questions is unimportant. The fact that we define the question categories on the basis of meaning rather than form is consistent with some other taxonomies of questions in the cognitive sciences (Graesser, Lang, & Horgan, 1988; Lehnert, 1978).

The taxonomy in Table 9.1 was developed to handle inquiries. Our primary focus in this chapter lies in mechanisms that generate genuine information-seeking questions, so we need a taxonomy that emphasizes inquiries rather than interrogative expressions per se. Moreover, the taxonomy was not developed on the basis of a fortuitous sample of observations. The taxonomy has foundations both in theory and in empirical research, as discussed in the following.

1. *Theory.* Two theories provided most of the categories in the taxonomy. D'Andrade and Wish (1985) identified eight major speech act categories that can be used to categorize virtually all speech acts in conversations: question (equivalent to interrogative), assertion, request/directive, reaction, expressive evaluation, commitment, and declaration. These eight categories were abstracted from speech act theories in philosophy, linguistics, and sociology (Austin, 1962; Labov & Fanshel, 1977; Searle, 1969). Our proposed taxonomy includes questions, assertions, and requests/directives because these were the only categories that provide genuine inquiries.

The major category of "questions" is segregated further into subcategories. Most of these question subcategories were extracted from Lehnert's (1978) set of 12 question categories. Lehnert's categories were motivated by a computational theory of question answering in artificial intelligence (called QUALM). The QUALM model answers questions that a user might ask after comprehending a short narrative passage. In addition to Lehnert's categories, there is a "comparison" category (which was investigated by Lauer & Peacock, 1990), a "definition" category, an "example" category, and an "interpretation" category.

2. *Empirical completeness.* The set of categories in the taxonomy is able to accommodate virtually all inquiries that occur in discourse. Graesser et al. (1988) used a subset of this taxonomy to analyze questions generated in three contexts:

when college students read passages, when individuals use a computer, and when citizens ask questions in television and newspaper media. All of the questions in this corpus could be handled by the taxonomy. In a recent project, we analyzed the speech acts in tutoring sessions. The sessions spanned a variety of topics, including basic mathematics, statistics, research methods, a computer network, climate, agricultural products, and population density. Our taxonomy was sufficiently complete to accommodate nearly all of the inquiries in these tutoring sessions.

3. *Scoring reliability.* Trained judges have very little difficulty identifying inquiries in conversations. We have tested this by having four trained judges analyze a sample of the tutoring sessions. The conversations were segmented into speech acts expressed by the student or tutor. The judges decided whether each speech act was or was not an inquiry. Reliability scores were extremely high in the sample of tutoring sessions (Cohen's kappa = .96 or higher).

Trained judges can reliably categorize inquiries according to the taxonomy in Table 9.1. The same four trained judges used this taxonomy to categorize the inquiries identified in the sample of tutoring sessions. Reliability scores were .63 or higher among the sessions. It should be noted that we selected the D'Andrade and Wish (1985) taxonomy of speech acts because it is the only taxonomy of speech acts that has achieved a high degree of reliability and that is theoretically motivated.

The taxonomy in Table 9.1 can be used either as a *monothetic* or a *polythetic* classification scheme (Stokal, 1974). In a polythetic scheme, a particular speech act could be assigned to more than one category. For example, the following speech acts can be assigned to multiple categories.

Did the freeze in 1989 cause an increase in citrus prices?
(verification + causal antecedent)
What are the consequences of profits being higher in 1988 than 1989?
(comparison + causal consequence)

However, in a monothetic scheme, the categories are mutually exclusive so any given speech act can be assigned to one and only one category. Precedence rules need to be established in order to break ties in observations such as those just shown. For example, we have found that verification categories and comparison categories are frequently combined with other categories in "hybrid" questions. In our analyses, verification and comparison questions have lower precedence than the other categories. Therefore, the preceding two example questions would be assigned to the categories of causal antecedent and causal consequence, respectively.

TABLE 9.1
A Taxonomy of Inquiries

Question	Abstract Specification	Examples
1. Verification	Is a fact true? Did an event occur?	Is an F-test a type of statistic? Did it rain yesterday?
2. Comparison	How is X similar to Y? How is X different from Y?	In what way is Florida similar to China? How is an F-test different from a t-test?
3. Disjunctive	Is X or Y the case? Is X, Y, or Z the case?	Do the mountains increase or decrease the rain in Oregon? Did he order chicken, beef, lamb, or fish?
4. Concept completion	Who? What? When? Where? What is the referent of a noun argument slot?	Where are the large population densities in North America? Who wrote the song? What did the child steal?
5. Definition	What does X mean? What is the superordinate category and some properties of X?	What is a factorial design? What does interaction mean?
6. Example	What is an example of X? What is a particular instance of the category?	What is an example of an ordinal scale? What experiment supports this claim?
7. Interpretation	How is a particular event interpreted or summarized? How is a pattern of information interpreted or summarized?	Does that graph show a main effect for "A"? What happened yesterday?
8. Feature specification	What qualitative attributes does entity X have? What is the value of a qualitative variable?	What is George like? What color is the dog?

#	Category	Specification	Examples
9.	Quantification	What is the value of a quantitative variable? How much? How many?	How many rooms are in the house? How much profit was made last year?
10.	Causal antecedent	What caused some event to occur? What state or event causally led to an event or state?	How does warm air get to Ireland? Why is the kite going backwards?
11.	Causal consequence	What are the consequences of an event or state? What causally unfolds from an event or state?	What happens to the warm winds when they reach the mountains? What are the consequences of double-digit inflation?
12.	Goal orientation	What are the motives behind an agent's action? What goals inspired an agent to perform an action?	Why did Roger move to Chicago? What was the purpose of the city's cutting taxes?
13.	Enablement	What object or resource enables an agent to perform an action?	What device allows you to measure an earthquake? What do I need to bake this fish?
14.	Instrumental/ Procedural	How does an agent accomplish a goal? What instrument or body part is used when an agent performs an action?	How does a person perform long division? How do you move a mouse on a computer?
15.	Expectational	What plan of action accomplishes an agent's goal? Why did some expected event not occur?	Why wasn't there a war in Iraq? Why doesn't this doll have a mouth?
16.	Judgmental	The questioner wants the answerer to judge an idea or to give advice on what to do.	What do you think about the new taxes? What should I do to stop the fight?
17.	Assertion	The speaker expresses that he or she is missing some information.	I don't understand what this message on the computer means. I need to know how to get to the Newark airport.
18.	Request/Directive	The speaker directly requests that the listener supply some information.	Please tell me how to get a printout of this file.

MECHANISMS THAT GENERATED INQUIRIES

This section presents a catalogue of mechanisms that generated questions. We have clustered the mechanisms into four major groups: (a) correction of knowledge deficits, (b) monitoring common ground, (c) social coordination of action, and (d) control of conversation and attention. Table 9.2 lists these four groups of mechanisms.

We did not discover the questioning mechanisms in a vacuum. A few of the mechanisms already existed in computer models of question generation, problem solving, and reasoning, such as AQUA (Ram, 1989; Reisbeck, 1988), SWALE (Schank, 1986), SOAR (Laird, Newell, & Rosenbloom, 1987), and SDDS (Klahr & Dunbar, 1988). Some insights about potential question-generation mechanisms were inspired by theories of natural language comprehension and conversation (Allen, 1983; Clark & Schaefer, 1989; Litman & Allen, 1987) and by some theories of learning (Collins, 1988; Palincsar & Brown, 1984; Sleeman & Brown, 1982; Wenger, 1987), although most of these research efforts have not focused on question-generation mechanisms directly. Graesser et al. (1988) identified some of the mechanisms when they analyzed transcripts of a computer help system, talk shows (e.g., Phil Donahue), and letters to the editor of a newspaper. In addition to these contributions, we discovered mechanisms when we analyzed transcripts of tutoring sessions. Tutoring sessions provide a wealth of useful information because the student occasionally asks questions during the course of knowledge acquisition and because the tutor frequently asks questions in order to guide the student's learning.

Colleagues contributed transcripts of some of the tutoring sessions. Allan Collins provided transcripts of interactions between an expert and novices who wanted to learn how to use the ARPANET computer network; the two adults communicated on computer terminals that were isolated from one another. Collins also provided transcripts of conversations between a professor and undergraduates about climate, population density, and agricultural products (Collins, Warnock, Aeillo, & Miller, 1975). Stellen Ohlsson furnished tutoring transcripts of academically weak fifth graders who learned fractions from a computer-based learning environment called Fractions Tutor (Ohlsson, Bee, & Zeller, 1989). Kurt van Lehn furnished tutoring transcripts of second and third graders learning multiplication skills from an adult (van Lehn, 1989). In addition to these tutoring protocols supplied by colleagues, we collected transcripts of tutoring sessions on research methods (i.e., statistics and operational definitions of variables). The students were undergraduates in a research methods class whereas the tutors were graduate students in psychology. The aforementioned set of transcripts provided a broad, representative sample of tutoring sessions.

This section describes each of the tutoring mechanisms presented in Table 9.2. An example is provided for each mechanism. Almost all of the examples

174

TABLE 9.2
Summary of Question-Generation Mechanisms

Correction of Knowledge Deficit

1. Obstacle in plan or problem solving
2. Deciding among alternatives that are equally attractive
3. Gap in knowledge that is needed for comprehension
4. Glitch in explanation of an event
5. Contradiction

Monitoring Common Ground

6. Estimating or establishing common ground
7. Confirmation of a belief
8. Accumulating additional knowledge about a topic
9. Comprehension gauging
10. Questioner's assessment of answerer's knowledge
11. Questioner's attempt to have answerer generate an inference

Social Coordination of Action

12. Indirect request
13. Indirect advice
14. Asking permission
15. Offer
16. Bargaining

Control of Conversation and Attention

17. Greeting
18. Reply to summons
19. Change in speaker
20. Focus on agent's actions
21. Rhetorical question
22. Gripe

were extracted from actual transcripts in the preceding corpus of tutoring sessions. In each example, the generated question is highlighted in italics.

Correction of Knowledge Deficit

The questioner discovers that his or her knowledge base is either incomplete or in error. In order to correct such a knowledge deficit, the questioner asks a question and hopes that the answerer will supply information that rectifies the knowledge deficit. In most cases, the answerer is a person who is believed to have useful, relevant information. Alternatively, the answerer may be a computerized information system. In some cases, the answerer is also the questioner; after posing the question to himself or herself, the questioner observes the environment or executes cognitive strategies in search of an answer.

Obstacle in Planning or Problem Solving.   An individual encounters an obstacle during the process of planning or problem solving. The individual asks a question in order to obtain information that removes or circumvents the obstacle. For example, when a person needs to be somewhere and gets lost, the person asks a stranger for directions. The following excerpt is extracted from a tutoring session on fractions.

Tutor: You might have to pick that up.
Student: Oh.
Tutor: And now we've got to move it down.
Student: *How do you move it down?*

Deciding Among Alternatives That Are Equally Attractive.   An individual has a set of options and must decide which option to select. Each of the options is equally attractive so additional information is needed to break the tie. The individual asks a questions in an effort to obtain the new information. For example, when a customer in a restaurant cannot decide which entrée to order, the customer asks the waiter how each entrée is prepared. The following excerpt is extracted from a tutoring session on variables.

Tutor: That's how you plot values on a graph to determine if there is a curvilinear
         or a linear relationship.
Student: *Are they called levels or values?*
Tutor: When you are talking about levels of variables or values of variables,
         you're referring to the same thing.

Gap in Knowledge That Is Needed for Comprehension.   An individual discovers a critical gap in his or her knowledge while attempting to comprehend a written message, an event in the world, or a conversation. The individual asks a question in an effort to fill the gap. For example, when a speaker uses a rare word in a conversation, the listener often asks the speaker what the word means. The following excerpt was extracted from a tutoring session on statistics in which the tutor is trying to explain the difference between an F-test and a t-test.

Tutor: An F-test is an extension of a t-test.
Student: *What is a t-test?*

Glitch in an Explanation of an Event.   An individual observes an event that cannot be explained in the context or situation under consideration. The individual has trouble explaining the event, so the person asks a question in search for an explanation. The following example was selected from a tutorial on multiplication.

Tutor: You start multiplying by the hundreds number. Okay? And then you go on and you say 1 times 3 is 3, 1 times—
Student: (Interrupting) *How did that 406 get there?*

Contradiction.   An individual identifies a contradiction between two knowledge structures or between two lines of reasoning. A question is asked in an effort to resolve the contradiction. This mechanism often occurs in arguments and in debates. It is also at the heart of the Socratic teaching method. The following excerpt was extracted from a tutorial on climate and geography.

Tutor: Do you know why it rains a lot in Oregon and Washington?
Student: There is a warm current passing over cool land.
Tutor: Do the Cascade Mountains there affect the amount of rainfall?
Student: No, no, no.
Tutor: *How can the Andes affect the amount of rain in the Amazon and the Cascades not affect the rain in Oregon?*

Monitoring Common Ground

Successful communication requires that the speech participants keep track of what information is in the common ground (Clark & Marshall, 1981; Clark & Schaefer, 1989). Knowledge in the common ground (i.e., *CG-knowledge*) is shared by the questioner and answerer. The speech participants identify or estimate CG-knowledge in several ways. CG-knowledge includes information that is explicitly covered in the current conversation or any previous conversations between the two individuals. CG-knowledge includes information that is shared by most, if not all, members of the culture that speech participants are part of (e.g., how to mail a letter, the major countries of the world). CG-knowledge is also inferred by virtue of the professions, roles, trait stereotypes, and interests of each speech participant. For example, if both speakers are cognitive psychologists, then there is a great deal of CG-knowledge about thinking mechanisms; this CG-knowledge would not exist if a cognitive psychologist had a conversation with a plant biologist.

Speech participants must constantly update, verify, and monitor the knowledge in the common ground. They must also estimate the topics and amount of knowledge of each speaker that is *not* in the common ground. For the present purposes, we define *Q-knowledge* as that knowledge which the questioner has, but the answerer does not have. Similarly, *A-knowledge* is knowledge that the answerer has, but the questioner does not have. We acknowledge that it is difficult for speech participants to assess the CG-knowledge, the Q-knowledge, and the A-knowledge in some situations. Nevertheless, the problem of accuracy is a separate issue from the question-generation mechanisms in this section.

Estimating or Establishing Common Ground.   An individual may ask a question in order to estimate the amount of knowledge that the answerer has about a topic, as illustrated in the context of a computerized tutorial on fractions.

Tutor: Okay, we'll get started now. *Have you ever worked on a computer before?*

The tutor needed to find out whether "computer usage" could be in the common ground of the student and tutor. Whereas CG-knowledge was estimated at a general level in the preceding example, speech participants often need to have a fine-tuned assessment of each other's knowledge. The following example is an excerpt from an ARPANET tutoring session.

Tutor: *Do you know the difference between "LOCAL" and "REMOTE" modes of TELNET?*

In some cases, the questioner needs to verify that the questioner's CG-knowledge is in close synchrony with the answerer's CG-knowledge (Edwards & Mercer, 1989). The following example is an excerpt from a tutoring session on research methods.

Student: *Is there anything that stands out that I need to know about this?*

In this example, the student wanted to know whether she was perceiving a problem in the same way that the tutor was.

Confirmation of a Belief.   An individual asks a question in order to confirm that the answerer's belief about something is the same as the questioner's. The following excerpt was in a tutorial on multiplication.

Student: 3 times 4. (pause) *Is that 12?*

The answerer is expected to give feedback on the truth or falsity of the belief. In some cases, the questioner wants evaluative feedback on an action that the questioner is performing (i.e., is the action correct, sloppy, or incorrect). The questioner believes the action is correct, but wants to verify that the answerer also believes the action is correct. The following excerpt is from a research methods tutoring session in which the student is pointing to a graph on a blackboard.

Student: (While pointing and writing on the board) *So does this point represent female and this point male?*
Tutor: No. The entire top line is male and the entire bottom line is female.

Accumulating Additional Knowledge About a Topic. In some cases, the questioner knows far less about a topic than the answerer. This is precisely the case when the questioner is the student and the answerer is the tutor. Under these circumstances, (a) the questioner's Q-knowledge is less than the answerer's A-knowledge and (b) the questioner may want to expand his or her knowledge about a topic so that the CG-knowledge includes more of the A-knowledge. The questioner asks questions in order to expand the common ground. The following excerpt is extracted from a geography and climate tutorial.

Tutor: They [eastern Amazon, Congo] have heavy rain. Why?
Student: The air is super-saturated.
Tutor: Yes, and the air is cooled some as it comes in over the land.
Student: Are we talking about the Congo, Eastern Amazon, or Northern Africa?
Tutor: The region from 15 to 35 on the east of the Atlantic.
Student: *Aren't there some mountains along the western coast of Central America?*

It should be noted that the questioner may not really need to know the new knowledge accumulated about the topic. The questioner merely wants to augment his or her knowledge base and is convinced that the answerer already has this information.

Comprehension Gauging. The questioner wants to know whether the answerer is comprehending some information or line of reasoning. The questioner asks a question that permits the questioner to gauge the answerer's degree of comprehension. In the typical situation, the questioner knows more about the topic than the answerer. The questioner might ask a global comprehension gauging question, for example, "Do you understand this?" Sometimes the comprehension gauging question focuses on a more specific problem, as illustrated in the following excerpt from a multiplication tutorial.

Tutor: Just think to yourself, 203 times 2. So you say 2 times 3 is 6, 2 times 0 is 0, 2 times 2 is 4. Okay? *Do you see where I got that?*

At times the questioner may know less than the answerer; the questioner seeks feedback from the answerer by asking whether the questioner is understanding the material. In these cases, the questioner might ask "Am I understanding this?"

Questioner's Assessment of Answerer's Knowledge. In this case, the questioner is more knowledgeable about a topic than the answerer. The questioner inquires whether the answerer knows about some particular Q-knowledge. The following excerpt was from a tutorial on research methods and factorial designs.

Tutor: *What is a main effect? What does it tell you?*

There is a subtle difference between this mechanism and that of comprehension gauging. Comprehension gauging questions are normally verification questions that call for yes or no answers. The present category involves open-ended questions, such that the answerers must demonstrate their understanding by giving more lengthy answers.

Questioner's Attempt to Have Answerer Generate a Particular Inference. Once again, the questioner is more knowledgeable than the answerer. The questioner wants the answerer to arrive at a particular conclusion but does not want to tell the answerer directly. The questioner wants the answerer to arrive at the conclusion by inference, so the questioner asks one or more leading questions (Emihovich & Miller, 1988). The following excerpt was extracted from a tutoring session on research methods and factorial designs.

Tutor: How many independent variables does a 2×3 have?
Student: Six.
Tutor: Remember we just went over this. How many independent variables does a 2×2 have?
Student: Two with, oh yeah, two levels on each independent variable.
Tutor: *So how many independent variables does a 2×3 have?*
Student: Two, too. But one independent variable has three levels. Right?

The Socratic teaching method emphasizes this question-generation mechanism.

Social Coordination of Action

Questions are frequently generated to coordinate actions performed by speech participants. For example, an individual may need permission to do something or may need to get another person to do something. Thus, speech acts are often performed to manipulate people or to coordinate actions within a group of people (Austin, 1962; Francik & Clark, 1986; Gibbs & Mueller, 1988; Gordon & Lakoff, 1971; Searle, 1969). The question-generation mechanisms in this section are organized around actions that are significant in a social context.

Indirect Request. The questioner wants the answerer to do something on behalf of either the questioner, the answerer, or some third party. Instead of issuing a command, the questioner produces an indirect request that often is in the form of a question. Commands are sometimes rude and presumptuous, especially when there is a large difference in status between questioner and answerer. An indirect request is more polite. In the following excerpt from a tutoring session on statistics, the tutor wants to see the numbers that the student is discussing.

Tutor: *Can you write them down for me?*

The tutor is not merely inquiring whether the student is *capable* of writing down the numbers; the tutor is requesting the student to perform an action.

Indirect Advice.   The speaker is advising the listener to perform a particular action. The advice is indirect rather than direct. In the following excerpt from a tutoring session on multiplication, the student is uncertain about multiplying with zeros so the tutor advises the student to apply a procedure that the student had used previously.

Student: Would I put another zero down here, two zeros, or something else down here?
Tutor: Okay, *wouldn't you do this one exactly the same way as you did the last one?*

Asking Permission.   The questioner wants to do something and seeks permission from the answerer. The following excerpt was extracted from a tutoring session on fractions.

Tutor: See, it divided into three parts.
Student: *Can I try that?*

Offer.   The questioner wants to do something for the answerer and asks whether this is acceptable to the answerer. For example, the following excerpt would occur in many tutoring sessions.

Tutor: *Would you like me to help you?*

Negotiation.   Questions are often generated during the process of a negotiation or exchange of resources. That is, Person A is willing to do something if Person B does something. For example, "Would you leave if I buy this from you?" Alternatively, Person A is willing to do something for B if Person A gets to do something for A. The following excerpt was in a tutoring session on research methods.

Student: *If I do two more problems, can I stop?*

Control of Conversation and Attention

Questions are often asked in order to monitor the flow of conversation among speech participants. This includes both maintaining attention on a particular speaker and changing speakers. Whenever a questioner asks a question, there is an element of conversational control because the answerer is obligated to reply. Asking a question is one way of shifting the conversational spotlight onto the answerer. The tutoring sessions had very few mechanisms in this last group of question mechanisms because there were only two speech participants (tutor and student) and the ground rules of conversation were somewhat constrained. However, the following fictitious examples illustrate how speakers use questions to monitor conversational flow and to fight for the floor.

Greeting.   A speaker either initiates or acknowledges a conversation with another speaker by expressing a gesture. These greetings are sometimes expressed as questions.

Tutor: *How are you?*

Reply to Summons.   When Person A summons Person B, Person B sometimes acknowledges Person A by expressing a question. This often occurs when two individuals first address each other, as illustrated in the following.

Person A: Hey Joe.
Person B: *Yeah?*

A reply to a summons is one of the frequent adjacency pairs that were identified by Sacks and Schegloff (1979).

Change Speaker.   Conversations are frequently most rewarding when several individuals have the opportunity to contribute. Monologues can be difficult to tolerate, especially when they are not very stimulating. One way of shifting attention away from a person hogging the floor is to ask another individual a question.

Alex: bla bla bla bla . . . . .
Bert: Excuse me Alex. *Chris, did you ever call that person who wanted to buy your house?*
Chris: Yes I did. bla bla bla bla . . . . .

Focus on Agent's Actions.   Speakers sometimes want to grab the floor and maintain the conversational spotlight. This is accomplished by questions of the following sort.

Person A: *You know what I'm gonna do?*
Person B: No. What?
Person A: I'm gonna bla bla bla . . . .

Rhetorical Question.   The questioner neither expects nor desires an answer to the question. If this speech act is delivered appropriately, the listener recognizes that an answer is not called for. In many (but not all) instances of rhetorical questions, an answer would not be found in either the CG-knowledge, the Q-knowledge, or the A-knowledge. The questioner sometimes generates a rhetorical question in order to convey some message or to persuade the listener to believe something. We did not find a rhetorical question in our sample of tutoring sessions. However, one might imagine a tutor producing the following rhetorical question.

Tutor: *How do you expect to pass your exam if you don't study?*

Gripe.   Gripes are sometimes expressed in the form of a question (e.g., "Why do I always have bad luck?"). As is the case with rhetorical questions, an answer is not expected when gripes are formulated as questions.

SOME PRACTICAL IMPLICATIONS FOR INFORMATION SYSTEMS

This chapter has identified the types of questions and question-generation mechanisms in naturalistic conversations. We found instances of most of these mechanisms in the transcripts of tutoring sessions. This final section briefly discusses some ways that this research is useful for improving the design of computerized information systems. The first three clusters of question-generation mechanisms (i.e., correction of knowledge deficit, monitoring common ground, and social coordination of action) have straightforward applications to information systems whereas the fourth cluster (i.e., control of conversation and attention) would not have any obvious relevance to the design of computerized information systems.

Many computerized information systems have a question-answering facility. The user selects a question and then the computer supplies an answer. As discussed earlier in this chapter, the quality of the computer-generated answers has been very unimpressive in expert systems and intelligent decision support systems (Lang et al., 1990). The research reported in this chapter provides a new foundation for improving question-answering facilities on computers. In essence, a good answer to a question should address the question-generation mechanism that inspired the user's question. An improved intelligent Q/A facility would have the following three components.

1. Recognition of user's goals and knowledge.
2. Identification of relevant question-generation mechanisms on the basis of Component 1 and the user's question.
3. Formulation of an answer based on Components 1 and 2, in addition to the knowledge base.

The proposed Q/A facility would need to be extremely intelligent if it were to identify the goals and knowledge of individual users (Allen, 1983; Wenger,

1987). A more practical solution would be to analyze the typical goals and knowledge of generic users of the computer system (or N different categories of generic users).

Most information systems have a domain-specific knowledge base. For example, medicine was the domain-specific knowledge in the MYCIN expert system (Buchanan & Shortliffe, 1984), whereas the LISP computer language was the domain-specific knowledge in Anderson's LISP tutor (Anderson, Boyle, & Reiser, 1985). It would be informative to identify the question categories that are relevant and illuminating in particular knowledge domains. This could be accomplished in a brute force empirical way. That is, researchers could observe what questions are generated when users interact with MYCIN or with Anderson's LISP tutor. However, it would be more impressive to have a theory that predicted a priori what questions would be appropriate for a particular knowledge domain. We have indeed made some headway in formulating such a theory, but it was beyond the scope of this chapter to present it. In brief, our theory first identifies what types of knowledge are emphasized in the specific knowledge domain, for example, taxonomic knowledge, spatial knowledge, goal hierarchies, and causal mechanisms. Associated with each type of knowledge is a set of relevant question categories (i.e., a subset of the categories shown in Table 9.1) and a set of typical question mechanisms (i.e., a subset of the mechanisms listed in Table 9.2). For example, suppose that the knowledge domain involves a goal structure and planning, such as building a house. The important types of questions would be goal orientation and instrumental/procedural questions. The important questioning mechanisms would be an obstacle in problem solving and deciding among two equally attractive alternatives.

Whenever researchers develop an expert system or intelligent tutoring system, they normally interview human experts in an effort to extract the expertise. Knowledge elicitation methods are implemented in order to elicit systematically the precious knowledge. One method that has been implemented is the question-probe technique (Gordon & Gill, 1989, chap. 3 in this volume). The knowledge engineer essentially probes the expert with hundreds of questions about the knowledge domain. What is needed is a theory that predicts a priori what questions yield a high density of useful expertise. Once again, we have made some headway in developing such a theory to the extent that we have mapped (a) relevant question categories in Table 9.1 to (b) types of knowledge, for example, causal mechanisms, goal/plan hierarchies, taxonomic knowledge, and spatial knowledge.

Some information systems are designed to support learning. The present research provides some foundation for developing a human-computer interface that encourages the learner to be more active by asking questions. We believe that the designer needs to tap into the relevant question-generation mechanisms in order to surmount the normal barrier to inquisitiveness that prevents people from asking questions. Once these question-generation mechanisms are stimulated, learner-generated questions will naturally flow. Therefore, the key is to worry about question-generation mechanisms when designing the human-computer interface, the content of the computer displays, and the structure of the computer-user dialogue. For example, the computer might flag contradictions and discrepancies in the knowledge base because these trigger questions. As yet another example, the computer could promote a "mixed initiative dialogue" by having the computer autonomously give advice and ask the user questions.

Our ultimate and perhaps idealistic design objective is rather simple. We would like the user to have a natural conversation with the computerized information system. A deep understanding of questioning mechanisms is absolutely essential for meeting this far-reaching, if not illusory objective.

ACKNOWLEDGMENTS

This research was funded by grants awarded to the first author by the Office of Naval Research (N00014-88-K-0110 and N00014-90-J-1492).

REFERENCES

Allen, J. (1983). Recognizing intentions from natural language utterances. In M. Brady & R. C. Berwick (Eds.), *Computational models of discourse* (pp. 107–166). Cambridge, MA: MIT Press.

Anderson, J. R., Boyle, C. F., & Reiser, B. J. (1985). Intelligent tutoring systems. *Science, 228*, 456–462.

Austin, J. L. (1962). *How to do things with words.* Oxford, England: Oxford University Press.

Buchanan, B. G., & Shortliffe, E. H. (Eds.). (1984). *Rule-based expert systems.* Menlo Park CA: Addison-Wesley.

Clark, H. H., & Marshall, C. R. (1981). Definite reference and mutual knowledge. In A. Joshi, B. Weber, & I. Sag (Eds.), *Elements of discourse understanding* (pp. 10–63). Cambridge, MA: Cambridge University Press.

Clark, H. H., & Schaefer, E. F. (1989). Contributing to discourse. *Cognitive Science, 13*, 259–294.

Collins, A. (1988). Different goals of inquiry teaching. *Questioning Exchange, 2*, 39–46.

Collins, A., Warnock, E. H., Aiello, N., & Miller, M. L. (1975). Reasoning from incomplete knowledge. In D. G. Bobrow & A. Collins (Eds.), *Representation and understanding* (pp. 383–416). New York: Academic Press.

Coombs, M. H., & Alty, J. L. (1980). Face-to-face guidance of university computer users-II. Characterizing advisory interactions. *International Journal of Man-Machine Studies, 12*, 407–429.

D'Andrade, R. G., & Wish, M. (1985). Speech act theory in quantitative research on interpersonal behavior. *Discourse Processes, 8*, 229–259.

Dillon, J. T. (1987). Question-answer practices in a dozen fields. *Questioning Exchange, 1*, 87–100.

Dillon, J. T. (1988). *Question and teaching: A manual of practice.* New York: Teachers College Press.

Edwards, D., & Mercer, N. M. (1989). Reconstructing context: The conventionalization of classroom knowledge. *Discourse Processes, 12*, 91–104.

Emihovich, C., & Miller, G. E. (1988). Talking to the turtle: A discourse of logo instruction. *Discourse Processes, 11,* 183–201.

Flammer, A. (1981). Towards a theory of question asking. *Psychological Research, 43,* 407–420.

Francik, E. P., & Clark, E. H. (1986). How to make requests that overcome obstacles to compliance. *Journal of Memory and Language, 24,* 560–568.

Gibbs, R. W., & Mueller, R. A. G. (1988). Conversational sequences and preferences for indirect speech acts. *Discourse Processes, 11,* 101–116.

Gordon, S. E., & Gill, R. (1989). Question probes: A structured method for eliciting declarative knowledge. *AI Applications in Natural Resource Management, 3,* 13–20.

Gordon, P., & Lakoff, G. (1971). Conversational postulates. *Papers from the seventh regional meeting, Chicago Linguistics Society, 7,* 63–84. Hillsdale, NJ: Lawrence Erlbaum Associates.

Graesser, A. C., Lang, K. L., & Horgan, D. (1988). A taxonomy for question generation. *Questioning Exchange, 2,* 3–15.

Kerry, T. (1987). Classroom questions in England. *Questioning Exchange, 1,* 32–33.

Klahr, D., & Dunbar, K. (1988). Dual search space during scientific reasoning. *Cognitive Science, 12,* 1–48.

Labov, W., & Fanshel, D. (1977). *Therapeutic discourse: Psychotherapy as conversation.* New York: Academic Press.

Laird, J., Newell, A., & Rosenbloom, P. S. (1987). SOAR: An architecture for general intelligence. *Artificial Intelligence, 33,* 1–64.

Lang, K. L., Graesser, A. C., & Hemphill, D. D. (1990). The role of questioning in knowledge engineering and the interface of expert systems. *Poetics, 19,* 143–166.

Lauer, T. W., & Peacock, E. (1990). An analysis of comparison questions in the context of auditing. *Discourse Processes, 13,* 349–361.

Lehnert, W. G. (1978). *The process of question answering.* Hillsdale, NJ: Lawrence Erlbaum Associates.

Litman, D. J., & Allen, J. F. (1987). A plan recognition model for subdialogues in conversations. *Cognitive Science, 11,* 163–200.

Miyake, N., & Norman, D. A. (1979). To ask a question, one must know enough to know what is not known. *Journal of Verbal Learning and Verbal Behavior, 18,* 357–364.

Neber, H. (1976). Training epistemic questioning behavior of elementary students. In W. R. Minsel, W. Royal, & B. Minsel (Eds.), *Verhaltenstraining* (pp. 360–374). Trier, Germany: Universitat.

Ohlsson, S., Bee, N. V., & Zeller, P. A. (1989). *Empirical evaluation of a computer based-learning environment for fractions* (Tech. Rep. No. Kul-89-07). Learning Research and Development Center, University of Pittsburgh, Pittsburgh, PA.

Palincsar, A. S., & Brown, A. L. (1984). Reciprocal teaching of comprehension-fostering and comprehension-monitoring activities. *Cognition and Instruction, 1,* 117–175.

Ram, A. (1989). *Question-driven understanding: An integrated theory of story understanding, memory and learning* (Research Rep. #710). Ph.D. thesis, Yale University, New Haven, CT.

Reisbeck, C. K. (1988). Are questions just function calls? *Questioning Exchange, 2,* 17–24.

Sacks, H., & Schegloff, E. (1979). Two preferences in the organization of reference to persons in conversation and their interaction. In G. Psathas (Ed.), *Everyday language: Studies in ethnomethodology* (pp. 15–21). New York: Irvington.

Schank, R. C. (1986). *Explanation patterns: Understanding mechanically and creatively.* Hillsdale, NJ: Lawrence Erlbaum Associates.

Searle, J. R. (1969). *Speech acts.* London: Cambridge University Press.

Sleeman, D. H., & Brown, J. S. (Eds.). (1982). *Intelligent tutoring systems.* New York: Academic Press.

Stokal, R. R. (1974). Classification. *Science, 185,* 115–123.

van der Meij, H. (1987). Assumptions of information-seeking questions. *Questioning Exchange, 1,* 111–117.

van Lehn, K. (1989). *Felicity conditions for cognitive skill acquisition: Tutorial instruction does not need them.* Unpublished manuscript, Carnegie Mellon University, Departments of Psychology and Computer Science, Pittsburgh, PA.

Wenger, E. (1987). *Artificial intelligence and tutoring systems.* Los Altos, CA: Morgan Kaufman.

10 Interpretation of Textual Queries Using a Cognitive Model

Kathleen Dahlgren
Intelligent Text Processing, Inc., Santa Monica, CA

The volume of machine-readable text is growing exponentially. In news media, the government, medicine, law, and other fields, machine-readable texts or abstracts have been stockpiled for decades. Wire and news services make text available in real-time across worldwide networks. This information explosion has reached proportions in which institutions and busy professionals are unable to read and incorporate the unanalyzed glut of news, memos, and articles. This chapter explores the problem of computationally asking questions about text and of text. Current text retrieval systems are based on pattern matching of key words to the text words. However, these methods have proven to be inaccurate, with hit rates as low as 20% recall (Blair & Maron, 1985). Experienced users express dissatisfaction with these offerings in several areas: the types of questions that can be asked, the representation language of the query, and the relevance of replies. In the typical key word-based text retrieval system, the user begins a session with few key words and is inundated with irrelevant references. As the user adds more key words, the number of documents that contain all of the key words very rapidly declines to zero in a "cross-section" effect.

This chapter describes a text retrieval system, Interpretext. Interpretext was built by the author and colleagues who were originally at IBM (Dahlgren, McDowell, & Stabler, 1989; Lord & Dahlgren, 1989) and at Intelligent Text Processing. The goal of the system is to improve dramatically on existing text retrieval performance, both in user-friendliness and in accuracy, by introducing the findings of modern linguistics and cognitive science into software algorithms. Planned applications range from the less challenging tasks of text selection (archiving or clipping service) and text routing (real-time delivery of messages to all and only the interested parties), to the quite difficult task of text querying (retrieving facts from text). Text querying in another guise can be enhanced to perform textual data base updating, in which a program reads text and maintains a standard format data base.

Picture the busy professional, such as an official who digests world political events as they unfold and ensures that appropriate superiors are informed of important events to which the government must respond. The present scenario for such an official is that each morning he or she sits down to a desk full of printed pages of news and message items produced by a key word-based text retrieval system. Two-thirds of the stack is irrelevant to topic domain and must be tossed. Similarly, throughout the day the official weeds out irrelevant incoming clippings. For example, suppose the domain is Latin American terrorism. The domain is defined in a profile of key words intended to cull from the incoming news and messages those that concern Latin American terrorism. Unfortunately, the text retrieval program clips many irrelevant articles because they contain the words *Latin, American* and *terrorism*. On the other hand, relevant and important articles are missed because they do not happen to contain exactly those words. Unlike humans, the program cannot recognize that the mention of any Latin American country, major city, or government official classifies a news report as about Latin America.

Enhancements of such systems include the addition of more key words in boolean expressions, that is, those which include both "ANDing" and "ORing" of key words. In our example, the official might develop an "ORed" list of all Latin American countries, capitals, and major government officials, in effect saying that any article that contains the expressions *Latin America* OR *Mexico* OR *Rio de Janeiro* is relevant to our official's profile. This list could be "ANDed" with the expression *terrorism*, yielding a profile that culls all articles with both an expression from the Latin America list and the term *terrorism*. One of the known problems with this enhancement is that even highly educated professionals find working with booleans difficult and unnatural. One solution has been the introduction of knowledge engineers or text librarians as intermediaries who assist in accessing the data base. At one installation, 65 knowledge engineers are employed to formulate queries to a text retrieval system. Another enhancement has been the introduction of weightings to the key word queries, as in Verity. However, this solution again requires software engineers.

Interpretext addresses these problems in three significant ways. First, the interpretation of the incoming *target* text uses several levels of linguistic analysis to produce "deep natural language understanding," that is, the most refined level of computer computational understanding possible given the limitations of modern linguistics and computer science. Secondly, the query or profile is stated in English, making the system much more easily and directly usable by the busy professional. Thirdly, the system employs a cognitive model of both the query and the target text. The cognitive model is constructed by drawing on naive semantics, a representation of the world knowledge people use to disambiguate text.

The first section of the chapter describes the particular linguistic theory employed in Interpretext. The second section runs through the program architecture, which takes English as input and translates it several times, applying several different levels of linguistic analysis. The third section takes up illustrative examples of linguistic analysis at a few of the levels, and demonstrates their importance in achieving accurate and relevant replies to queries. The chapter briefly sketches the treatment of such problems in alternative systems.

COGNITIVE MODELS IN INTERPRETEXT

The particular approach in Interpretext is a model of natural language interpretation that incorporates all levels of linguistic processing that are known to exist in text interpretation by people: syntax, formal semantics, and world knowledge. The model addresses the interface between formal structures in language interpretation and memory structure (or the content of language). Other approaches are narrower. Either they can handle parsing (just syntactic form) OR world knowledge (just content, not form), as in Schank's (1982) conceptual dependencies and MOPs, OR formal syntax and formal semantics (just form, no content), as in the SRI approach (Shieber, van Noord, Moore, & Pereira, 1989). A representation of content requires a cognitive model that represents more than syntactic structure (Johnson-Laird, 1983; Morrow, Greenspan, & Bower, 1987). A cognitive model reflects both an interpretation of the explicit linguistic form and those inferences that must be drawn in order to interpret the form. The text in Table 10.1a is used to illustrate the claims of the chapter. In Table 10.1a, the reader's interpretation includes not only the structural assignment of *the U.N.* to subject of the first sentence constituent (S), but also an understanding that the U.N. is said to have accused Guatemala. Evidence that this inference is a required element of the interpretation lies in the next sentence, which begins with the pronoun *they*. To determine that *they* in the second sentence has *the U.N.* as antecedent rather than Guatemala, the reader must understand that both charging and citing are types of accusing, and that the citing activity was probably done as part of the charging activity. The reader can then infer that both activities have the same agent—*the U.N.* This is the kind of inferential information included in the cognitive model and not in structure-only models. Cognitive models are distinctly different from and more powerful than simple parse trees on the one hand, and semantic net representations on the other. The cognitive model is built on the output of the parser in the following levels:

1. Syntax (with syntactic disambiguation);
2. Sentential Formal Semantics;
3. Discourse Formal Semantics;
4. Cognitive Model.

TABLE 10.1
Sample Text and Levels of Representation

---

a. English Text: Guatemala was charged today by the U.N. They cited an illegal
   attack on a newsman.

b. Parse: s(np(det(the) & (un) & vp (v(charge) &
   np(n(guatemala))) & adv (today))

c. DRS for one sentence: el, un, g

---

charge6 (el, un, g)
today (el)

d. DRS for text: $el, un, g, e2, they1, e3, al$

---

charge6 (el, un, g)
today (el)
cite ($e2, they1, e3$)
attack2 ($e3$)
illegal ($e3$)
on ($e3, al$)
newsman (al)
  $they1 = un$

e. Cognitive preference: constituency ($e1, e2$)

f. First Order Logic: $\exists el$(charge6 (el, un, g) & today (el)

g. Prolog: charge6 (el, un, g)

The Interpretext system translates the cognitive model further for processing
purposes as follows:

5. First Order Logic;
6. Prolog;
7. Reasoner;
8. Relevance, Problem Solver, or Data base Update.

The ensuing subsections outline the analysis of Table 10.1a at each of the levels
(1–8).

Parse

A parse tree for the first sentence analyzes the grammatical parts of the sentence
and their roles relative to each other. Although the surface order of the words has
Guatemala as subject, the simplified parse in Fig. 10.1 shows that the deep
grammatical subject is *the U.N.* The serial form of such a parse looks like Table
10.1b.

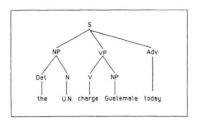

FIG. 10.1. A simplified parse tree.

Sentential Formal Semantics

A parse captures only the grammatical structure of a sentence. Another level of information conveyed by the form of linguistic elements are truth conditions. The formal semantic level provides a formula expressing the conditions in the actual world (or some possible world) that would have to exist in order for a sentence to be true. In the first sentence of Table 10.1a, there are entities (*the U.N., Guatemala*), an event (*of charging*), and a relation between them (*the U.N.* and *Guatemala* stand in a "charging" relation). A translation function based on Discourse Representation Theory of Kamp (1981) and Asher (1987) produces from the parse the Discourse Representation Structure (DRS) in Table 10.1c. The entities in the sentence are listed in the top part of the box. Each of these denotes an individual or set of individuals, an event or set of events in a world model. It might be noted that the world model is represented as an entity-attribute data base. The lower part of the box contains predictions on these entities and the relations among them. Thus, we see that event *e1* is the one in which entity *un* (the U.N.) relates to entity *g* (Guatemala) as the charger in a charging event in which entity *g* is the chargee. Similarly, we find that event *e1* occurred today (the day the text was written).

Discourse Formal Semantics

This level represents the truth conditional properties of the entire discourse. It tracks and equates entities across text as they are mentioned over and over again (this is called *anaphor resolution*). The DRS for both sentences of Table 10.1a contains the resolution of the anaphoric device *they* and shows that it corefers with *U.N.* to the entity *un*. This identity is expressed in the equation *they1 = un*, as in Table 10.1d. Notice that entities (or instantiations), and sorts of things like *newsman* are distinguished in the DRS, as needed for knowledge-base reasoning (Brachman & Schmolze, 1985). Table 10.1d omits temporal equations also provided in the DRS, which indicate the time relations between events. In Table 10.1d, the equations would indicate that events *e1* and *e2* overlap in time, as in Partee (1984).

The DRS provides a formal representation of the events described in the text, and a method for assigning truth conditions to the assertions of the text. In other words, given the first order representations in the DRS, whether the world conformed on that day to the assertions in the text can be checked by the application of formal logical rules to a model produced by a mapping from the DRS. If entities in the model of the.actual world had the relations expressed in the DRS, then the assertions in the text are true. This level of representation is very important in computational text understanding, especially for the ultimate goal of extracting data base knowledge from text. The DRS is translatable into first order logic and then into a programming language or computational knowledge base. The assertions in the text can then be checked against data bases or used to update them, which is exactly the knowledge acquisition procedure in Interpretext.

Formal semantic properties of natural language include the capability of expressing unqualified assertions, such as "The guerrillas attacked the base." In addition, assertions can be qualified in a large number of ways. Models affect the force of assertions, as in "The guerrillas might attack the base." The latter sentence does not imply a world model in which the base has actually been attacked. Operators such as negation reverse the force of an assertion, as in "The guerrillas did not attack the base." Formal semantic properties such as these are treated in the Interpretext program, but will not be explored in depth in this chapter.

Cognitive Model

Another level of representation in the theory is the *cognitive model,* so called because it infers the intended content from what the text says directly and because it incorporates world knowledge. The clauses of a text are written with the intention that the reader draw some relationship between them. For purposes of economy, language is both highly ambiguous and highly telescopic. A given form of words in English can make a large number of different assertions, depending on the situation being referred to (Barwise & Perry, 1983). This ambiguity of the English language requires that the human interpreter reason about the likely situation to which the writer might be referring. So a mandatory aspect of text interpretation for humans is drawing inferences about the connections between the contents of individual sentences. The sentences in (1a) describe a likely situation, whereas those in (1b) do not. Furthermore, the second sentence in (1a) disambiguates the first sentence, which has a possible interpretation concerning finances rather than legalities.

(1a) "Guatemala was charged today by the U.N. They cited an illegal attack on a newsman."

(1b) "Guatemala was charged today by the U.N. They ate oranges."

The two events are unrelated. The reader cannot even decide whether "they" corefers with Guatemala or the U.N. In contrast, with (1a) the reader uses knowledge that charging and citing are related events to infer that the U.N. is the grammatical subject of both *cite* and *charge*. Furthermore, the human reader guesses that the charging event is the broader one, and that part of it was a subevent of citing. The representation of the cognitive model for (1a) as built by Interpretext is pictured in Table 10.1d, with the added inference 1e that the two events of citing and charging cohere under the relation "constituency." This inference states that the citing event *e2* occurred as part of the charging event *e1*.

Other inferences are added to the cognitive model to break longer texts into coherent segments (not paragraphs, which may or may not coincide with coherent segment breaks). In addition, the cognitive model contains an indication of which event is the topic event of the text, and which are the main participants in the topic event (see Dahlgren, 1989). In summary, the cognitive model contains a list of discourse entities (individuals and events) and a list of predicates. The latter represent: properties of the discourse entities; relations between those entities directly expressed in the text; temporal equations; coherence relations between events inferred from both the text and world knowledge; and textual structure (topic and segments).

First-Order Logic

The cognitive model in Interpretext is translated into first-order logic formulas. First-order logic has the important advantage, as a representational language, that its proof properties have been well-known for a century. Translation of English to first-order logic results in a representation to which standard proof methods can be applied. In contrast, translation to a special knowledge representation language requires special reasoning modules that become large, slow, and unpredictable in their behavior. The first-order logic form for the first sentence of Table 10.1a is shown in Table 10.1f. This means "there is an event *e1* such that the individual *un* (in the world model) charged the individual *g* (in the world model) during the event *e1*, and *e1* occurred today." The cognitive model is translated to first-order logic.

Prolog

The first-order logic form is an intermediate representation between the cognitive model and Prolog. First-order forms contains quantifiers $\exists$ (there exists) and $\forall$ (for all). The translation eliminates these because they introduce infinite chains of reasoning. The translation function transforms first-order logic (e.g., Table 10.1f) into Prolog (e.g., Table 10.1g). The Prolog form is the data base used by the reasoning module to answer questions. The Reasoner and higher level modules are explored in the Architecture section.

NAIVE SEMANTICS

The approach to lexical knowledge in Interpretext is called Naive Semantics (NS) and is fully described and defended in Dahlgren (1988). NS is fundamental to the construction of the cognitive model. It is based on the observation that a reader draws on world knowledge to disambiguate and clarify text, selecting the most plausible interpretation from among the infinitely many possible ones. Although extensive world knowledge can, in principle, affect the choice of an interpretation, NS is just the shallow layer of knowledge speakers must use in production and interpretation of language. The nature of the required shallow layer of knowledge is carefully and projectibly defined. Lacking this knowledge, they are incompetent in the language. Operationally, NS knowledge consists of characteristics of objects and the implications of events produced by subjects in psycholinguistic experiments.

An informal example of a naive semantic concept is the following description of the typical lawyer, drawn from a psychological study of concepts (Dahlgren, 1985).

> If someone is a lawyer, typically they are well-dressed, use paper, books and brief cases in their job, have a high income and high status. They are well-educated, clever, articulate, knowledgeable, as well as contentious, aggressive, and ambitious. Inherently lawyers are adults, have gone to law school, and have passed the bar. They practice law, argue cases, advise clients, and represent them in court. Conversely, if someone has these features, he/she probably is a lawyer. (p. 57)

Concepts are called naive in NS because they are not always objectively true and bear only a distant relation to scientific theories. They are probabilistic rather than formulaic in force. In other words, if the meaning of *lawyer* is that a lawyer typically negotiates settlements, then a sentence "John is a lawyer" only probabilistically implies that John negotiates settlements. The success of communication with a vague and ambiguous vehicle is explained by the fact that natural language is anchored in the real world. Real objects and real events are referred to using words that have meaning representations that are close enough to the truth, enough of the time, to make reference possible (Boyd, 1986). The stability of the extensional world is also what makes NS representations portable to other languages. A car is a car in the U.S. and Japan. People do not have radically different naive views of them in modern industrial societies.

NS differs from approaches that employ exhaustive decompositions into primitive concepts. In these decompositional approaches, a term such as *lawyer* has a meaning representation like *adult* and *human* and *counselor*. All and only those objects that have those features are lawyers. Thus, the meaning representation of a word forms a set of conditions which all members of the set of objects which the word names share. This is essentially the approach in many knowledge representation schemes such as KL-ONE (Brachman & Schmolze, 1985) and AI approaches to natural language (Schank, 1982). In contrast, NS representations are not limited to a set of primitives, but contain many English words as feature values. Furthermore, the feature values correspond to naive theories about the nature of the world, which may or may not be correct. A meaning representation in NS consists of those properties of things that most believe to be true. The result is richer representations with more content, which are not treated as logical formulas (which are true of all objects named by a word). For example, in the representation of "lawyer" a feature "function, defends clients in court" appears. Although this property is typical of lawyers, it is not a logical necessity that if someone is a lawyer he or he must defend clients in court. Some lawyers do not. The result is that NS representations of word meaning contain more information than is found in alternative approaches.

NS representations are of two types, ontological and generic. Ontological classes reflect naive beliefs concerning the structure of the actual world and the significant "joints" in that structure, such as animate versus inanimate and real versus abstract. A piece of this knowledge is illustrated in Fig. 2. This piece of the ontology shows that "lawyer" is a social role. In many AI and psychological theories this is called a taxonomy or semantic net.

Generic knowledge contains features of objects and implications of events, the knowledge that a generation of psycholinguistic studies has shown to be the cognitive structure of nouns and verbs (Graesser & Clark, 1985; Rosch & Mervis, 1975). Generic knowledge is represented as two lists, one of inherent and one of typical features. For the knowledge base, these get translated into indi-

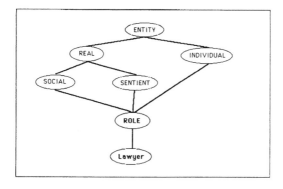

FIG. 10.2. A piece of the ontology.

vidual ground clauses in Prolog. Each feature is typed. For nouns there are 59 types: size, shape, color, function, and so on. Part of the representation for "lawyer" looks as follows:

lawyer

typically -	internal__trait(articulate), function(defend(noun,Y) & client(Y)), income(high), function(negotiate)
inherently -	education(school(X) & law(X)), function(represent(noun,Y) & client(Y))

For verbs there are very few types: cause, goal, enable, consequence, what happened next, where, when, how, implies, and selection restriction. Alternative senses of ambiguous words have different entries, indexed by sense numbers.

Generic knowledge for nouns and verbs are collected using a computer program that asks a native speaker of American English intuitively to fill values for feature types. The feature types for a noun are narrowed to those that have been established empirically to be found under a given node in the ontology. For example, under the Social Role node of the ontology, several feature types are applicable. A knowledge engineer is prompted for these, as illustrated in (2). The values are some of those for "lawyer."

(2)

Feature type	Feature value
Function	negotiate
Function	represent(X,Y) & client(Y)
Education	school(X) & law(X)
Income	high
Internal trait	articulate

NS can be encoded easily for computational purposes because it is limited to a relatively small number of types of features (though feature values are unlimited), and nonprofessionals can be taught to encode it. Such entries are translated by computer program into a Prolog knowledge base, so that each feature for a word has a format like (3) in Interpretext.

(3) lawyer(income,high,typical).

ARCHITECTURE AND OPERATION

Interpretext reads text or queries as input and processes both of these with the same modules until the very last component (the reasoner) is executed. Figure 10.3 shows the flow. Taking text Table 10.1a as an example input, the parser first produces a labeled bracketing as in Table 10.1b for the first sentence. The

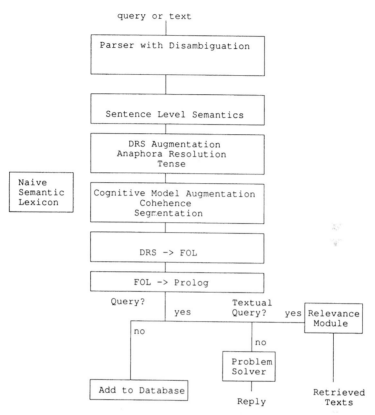

FIG. 10.3.   Flow chart of interpretext.

disambiguation step of the parsing disambiguates the parse tree structurally (which is not necessary for this sentence). It also selects from among the available senses for each noun and verb. In the first sentence of Table 10.1a, the legal sense of "charge" is chosen, rather than the monetary or physical senses. Then the DRT module (Sentence Level Semantics) builds a DRS from the parse tree as in Table 10.1c. At this point, DRS augmentation and cognitive model augmentation are irrelevant because they are discourse-level modules and not enough sentences have been received. Next, the DRS to first-order logic translator produce Table 10.1f, and the first-order logic to Prolog translator produces Table 10.1g. At this point, the reasoning module is not called because not all of the input has been processed. Instead, the interpretation process begins anew with parsing for the second sentence in the incoming text. It is processed through all of the levels in exactly the same way as the first sentence up until anaphor resolution in the DRS augmentation module.

For the second sentence, discourse-level processing is necessary. DRS augmentation first invokes anaphor resolution, which uses both syntactic rules (such as number agreement) and world knowledge (such as the relatedness of charging and citing), to infer that the antecedent of *they1* is *the U.N.* Next, it invokes temporal reasoning to produce tense equations reflecting both that the charging (*e1*) happened the same day as the text was written, and that the citing (*e2*) happened during a time interval included in the time of *e1*. The Reasoning module is invoked and inspects whether this is text or query. Finding that it is text, it invokes the data base updating module, which adds Table 10.1g to the Prolog workspace. This is available to answer questions such as "What did the U.N. do?"; "What did Guatemala do?"; "When did the U.N. charge Guatemala?" For such queries, again the input is parsed and translated as for the first sentence of Table 10.1a. When the translation reaches the first-order logic to Prolog module, it is converted into a Prolog command to query the data base, and the answer is produced by the Problem Solver module. If the query is a text retrieval query, the Relevance module is invoked. In this case, it determines precisely that Table 10.1a is about the U.N.'s act of charging Guatemala with illegal attack, rather than about heart attacks, monetary fees, or book citations, all of which would be possibilities for key-word-based systems. At each stage of the analysis, the system is forced to choose among possible structures and interpretations in accordance with preference strategies (i.e., it selects which one is most plausible or typical).

LEVELS OF INTERPRETATION

Turning to a defense of deep natural language understanding, a number of major figures in the field, most notably Fodor (1987), have claimed that a rich, open-ended approach such as NS is logically infeasible. Happily, the prototyped Interpretext demonstrates the model's feasibility. Others argue that any sort of linguistic analysis requires too much reliance on inadequate theories and hand-encoding of representations, so that the only answer is to treat language as a massive pattern like visual or audio input (Streeter, 1990). In this section, I demonstrate the value and feasibility of multilevel linguistic analysis of text by examples from several levels of analysis. I explore parsing, structural disambiguation, word sense disambiguation, synonymy, anaphor resolution, and reasoning for relevance in order to illustrate their importance in achieving precise answers to questions.

Parsing

Parsing is needed to translate the surface string of words into the argument structure of the query or text. In queries such as (4) and (5), a system needs the syntactic fact that *Guatemala* is object rather than subject of the sentence. It can thereby look for instances of Guatemala being invaded, rather than of Guatemala invading some other country.

(4) "Who invaded Guatemala?"

(5) "Did the U.S. invade Guatemala?"

Similarly, in trying to answer a query about murder of government officials, a system with no parsing can be fooled into selecting any of the following texts as relevant:

(6) "The CIA murdered officials of the government."

(7) "The government murdered officials."

(8) "The government has made murder an official policy."

(9) "The government tried the official for murder."

(10) "Government officials charged the death squads with murder."

In contrast, a system with parsing converges only on (6), because *officials* is the object of *murder*, and *officials* is modified by *government*.

Thousands of English words have syntactic roles of both noun and verb, and have different meanings in these roles. One product of parsing is that it assigns each word in the string to a part of speech. When a query is parsed, the correct thematic role for each word must be assigned. Thus *charge* is a verb in (11), yet a noun in (12). Only (11) is relevant to a query such as (13).

(11) "Guatemala charges that the U.N. interfered."

(12) "The charges against Guatemala were dropped."

(13) "What did Guatemala charge?"

Structural Disambiguation

Natural language structure is highly ambiguous, so the parse output is also ambiguous (or, alternatively, for each sentence many parses must be produced). Structural ambiguities arise in sentences with prepositional phrases (PPs) after the object of the verb because the first PP after the object can modify either the object, the verb, or the sentence constituent. Such sentences have at least three readings due to structure alone. Consider this structure in (14). The three readings are illustrated with different words after the preposition.

(14) "Guerrillas attacked the outpost with (a) a sentry

                                                 (b) grenades.

                                                 (c) fury.

In (14a), the PP *with a sentry* modifies *the outpost;* the outpost is the one with a sentry. In (14b), *with grenades* modifies *attack;* the attacking had grenades as instrument. In (14c), *with fury* modifies the whole sentence; the guerrilla attack was done in a furious manner. These structural alternatives are illustrated in Fig. 10.4. If the structural ambiguity is not resolved, a system cannot accurately answer questions. For example, the answer to "Which outpost did the guerrillas attack?" is found in (14a) and not (14b) or (14c), whereas the answer to "What did the guerrillas use to attack?" is in (14b) and not (14a) or (14c). In sentences with two PPs after the object of the verb, the number of possible structures rises to seven. Computational linguists are fond of generating examples that illustrate exponential growth in the number of readings for sentences in which various structural ambiguities interact. Apparently simple sentences can have hundreds of potential parse trees. A computational system that tries to interpret text without human intervention must apply "preference strategies" to select among the trees. Preference in this phrase alludes to the fact that lacking a human reasoning capacity, the program must guess and try to come as close as possible to the selection of the correct reading with whatever information and algorithms it has at its disposal.

We have developed a computational method for PP disambiguation using preposition-specific rules, syntax, and naive semantics (Dahlgren & McDowell, 1986). The algorithm was found to be 97% accurate in a corpus of 12,000 words of geography and newspaper text. To illustrate its function, consider example (14b). In this case, global rules are tried and fail, such as a rule that assigns S-attachment to PPs with temporal nouns, and VP-attachment to motion verbs with certain prepositions. Then the preposition-specific "with" rule is tried and it attempts to prove VP-attachment by checking whether in the NS lexicon the head of the PP is a typical instrument of the verb *attack*. In this case, it is, so the parse is reformed with the PP attached to the VP. In (14a), the "with" rule checks in the NS lexicon to see whether a typical part of an outpost is a sentry, and finds that it is, so it assigns the "with" phase as a modifier of the object NP *the outpost*. In example (14c), none of the specific cases in the "with" rule applies, so the default is taken. The default assigns the "with" phrase as a sentence-

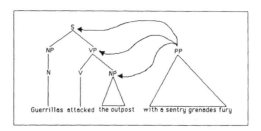

FIG. 10.4.   Possible attachment sites for a prepositional phrase.

modifier. The algorithm also records the case role, by replacing the preposition with *instrument* for (14b) and *manner* for (14c).

In sentences with both PPs and ambiguous words, the algorithm disambiguates words in relation to the structure it selects. In (14b) the verb *attack* has several different senses. Two of them are "attack physically" and "attack verbally." The physical sense is the one that has *grenades* as instrument, not the verbal sense. Thus, the algorithm selects the physical reading for *attack* and puts the word-sense index on it as part of the processing. When the word-sense disambiguation module processes the sentence, it ignores previously disambiguated words.

Another type of structural ambiguity arises with conjunction. Conjoined noun phrases and verb phrases allow for a variety of interpretations. Consider (15) versus (16). In (15), the most probable interpretation is one in which there is one event of driving to Guatemala, and John and Mary do it together. In (16), such a collective interpretation is plausible, but equally plausible is a distributive interpretation in which there are two separate events of visiting Guatemala, one by John and another by Mary. Verb phrase conjunctions also introduce ambiguity, as in (17). A plausible interpretation has one wife for each man, but an allowable interpretation has only one woman that both love.

(15) "John and Mary drove to Guatemala."
(16) "John and Mary visited Guatemala."
(17) "John loves his wife, and Bill does, too."

Similarly, conjunctions have multiple interpretations in queries. In (18), there may be only one, or there may be two, individuals to identify.

(18) "Who criticized the dancing and praised the singing?"

Therefore, conjunction introduces the problem of determining how many individuals are referred to by a sentence. To resolve these ambiguities, we can assume a tendency to infer collective interpretations, because the conjunction construction implies the formation of sets. Furthermore, NS filtering can be used to discover cases where the distributive interpretation is more plausible. In (15), a joint event of driving somewhere is a typical situation, so that the collective interpretation is preferred. In (19), people typically read books by themselves, so the distributive interpretation is more plausible.

(19) "John and Mary read *Lord of the Flies*."

Conjoined verb phrases also introduce ambiguity, as in (20).

(20) "John ate fish and Mary had veal."

As with conjoined noun phrases, conjoined verb phrases similarly imply a single broader event. In (20) the broader event is a meal that John and Mary had together. We are working on the development of a preference strategy for conjunction disambiguation using structural probability and NS filtering.

Word-Sense Disambiguation

Ambiguity of word senses is a critical problem in query interpretation and data base searching. Irrelevant replies stemming from ambiguity in the text or query are the source of most of the precision problem in text retrieval. Gentner (1981) reported that the 20 most frequent nouns in English have an average of 7.3 senses, and the 20 most frequent verbs have an average of 12.4 senses. Dahlgren (1987) noticed that the word *hand* has 16 senses, 10 of which are uses in any type of text. The verb *work* has 8 intransitive senses.

Word-sense ambiguity is a problem for question-answering and text retrieval systems, even when vocabulary has been restricted to a specific domain. Suppose that (21) is a target text, and there are three queries to it (22)–(24).

(21) "Garcia moved that the people evacuate to the countryside."
(22) "Did Garcia move the action be taken?"
(23) "Did Garcia move the people to action."
(24) "Did Garcia move the people to the countryside?"

Each of the queries has a different reading for transitive *move:* the parliamentary, the mental, and the physical. Without disambiguation, a query system could easily be fooled into erroneous affirmative responses to both (23) and (24).

The Interpretext word-sense disambiguation method employs three levels of knowledge: frequency, syntax, and naive semantics. The algorithm was developed by studying the syntactic and semantic environments of word senses for 16 words in live text. The system has a list of sense numbers for ambiguous words. Words with no such list are unambiguous.

First, the algorithm tries fixed and frequent phrases that have only one reading, and occur often enough to be recorded: *by hand, for once, in hand, leveraged buyout, human rights,* and so on. If an ambiguous word does not occur in any such phrase, syntactic tests are tried. Some syntactic environments reduce or eliminate ambiguity (e.g., in the case of noun senses being sensitive to the presence or absence of determiners). For example, the electoral sense of *office* is the only sense possible when there is no determiner ("for office," "in office"). Some noun senses are sensitive to the presence of quantifiers. "Many interests" cannot have the financial reading, but may have the sentient or abstract readings. Other noun senses are selected by particular prepositions. "In the office" or "at

the office" must have the place reading, not the sentient (institutional) or electoral readings.

For verbs, various syntactic constructions help disambiguate the word, such
as certain modals and complement constructions. This is illustrated with several
senses of the verb *charge* in (25).

(25) (a) physical   to attack
      (b) physical   to replenish (as electricity)
      (c) social,financial   to impose a tax or fine
      (d) social,financial   to debit
      (e) social   to entrust
      (f) social, mental   to accuse
      (g) social, legal   to indict
      (h) social, mental   to direct

"Someone charges that . . ." can only have the mental reading (25f) for *charge*,
as opposed to physical or financial readings. Prepositions may help select senses
of verbs. In combination with prepositions, these senses are partially or fully
selected. "Charge with" has legal (25g) or financial readings (25c,d), whereas
"charge toward" has the physical reading (25a). Some adverbs help select senses
of verbs. "Charge heavily" has the electrical (25b), financial (25c,d), or legal
readings (25g); "charge vehemently" the verbal reading (25f); "charge con-
tinually" the electrical reading (25b); and "charge abruptly" the physical reading
(25a).

The third layer of reasoning for word-sense disambiguation is the application
of NS knowledge. This knowledge suffices to disambiguate almost all of the
cases (98%) that were not disambiguated by either (a) fixed and frequent phrases
or (b) syntactic tests (Dahlgren, 1987). In (26), the algorithm is able to select
reading (25f). The algorithm uses knowledge that in the accusation reading
(25f), typically the head noun of a PP is an event (e.g., *interference*), whereas
for the other senses, typical head nouns of PPs are different. For example,
typically a "with" phrase after the physical reading (25a) is a weapon. On the
other hand, for (27) the algorithm selects the financial sense (25d) because the PP
contains a financial word. In (28), sense (25d) is selected over (25c) because
typical subjects of that reading are financial institutions, and typical objects are
assets. The two financial senses are distinguished by subject selectional re-
strictions in the verb generic knowledge. Typical subjects of sense (25c) are
governments or government officials, whereas typical subjects of sense (25d) are
individual persons, merchant roles, or financial institutions.

(26) "The U.S. charged Guatemala with interference."
(27) "The U.S. charged Guatemala with interest."
(28) "The bank charged Guatemala interest."

Synonymy

Precision of question-answering systems requires mechanisms for recognizing synonymy. Some systems for text retrieval address this through concept clustering. Sets of vocabulary words that are found in texts on similar topics are identified. These sets of synonyms are treated as though they were the same word in the retrieval task. However, this statistical method ignores word-sense differences. Returning to our verb *charge*, only sense (25b) is quasi-synonymous with *electrify, energize,* and *power up.* Only in sense (25a) is *charge* quasi-synonymous with *attack* and *set upon.* When query (29) is applied to textual data base (30), the relevance of (30) is recognizable only in relation to disambiguated *charge,* because only in that reading is it synonymous with *accuse.*

(29) "Who charged Guatemala with violations?"
(30) "The U.S. accused Guatemala of abrogations of human rights."

Anaphor Resolution

Pronouns, demonstratives, or definite noun phrases often need to be equated with some entity mentioned previously in the text. Texts with such anaphoric expressions are uninterpretable without anaphor resolution. In (31) the pronoun *they* must be correctly resolved before (32) can be answered.

(31) "Guatemala criticized the U.S., and they responded by cutting off aid."
(32) "What did the U.S. do to Guatemala?"

Pronouns refer to events as well as individuals. In (33), the antecedent of *it* is the event of dropping a bomb on the village. An algorithm must make this assignment despite the presence of three other potential antecedents in the sentence which match "it" in gender and number (Guatemala, bomb, village). The correct selection is required for answering the question in (34).

(33) "Guatemala dropped a bomb on the village. It shocked Latin America."
(34) "What shocked Latin America?"

Pronouns are important for series of queries. Otherwise the user is forced to repeat names and full NP's, which is experienced as awkward and redundant. This is illustrated in the query session in (35).

(35) "What did the President do yesterday?"
      —"He made an announcement."
      "Who is the ambassador to Guatemala?"
      —"White."

"Did he make the announcement with him?"
—"Yes."
"Where did he make it?"
—"On television."

For Interpretext we have built an anaphor resolution method that combines agreement criteria, syntactic and structural factors, and NS filters to resolve anaphors (Dahlgren, Lord & McDowell, 1990; Lord & Dahlgren, 1989). The input to the anaphor resolution algorithm is the DRS, as described in the Architecture section. The DRS directly and recursively exhibits which entities in the prior discourse are available as antecedents. The details of this formalism and the theory behind it are far beyond the scope of this chapter. Suffice it to say that the anaphor resolution module applies rules to narrow an incoming list of available antecedent using the factors previously listed until it converges on a best guess for the antecedent of an anaphor. The familiar agreement criteria are number, gender, and animacy. With naive semantics, the algorithm has knowledge that certain animals can corefer with *he, she,* or *it*. There are two syntactic tests. One makes sure that nonreflexive pronouns in most syntactic positions do not find their antecedent in the same clause. For example, in "The Guatemalans criticized them," the antecedent of *them* cannot be *Guatemalans*. The second syntactic test guarantees that if a pronoun is in the subject position, antecedents that are in subject positions are preferred. NS filters test antecedents for contextual plausibility. In (36), both the President and his colleague satisfy agreement tests for *he*.

(36)   "The Ambassador stopped to see the President, who was sitting at his desk. He rose and greeted him."

But NS knowledge of *sit* has an implicational feature that "what happens next" is typically to *rise* or *stand up*. Structure prefers the Ambassador over the President. However, naive semantic filters indicate that the President rose, after sitting, so President is selected as antecedent of *he*.

Relevance

Precision has eluded existing text-retrieval systems. They return from 35% to 80% irrelevant references (Blair & Maron, 1985). In the text-retrieval task, the objective is to find all and only those texts in a target data base or a stream of incoming messages that are *relevant* to a query. Existing key-word-based systems such as Verity and enhancement from Thinking Machines have achieved success in ordering a file of texts (or a series of messages) in a relevance ranking. A file of 100 texts is ranked from 1 to 100 for relevance to the query. In a process called *relevance feedback* the user selects one of the high-ranking texts as most relevant to the query, and the system processes entire text as though it were a query to order more accurately the remaining texts. The second ranked list tends to more accurately reflect the user's interests.

A full cognitive model makes possible a significant improvement in precision because it builds a more precise representation at each level of linguistic analysis. Interpretext is intended to process queries stated in English rather than key words, and to return the short, accurate list of all and only the articles that are relevant without a feedback step. Another interesting possibility would be to use the sophisticated and computation-heavy reasoning of Interpretext to select from a rank-ordered list produced by a key-word-based system. Returning to our state department official in the introduction, suppose the task is to match a profile that describes the official's domain of interest, as in (37).

(37) "I want to read about acts of terrorism in Latin America perpetrated either by governments or guerrillas, but not by armies."

Interpretext has the immediate advantage over competitors because it can read English queries or profiles. Thus, the relevance task becomes one of comparing two Prolog data bases, the query and the target texts or messages. There are three elements of relevance reasoning that Interpretext can handle in matching target texts to this query:

1. Concept Clustering;
2. Ontological Similarity; and
3. Topic Extraction.

Each of these is sketched in the following. In each case, the NS lexicon and cognitive model make possible very precise forms of relevance reasoning.

Concept Clustering

A number of systems have shown that valuable data structure in text retrieval algorithms is the concept cluster or synonymy group. Used alone, the concept cluster has the same problems of precision and recall as other key-word-based reasoning. However, it can be a valuable filter for higher-level relevance reasoning. Interpretext's Word-Sense Disambiguation module makes more precise because it factors out irrelevant word senses. Furthermore, NS representations yield concept clusters for free. Very often the associated concepts are mentioned in the NS generic information. For example, the words *borrow, credit, debt1* (the financial sense), *owe, bank2* (the financial sense), *debtor, loan1* (the financial sense), *principal2* (the financial sense), *lend, pay, service3* (the financial sense), and *deposit* all have the others as feature values in the NS generic lexicon. In particular, function features of nouns mention *loan* and *money;* "how" and "why" features of verbs mention *money, owe,* and *have.* Thus the "financial" concept cluster is fully represented without additional work or analysis, and simply falls out the cognitive approach to word meaning. Similarly, NS knowledge associated with proper names aids concept clustering. In Guatemala we find Latin America and Third World. Clearly, with such relationships encoded, the user does not need to provide Interpretext with list of Latin America terms, as in our introductory scenario.

Ontological Similarity

Ontological similarity refers to relationships in the ontology that makes near-nodes in the lower reaches of the ontology similar to each other. For example, the lower portion under the node "automobile" branches into a subtree with "sedan," "sports car," "four-wheel drive," and so on. Any of the nodes under "automobile" counts as ontologically similar to the others because they are sisters in the ontology. If a text-retrieval system user is interested in texts about automobiles, any of the words *sedan, sports car,* or *four-wheel drive* should count as in the domain of interest of the user. The Interpretext ontology permits the use of one of the ontologically similar words in the query, and all of the others will count equally well in determining the relevance of texts to the query. This is done automatically. The user need not recall all of the similar words of English to form a boolean expression mentioning all of the words that count as automobiles in the texts of interest.

Topic Extraction

In topic extraction, detailed and exhaustive linguistic analysis pays off. The cognitive model of the target text contains several types of information that are important indicators of topic: argument structure, discourse entities and events, and coherence relations. The topic of a text is the event that the text is about, at least for those genres of text that have a topic. We have analyzed a corpus of 20 newspaper articles, a novel, and a number of other texts for topic. The topic of segments of text is identifiable as the event that is most often referred to (i.e., the event for which the discourse entity symbol [e.g., e1] occurs most often). In the DRS, the anaphor resolution process identifies all instances of the same event with each other. For example, in (38) the words *charge, move,* and *it* all corefer to the event of U.N.'s charge.

> (38) "The U.N.'s charge came as a shock to the Guatemalan government. The move stunned the President. It causes a flurry of denials."

We have found that the event most often mentioned in any predicate in the cognitive model is the topic event. This is related to the fact that the cognitive model contains coherence relations that connect each of the clauses to some other clause. This assumption is consistent with some psychological studies that have tested the notion that text contains a causal chain in which the most salient event is that which is most related to all others in the text (Black & Bower, 1980; Graesser & Clark, 1985; Kintsch, 1988). Although a counting mechanism seems simplistic, it works because of the psychologically justified layers of analysis that produce the reference markers to be counted. Precisely because the theory and the program attempt to model human linguistic reasoning at all levels, the resulting representation easily performs the task of extracting the topic or gist.

SUMMARY AND CONCLUSIONS

In this chapter I have described a multilevel, deep natural language analysis approach to queries. I have shown that many of the ambiguities that plagued earlier approaches to natural language understanding can be overcome when a shallow layer of world knowledge is encoded and used in disambiguation algorithms. The power of an approach that incorporates the findings of modern linguistics and artificial intelligence was illustrated with examples from several of the levels of analysis. The approach appears to be feasible because it has been implemented as a computational system. All of the components of this analysis are presently prototyped and running in Prolog, with the exception of the temporal equations and the relevance reasoning for queries.

REFERENCES

Asher, N. (1987). A typology for attitude verbs and their anaphoric properties. *Linguistics and Philosophy, 10,* 125–198.

Barwise, J., & Perry, J. (1983). *Situations and attitudes.* Cambridge, MA: MIT Press.

Black, J. B. & Bower, G. H. (1980). Story understanding as problem-solving. *Poetics, 9,* 223–250.

Blair, D. D., & Maron, M. E. (1985). An evaluation of retrieval effectiveness for a full-text document retrieval system. *Communications of the Association of Computer Machinery, 28,* 289–299.

Boyd, R. (1986). Natural kinds, homeostasis and the limits of essentialism. Unpublished manuscript.

Brachman, R. J., & Schmolze, J. G. (1985). An overview of the KL-One knowledge representation system. *Cognitive Science, 9,* 171–216.

Dahlgren, K., & McDowell, J. P. (1986). Using commonsense knowledge to disambiguate prepositional phrase modifiers. *Proceedings American Associations of Artificial Intelligence.* pp. 589–593.

Dahlgren, K. (1985). The cognitive structure of social categories. *Cognitive Science, 9,* 379–398.

Dahlgren, K. (1987). Using commonsense knowledge to disambiguate word senses. In V. Dahl & P. Saint-Dizier (Eds.), *Natural language understanding and logic programming,* II. Amsterdam: North-Holland.

Dahlgren, K. (1988). *Naive semantics for natural language understanding.* Norwell, MA: Kluwer Academic Press.

Dahlgren, K. (1989). Coherence relation assignment. *Proceedings Cognitive Science Society* pp. 588–596.

Dahlgren, K., McDowell, J. P., & Stabler, E. P., Jr. (1989). Knowledge representation for commonsense reasoning with text. *Computational Linguistics, 15*, 149–170.

Dahlgren, K., Lord, C., & McDowell, J. P. (1990). *Lexical Knowledge for Accurate Anaphora Resolution*. Unpublished manuscript.

Fodor, J. (1987). Modules, frames, fridgeons, sleeping dogs, and the music of spheres. In J. Garfield, (Ed.), *Modularity in knowledge representation and natural language understanding* (pp. 1–15). Cambridge, MA: MIT Press.

Gentner, D. (1981). *Some interesting differences between nouns and verbs. Cognition and Brain Theory, 4*, 161–178.

Graesser, A., & Clark, L. (1985). *Structures and procedures of implicit knowledge*. Norwood, NJ: Ablex.

Johnson-Laird, P. N. (1983). *Mental models*. Cambridge, England: Cambridge University Press.

Kamp, H. (1981). *A theory of truth and semantic representation*. In J. Groenendijk, T. Janssen, & M. Stokhof (Eds.), *Formal methods in the study of language*. Mathematisch Centrum, Amsterdam.

Lord, C., & Dahlgren, K. (1989). *Tracking participants and events in newspaper articles*. Unpublished manuscript.

Morrow, D. G., Greenspan, S. L., & Bower, G. H. (1987). Accessibility and situation models in narrative comprehension. *J. Memory and Language, 26*, 165–187.

Partee, B. H. (1984). Nominal and temporal anaphora. *Linguistics and Philosophy, 7*, 243–286.

Rosch, E., & Mervis, C. (1975). Family resemblances. *Cognitive Psychology, 7*, 573–605.

Schank, R. (1982). Reminding and memory organization: An introduction to MOPs. In W. Lehnert & M. Ringle (Eds.), *Strategies for natural language processing* (pp. 120–156). Hillsdale, NJ: Lawrence Erlbaum Associates.

Shieber, S., van Noord, G., Moore, R., & Pereira, F. C. N. (1989). A semantic-head-driven generation algorithm for unification-based formalisms. *Proceedings Association of Computational Linguistics*. 7–17.

Streeter, L. (1990). Learning a lesson from the law of large numbers. *Proceedings American Association Artificial Intelligence Symposium on Text-Based Intelligent Systems*. 91–92.

11

WHEN: A Model for Answering "When" Questions About Future Events

Jonathan M. Golding
University of Kentucky

Joseph Magliano
Memphis State University

Darold Hemphill
Carnegie Mellon University

Information about the timing of future events is critical for the completion of goals in our daily lives. This temporal information spans different levels of grain size such as clock time, days of the week, and calendar dates. Without accurate bookkeeping of temporal information we would not be able to plan our schedules and to undertake these planned activities.

For example, suppose you needed to know the time of an important meeting so that you could arrange your schedule and attend the meeting. You could find out the meeting time by asking another person in the work setting. Alternatively, if meetings were posted in a computer system's bulletin board, you could query the computer system, perhaps in natural language: "When is the meeting on salary increases?" Whether you query a person or a computer, a good answer to the question should address the questioner's goals, and should supply information that facilitates some plan to achieve the goals (Allen, 1983; Francik & Clark, 1985; Kaplan, 1983). To illustrate the extent to which various answers to the previous question meet the criteria for a good answer, consider the following answers:

1. "At 8:00 P.M."
2. "In 42,898 seconds."
3. "Next Friday."
4. "In a week."
5. "On July 3."

6. "This year."
7. "This century."
8. "Soon."

All of these answers are technically correct. The answers, however, vary in specificity, informativeness, grain size, and relevance to the questioner's goals. Perhaps the best answer would be a combination of 1 and 3 ("Next Friday at 8:00 P.M.") or 1 and 5 ("On July 3 at 8:00 P.M."). Answer 2 would be accurate but too difficult for the questioner to decode (although easy for a computer to compute!). The grain size of Answers 4, 6, 7, and 8 are too coarse or too vague to be useful. Indeed, Answers 6, 7, and 8 would probably be construed as sarcastic or humorous.

How does the answerer select an appropriate reply to a "when" question among the bewildering array of options? The answer to this question is far from settled. Unlike other types of questions (e.g., "why," "how," and "where" questions), the procedures that generate answers to "when" questions about future events have not been studied extensively. We suspect that an adequate procedure for answering "when" questions would depend on pragmatics, that is, the communicative rules that are followed during a conversation and that foster a cooperative exchange of information between participants (Allen, 1983; Green, 1989; James, 1990; Kaplan, 1983; Keenan, MacWhinney, & Mayhew, 1977). The effect of pragmatics on question answering in general has been investigated and discussed in a number of studies (Allen, 1983; Clark, 1979; Clark, Schreuder, & Buttrick, 1983; Francik & Clark, 1985; Freyd, 1983; Isaacs & Clark, 1987; Kaplan, 1983; Miyake & Norman, 1979; Newman & Bruce, 1986; Norman, 1973; Shanon, 1983), but the effect of pragmatics on answering "when" questions has yet to be fully investigated.

The purpose of the present chapter is to present a model of answering "when" questions (called WHEN). This model sheds light on the procedures that individuals use when they answer "when" questions about future events. We propose that the same procedures could be used in the question-answer interface of a computerized information system.

PREVIOUS STUDIES OF "WHEN" QUESTIONS

There has been relatively little research on psychological processes that might explain how individuals answer "when" questions about future events. This is perhaps surprising given that (a) the issue of time has been of great interest to psychologists for a number of years (e.g., Fraisse, 1984; Michon & Jackson, 1986) and (b) answers to "when" questions have been collected in previous psychological studies. Previous research has generally been confined to the perception of time and memory for time duration (e.g., Fraisse, 1984; Michon, 1986). There are a few insights about the use of conventional time measurement devices (i.e., calendars and clock time) to express temporality (Ames, 1946; Harner & Nelson, 1989). For example, Fraser (1987) stated that time measurement devices allow humans to understand time beyond the biological horizons of the body.

Psychological studies that have asked "when" questions have used such questions in investigations of memory and of conceptual development in children. Those studies investigating the storage and retrieval of information in memory have examined how individuals extract temporal information when they attempt to remember past events (Baddeley, Lewis, & Nimmo-Smith, 1978; Brown, 1990; Brown, Rips, & Shevell, 1985; Ferguson & Martin, 1983; Friedman, 1987; Friedman & Wilkins, 1985; Huttenlocher, Hedges, & Bradburn, 1990; Linton, 1975; Thompson, 1982; Underwood, 1977). In a typical experiment, individuals are asked to remember the exact date and time of a historical event (e.g., "When was John F. Kennedy shot?") or a personal event ("When was your last visit to the lab?"). Developmental studies using "when" questions have investigated the understanding of relational terms, such as *before* and *after* (Cairns & Hsu, 1978; Clark, 1971; French, 1989). These studies present children with sequences of causal events and ask when a specific event occurred. The use of relational terms by the children reveal whether specific stages in development have been reached.

Researchers in cognitive science have recently developed models of question answering (Allen, 1983; Graesser & Clark, 1985; Graesser & Murachver, 1985; Lehnert, 1977, 1978; Lehnert, Dyer, Johnson, Young, & Harley, 1983). These models specify the knowledge structures that supply answers to questions, and the procedures that select appropriate answers from the knowledge structures. In Lehnert's models (QUALM, BORIS), "when" questions are classified as "Concept Completion" questions. These questions refer to a particular event and invite the answerer to fill in the time index slot that situates the event in time. For example, the question "When did John leave Paris?" (Lehnert, 1978, p. 70) refers to a particular event (i.e., John leaving Paris), and invites the listener to specify the time when the event occurred (e.g., on Tuesday). According to the computer models, answering this type of question involves searching script structures, planning structures, and causal chain representations for a value of the unknown time slot that is presumably stored directly in the structures. However, the procedures that generate inferred values of the time slot were not specified in Lehnert's models.

In Graesser's models (Graesser & Clark, 1985; Graesser & Murachver, 1985), the procedure for answering a "when" question in the context of a narrative passage frequently involves a comparison of the queried event with other queried events. That is, the target event is related to another event in the chronological sequence (i.e., the target event occurred *before, during,* or *after* another event).

Graesser's models also allow for time indices as answers (e.g., "In the afternoon."); these were essentially the same as Lehnert's concept completion answers.

In Allen's (1983) model of question answering, answers to "when" questions satisfy the questioner's goals. Answers may address the goal structure rather than, or in addition to, the information requested in the query. His computerized question-answering system answered questions about train schedules. An example question and answer is provided in the following:

> Customer: When does the train to Lexington leave?
> Computer: At 10:10 A.M., gate 7.

Note that the location information is provided in the answer even though it is not directly asked for. The computer recognized that the customer has two goals: getting to the correct location of the train and getting there on time. An answer formulated by the computer addresses both of these goals.

These initial attempts to model question answering have offered important insights about the generation of answers to "when" questions. However, current models have not completely explained how or why one correct answer is chosen over another correct answer. These models have not specified how the answerer formulates an answer at the appropriate grain size and level of accuracy, given the goals and situational context of the speech participants. The proposed model is an initial attempt to specify further the procedures that are used in answering "when" questions about future events. The WHEN model attempts to explain how the answers are expressed at the correct grain size and level of accuracy, but it does not directly explain how the goals and plans of the conversational participants affect the answers.

DATA COLLECTION

We collected some data to investigate the procedures that individuals use to answer "when" questions about future events. Specifically, we manipulated the temporal duration between the present point in time and the future-event point in time. This was done because we expected intuitively that temporal duration would have a radical impact on the generation of answers. For example, answering a "when" question about an event that is 1 day away from the present should lead to a different answer (e.g., "Tomorrow at 10:00 in the morning.") than a "when" question about the same event when it is 90 days away from the present (e.g., "July 3.").

We have conducted several experiments with college students using scenarios describing everyday situations. As seen in Table 11.1, each scenario included a present setting (PRESENT SETTING) and an event setting (EVENT SETTING). We

TABLE 11.1
Example Event Scenario

PRESENT SETTING

Location:	Hallway of the classroom building
Day of week:	Thursday
Date:	February 2, 1989
Time:	10.00 A.M.

EVENT SETTING

Event:	Research presentation
Location	Washington, D. C.
Day of week:	Thursday
Date:	February 9, 1989
Time:	11:00 A.M.

CIRCUMSTANCES and QUESTION:

Before class you tell your best friend that you are going to present your research findings at a session for undergraduates at the American Psychological Association convention. You are honored because this is not an opportunity afforded to many students. Your best friend asks, "When are you making this research presentation?"

---

varied the temporal duration between the PRESENT SETTING and the EVENT SETTING. In addition, each scenario included (a) a description of the circumstances surrounding the asking of a "when" question (CIRCUMSTANCES) and (b) the "when" question itself (QUESTION).

In one experiment, college students read scenarios in which the temporal duration could be described as relatively "regular." In other words, the duration between the PRESENT SETTING and the EVENT SETTING could be described by a frequently used linguistic expression (i.e., temporal durations of 1 day, 1 week, 1 month, and 3 months). When an EVENT SETTING was either 1 day or 7 days from the PRESENT SETTING, it always occurred within the same month as the PRESENT SETTING. In a second experiment, temporal durations were relatively "irregular." That is, the duration between the PRESENT SETTING and the EVENT SETTING could not be described by a frequently used linguistic expression (i.e., temporal durations of 4 days, 11 days, 17 days, and 43 days). When an EVENT SETTING was 4 days, 11 days, or 17 days from the PRESENT SETTING, it always occurred within the same month as the PRESENT SETTING. In a third experiment, the scenarios included both regular and irregular temporal durations (i.e., temporal durations of 1 day, 4 days, and 17 days), but each EVENT SETTING was always in the month following the month containing the PRESENT SETTING. It should be noted that in none of the experiments did the PRESENT SETTING or EVENT SETTING coincide with a holiday (e.g., Christmas, Thanksgiving).

In all three experiments subjects were presented the scenarios in a booklet and were asked to read the PRESENT SETTING, EVENT SETTING, CIRCUMSTANCES, and QUESTION. After reading, they were required to write down an answer to the "when" question. They were explicitly instructed to generate an answer that they would produce in "real life."

The question-answering protocols collected from the college students were used to determine how often an answer included particular pieces of information. First, the protocols were scored for the mention of the date (*July 3*) or the day of the week (*Wednesday*). Second, we scored how often the words *day, week,* or *month* were generated. Third, we scored how often words such as *this, next, few,* or *about* were mentioned. Fourth, we scored the protocols for occurrences of any number word (e.g., *one, three*). Finally, we observed whether the protocols mentioned the exact time of day (e.g., *10:00*).

THE WHEN MODEL

The experiments revealed that the answers to "when" questions were neither uniform (i.e., the same answer being generated regardless of temporal duration) nor random, but varied systematically as a function of temporal duration. Based on these results, the proposed WHEN model was developed to account for the effect of temporal duration on the generation of these answers. As seen in Fig. 11.1, the model has various stages. Each of these stages is guided by production rules (Anderson, 1983), which will be presented later. Each of the stages is

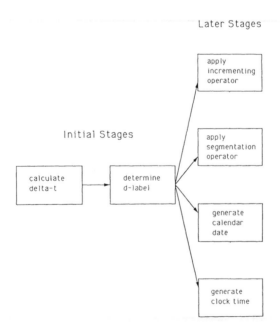

FIG. 11.1. The stages of the WHEN model.

discussed in detail, explaining how the productions operate to generate the observed answers, and how the productions could operate in contexts other than those investigated in the present experiments. The initial stages of generating an answer occur in a set order: (a) calculating δ-t and (b) determining a temporal duration label (d-label). The later stages of answer generation occur in parallel. These stages include the application of incrementing operators to the d-label, the application of a segmentation operator, the generation of calendar date, and the generation of the clock time.

The Initial Stages

Calculating Delta-t.   The first step in the generation of an answer involves the computation of the temporal duration (δ-t) between the PRESENT SETTING and the EVENT SETTING. That is, the individual must determine the time that will elapse before the EVENT SETTING is to occur (see also Huttenlocher et al., 1990).

Delta-t is expressed in terms of a specific temporal primitive that is appropriate for the context of the scenario. Alternative primitives are *millisecond, second, day, year, month,* and *century.* The temporal primitive that is used to express δ-t depends on the context in which the "when" question is asked. For example, in the present experiments the "when" questions were asked in the context of specific events occurring within the yearly calendar. The use of the calendar in this context makes the temporal primitive of *day* most appropriate. Therefore, in this chapter the primitive for δ-t is the *day* unit. The production rule that is applied to calculate δ-t is presented in the following:

IF [δ-t unknown] THEN [δ-t = EVENT SETTING (in days) − PRESENT SETTING (in days)]

Other contexts involving "when" questions, however, would require different temporal primitives. For example, a "when" question in the context of discussing upcoming presidential elections (e.g., "When will the Democrats have their next chance to recapture the White House?") would probably involve *year* as the temporal primitive. "When" questions in the context of future civilizations would adopt *century* as the temporal primitive. At the other end of the spectrum, "when" questions in the context of electronic devices would use the temporal primitive of *nanosecond.*

There are two important points to note about determining δ-t. First, it is critical that the temporal primitive for δ-t matches for the questioner and answerer. One can only imagine the difficulty in communicating if the temporal primitive between the conversational participants was different. For example, the question "When is the meeting on salary increases?" usually leads to an answer that adopts the temporal primitive of *day* for the questioner. However, if the answerer (e.g., a computer) has adopted the temporal primitive of *minute* and responds *in 4,690 minutes,* there will be a communication breakdown.

Second, the ability to calculate δ-t depends on successful time orientation (Koriat & Fischoff, 1974; Shanon, 1979). An answer to a "when" question requires awareness that the question is being asked at a certain point in time (i.e., the PRESENT SETTING), awareness that the EVENT SETTING will occur at another point in time, and accuracy in computing the time points. In the present experiments, the issue of time orientation was not a major concern because subjects were supplied with both the correct PRESENT SETTING and the correct EVENT SETTING. In other contexts, however, the matter of time orientation might be problematic. For example, if you were asked a "when" question but did not have your datebook to verify the EVENT SETTING, you might not calculate δ-t accurately.

Determining a Temporal Duration Label (d-label).   The experiments revealed that answers to "when" questions do not simply involve expressing the δ-t value (e.g., *in 17 days*). Instead, the answers were discussed in terms of well-established labels (i.e., d-labels) that designate a specific temporal duration. In the present scenarios, the alternative d-labels were *day, week,* and *month.* The determination of a d-label involves the following production rules:

IF [δ-t ≤ 7 days] THEN [d-label = day]
IF [3 days ≤ δ-t ≤ 29 days] THEN [d-label = week]
IF [15 days ≤ δ-t ≤ 90 days] THEN [d-label = month]

Note that values of δ-t can be included in one of two of the preceding production rules, so the above rules allow for alternative answers. For example, if δ-t = 17, an answer could be *in a few weeks* (d-label = week) or *this month* (d-label = month).

The Later Stages

Applying Incrementing Operators to the d-label.   Once a d-label is determined, an individual can apply incrementing operators to the d-label to specify further time duration. The increment can involve either of two types of scales: interval or ordinal. Interval operators apply numbers on a number scale: 1, 2, 3, 5, 10, and so on. These interval operators are typically used when the value of δ-t is an even multiple of the d-label, such as 1 week (δ-t = 7), 2 weeks (δ-t = 14), or 4 weeks (δ-t = 28). It should be noted that the value *1* is sometimes expressed as *a* (e.g., *a week* = *1 week*). The application of interval operators involves the following production rule:

IF [δ-t = integer (N) * d-label value]
THEN [answer = N + d-label]

This production rule would generate the following expressions:

in 2 days (δ-t = 2)
in 3 days (δ-t = 3)
in 1 week (δ-t = 7)
in a week (δ-t = 7)
in 3 weeks (δ-t = 21)
in 2 months (δ-t = 60)

The second type of operator is called an *ordinal operator* because these values are on an ordinal scale. The values of these operators include *this, next, several,* and *in a few*. These operators are used under the same conditions as interval operators, except that values are not evenly spaced and are more qualitative. Ordinal operators are frequently used when δ-t is not equal to the number of days associated with either the d-label or a multiple of the d-label. The following production rules are applied when ordinal operators are used:

> IF [δ-t < 1 * d-label value]
>> THEN [answer = *this* + d-label]
> IF [1 * d-label value < δ-t < 2 * d-label value]
>> THEN [answer = *next* + d-label]
> IF [δ-t > 2 * d-label value]
>> THEN [answer = {*several* or *in a few*} + d-label]

Example expressions generated by the preceding production rules are presented in the following:

this week (δ-t = 4)
next week (δ-t = 11)
in several days (δ-t = 5)
in a few weeks (δ-t = 20)
next month (δ-t = 41)

The use of both the interval and ordinal incrementing operators has two important exceptions involving special linguistic terms in the English language. First, when δ-t = 0, individuals use *day* as their d-label and express this with the answer *today*. Second, when δ-t = 1, individuals use *day* as their d-label and express this with the answer *tomorrow*. These exceptions can be expressed using the following production rules:

> IF [*this day* is generated] THEN [*this day* = *today*]
> IF [*next day* is generated] THEN [*next day* = *tomorrow*]

Applying Segmentation Operators.   One of the useful aspects of the calendar is that it is hierarchically organized. This type of organization allows for the segmentation of the year into various units that are generally perceived as approximately equivalent. The year unit is superordinate to the 12 months of the year; each of the 12 months is superordinate to the 4 weeks of the month; each week is superordinate to the 7 days of the week. Our knowledge of certain aspects of this hierarchical structure appear to be extremely well-established, having been learned in elementary school. In fact, Harner and Nelson (1989) have found that 89% of second graders knew all the days of the week and 70% knew all the months of the year.

The individuals in our study were found to make extensive use of segmentation operators when they generated answers to "when" questions. For example, a δ-t of 11 is not a multiple of a week incrementer (e.g., 7, 14, 21, etc.), so an appropriate expression might be *next week on Friday*. In this case, *week* is the d-label, *next* is a product of the ordinal incrementing operator, and *on Friday* is the product of the segmentation operator. The type of segmentation observed most often in the current set of protocols was that of categorical segmentation (i.e., segmenting the week into categories of Sunday, Monday, Tuesday, etc.). This was especially evident when δ-t was less than or equal to 14 days. Instead of generating an answer that specified the exact calendar date (e.g., *on July 3*) or using an interval operator to note how many days away the EVENT SETTING was from the PRESENT SETTING (e.g., *in 11 days*), subjects generated answers that specified the day of the week using the following production rule:

IF [2 days < δ-t < 14 days]
    THEN [embellish answer with *on* + {Monday, Tuesday, . . .}]

For example, the following expressions would be generated for the scenario in Table 11.1 when both the incrementing operator and the segmentation operator are applied to different values of δ-t:

this week on Friday (δ-t = 4)
next week on Friday (δ-t = 11)

Some of the words in the preceding expressions may be deleted elliptically. In the first expression, the word *this* may be deleted. The words *week on* are frequently deleted in both expressions as shown in the following:

Friday (δ-t = 4)
next Friday (δ-t = 11)

Categorical segmentation could include other means of segmentation. These would depend on the d-label and the context in which the when-question was asked. For example, a month could be segmented into the specific week of the month (e.g., *the third week of this month*). In addition, when the d-label is *year*, segmentation could involve either the 12 months of the year or the 4 seasons of the year (e.g., *in May, in winter*).

Segmentation may have values on an ordinal scale rather than a categorical scale. Ordinal segmentation was not found very often in the present protocols, but it is sometimes appropriate, especially when there is no categorical scale. For example, ordinal segmentation operators may generate answers that indicate the beginning, middle, and end of the work week. Some production rules that produce these answers are shown in the following:

> IF [EVENT SETTING = Monday or Tuesday]
> THEN [answer = *beginning of the week*]
> IF [EVENT SETTING = Wednesday]
> THEN [answer = *middle of the week*]
> IF [EVENT SETTING = Thursday or Friday]
> THEN [answer = *end of the week*]

The Use of Calendar Dates. Calendar dates (e.g., *July 3*) express very specific information and might be the most efficient answer to a "when" question about a future event. However, the results from our experiments revealed that the use of calendar dates varies systematically as a function of δ-t. Specifically, the probability of generating a calendar date increases as a function of δ-t. In fact, the probability increases dramatically when δ-t exceeds 14 days.

Within the 14-day limit, an answer normally includes the d-label, with applications of the incrementing and segmentation operators. However, after 14 days, these same production rules generate lengthy expressions that would be difficult for the comprehender to encode (e.g., *the second week of next month on Thursday*). When the generated expression begins to be cumbersome, the answerer resorts to producing calendar dates because there are fewer words in the answer and the answers are precise. This result suggests that the answerer is guided by one of Grice's conversational maxims (Grice, 1975), namely that of manner (i.e., an individual should be clear and should try to avoid obscurity and wordiness). Beyond the 14-day point, calendar dates were generally provided if the δ-t was not equal to or a multiple of a value typically associated with a d-label. Thus, if an EVENT SETTING was 30 days from the PRESENT SETTING (δ-t = 30), subjects were most likely to respond *"in a month."* If δ-t was 43, however, the calendar date was generated (e.g., *July 3*). Therefore, the following production rule is applied in such cases:

> IF [δ-t > 14 days and δ-t ≠
> Integer (N) * d-label]
> THEN [answer = calendar date]

Calendar dates may also serve another important function with regard to answering "when" questions about future events, although this function was not explicitly tested in the present experiments. A calendar date can sometimes be designated as a "landmark calendar date" or a "critical date" (Fraisse, 1963). These landmark calendar dates include any date for which there is an event that holds personal or common interest. An example of the former is one's birthday, an example of the latter is a holiday (e.g., Christmas). Landmark calendar dates are probably not generated as answers to questions; the event that occurs on that calendar date is generated instead. This is also probably the result of the conversational postulate of manner (Grice, 1975). For example, if asked a "when" question about an event on December 25, an answer would probably be "Christmas" instead of "on December 25." Therefore, landmarks are relatively salient and accessible from memory, and have precedence over calendar dates.

Indicating the Exact Clock Time.   Based on the results of our study, the probability that individuals generate the exact clock time (e.g., 11:00 A.M.) associated with the upcoming event is a function of δ-t. Specifically, as δ-t increases past 3 days, there is a dramatic decrease in the probability of the exact clock time being generated. It appears that individuals are not willing to provide the "excess baggage" of exact clock time when discussing events that are relatively far in the future. Therefore, individuals follow the Gricean conversational maxim of quantity (i.e., make your contribution as informative as is required, but not more informative than is required). Conversely, when events are close in time to the PRESENT SETTING (i.e., they have a relatively small δ-t), providing the exact clock time helps the questioner fulfill his or her goal of establishing an hour-by-hour schedule during the subsequent few days. Of course, providing clock time would be useful in all cases if the questioner had his or her calendar physically available.

Note that the exact clock time was not generated as an answer to a "when" question by itself. It was always generated as part of the answer (e.g., *"tomorrow at 11:00 A.M."*). Clock time would be more relevant when the grain size is smaller (e.g., hours instead of days). For example, if asked "When is the meeting today?" an answer would include only the clock time. The following is the production rule for generating an answer that includes the exact clock time:

IF [δ-t < 3 days]
THEN [embellish answer with clock time]

SUMMARY AND CONCLUSION

The WHEN model for answering "when" questions about future events assumes that the generation of answers to such questions is neither a simple task, nor a random one. Individuals do not merely generate a uniform answer (e.g., a calendar date) to every "when" question, nor do they generate an answer at random from the population of possible answers to these questions. Instead, individuals' answers were sensitive to temporal duration. In the present experiments, temporal duration was manipulated by presenting the EVENT SETTING at different temporal durations from the PRESENT SETTING. Subjects used the temporal durations to decide which of many possible answers would be generated as responses to the "when" questions.

WHEN is an advance over previous models of question answering that have dealt with "when" questions. By focusing on how individuals generate different answers to "when" questions as a function of temporal duration, WHEN presents a more detailed specification of concept completion than have previous models of question answering (Allen, 1983; Graesser & Clark, 1985; Graesser & Murachver, 1985; Lehnert, 1977, 1978; Lehnert et al., 1983).

In addition to uncovering some of the procedures that are used in generating answers to "when" questions, the experimental studies have important methodological implications. The results indicate that college students are able to construct cognitively scenarios in a naturalistic context and formulate natural answers to "when" questions. That is, they are able to put themselves in the hypothetical role of a conversational participant and to answer the "when" question based on their knowledge of the temporal duration between the PRESENT SETTING and the EVENT SETTING. It is hoped that this methodology can be used as effectively in future studies.

The WHEN model could be expanded (through additional research) and then applied to information systems as the basis for a question-answer interface. The computerized natural language generation system would be set up, using the WHEN production rules, to generate appropriate answers to queries. There are at least four examples of such applications to the domain of information systems. First, as discussed earlier, an individual would be able to query the system about specific events that were to occur in the future by asking a "when" question on his or her computer. Thus, the WHEN model would provide a natural method for managing and planning schedules around events that had definite time frames.

Second, the question-answer interface could be used in situations in which scheduling involved multiple agents. In such a situation, the agents must work together to find a time in which all agents are free to meet. This would probably be a mixed initiative system in which the system would sometimes query the user. For example, the system might ask "When can you meet next for the committee meeting?" The system would need to be able to handle various responses (e.g., "next week," "Any Monday or Wednesday afternoon") from the users. In addition, the system would have to produce answers that were meaningful. This last requirement would probably involve the system having to gradually decrease the grain size of the answers as the schedule is negotiated among the committee members.

A third possible application of the WHEN model would be to a manufacturing context. A flexible manufacturing system requires efficient scheduling of material, equipment, and personnel so that production or profit can be maximized (see Barr, Cohen, & Feigenbaum, 1989). The WHEN model could be integrated into such a system to help with scheduling. For example, it may be critical to know when production is finished on one part of a product so that the plant may be readied to begin production on the next part; new material might have to be purchased, equipment readied, and personnel reassigned to prepare for the production of the second part.

Finally, the use of a question-answer interface could be used in expert systems that require time-dependent information, such as an auditing expert system (see Messier & Hansen, 1987). Such a system requires temporal information in the context of (a) regular intervals ("When are employees paid?"); (b) irregular intervals ("When do employees take vacations?"); and (c) events triggered by other events ("When are bills paid?").

The preceding four examples of applications of the WHEN model indicate the powerful potential of this model with regard to information systems. Additional research will be needed to specify further the production rules that drive the WHEN model. Further research may also suggest other applications of this model. In sum, the WHEN model is a promising one, in both its potential for helping us to understand the procedures used to answer "when" questions about future events and in its application to information systems.

REFERENCES

Allen, J. F. (1983). Recognizing intentions from natural language utterances. In M. Brady & R. C. Berwick (Eds.), *Computational models of discourse* (pp. 107–166). Cambridge, MA: MIT Press.

Ames, L. B. (1946). The development of the sense of time in the young child. *Journal of Genetic Psychology, 68,* 97–125.

Anderson, J. R. (1983). *The architecture of cognition.* Cambridge, MA: Harvard University Press.

Baddeley, A. D., Lewis, V., & Nimmo-Smith, I. (1978). When did you last . . . ? In M. M. Gruneberg & R. N. Sykes (Eds.), *Practical aspects of memory* (pp. 77–83). London: Academic Press.

Barr, A., Cohen, P. R., & Feigenbaum, E. A. (1989). *The handbook of artificial intelligence* (vol. 4). New York: Addison-Wesley.

Brown, N. R. (1990). Organization of public events in long-term memory. *Journal of Experimental Psychology: General, 119,* 297–314.

Brown, N. R., Rips, L. J., & Shevell, S. K. (1985). The subjective dates of natural events in very-long-term memory. *Cognitive Psychology, 17,* 139–177.

Cairns, H. S., & Hsu, J. R. (1978). Who, why, when, and how: A developmental study. *Journal of Child Language, 5,* 477–488.

Clark, E. V. (1971). On the acquisition of the meaning of *before* and *after. Journal of Verbal Learning and Verbal Behavior, 10,* 266–275.

Clark, H. H. (1979). Responding to indirect speech acts. *Cognitive Psychology, 11,* 430–477.

Clark, H. H., Schreuder, R., & Buttrick, S. (1983). Common ground and the understanding of demonstrative reference. *Journal of Verbal Learning and Verbal Behavior, 22,* 245–258.

Ferguson, R. P., & Martin, P. (1983). Long-term temporal estimation in humans. *Perception and Psychophysics, 33,* 585–592.

Fraisse, P. (1963). *The psychology of time*. New York: Harper & Row.

Fraisse, P. (1984). Perception and the estimation of time. In M. R. Rosenzweig & L. W. Porter (Eds.), *Annual review of psychology* (vol. 35, pp. 1–36). Palo Alto, CA: Annual Reviews.

Francik, E. P., & Clark, H. H. (1985). How to make requests that overcome obstacles to compliance. *Journal of Memory and Language, 24*, 560–568.

Fraser, J. T. (1987). *Time the familiar stranger*. Amherst, MA: University of Massachusetts Press.

French, L. A. (1989). Young children's responses to "when" questions: Issues of directionality. *Child Development, 60*, 225–236.

Freyd, J. J. (1983). Shareability: The social psychology of epistomology. *Cognitive Science, 7*, 191–210.

Friedman, W. J. (1987). A follow-up to "Scale effects in memory for the time of events": The earthquake study. *Memory and Cognition, 15*, 518–520.

Friedman, W. J., & Wilkins, A. (1985). Scale effects in memory for the time of events. *Memory and Cognition, 13*, 168–175.

Graesser, A. C., & Clark, L. F. (1985). *Structures and procedures of implicit knowledge*. Norwood, NJ: Ablex.

Graesser, A. C., & Murachver, T. (1985). Symbolic procedures of question answering. In A. C. Graesser & J. B. Black (Eds.), *The psychology of questions* (pp. 15–88). Hillsdale, NJ: Lawrence Erlbaum Associates.

Green, G. M. (1989). *Pragmatics and natural language understanding*. Hillsdale, NJ: Lawrence Erlbaum Associates.

Grice, H. P. (1975). Logic and conversation. In P. Cole & J. Morgan (Eds.), *Syntax and semantics* (vol. 3, pp. 41–58). New York: Academic Press.

Harner, L., & Nelson, K. (1989, July). *Conventional time knowledge in early childhood*. Presented at the Annual Meeting of the American Psychological Society, Arlington, VA.

Huttenlocher, J., Hedges, L. V., & Bradburn, N. M. (1990). Reports of elapsed time: Bounding and rounding processes in estimation. *Journal of Experimental Psychology: Learning, Memory, & Cognition, 16*, 196–213.

Isaacs, E. A., & Clark, H. H. (1987). Reference in conversation between experts and novices. *Journal of Experimental Psychology: General, 116*, 26–37.

James, S. L. (1990). *Normal language acquisition*. Boston: College Hill.

Kaplan, S. J. (1983). Cooperative responses from a portable natural language data base query system. In M. Brady & R. C. Berwick (Eds.), *Computational models of discourse* (pp. 167–208). Cambridge, MA: MIT Press.

Keenan, J. M., MacWhinney, B., & Mayhew, D. (1977). Pragmatics in memory: A study of natural conversation. *Journal of Verbal Learning and Verbal Behavior, 16*, 549–560.

Koriat, A., & Fischoff, B. (1974). What day is today? An inquiry into the process of time orientation. *Memory and Cognition, 2*, 201–205.

Lehnert, W. G. (1977). Human and computational question answering. *Cognitive Science, 1*, 47–73.

Lehnert, W. G. (1978). *The process of question answering*. Hillsdale, NJ: Lawrence Erlbaum Associates.

Lehnert, W. G., Dyer, M. G., Johnson, P. N., Young, C. J., & Harley, S. (1983). BORIS—An experiment in in-depth understanding of narratives. *Artificial Intelligence, 20*, 15–62.

Linton, M. (1975). Memory for real world events. In D. A. Norman & D. E. Rumelhart (Eds.), *Explorations in cognition* (pp. 376–404). San Francisco: W. H. Freeman.

Messier, W. F., & Hansen, J. V. (1987). Expert systems in auditing: The state of the art. *Auditing: A Journal of Practice & Theory, 7*, 94–105.

Michon, J. A. (1986). The compleat time experiencer. In J. A. Michon & J. L. Jackson (Eds.), *Time, mind, and behavior* (pp. 20–52). New York: Springer-Verlag.

Michon, J. A., & Jackson, J. L. (1986). *Time, mind, and behavior*. New York: Springer-Verlag.

Miyake, N., & Norman, D. A. (1979). To ask a question, one must know enough to know what is not known. *Journal of Verbal Learning and Verbal Behavior, 18,* 357–364.

Newman, D., & Bruce, B. (1986). Interpretation and manipulation in human plans. *Discourse Processes, 9,* 167–195.

Norman, D. (1973). Memory, knowledge and the answering of questions. In R. Solso (Ed.), *Contemporary issues in cognitive psychology* (pp. 135–165). Washington, DC: Winston.

Shanon, B. (1979). Yesterday, today and tomorrow. *Acta Psychologica, 43,* 469–476.

Shannon, B. (1983). Answers to where-questions. *Discourse Processes, 6,* 319–352.

Thompson, C. P. (1982). Memory for unique personal events: The roommate study. *Memory and Cognition, 10,* 324–332.

Underwood, B. J. (1977). *Temporal codes for memories: Issues and problems.* Hillsdale, NJ: Lawrence Erlbaum Associates.

12 Answering Questions About Information in Databases

Arthur C. Graesser
Paul J. Byrne
Michael L. Behrens
Memphis State University

When individuals answer questions, they tap multiple sources of information that embody world knowledge. We assume that each information source is a structured database containing content *nodes* that are connected by relational *arcs*. Structured databases are incorporated in various types of information systems, such as intelligent tutoring systems, expert systems, and decision support systems. We also assume that there are a variety of question-answering strategies that produce good answers by accessing particular information sources and systematically selecting nodes within each information source. A psychological theory of question answering would (at minimum) document the question-answering strategies that are associated with different categories of questions.

Consider a scenario in which an experienced computer user is teaching a novice how to use a computer system. Suppose that the novice asks the following question: "Why do you save your program every 15 minutes?" One strategy of answering this question consists of a logical trace of facts and rules that justifies the action of saving the program. This strategy is precisely the one that many rule-based expert systems execute when "why" questions are answered (Buchanan & Shortliffe, 1984). This logic-based strategy could produce Answer 1 as follows.

Answer 1. There is some likelihood that the computer will crash (1). The amount of wasted programming work should be minimized (2). If the computer system crashes, you will lose all work since the last time you saved the program (3). If you save your program frequently, you will minimize the amount of wasted programming work (4). Therefore, you should save your program frequently (5).

The conclusion sentence (5) is derived logically from the facts (Sentences 1 and 2) and rules (Sentences 3 and 4).

Unfortunately, a logical trace of generic facts and rules does not provide a good answer to a "why" question (Lang, Graesser, & Hemphill, 1990; Schank, 1986; Young, 1989). A logical trace can provide useful information for other types of tasks, such as debugging program logic. However, it does not provide a coherent explanation of why computer work needs to be saved frequently. A more satisfying explanation would provide information about the programmer's goal structure and planning (Baudet & Denhiere, 1989; Clancey, 1982; Ram, 1990), as illustrated in Answer 2.

> *Answer 2*. A program needs to be saved in order to store the most recent version of your program in permanent memory. It needs to be stored frequently in order to minimize losing your work if the computer crashes.

Answers 1 and 2 are products of question-answering strategies that access general facts, rules, and goal structures. Instead of accessing general knowledge, some question-answering strategies access particular cases stored in memory. This case-based strategy is illustrated in Answer 3.

> *Answer 3*. One day two years ago I spent eight hours working on a program that sorts addresses on a mailing list. Then the computer crashed because of a power failure. All eight hours of my work were wasted—I was so angry. I decided at that point that I would never face that again. Now I save my program every 15 minutes.

One way of justifying an action is to tell a story that illustrates the virtues of performing the action (Dyer, 1983; Schank, 1986). For example, action A is justified if such an action previously solved a problem, circumvented a bottleneck, or prevented an unfortunate event. Cases have a high likelihood of being stored in memory if they present interesting dilemmas, novel solutions, and challenging problems (Hammond, 1986; Kolodner, 1984; Schank, 1986). The answerer is reminded of these specific cases when the person justifies why an action is performed in a new situation.

There is yet another strategy of justifying why an action is performed. This additional strategy simply identifies an expert who recommended the action, as illustrated in Answer 4.

> *Answer 4*. When my computer instructor taught me how to use the computer, he told me to save the program every 15 minutes.

The expert could be a knowledgeable person, a book, a manual, an institution, or some other highly regarded source of knowledge.

The preceding question and answers illustrate the diverse information sources and question-answering strategies that may operate when a person answers a "why" question. As cognitive scientists, our goal is to specify the knowledge structures that are activated and cognitive procedures that are executed when people answer various categories of questions. We are entirely convinced that a psychological theory of question answering would be highly beneficial to designers of query-based interfaces for information systems. That is, computers should formulate human-like answers in expert systems, decision support systems, and intelligent tutoring systems. The expert system enterprise might have benefitted greatly if knowledge engineers had known that the logic-based answers to "why" questions (e.g., Answer 1) were comparatively unnatural for the human mind. Had there been a psychological theory of question answering 10 years ago, the question-answering facilities of modern information systems might not have been so inept.

The adequacy of a question-answering (Q/A) system can be evaluated on a number of dimensions. The Q/A system should have a high *hit rate*. That is, the answer should include most, if not all, of the information in the database that is relevant to the question. The Q/A system should have a low incidence of *false alarms* (i.e., irrelevant answers) and *errors* (i.e., incorrect answers). Sometimes several answers are produced in response to a question, that is, a cogent explanation in answer to a "why" question. A complex response should be *coherent* in the sense that the ideas hang together conceptually. A Q/A system should minimize the *response time* to answer a question. It is very difficult to design a Q/A system that satisfies all of these criteria.

The format of the database is a critical consideration in the design of Q/A systems (see Lang, Graesser, Dumais, & Kilman, chap. 8 this volume). Unstructured text is the easiest database format to implement because it is simply a copy of the information content under consideration (e.g., a copy of an encyclopedia article). Unfortunately, it is extremely difficult (if not impossible) to access relevant information and to compose cogent answers to most questions when the database is unstructured. For this reason, unstructured databases are essentially never used in intelligent tutoring systems, expert systems, and intelligent decision support systems. At the other end of the continuum, structured databases impose organization on the information. That is, the information is segmented into theoretical units (e.g., words, propositions, statements, rules), sets of units are grouped into "packages" of information (i.e., higher order units), and units are connected by relations. It is possible to access relevant information and to formulate coherent answers when the database is structured. However, substantial effort must be devoted to organizing the knowledge in a special way that makes it easy to retrieve during question answering.

This chapter presents highlights of a model of human question answering, named QUEST. QUEST simulates the psychological processes and answers of adults when they answer questions. QUEST handles many question categories, but the major focus has been on *open-class* questions, such as "why," "how," "when," "where," and "what-if" questions. Open-class questions invite replies with elaborate verbal descriptions, such as Answers 1–4 shown earlier. In contrast, appropriate answers to *closed-class* questions are restricted to a limited number of alternatives that are usually short. For example, answers to verification questions are "yes," "no," "maybe," and "I don't know."

Previous studies have tested whether QUEST (and its predecessor models) can account for answers that adults give to open-class questions. In a typical study, adults first read a passage and then answer a series of open-class questions. Alternatively, questions are answered in the context of a generic concept (e.g., kitchen, computer). These studies have evaluated whether the answers produced by QUEST are the same as the answers produced by adult subjects. That is, there should be a high overlap between (a) QUEST's distribution of answers to a particular question and (b) the distribution of answers generated by people. We gain more confidence in QUEST to the extent that this overlap approaches 100%. QUEST has been tested in the context of narrative passages (Golding, Graesser, & Millis, 1990; Graesser & Clark, 1985; Graesser, Lang, & Roberts, 1991; Graesser & Murachver, 1985; Graesser, Robertson, & Anderson, 1981; Graesser, Robertson, Lovelace, & Swinehart, 1980), expository texts on scientific mechanisms (Graesser & Hemphill, 1991; Graesser, Hemphill, & Brainerd, 1989), scripts and other generic concepts (Graesser, 1978; Graesser & Clark, 1985), and everyday social interactions (Graesser, Roberts, & Hackett-Renner, 1990). Therefore, QUEST holds some promise in accounting for empirical data.

This chapter summarizes the components of QUEST rather than providing an exhaustive account of the technical details and empirical evidence. We refer to previous reports for a more complete description of QUEST (Graesser, 1990; Graesser & Franklin, 1990; Graesser, Gordon, & Brainerd, in press; Graesser, Lang, & Roberts, 1991) and for coverage of the empirical support (Graesser, 1990; see Graesser references).

OVERVIEW OF THE QUEST MODEL
OF HUMAN QUESTION ANSWERING

It is convenient to segregate QUEST into four major components (see Fig. 12.1). The first component translates the question into a logical form and assigns it to one of several question categories. The second identifies the information sources that are relevant to the question. The information sources are represented as conceptual graph structures that contain goal/plan hierarchies, causal networks, taxonomic hierarchies, and descriptive structures. In the third component, convergence mechanisms compute the subset of nodes within each information source that serves as relevant answers to the particular question. The fourth component considers pragmatic features of the communicative interaction, such as the goals and the common ground of the speech participants. Although we

COMPONENTS OF QUEST

INTERPRETING THE QUESTION
Parsing the question into a logical form
Identifying the appropriate question category

INFORMATION SOURCES
Episodic knowledge structures (text experience)
Generic knowledge structures (concepts, scripts, frames, etc.)
Knowledge represented as conceptual graph structures

CONVERGENCE MECHANISMS
Intersection of nodes from different information sources
  (plus structural distance)
Arc search procedures
Structural distance gradient
Constraint satisfaction

PRAGMATICS
Goals of questioner and answerer
Common ground
Informativity of answer

FIG. 12.1. Components of the QUEST model of human question answering.

segregate question answering into these four components, we acknowledge that an adequate model of question answering would integrate these components in a highly interactive fashion (Dyer, 1983; Lehnert, Dyer, Johnson, Young, & Harley, 1983; Robertson, Black, & Lehnert, 1985).

QUEST was not developed to account for the linguistic features of question answering. QUEST does not explain the process of parsing the question syntactically and the process of articulating replies linguistically. Instead, QUEST was developed to account for the conceptual content of answers.

We should acknowledge some of the models and research that assisted us in developing the QUEST model. Cognitive psychologists have investigated the process of answering closed-class questions at considerable depth (Glucksberg & McCloskey, 1981; Reder, 1987; Singer, 1986, 1990). Some of the mechanisms that are part of answering closed-class questions are also relevant to the answering of open-class questions. Progress in investigating the answering of open-class questions has been comparatively slow in psychology, but there have been some major contributions (Collins, Warnock, Aiello, & Miller, 1975; Graesser & Black, 1985; Norman, 1973; Norman & Rumelhart, 1975; Piaget, 1952; Shanon, 1983; Trabasso, van den Broek, & Liu, 1988).

The fields of artificial intelligence and computational linguistics have furnished detailed models of question answering that account for the content of answers and the world knowledge that supplies the content (Allen, 1983; Bruce, 1982; Dahlgren, 1988; Dyer, 1983; Kaplan, 1983; Lehnert, 1978; Lehnert et al., 1983; McKeown, 1985; Ram, 1990; Schank, 1986; Schank & Abelson, 1977; Souther, Acker, Lester, & Porter, 1989; Woods, 1977). In most of these models, texts and world knowledge are organized in the form of structured databases. The Q/A procedures access these information sources and search through the structures systematically. The Q/A mechanism ultimately constructs an informative coherent answer to a particular question.

QUESTION CATEGORIZATION

QUEST assumes that there is a finite set of question categories, that each question category has a unique set of Q/A strategies, and that a particular question is assigned to one of the question categories (see also Lehnert, 1978). For example, the question "Why do you save your program every 15 minutes?" is a *goal-orientation* question that probes for the reasons and motives behind an agent's intentional action. The question "How do you save your program?" is an *instrumental/procedural* question that elicits the plan, procedure, or style of executing an action. The chapter by Graesser, Person, and Huber (chap. 9 in this volume, Table 9.1) presents a set of question categories that would be included in QUEST's catalogue of questions.

In order to complete question categorization successfully, it is necessary to determine the *question focus,* the element or expression that constitutes the target of the question. In most cases there are many nodes in a question, so there needs to be a way to select the question focus. In the question "How do you save a program?", the question focus is the *statement node* "you save program." A statement node contains one predicate (e.g., save) and one or more arguments (you, program). The question focus may be an argument of a statement node rather than the statement as a whole. In the question "Who saved the program?" the focus is the agent slot (X) of the statement node "X saved program." In a long-winded question there are many statement nodes, only one of which would be selected as the question focus. For example, consider the following question and its three statement nodes:

> How do you save a program when there is a blackout and the computer crashes?
> S-Node 1: You save program.
> S-Node 2: A blackout occurs.
> S-Node 3: The computer crashes.

Statement Node 1 would be the question focus in this example, whereas Nodes 2 and 3 furnish context. The focusing mechanism is a rather complex process that considers semantic and pragmatic constraints. QUEST assumes that focusing is successfully completed but does not currently explain the operation of the focusing mechanism.

INFORMATION SOURCES

An information source is a structured database that furnishes answers to a question. Whenever a question is asked, QUEST computes an expression with three slots:

QUESTION (<Q-category>, <question focus>, <information source>)

The expression for "Why do you save your program?" is presented in the following:

QUESTION (goal-orientation, you save program, <information source>)

The third slot supplies the world knowledge structures that are tapped for answers to the question. At least one information source must be accessed before the question can be fully interpreted and answered. Without an information source, it is difficult, if not impossible, to understand the question and to identify the question focus.

When most questions are answered, several information sources are relevant to the question. There are *episodic knowledge structures* (EKSs) that correspond to particular episodes, cases, or exemplars that a person experienced in the past. For example, Answer 3 referred to a particular episode of a person losing 8 hours of work when the computer crashed. In addition to a vast inventory of EKSs, there are thousands of *generic knowledge structures* (GKSs) in long-term memory. A GKS is a more abstract representation that summarizes the typical properties of the concept it represents. Two GKSs relevant to the example question are "computer program" and "saving."

The content of a GKS is undoubtedly derived from the family of EKSs that are associated with the GKS (Kolodner, 1984; Schank, 1986; Smith & Medin, 1981). For example, the generic concept (GKS) that a person has for "computer program" is a product of thousands of EKSs that are created from particular experiences with particular programs. QUEST does not make any informative or controversial claims about the relationship between a GKS and its associated family of EKSs. Presumably, there is a family of EKSs associated with the GKS, such that each EKS has some features that are common with the GKS and some features that distinguish the particular EKS from others in the family. For example, there may be 1000 EKSs involving computer programs, but only one of these EKSs involves a computer program that controls a sprinkler system in a house (e.g., EKS-118). EKS-118 would be indexed with unique, distinctive features (see Kolodner, 1984, 1989; Schank, 1986) that set it apart from other EKSs.

Many of the information sources for a question are accessed by the content words in the question, such as nouns, main verbs, and adjectives. Those information sources that are accessed by content words are termed *word-activated* information sources. In contrast, *pattern-activated* information sources are activated by the features that accumulate from (a) the context of the question, (b) the goals of the speech participants, and (c) the combinations of content words that are mentioned in the discourse.

The information sources for a particular question consist of a family of GKSs and EKSs that are relevant to the question. Each information source is a structured database with dozens, even hundreds of nodes. Therefore, working memory is crowded with a wealth of information during question answering. If there were five information sources, with 100 nodes per source, then 500 nodes would be activated in working memory. Obviously, most of these nodes would not be produced as answers to the question. Only a small set of answers (fewer than 10) is normally produced when an adult answers an open-ended question. QUEST's *convergence mechanisms* begin with the 500 nodes in the node space and prune the space to approximately 10 good answers. These convergence mechanisms are discussed later in this chapter.

REPRESENTATION OF INFORMATION SOURCES

Each information source is a package of highly structured nodes. In the representational system adopted by QUEST, an information source is a database that is organized in the form of a *conceptual graph structure*. A conceptual graph structure consists of a set of nodes that are categorized and that are interrelated by labeled, directed arcs. There are five basic node categories, which are specified in the following:

1. *Concept*. An entity that is normally expressed as a noun (e.g., computer, tree, time).
2. *State*. An ongoing characteristic that remains unchanged within the time frame under consideration (e.g., the computer has an on/off switch, George knows how to run the program).
3. *Event*. A state change within the time frame under consideration (e.g., George presses the wrong key, the computer crashes).
4. *Goal*. An event or state that an agent desires (e.g., George wants to save the program).
5. *Style*. The speed, intensity, force, or qualitative manner in which an event unfolds (e.g., an event occurs quickly, in circles).

An *action* is an amalgamation of a goal node and an event, state, or style specification that achieves the goal; the agent must have done something that causally led up to the successful outcome.

There are several arc categories in QUEST's representational system. Table

12.1 presents a list of 14 arc categories that have been adopted by QUEST. Table 12.1 defines each arc category and presents examples. One or more composition rules are associated with each arc category. A composition rule declares which node categories can be connected by the particular arc. For example, a Reason arc connects only goal nodes whereas a Consequence arc never connects goal nodes. Except for And/Or arcs, all arcs are directed, such that the end node is connected to the head of the arc and the source node is connected to the tail:

$$(source node)—arc\rightarrow (end node)$$

A more complete specification of the arc categories is provided in other reports (Graesser & Clark, 1985; Graesser & Franklin, 1990; Graesser, Gordon, & Brainerd, in press).

We have devoted much of our past research efforts at understanding four types of knowledge structures:

1. *Causal networks* contain event chains, along with states that enable the events to occur; there is a high density of Consequence and Manner arcs.

2. *Goal hierarchies* convey the goals, plans, and intentional actions of agents, along with events/states in the world that initiate the goal hierarchies; Reason, Manner, Initiate, and Outcome arcs are very prevalent in goal hierarchies.

3. *Taxonomic hierarchies* express (a) what classes of entities are nested within other classes and (b) those properties that are both distinctive and characteristic of each concept; there is a high density of Isa and Property arcs.

4. *Spatial region hierarchies* express what regions are embedded within other regions and how regions are directionally related (e.g., X North-of Y, X Left-of Y, X On-top-of Y.).

We acknowledge that a particular information source is an amalgamation of these and other types of knowledge structures. The purpose of segregating these types of substructures is to identity the systematic characteristics of both the structures and the Q/A procedures that operate on the structures.

Figure 12.2 shows an example information source that contains a goal hierarchy and a causal network. Nodes 1–7 consist of a hierarchical structure of goals that are connected by Reason arcs. The most superordinate goal is Node 1 ("George uses program whenever George wants to"), whereas the most subordinate goal is Node 7 ("George makes up file name"). Whenever a goal is achieved, a goal node is linked to an event or state with an Outcome arc, and the event/state signifies a positive outcome. Goals 4, 5, and 7 are achieved because there are positive outcomes in Nodes 10, 11, and 12, respectively. There are no outcomes associated with Nodes 1–3 because these goals are not achieved. Goal

TABLE 12.1

Definitions and Composition Rules for Fourteen Categories of Arc

Arc Category	Definition and Temporal Constraints	Composition Rules	Example
Consequence (C)	A causes or enables B A precedes B in Time	(event / state / style)-C--> (event / state / style)	(Event: George presses the wrong key)-C--> (Event: The screen goes blank)
Implies (Im)	A implies B A and B overlap in time	(event / state / style)-Im--> (event / state / style)	(Event: The screen goes blank)-Im--> (Event: The computer crashed)
Reason (R)	B is a reason or motive for A B is a superordinate goal of A A is achieved before B is achieved	(goal)-R-->(goal)	(Goal: George types "save")-R--> (Goal: George saves program)
Outcome (O)	B specifies whether or not the goal A is achieved A precedes B in time	(goal)-O-->(event / state / style)	(Goal: George types "save")-O--> (Event: "Save" is typed)
Initiate (I)	A initiates or triggers the goal in B A precedes B in time	(event / state / style)-I-->(goal)	(State: George knows how to save program)-I--> (Goal: George saves program)
Manner (M)	B specifies the manner in which A occurs A and B overlap in time	(goal)-M-->(goal / style) (style)-M-->(style) (event)-M-->(event / style)	(Event: George pressed a key)-M--> (Style: The key was pressed hurriedly)

Relationship	Description	Form	Example
Before / After / During: Temporal relationship	A has a temporal relationship with B	(goal)-Before-->(goal) (event / state)-Before--> (event / state)	(Goal: George types "save")-Before--> Goal: George types space)
And / Or	Both A and B exist / occur Either A or B exists / occurs	(concept)-Or-->(concept) (goal)-Or-->(goal) (event / state)-Or-->(event / state)	(State: George had a deadline)-And--> (Event: The computer crashed)
Is a (Isa)	A is a kind / type / instance of B	(concept)-Isa-->(concept)	(Concept: computer)-Isa--> (concept: electronic device)
Has As Part (HAP)	A has as a part B	(concept)-HAP-->(concept)	(Concept: computer)-HAP--> (Concept: keyboard)
Property (P)	A has a property P	(concept)-P-->(state / event / goal)	(Concept: Macintosh)-P--> (State: computer has iconic interface)
Referential Pointer (Ref)	An argument of A refers to a concept B	(state / event / goal)-Ref--> (concept)	Noun argument of (Event: The computer crashed)-Ref-->(Concept: computer)
Contains (Cont)	A contains B	(concept)-Cont-->(concept)	(Concept: computer case)-Cont--> (Concept: disk drive)
Spatial relationship Left-of / Right-of Top-of / Bottom-of East-of / West-of North-of / South-of Touch / Connect	A has a spatial relationship with B	(concept)-East-of-->(concept)	(Concept: computer case)- Top-of-->(Concept: table)

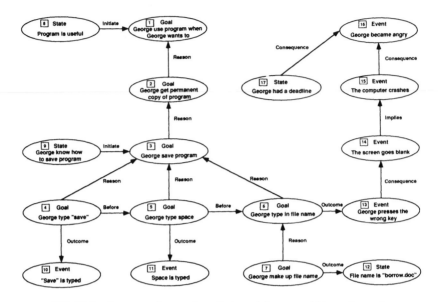

FIG. 12.2.   An example structure that contains a goal hierarchy and a causal network.

6 ("George types in file name") has an outcome node, but the outcome is negative (Node 13, "George presses wrong key"). In addition to the goal hierarchy and outcome nodes, there are states and events that initiate the goal hierarchy. For example, the goal hierarchy (Nodes 1–7) is initiated by States 8 and 9 via the Initiate arc. Finally, Fig. 12.2 contains a causal network (Nodes 13–17). The event chain begins with George pressing the wrong key and ends with George becoming angry.

Figure 12.3 shows a taxonomic structure for computers and tools. There is a hierarchy of concept nodes that are connected by *Isa* arcs (Nodes 1–10). The most superordinate concept is *tool* whereas *Macintosh, IBM/XT,* and *Cray* are the most subordinate concepts. Most of the concept nodes have properties (via Property arcs). A property is not only very typical of the concept to which it is connected; it is also distinctive in the sense that it is typical of concept C, but atypical of the sibling nodes of C. For example, a microcomputer is inexpensive (Node 14) but inexpensiveness is not a property of supercomputers and Connection Machines.

Figures 12.2 and 3 furnish an impression of conceptual graph structures, their node categories, and their arc categories. We emphasize that these structures are not composed haphazardly according to idiosyncratic intuitions of the investigator. There are specific constraints that must be satisfied when one node is connected to another node by a particular arc category (see Table 12.1). These are captured by each arc's definition, temporal constraints, and rules of composition.

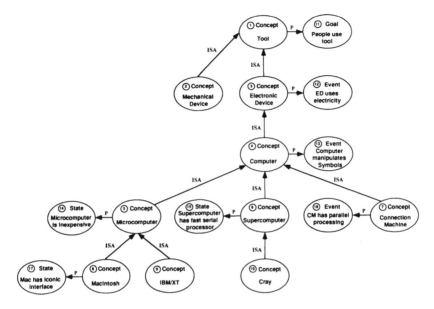

FIG. 12.3. An example taxonomic hierarchy.

The selection of arc categories and their constraints is based on cognitive theories of knowledge representation that are beyond the scope of this chapter.

CONVERGENCE MECHANISMS

When a particular question is asked, QUEST activates several information sources in working memory and each information source has dozens, or hundreds, of nodes. Convergence mechanisms narrow down the node space from hundreds of nodes to approximately 10 good answers. Convergence is accomplished by four components: (a) an intersecting node identifier, (b) an arc search procedure, (c) a structural distance gradient, and (d) constraint satisfaction.

Intersecting Node Identifier

This component isolates those nodes from different knowledge structures that intersect (i.e., match, overlap). For example, the statement node "X presses wrong key" might be stored in three distinct information sources within working memory: in two GKSs (as "X presses wrong key" in two different structures) and one EKS (as "George presses wrong key" in Fig. 12.2). Node matches are accomplished very quickly in the cognitive system by virtue of pattern matching processes that impose very little cost to working memory (Anderson, 1983). It is important to note that two nodes may match by virtue of argument substitution (e.g., X is substituted for George).

The intersecting node identifier isolates all nodes in working memory that overlap. These intersecting nodes have a privileged status. There is evidence that these intersecting nodes have a higher likelihood of being produced as answers than nonintersecting nodes (Golding et al., 1990; Graesser & Clark, 1985; Graesser, Lang, & Roberts, 1991).

Arc Search Procedure

Each question category has its own arc search procedure that operates on the information sources relevant to a question and that produces candidate answers. When an information source is accessed, the arc search procedure is applied to each of the "entry nodes" in the information source. An entry node usually consists of a node in the structure that matches the question focus in the question. Suppose that the question is "Why does a person save a program?" and the information source is Fig. 12.2. The entry node would be Node 3 in Fig. 12.2 because the question focus (i.e., person saves program) matches Node 3 ("George saves program") by virtue of argument substitution. In some cases, the entry node is one of the intersecting nodes that was extracted by the intersecting node identifier. For example, Nodes 1 and 8 may be intersecting nodes that are stored both in the EKS for Fig. 12.2 and the GKS for computer program.

Once an entry node is located in an information source, the arc search procedure executes a breadth first search from the entry node by traversing legal arcs that radiate from the entry node. For each question category, there is a particular set of arc categories and arc directions that is legal. For example, the arc search procedure for a goal orientation question is specified in the following:

> *Arc search procedure for goal orientation question:* Generate superordinate goals (via paths of forward Reason arcs and backward Manner arcs) and goal initiators (connected to the entry node and superordinate nodes via backward Initiate arcs).

Consider, for example, the goal-orientation question "Why does a person save a program?" If this question were interpreted in the context of the structure in Fig. 12.2, the entry node would be Node 3 and the following nodes would be legal candidate answers:

> "In order to get a permanent copy of the program" (Node 2).
> "In order to use the program whenever the user wants to" (Node 1).
> "Because the program is useful" (Node 8).
> "Because the person knows how to save the program" (Node 9).

All of the other nodes in Fig. 12.2 are illegal. Given that there are 16 possible answers, but only 4 are legal answers, the arc search procedure has reduced the node space to 25% of the possible nodes.

Instrumental/procedural questions have a completely different arc search procedure.

Arc search procedure for instrumental/procedural question: Generate subordinate goals and style specifications (via paths of backward Reason and forward Manner arcs).

When this arc search procedure is applied to the question "How does a person save a program?" in the context of Fig. 12.2, the following legal answers are generated.

"You type save" (Node 4).
"You type a space" (Node 5).
"You make up a file name" (Node 7).
"You type in the file name" (Node 6).

Therefore, answers to instrumental/procedural questions include subordinate goals in the goal hierarchy whereas answers to goal-orientation questions include superordinate goals.

The arc search procedures for causal antecedent and causal consequence questions are normally applied to events and states.

Arc search procedure for causal antecedent question: Generate nodes on paths with the following arcs: backwards Consequence, forward and backward Implies, backward Initiate, and backward Outcome.

Arc search procedure for causal consequence question: This procedure is the inverse of that of causal antecedent questions: forward Consequence, forward and backward Implies, forward Initiate, and forward Outcome.

The causal antecedent question "Why did the screen go blank?" would generate the following legal answers when applied to the Fig. 12.2 structure:

"Because the computer crashed" (Node 15).
"Because the person pressed the wrong key" (Node 13).
"The person wanted to type the file name" (Node 6).

The causal consequence question "What were the consequences of the screen going blank?" would generate the following legal answers:

"The computer crashed" (Node 15).

"George became angry" (Node 16).

The arc search procedure for the causal consequence question is probably incomplete, as it has been formulated so far. Good answers to such questions also should include goal failures (i.e., "George was not able to save his program," negated Node 3) and failed obligations (e.g., "George missed his deadline," negated Node 17).

Why, how, and consequence questions are very natural for goal hierarchies and causal networks. A different set of questions is natural for taxonomic structures. Definition questions are frequently asked about the concept nodes in taxonomic hierarchies: "What does X mean?" and "What is an X?". The arc search procedure for these definition questions consists of a genus-differentiae frame, which is adopted in most dictionary definitions.

Arc search procedure for definition questions: Generate the immediate superordinate node of concept X (via the forward Isa arc) and the properties directly linked to X (via the forward Property arc).

The question and answer is articulated as follows:

"What is an X?"

"An X is a <superordinate node>that<property 1> . . . .<property n>"

QUEST would generate the following answer to the question "What is a computer?" when the database is Fig. 12.3: "A computer is an electronic device that manipulates symbols." Whereas definition questions produce concepts that are superordinate in the Isa hierarchy, subordinate concepts are produced when answering the question "What is an example of X?" Legal answers to the question "What is an example of a computer?" would be a microcomputer, a supercomputer, and a Connection Machine.

Comparison questions are frequently asked about concepts in taxonomic hierarchies, that is, "How is X similar to Y?" and "How is X different from Y?". The answers include properties that either compare or contrast the two concepts (X and Y). When these properties are computed, QUEST considers the properties that are inherited from its superordinate concepts as well as properties directly linked to the concept. For example, the concept computer has Node 13 directly linked to it whereas Nodes 11 and 12 are inherited properties:

"A computer manipulates symbols" (Node 13).

"A computer uses electricity" (substituting computer for electronic device in Node 12).

"People want to use computers" (substituting computer for tool in Node 11).

The arc search procedure for comparison questions selects the appropriate properties from the total set of properties of X and Y (both directly linked and inherited). However, the procedure for selecting these properties will not be specified in this chapter (see Graesser, Gordon, & Brainerd, in press).

The arc search procedures in QUEST are compatible with some theories of question answering in artificial intelligence that have emphasized the importance of knowledge organization and of restricting search by pursuing nodes that are linked by particular conceptual relations (Lehnert, 1978; Lehnert et al., 1983; Schank & Abelson, 1977; Souther et al., 1989). There also is extensive empirical evidence that the arc search procedures robustly predict what answers adults produce to questions (Golding et al., 1990; Graesser, 1990; Graesser & Hemphill, 1991; Graesser et al., 1989; Graesser, Lang, & Roberts, 1991; Graesser & Murachver, 1985; Graesser et al., 1981).

Structural Distance

When an information source is tapped for answers to a question, there is a structural distance score associated with each candidate answer. Structural distance consists of the number of arcs between the entry node and the candidate answer node. For example, in Fig. 12.2 the distance between Nodes 3 and 13 is two whereas the distance between Nodes 3 and 17 is six.

There is some evidence that the likelihood of a node being produced as an answer decreases as a function of its distance from the entry node in the information source (Golding et al., 1990; Graesser & Clark, 1985; Graesser & Hemphill, 1991; Graesser et al., 1989; Graesser, Lang, & Roberts, 1991). The decrease appears to be exponential. If d is structural distance and t is the likelihood of traversing a single arc, then the likelihood is t^d of producing a node as an answer (given that it is a legal answer that passed the arc search procedure). The value of t was 0.67 in the study by Graesser et al. (1989). If the candidate answer were four arcs away from the entry node, then the likelihood of it being produced as an answer would be $0.67^4 = 0.21$.

The predicted effects of structural distance on answer production are consistent with models of question answering other than QUEST (Shanon, 1983; Winston, 1984). For example, Winston described a Q/A model that answers "why" and "how" questions in the context of goal hierarchies and problem spaces. His Q/A algorithm specifies that good answers are only one arc away from the question focus. QUEST assumes there is an exponential gradient rather than assuming the single arc rule. Theories of marker passing and spreading activation also would predict the exponential distance gradient (Anderson, 1983).

Constraint Satisfaction

The semantic content of the answer should not be incompatible with the content of the question focus. Constraint satisfaction discards those candidate answers in the node space that are incompatible with the question focus. Stated differently, the question focus has semantic and conceptual constraints that are propagated among the nodes in the information sources, ultimately pruning out the incompatible nodes.

There are several ways in which a candidate answer could be incompatible with the question focus (Graesser & Clark, 1985). Suppose that the question focus is "X saves program." A node is pruned if it directly contradicts the question focus (e.g., "X lost the program"). A node is pruned if it is in the wrong time frame (e.g., "X was born"). Incompatibilities in planning may occur when a plan conveyed in the candidate answer cannot be executed when the action in the question focus is executed (e.g., "X went to sleep"). An answer may be pruned if it is not causally related to the question focus. A candidate answer is not produced if it has incompatibilities on one or more of these dimensions.

Once again, the above four components of convergence are capable of narrowing the node space from hundreds of nodes in working memory to a handful of good answers to a question. Graesser, Gordon, and Brainerd (in press) analyzed convergence mechanisms in a study that involved answering "why," "how," and consequence questions in the context of simple short narrative passages (150 words). A convergence score was defined as the proportion of nodes in the node space that constituted good answers to a question after application of the following convergence mechanisms: arc search procedure, structural distance, and constraint satisfaction. The arc search procedures reduced the node space to 10% of the original nodes. The structural distance component reduced the node space further; 38% of the above 10% of the nodes passed the structural distance component, yielding 3.8%. Constraint satisfaction reduced the node space to 55% of the remaining 3.8% of the nodes. Therefore, the overall constraint satisfaction score was 2.1%. If the information source were a text structure with 200 nodes, then convergence mechanisms would have produced four good answers to the question. This estimate is quantitatively close to available studies on human question answering (Graesser & Clark, 1985; Graesser & Murachver, 1985).

PRAGMATICS

The pragmatic components of QUEST address the social and communicative functions of answering a question. One key component considers the goals of the questioner and answerer. From the perspective of the questioner, a question may be asked to solve a problem, to assess how much the answerer knows, to persuade, to control a conversation, and so on. From the perspective of the answerer, the answer may be formulated to inform the questioner, to let the questioner know the answerer knows something, to entertain the questioner, and so on. A complete model of question answering would consider the goals of the speech participants in the discourse context and would tailor answers to achieve these goals (Allen, 1983; Bruce, 1982; Francik & Clark, 1985; Kaplan, 1983).

One important goal to assess is whether the questioner genuinely seeks the information invited by the question. Some questions are not genuine information-seeking questions: Indirect requests (e.g., "Could you delete this file?"), greetings ("How are you doing?"), gripes ("Why does this always happen to me?"), and rhetorical questions. Van der Meij (1987) has identified the preconditions that must be met before an utterance constitutes a genuine information-seeking question.

1. The questioner does not know the information asked for with the question.
2. The questioner believes that the presuppositions of the question are true.
3. The questioner believes that an answer exists.
4. The questioner wants to know the answer.
5. The questioner can assess whether a reply constitutes an answer.
6. The questioner poses the question only if the benefits exceed the costs. The benefits of knowing the answer must exceed the costs of asking the question. The benefits of knowing the answer must exceed the benefits of not knowing the answer.
7. The questioner believes the answerer knows the answer.
8. The questioner believes that the answerer will not give an answer in absence of the question.
9. The questioner believes that the answerer will supply an answer.

To the extent that these nine preconditions are violated, a speech act would not be a genuine information-seeking question.

A second pragmatic component is the common ground (i.e., shared knowledge) between the questioner and answerer (Clark & Marshall, 1981; Clark & Schaefer, 1989; Miyake & Norman, 1979; Shanon, 1983; Sleeman & Brown, 1982). The answerer first estimates the common ground between speech participants and then selects an answer that moderately extends the boundaries of the common ground. That is, the answer should be somewhat more informative, elaborate, or detailed than the common ground, but should not be (a) entirely within the sphere of the common ground or (b) substantially more detailed than the common ground.

In principle, QUEST could keep track of the common ground between the questioner and answerer. QUEST would identify those information sources that each participant has stored in memory, and what nodes are stored in each information source. The fringe or boundary of knowledge also can be computed in a straightforward manner. A fringe answer would be one or two arcs away from a node in the common ground.

Common ground could have some counterintuitive effects on answer production. If the common ground is high and the answerer wants to be informative by supplying information that the questioner does not already know, then the answerer would avoid nodes that are in multiple information sources. Surprisingly, this would yield a negative correlation between answer production and the number of information sources that supplied the answer. Common ground also might have an interesting prediction regarding the impact of structural distance on answer production. There might be a preference for distant nodes because proximate nodes would be easy to infer. Perhaps the net effect would yield a curvilinear relationship, with answers at intermediate distances being better than answers at close and at far distances from the entry node in the information source.

The impact of pragmatic components on question answering should not be taken lightly. Indeed, there are ample reasons for being skeptical about the external validity of QUEST's convergence mechanisms when questions are embedded in conversations. The context and constraints of a conversation can potentially modify the literal meaning of a question and thereby radically alter appropriate replies. Suppose, for example, that a customer visits a used car lot, points to a car, and asks the salesperson "Why is this 1985 Chevy so expensive?" Some replies are presented in the following:

1. The engine has only 2,000 miles on it.
2. This 1983 Buick is in good condition.
3. Why don't you look at this 1983 Buick?
4. What price range are you considering?

Reply 1 would be produced by QUEST because it specifies a causal antecedent to the Chevy's being expensive. Replies 2, 3, and 4 would be reasonable replies to the question in the conversation, but these replies would not be generated by QUEST. Reply 2 does not address the customer's question directly; the salesperson inferred that the customer could not afford the Chevy so the salesperson recommended a less expensive car. Reply 3 is syntactically a question, but functionally an indirect request. Neither of these speech act categories are produced as answers by QUEST; assertions are the only appropriate replies to questions in the QUEST model. Reply 4 is a question, both syntactically and functionally, and therefore is beyond the scope of QUEST.

Answers to questions in naturalistic conversations are constrained by the goals and common ground of the speech participants. To the extent that these components are increasingly complex, questions are less likely to be information-seeking questions that can be accommodated by QUEST's convergence mechanisms. QUEST will fail when questions are functionally commands, indirect requests, gripes, sarcastic comments, conversation monitors, or rhetorical devices. These pragmatic considerations illustrate some limitations of QUEST but do not imply the model is useless. QUEST would hold up quite well in contexts where pragmatics does not play a major role. QUEST would be quite useful if it could account for many, although not all, the answers in naturalistic conversations. Graesser, Roberts, and Hackett-Renner (1990) reported that approximately 80% of the answers in naturalistic conversations were compatible with QUEST's arc search procedures. Accounting for 80% of the answers would be considered by some colleagues as either encouraging or impressive results.

It is easy to declare that a good answer must address the goals of the questioner and answerer. It is difficult to write a computer program that simulates the computational mechanisms that accomplish this requirement. We are currently exploring how the speech participants' goals impact on (a) the selection of good answers to a question and (b) the selection of the most relevant question-answering strategies. We are also investigating how the answerer pieces together the nodes from diverse information sources in an effort to formulate a coherent answer. A good long-winded answer is both coherent and informative. Unfortunately, we know next to nothing about the mechanisms that generate coherent, informative answers.

In closing, we believe that the QUEST model furnishes a promising start at developing an adequate theory of human question answering. However, we would not at all be surprised if we undertake extensive remodeling in the future.

ACKNOWLEDGMENTS

This research was funded by grants awarded to the first author by the Office of Naval Research (N00014-88-K-0110 and N00014-90-J-1492).

REFERENCES

Allen, J. F. (1983). Recognizing intentions from natural language utterances. In M. Brady & R. C. Berwick (Eds.), *Computational models of discourse* (pp. 107–166). Cambridge, MA: MIT Press.
Anderson, J. R. (1983). *The architecture of cognition.* Cambridge, MA: Harvard University Press.
Baudet, S., & Denhiere, G. (1989). Representation and acquisition of knowledge of functional systems. In *Proceedings of the Eleventh Annual Conference of the Cognitive Science Society* (pp. 546–552). Hillsdale, NJ: Lawrence Erlbaum Associates.
Bruce, B. C. (1982). Natural communication between person and computer. In W. G. Lehnert & M. H. Ringle (Eds.), *Strategies for natural language processing* (pp. 55–88). Hillsdale, NJ: Lawrence Erlbaum Associates.
Buchanan, B. G., & Shortliffe, E. H. (1984). *Rule-based expert systems: The MYCIN experiments of the Stanford heuristic programming project.* Reading, MA: Addison-Wesley.
Clancey, W. J. (1982). Tutoring roles for guiding a case method dialogue. In D. Sleeman & J. S. Brown (Eds.), *Intelligent tutoring systems* (pp. 201–225). New York: Academic Press.

Clark, H. H., & Marshall, C. R. (1981). Definite reference and mutual knowledge. In A. Joshi, B. Webber, & I. Sag (Eds.), *Elements of discourse understanding* (pp. 10–63). Cambridge: Cambridge University Press.

Clark, H. H., & Schaefer, E. F. (1989). Contributing to discourse. *Cognitive Science, 13,* 259–294.

Collins, A., Warnock, E. H., Aiello, N., & Miller, M. L. (1975). Reasoning from incomplete knowledge. In D. G. Bobrow & A. Collins (Eds.), *Representation and understanding* (pp. 383–415). New York: Academic Press.

Dahlgren, K. (1988). *Naive semantics for natural language understanding.* Boston: Kluwer Academic Publishers.

Dyer, M. G. (1983). *In-depth understanding: A computer model of integrated processing for narrative comprehension.* Cambridge, MA: MIT Press.

Francik, E. P., & Clark, H. H. (1985). How to make requests that overcome obstacles to compliance. *Journal of Memory and Language, 24,* 560–568.

Glucksberg, S., & McCloskey, M. (1981). Decisions about ignorance: Knowing that you don't know. *Journal of Experimental Psychology: Human Learning and Memory, 7,* 311–326.

Golding, J. M., Graesser, A. C., & Millis, K. K. (1990). What makes a good answer to a question?: Testing a psychological model of question answering in the context of narrative text. *Discourse Processes, 13,* 279–303.

Graesser, A. C. (1978). How to catch a fish: The memory and representation of common procedures. *Discourse Processes, 1,* 72–89.

Graesser, A. C. (1990). *Investigations of human question answering* (Technical Report #1 for Office of Naval Research contract, Memphis State University, Memphis, TN).

Graesser, A. C., & Black, J. B. (Eds.). (1985). *The psychology of questions.* Hillsdale, NJ: Lawrence Erlbaum Associates.

Graesser, A. C., & Clark, L. F. (1985). *Structures and procedures of implicit knowledge.* Norwood, NJ: Ablex.

Graesser, A. C., & Franklin, S. P. (1990). QUEST: A cognitive model of question answering. *Discourse Processes, 13,* 279–303.

Graesser, A. C., Gordon, S., & Brainerd, L. E. (in press). QUEST: A model of question answering. *Computers & Mathematics with Applications.*

Graesser, A. C., & Hemphill, D. D. (1991). Question answering in the context of scientific mechanisms. *Journal of Memory and Language, 31,* 186–209.

Graesser, A. C., Hemphill, D. D., & Brainerd, L. E. (1989). Question answering in the context of causal mechanisms. In *Proceedings of the Eleventh Annual Conference of the Cognitive Science Society* (pp. 621–626). Hillsdale, NJ: Lawrence Erlbaum Associates.

Graesser, A. C., Lang, K. L., & Roberts, R. M. (1991). Question answering in the context of stories. *Journal of Experimental Psychology: General, 120,* 254–277.

Graesser, A. C., & Murachver, T. (1985). Symbolic procedures of question answering. In A. C. Graesser & J. B. Black (Eds.), *The psychology of questions* (pp. 15–88). Hillsdale, NJ: Lawrence Erlbaum Associates.

Graesser, A. C., Roberts, R. M., & Hackett-Renner, C. (1990). Question answering in the context of telephone surveys, business interactions, and interviews. *Discourse Processes, 13,* 327–348.

Graesser, A. C., Robertson, S. P., & Anderson, P. A. (1981). Incorporating inferences in narrative representations: A study of how and why. *Cognitive Psychology, 13,* 1–26.

Graesser, A. C., Robertson, S. P., Lovelace, E. R., & Swinehart, D. M. (1980). Answers to why-questions expose the organization of story plot and predict recall of actions. *Journal of Verbal Learning and Verbal Behavior, 19,* 110–119.

Hammond, K. J. (1986). *Care-based planning: An integrated theory of planning learning and memory.* Ph.D. thesis, Yale University, New Haven, CT.

Kaplan, S. J. (1983). Cooperative response from a portable natural language system. In M. Brady &

R. C. Berwick (Eds.), *Computational models of discourse* (pp. 167–208). Cambridge, MA: MIT Press.

Kolodner, J. (1984). *Retrieval and organization strategies in conceptual memory: A computer model*. Hillsdale, NJ: Lawrence Erlbaum Associates.

Kolodner, J. (1989). Selecting the best case for a best-case reasoner. In *Proceedings of the Eleventh Annual Conference of the Cognitive Science Society* (pp. 155–162). Hillsdale, NJ: Lawrence Erlbaum Associates.

Lang, K. L., Graesser, A. C., & Hemphill, D. D. (1990). The role of questioning in knowledge engineering and the interface of expert systems. *Poetics, 19,* 143–166.

Lehnert, W. G. (1978). *The process of question answering*. Hillsdale, NJ: Lawrence Erlbaum Associates.

Lehnert, W. G., Dyer, M. G., Johnson, P. N., Young, C. J., & Harley, S. (1983). BORIS—An experiment in in-depth understanding of narratives. *Artificial Intelligence, 20,* 15–62.

McKeown, K. R. (1985). Discourse strategies for generating natural language text. *Artificial Intelligence, 27,* 1–41.

Miyake, N., & Norman, D. A. (1979). To ask a question, one must know enough to know what is not known. *Journal of Verbal Learning and Verbal Behavior, 18,* 357–354.

Norman, D. A. (1973). Memory, knowledge and the answering of questions. In R. Solso (Ed.), *Contemporary issues in cognitive psychology* (pp. 135–165). Washington, DC: Winston.

Norman, D. A., & Rumelhart, D. E. (1975). *Explorations in cognition*. San Francisco: Freeman.

Piaget, J. (1952). *The origins of intelligence in the child*. London: Routledge & Kegan Paul. (Original work published 1936).

Ram, A. (1990). Knowledge goals: A theory of intelligence. In *Proceedings of the Twelfth Annual Conference of the Cognitive Science Society* (pp. 206–214). Hillsdale, NJ: Lawrence Erlbaum Associates.

Reder, L. M. (1987). Strategy selection in question answering. *Cognitive Psychology, 19,* 90–138.

Robertson, S. P., Black, J. B., & Lehnert, W. G. (1985). Misleading question effects as evidence for integrated question understanding and memory search. In A. C. Graesser & J. B. Black (Eds.), *The psychology of questions* (pp. 191–218). Hillsdale, NJ: Lawrence Erlbaum Associates.

Schank, R. C. (1986). *Explanation patterns: Understanding mechanically and creatively*. Hillsdale, NJ: Lawrence Erlbaum Associates.

Schank, R. C., & Abelson, R. (1977). *Scripts, plans, goals, and understanding*. Hillsdale, NJ: Lawrence Erlbaum Associates.

Shanon, B. (1983). Answers to where-questions. *Discourse Processes, 6,* 319–352.

Singer, M. (1986). Answering yes-no questions about causes: Question acts and question categories. *Memory & Cognition, 14,* 55–63.

Singer, M. (1990). Answering questions about discourse. *Discourse Processes, 13,* 261–277.

Sleeman, D. H., & Brown, J. S. (Eds.). (1982). *Intelligent tutoring systems*. New York: Academic Press.

Smith, E. E., & Medin, D. L. (1981). *Categories and concepts*. Cambridge, MA: Harvard University Press.

Souther, A., Acker, L., Lester, J., & Porter, B. (1989). Using view types to generate explanations in intelligent tutoring systems. In *Proceedings of the Eleventh Annual Conference of the Cognitive Science Society* (pp. 123–130). Hillsdale, NJ: Lawrence Erlbaum Associates.

Trabasso, T., van den Broek, P. W., & Liu, L. (1988). A model for generating questions that assess and promote comprehension. *Questioning Exchange, 2,* 25–38.

van der Meij, H. (1987). Assumptions of information-seeking questions. *Questioning Exchange, 1,* 111–117.

Winston, P. H. (1984). *Artificial Intelligence* (2nd ed.). Reading, MA: Addison-Wesley.

Woods, W. A. (1977). Lunar rocks in natural English: Explorations in natural language question answering. In A. Zampoli (Ed.), *Linguistic structures processing* (pp. 201–222). New York: Elsevier North-Holland.

Young, R. (1989). Human interface aspects of expert systems. In L. A. Murray, & J. T. E. Richardson (Ed.), *Intelligent systems in a human context* (pp. 101–111). Oxford: Oxford University Press.

13 Question-Driven Information Search in Auditor Diagnosis

Thomas W. Lauer
Eileen Peacock
Oakland University

Auditing is a complex, ill-structured practical problem that is both exploratory and analytical. The auditor collects and analyzes evidence regarding an organization's operations, eventually arriving at an overall judgment. The auditor must come to a judgment about whether the company's annual and quarterly financial statements accurately portray its financial condition. If the evidence is provided by the company, various means of verifying its authenticity may be employed. Evidence is analyzed and statements of the company's financial condition are evaluated in light of the analysis.

This chapter focuses on the auditor's inquiry process. This initial stage of the decision process, wherein the auditor actively searches for information, is often taken for granted by researchers as they study the mechanics of decision making. In the present study, we recorded questions generated by audit managers who were conducting a preliminary analytic review of three companies. The corpus of questions was analyzed first by assigning each question to a question category. We subsequently classified groups of questions that were aimed at diagnosis and mapped these specific questions to phases of the diagnostic process. We found that auditors' questions manifest diagnostic activity and the distinctive features of the auditor's knowledge base. As would be expected, the auditor's diagnostic processes share some features with other diagnostic tasks, such as medical diagnosis and fault diagnosis in electronic devices. However, there are some important differences.

This chapter shows how auditors' questions elucidate properties of their knowledge base and the audit diagnostic task. The next section gives a general description of auditor's task. Following this, we discuss diagnosis in general and audit diagnosis in particular. Subsequently, we examine the relationship between auditors' questions and diagnosis. Finally, we make some suggestions for knowledge elicitation for audit expert systems.

THE AUDIT TASK AND THE AUDITOR'S KNOWLEDGE BASE

Any firm that is traded publicly must subject its financial records to examination and analysis by an independent auditor. This legal requirement was instituted as a result of the Securities Act of 1933 and the Securities and Exchange Act of 1934. The Acts protect stockholders from financial losses resulting from their basing actions on erroneous information about some publicly traded company. In order for accounting firms in the business of auditing to be profitable, they must be able to carry out an accurate audit without expending undue amounts of time or money. Thus, auditing is not like a scientific investigation in which the researcher can continue investigating until satisfied. The constraints of time and money make the rewards of accurate and efficient diagnosis considerable.

The auditor is guided in his work by Statements on Auditing Standards (SASs) designed to form the basis of the professional auditors responsibility. The standards mandate certain actions by the auditor, such as performing analytical review in the planning and final review stages of an audit (AICPA, 1988). The standards recommend certain actions such as seeking a specialist's help when the auditor lacks the relevant expertise (AICPA, 1976).

In order to accomplish the auditor's prime goal of giving credibility to an organization's financial statements, the auditor must evaluate the particulars of the client's financial condition from several standpoints, both general and specific. The auditor must have general knowledge about the client's industry, the prevailing economic climate, the legal environment, and the accounting regulations put forward by the financial accounting standards board (FASB). The auditor must also have specific detailed knowledge concerning financial ratios such as profit margin ratios or average collection periods. The accounting regulations, to which a company must adhere, are complex, far-reaching, and often under amendment. Even though the auditor has a fundamental understanding of these regulations, the auditor is expected to look for clarification of details for specific industries or situations.

The knowledge the auditor brings to bear on the audit is also a reflection of his experience. The audit manager's ability to question the details of the financial statements to a greater extent than a staff accountant is a function of the large inventory of past cases that accumulate from past audits.

Felix and Kinney (1982) described the cognitive processes that underlie the auditor's opinion formulation. In the first step (called orientation) the auditor learns about the setting of the client's organization and the operation of the organization. This includes collecting evidence about the geographic setting, industry characteristics, management of the firm, and attributes of the financial and accounting systems. In the second step, the auditor develops a preliminary evaluation of the client's system of internal controls. This involves assessing the error likelihoods for different components of the client's accounting system. Those areas in which there is a relatively high likelihood of error are scrutinized more carefully during the subsequent testing stages of the audit. The third step is the development of a plan of audit activities. During this step, the auditor specifies a set of audit procedures for collecting sufficient evidence to justify the formulation of an opinion. Subsequent steps include the testing and evaluation of controls, transactions, and balances.

The auditor eventually aggregates the results of the previous testing and evidence collection. In the final step, the auditor formulates an opinion. The opinion represents the auditor's judgment about whether the financial statements accurately represent the firm's financial condition. The opinion can be unqualified, which means that the firm's financial statements accurately reflect its condition. Alternatively, the qualified opinion describes specific areas of discrepancy. The auditor's opinion formulation is an example of a diagnostic problem.

DIAGNOSIS

Insights regarding diagnosis come from studies of various diagnostic tasks, for example, electronic fault diagnosis (Milne, 1987), medical diagnosis (Clancey, 1988), intelligent tutoring systems (Wenger, 1987), and scientific reasoning (Klahr & Dunbar, 1988). In this section, we present some observations about diagnosis in order to provide a basis for later claims that we make regarding auditor diagnosis.

A traditional view of diagnosis emphasizes inferring past causes from present or recent effects. For example, the diagnostic process can be broken down into three stages (Einhorn & Hogarth, 1982; Milne, 1987). The first involves the observation of some behavior that is recognized as abnormal or undesirable. These are symptoms or faults. During the second stage, hypotheses are generated to explain the cause of the symptom. The third stage involves the selection of the appropriate hypothesis by means of testing. A test may assume that a hypothesis is true and then test for other behaviors that should occur.

Some authors conceptualize diagnosis as the development of a mental model of the object of diagnosis. Developing the mental model includes a high-level diagnostic strategy that directs information gathering. The information enables the diagnostician to select hypotheses that best account for causal relationships involving the symptoms (Clancey, 1988; Klahr & Dunbar, 1988; Wenger, 1987). The diagnostic model supports the goal of producing an explanation that accounts for both deviant and normal behavior (Kuipers, 1987). Thus, an adequate diagnosis requires the ability to understand and explain the system in its normal state. Defects in the system structure are understood by comparison to the normal state.

Some researchers have analyzed diagnostic strategy by identifying three levels of conceptualizing the system under study: the structural level, the behavioral level, and the functional level (Chandrasekaran & Milne, 1985; Davis, 1983). The structural level identifies the components of the device and their interconnections. The behavioral level is a description of events that occur throughout the system as the components interact and inputs are converted into outputs. For physical systems, the functional level contains an account of how the system is to be used. If the system involves intentional actors, the functional level would include goals and plans of the actors.

Diagnosis is concerned with reasoning back and forth between behavior, structure, and function. Some information about the structure and the function of the evoking system is known a priori. In the case of a physical system such as a computer program, the program design specifications describe the structure of the system. When a person diagnoses faulty behavior of the program, the engineer infers deviations from the design that cause the faulty behavior (i.e., errors when the program is run). Debugging the program with only program specifications and a record of the errors is quite difficult. The task of diagnosing the error is made easier if the programmer has knowledge of the function of the program. This would include high-level specifications that describe the purpose of the program and contextual information about its relationship with other programs in the system.

The diagnostician's mental model includes information at all three levels: structural, behavioral, and functional. The basic inferential task of reasoning from symptom to cause serves to instantiate the model.

Audit Diagnosis

There are some characteristics of audit diagnosis that distinguish it from other diagnostic problems. Some significant features of audit diagnosis are: (a) there is no presenting problem, (b) it is difficult to determine what is normal, (c) there is no taxonomy of organizational diseases, (d) it is highly complex, and (e) at present, firms operate in unstable, rapidly changing environments. As a result, audit diagnosis will emphasize symptom identification to a greater extent than diagnosis in other fields.

The auditor is *not* presented with a specific diagnostic problem. This is in contrast to medical diagnosis where the patient comes with a specific set of presenting symptoms or to fault diagnosis of an electronic circuit or maintenance of a computer program, either of which fails for certain specific operations. The auditor is presented with general information and must search for specific symptoms that will provide an overall understanding of the firm's operations. In some cases, the firm's management is motivated to conceal the true state of affairs.

Understanding the system under study in its normal state provides the basis for determining what is symptomatic. Events or conditions that contrast markedly and in important ways from those of a normal system are considered symptomatic. For the auditor, normalcy is often determined by comparison to a relevant peer group of organizations. Determining which firms constitute the appropriate peer group is not always a straightforward process. This suggests that the auditor will concentrate a significant amount of information acquisition on determining what is normal. Clancey (1988) noted that asking general questions to determine what is normal and expected is important for evaluating medical findings.

If the problem area is well-understood, testing for certain deviant conditions becomes more workable. Diagnosis of errors in computer programs and electronic circuits is in theory a well-understood process. There is a formal specification that guides the search for the cause of the error. This formal specification identifies the normal state of the program or circuit. Medical diagnosis is simplified because it is based on the accumulated knowledge resulting from centuries of medical practice and medical research. In contrast, the auditor does not have available a taxonomy of organizational diseases or a well-developed science of organizational activity to guide diagnosis.

The diagnostic problem faced by the auditor is also very complex. From a system's viewpoint, complexity is a function of the number of components and the interactions between them. Intuitively, this is an indicator of the number of causal links in the system. Having to account for a single chief complaint even though the system is complex will reduce the complexity of the problem. Another way to think of the complexity of the system is to distinguish between the system's structure, behavior, and function. Complexity of the structure is a function of components and the interactions between them. Complexity of behavior is determined by the range of behavior that the system can manifest. Complexity of function is the range of goals and functions that the system can fulfill. From this standpoint, the auditor's problem is extremely complex. There are diverse organizations that conduct business in different ways. Some are primarily service organizations whereas others are manufacturers. Each organization can choose different strategies for competing within its particular market. There are numerous structural configurations for these organizations and therefore a wide range of economic behavior.

The overall complexity of audit diagnosis is compounded by the rapidly changing business environment. The last two decades have been marked by a series of dramatic changes within the business environment including: the globalization of business competition, an increasing rate of technological change, deregulation of many industries, and attempts of Eastern bloc nations to move toward a market economy. One effect of these extraordinary changes has been to increase difficulty of audit diagnosis.

It follows that there are several ways to simplify the diagnostic process. Bounding the diagnostic problem, operating in a well-specified relatively structured system, or having the benefit of a developed science simplifies the search for hypothesized causes for a particular problem. The five features of audit diagnosis discussed earlier force the auditor to conduct the search for symptoms and hypothesized causes over a wide area. In order to conduct the basic inferential task of determining causes of symptoms, considerable activity must be devoted to determining what is normal and what is symptomatic.

Structure, Behavior, and Function

The audit is an evaluation of the firm's financial condition based on the examination of evidence regarding business events and conditions. Inferences about both structural and functional aspects of the firm are drawn from records of business events and conditions. Defining the function and structure of the firm, as it relates to financial condition, does not lend itself to the level of precision found in a design specification for a computer program or electronic circuit. Two reasons for this are the changing organizational goals in response to environmental flux and the fact that organizational goals are determined by multiple stakeholders. In spite of this lack of precision, reasoning about the relationship between the behavioral, structural, and functional levels is part of the auditor's diagnostic process. By gaining a familiarity with the firm at the functional level, the expert auditor can conceptualize a "normal" firm and can draw inferences about the firm's structure that explain both normal and abnormal business events.

Some organizational theorists (Mintzberg, 1979) have examined the relationship between structure, behavior, and function as a way of evaluating organizational design. Mintzberg defined organizational structure as methods that organizations use to divide tasks and coordinate workflow in order to establish consistent and productive patterns of behavior. Translation of high-level strategic goals into structures consistent with those goals is crucial to the effective operations of an organization. This suggests a clear relationship among structure, behavior, and function in an ideal organization. However, the functional level can include goals and objectives of stakeholders that diverge somewhat from those formally stated by the organization. These individuals or groups can introduce modifications (informally perhaps) at the structural level. These modifications will in turn alter the events that occur at the behavioral level.

For the auditor, the behavioral level is composed of records of events that have occurred over a period of time. For example, the auditor must examine annual and quarterly financial reports. These reports consist of aggregations of quantities that make up the assets and liabilities of the firm as well as revenues and expenditures that show the profitability of the firm.

A firm can be thought of as transforming some set of inputs by adding value either through some production process or service into a set of outputs that are sold to a customer. For example, a computer manufacturer may purchase electronic components (inputs) and assemble them to produce a microcomputer. The manufacturer may then distribute the computers (outputs) to customers. The various primary activities necessary for bringing a product or service to a customer are value-adding processes (Porter, 1985). In the example, assembly and distribution are value-adding processes. In addition, there are a number of secondary supporting activities within a firm such as human resources management, accounting, and research and development that are not directly essential to the primary business activities. In the course of auditing a firm, the auditor examines financial records that relate to both the primary value-adding activities and the secondary supporting activities.

The structural level includes (a) formally defined work groups, (b) procedures for coordinating their activities among themselves, with suppliers, and with customers, and (c) accounting procedures. The different work groups can be associated directly or indirectly with value-adding processes. Accounting procedures provide a detailed account of how information is kept about various financial events. Depending on the particular accounting procedure chosen, the overall appearance of some set of financial events can change.

The functional level includes those features of the organization that define its raison d'être. At the superordinate level, function concerns the organization in relationship to its environment. The firm's industry, what it produces in that industry, characteristics of its market (such as geographical location and competitiveness), and state of the economy help to define the organization at the functional level. At a more specific level, the organization's culture, its overall strategic posture, goals, and objectives provide further functional definition. These may be translated more or less imperfectly into plans and structures that support the ongoing operations of the firm.

Our conceptualization of the structural, behavioral, and functional levels differs in one important respect from that of Milne (1987). He described these levels as strictly hierarchical with structure at the lowest level, behavior at the next level, and function at the highest level. They are hierarchical in that the knowledge representation for a level makes it possible to derive the next higher level of representation. In contrast, Fig. 13.1 shows that the three levels are highly interdependent. In an ideal sense, structure causes behavior, behavior illustrates function, and structure is developed or modified to fulfill the goals at the functional level. As a practical matter, the auditor must be concerned with other interactions between levels. For example, the intentional action of individuals can override procedures at the structural level. This suggests that the auditor's diagnostic reasoning may search for explanations for behavior at both the structural and the functional levels.

The intent of the preceding description is *not* to provide a rigorous theory of organizational function, structure, and performance. Rather it is to offer a backdrop for the discussion showing the relationship between the auditor's questioning strategy and knowledge structures that become apparent during diagnostic activity.

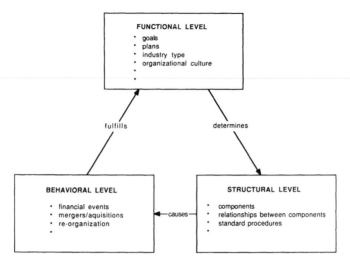

FIG. 13.1.   Organizational structure, behavior, and function.

QUESTIONING AND AUDITOR DIAGNOSIS

In this section, we describe an experiment that studied experienced auditors as they actively searched for information while they formulated an initial audit plan. Our objective was to show the relationship between the questioning strategies used by the auditors and the diagnostic process described earlier. We relate question types to the three steps of the basic diagnostic task of inferring the cause of a symptom: symptom identification, hypothesis generation, and hypothesis testing. The questions also reveal relationships among the structural, behavioral, and functional levels of organizational analysis.

Methodology

We analyzed approximately 1,600 questions generated by expert auditors who were conducting a preliminary examination of a company. They were presented with case material about three companies and were told that the company in the case was a new client. The case material provided general introductory information about a company, similar in form and content to the material an auditor would see during the initial planning stage of a new audit.

Each case consisted of nine pages of text and tables. Two pages of text described the company and industry background. Following this, a trial balance was split into balance sheet accounts and income statement accounts. The balance sheet shows the financial status of the firm in terms of assets and liabilities at some point in time. The income statement shows the accumulation of revenues and expenses during some time period (typically one year). The remainder of the case consisted of groups of financial ratios. These ratios show relationships between various components of the company's accounts, such as revenue, capital assets, expenses, inventory, and interest paid. They are presented along with industry averages to provide a basis for comparison. A major difference between the three companies in the cases was that one was financially healthy, one was marginally healthy, and the third was on the verge of bankruptcy.

Each of the 14 auditors who participated in the experiment was employed by one of the eight largest international accounting firms. All were audit managers. All but one had at least 5 years of experience. The experiment was conducted at the auditors' offices in a room that was insulated from interruptions. Their instructions were to examine the case material, one page at a time, and to verbalize any questions or requests for additional information.

Our initial analysis classified the questions by using the semantic categories in the Graesser, Lang, and Horgan (1988) taxonomy plus the comparison question category (Lauer & Peacock, 1990a). The taxonomy appears elsewhere in this volume (Graesser, Person, & Huber, chap. 9 in this volume; Paradice, chap. 15 in this volume). Comparison questions ask how two entities are similar or different. An explanation of how symptoms are identified by comparisons appears in the following.

In order to understand the auditor's problem-solving behavior, we examined sequences of questions within the individual protocols. Specifically, we were interested in determining the extent to which the auditor's early search and acquisition of information supported diagnostic processes. We identified two kinds of question group that were defined to be mutually exclusive: diagnostic groups and topic-related groups. Diagnostic groups were made up of contiguous questions addressing the same topic as a comparison question or statement. Topic-related groups were contiguous questions addressing the same topic that were also not diagnostic groups.

Comparison Questions and Symptom Identification

In the first step, the diagnostician searches out symptoms. What determines whether some variable or feature is symptomatic? Symptom identification involves comparison (Einhorn & Hogarth, 1982) in order to find abnormal or undesirable features and variables (Milne, 1987). We found that comparison questions were used to identify symptoms.

A task integral to symptom identification is the establishment of a referent for comparison. In a statement comparing Midway Airlines to American Airlines, Midway is called the subject and American is called the predicate element. It should be noted that comparing *a* to *b* is different from comparing *b* to *a*. For most people, comparison statements make the most sense when the more prominent or prototypical statement is the predicate element.

There are several points to be made with regard to the comparisons made during the symptom identification process. Comparisons may be made to establish an appropriate predicate element at a global level that provides the basis for the subsequent identification of individual symptoms. The predicate element is frequently a conceptual entity such as a prototypical firm from the same industry as the company under scrutiny and serves as the basis for determining what is normal. The prototype provides information about the firm's industry as well as historical information.

In auditing, many comparisons are strictly quantitative, such as comparison of ratios and comparison of profits over time. However, comparisons may also involve qualitative features (Tversky, 1977). For example, some subjects asked for comparisons of a company's product line with those of other companies in the same industry. Comparisons may be based on differences or similarities. One subject asked what the company was doing differently than others in the industry that led to slow payment of accounts receivable. The search for a global referent emphasizes similarities. For example, comparing product lines gives some measure of similarity for two companies in the same industry. Some subjects asked a number of general questions about product lines, markets, methods of distribution, and methods of production for the purpose of understanding the industry. One subject commented about this type of question.

> A lot of these questions may seem real general. But it's extremely helpful to understand where a company's coming from and where it's going, to see what their concerns are, and to be able to properly focus on where the risk is in the business, which helps with the risk in my audit.

After a good-fit prototype is selected, the ensuing search for symptoms involves comparison questions that focus on differences between the firm and the prototype. Quantitative differences play an important role. Many comparison questions ask whether some quantity exceeds some threshold ("Why is their collection period so much higher than the industry?"). Other comparison questions may examine differences in features ("What additional factors have negatively affected Infonet versus the industry in these two periods?" and "Who is it that they are selling to that they're out of whack with the rest of the industry?").

Hypothesis Generation

The reasoning from symptom to cause involves an examination of the relationship between structure, behavior, and function. However, there are different knowledge structures involved depending on whether explanations are found for behavior at the structural level or at the functional level. Reasoning from behavior to structure suggests causal knowledge structures. Cause-oriented knowledge structures are sequences of events where specific events are caused by previously occurring events together with certain enabling states or conditions (Graesser & Clark, 1985). Procedures (standard sequences of events) and work-group configurations (conditions) established at the structural level cause certain types of financial events to occur at the behavioral level. For example, one type of symptom could be an accounts receivable aging summary. This specifies the proportion of customers who pay their bills within certain time periods. This would be symptomatic if a large portion of the accounts receivable are outstanding. The cause could be one large customer who is slow in paying (an event). This in turn could be caused by an overly liberal credit policy (a condition).

At the stage of hypothesis generation, questions should reflect a search for causal relationships involving the symptom. Causal antecedent questions (questions that inquire about the cause of some event) indicate the search for a hypothesis. An example causal antecedent question is: "Why have receivables decreased from 1984 to 1985?" This question preceded three hypotheses: customers paying sooner, fewer customers, and institution of a new discount policy to reward early payment. Expectational questions also ask about a cause but indicate a greater degree of surprise regarding the outcome. The following example shows an expectational question: "Wouldn't you think that in this kind of market, receivables are probably more doubtful than they were last year?" This question followed the subject's observation that the allowance for doubtful accounts had declined from the previous year. Verification questions (questions that ask if a statement is true) presuppose the generation of a hypothesis by asking about a causal relationship, as shown in the following: "Inventory utilization is better than last year, better than industry. Is that just because we've written down the inventory, so the quantities are still there?" The verification question actually states a hypothesis regarding inventory utilization. The hypothesis is that there has been no real change in how effectively inventories are utilized. The cause of the apparent change is an accounting decision to reduce the value of the inventory. This represents a structural change in that the standing procedure for recording information about inventory has been altered.

Hypotheses that explain behavior at the functional level suggest goal-oriented knowledge structures. Goal-oriented structures provide the basis for intentionally executed plans and activities. Intentional actions that result in events or states are motivated by goals. The following example illustrates the search for hypotheses at the functional level: "They appear to maintain a very low level of debt. Are they making the proper expenditures for research and development? Will they make themselves less competitive in the marketplace in the long run?" Here, the auditor is concerned about the goals and long-term consequences of maintaining a low level of debt.

Furthermore, goals at the functional level may motivate the establishment of components or standing procedures at the structural level. The elements at the structural level may then lead to events at the behavioral level. Diagnosis may proceed by identifying hypotheses at the functional level to explain both structure and behavior. For example:

A lot of cash on hand at year's end, 90 million versus 21 million in '84. However, marketable securities are 20% of what they were the prior year, 9 million versus 54 million. Did they sell some securities or they matured and they didn't reinvest the money and just put it in cash? Do they have plans for that cash or (does it) just happen to be there at year's end and it's going to be reinvested? If so, in what?

In this example, the subject is examining the large amount of cash on hand. The subject notes that some marketable securities have either been sold or have matured. Two events have produced a symptom at the behavioral level, namely the presence of a large amount of cash. Securities were sold or matured and the proceeds were not reinvested. The large amount of cash may be on-hand due to timing, as a result of not having a plan, or because the firm is holding it in preparation for some major strategic initiative. Inquiries about the functional level will clarify which of these is true because specific goals are consistent with the presence of certain actions. Answers to these questions will motivate further inquiry or planning for future audit activities. If the subject finds there is no plan, then there will be no structural mechanism for reinvesting the funds. Alternatively, if the large amount of cash on-hand is due to timing, the structural mechanism for reinvestment will be in place. If the firm is holding the cash prior to investing in some large strategic project, the normal mechanisms for dealing with the proceeds from the securities will have been superceded by some executive action. The inquiry could also proceed by asking about what mechanisms exist for the reinvestment of proceeds from marketable securities (structural level). Depending on what is discovered about reinvestment procedures, the auditor could then ask about goals at the functional level.

Hypothesis Testing

The third step tests the hypotheses. In medical diagnosis, the physician develops a set of competing hypotheses. Testing involves gathering information that supports or refutes the hypotheses. Due to the nature of our experimental task, there is less evidence regarding the hypothesis-testing phase. The information in the cases provided a general overview of the company's activities. There may have been insufficient detail with which to derive tests warranted by the hypotheses that the subjects identified. The testing phase sometimes involves causal relationships that have multiple links with the hypothesis. A sequence of tests is often needed with each test contingent upon the results of the previous test.

When there is a single causal relationship, a verification question may capture the underlying test. An example is provided in the following: "Allowance for doubtful accounts is down. I would question that. I question that the relationship, the decrease in allowance compared to the decrease in accounts receivable is a consistent one. I want to look at that real hard." In this case, the subject seeks a verification that the decrease in allowance for doubtful accounts was accompanied by a like decrease in accounts receivable. This would indicate that the decrease in allowance for doubtful accounts was normal. However, a negative result would lead to a further hypothesis and test for potential deception.

In addition to verification questions, disjunctive questions and quantitative questions are likely markers of the test phase. Disjunctive questions may pose one alternative that is consistent with a hypothesis and one that rules it out as illustrated by the following example: "Why didn't they string out their payables a bit more if they're trying to control costs? Are they dealing with typical vendors or are they purchasing from one large vendor?" In this case, if the company is dealing with one large vendor, they may be forced to pay their bills promptly. The next example shows how answers to quantitative questions may support a hypothesis: "Inventories are down, which could consist of two things: quantities dropping or reevaluation of inventories. What are current year inventories calculated at last year's standards?" Answering this question will enable the auditor to determine how much of the drop in inventory is due to the new accounting procedure for calculating inventory value.

Diagnostic Groups and Topic-Related Groups

Diagnostic groups were identified by searching for comparison questions and comparison statements. Contiguous questions topically related to the comparison question or comparison statement together with that statement or question formed a group. The following is an example of a diagnostic group: "Property plant and equipment, way up. Twenty million dollars over prior year. What did they buy? How are they depreciating it? Does it relate to their increase in R & D expenses as well then?"

Topic-related groups are groups of contiguous questions related by some topic area that were not classified as a diagnostic group. The following is an example of a topic-related group:

Inventories, primarily is the same question. How many times do we turn over inventory annually? What's in inventory? Have we done a physical inventory observation? Are there any obsolete items in there, potentially discontinued items, any reserve set up for it? How do we account for inventories, on a LIFO or FIFO basis?

Three kinds of analysis suggest that the two groups serve a different function for the auditor. The topic-related groups provide the auditor with a general orientation to the company. The diagnostic groups are in response to specific conditions or events that require explanation.

Frequencies of the semantic categories of questions are significantly different for the two groups ($\chi^2 = 88.4$, $df = 11$, $p < .005$). Four of the categories accounted for the greatest differences: concept completion, instrumental/procedural, causal antecedent and expectational. The first two categories occur more in topic-related groups, whereas the causal type questions occur more in the diagnostic groups. The presence of more causal questions in the diagnostic groups is consistent with the previous discussion of diagnosis. The auditor identifies a symptom via comparison and then seeks to find a causal explanation for it. Most of the instrumental/procedure questions were asked to find out about the accounting procedures used by the firm. Greater numbers of concept completion and instrumental/procedure questions suggest that the topic-related groups are performing the function of orientation. Answers to these questions give the auditor a more complete understanding of the firm.

There were significantly more diagnostic groups for the cases that had inferior financial health ($\chi^2 = 44.2$, $df = 26$, $p < .01$). In contrast, there was no significant difference in the number of topic-related groups for the three cases ($\chi^2 = 20.5$, $df = 26$, $p = $ n.s.). The Felix and Kinney (1982) model predicts that topic-related groups should generally occur prior to diagnostic activity. The mean probability that a topic-related group occurred before diagnostic group was .67. This was significantly different from .5 ($t = 3.64$, $df = 28$, $p < .005$). Some 79.6% of the topic-related groups occurred during the first four pages of the cases. Only 53.7% of the diagnostic groups occurred during the first four pages.

The topic-related groups illustrate the orientation necessary to determine which audit evidence requires explanation. The amount of general information seeking, useful for determining what is normal, is not sensitive to the financial health of the company. This orientation generally occurs prior to the information seeking that supports diagnostic inference. In contrast, the amount of diagnostic activity is influenced by the financial health of the firm.

EXPERT SYSTEMS IN AUDITING

During the last decade, there has been increasing interest in developing expert systems to support various phases of the audit judgment process. For example, expert systems have been developed to assess audit risk (Graham, Damens, & Van Ness, 1990), to determine the adequacy of loan-loss reserves (Kelly, Ribar, & Willingham, 1986), to make going-concern judgments, judgments regarding the company's ability to stay in business, (Biggs & Selfridge, 1986), and to evaluate internal controls (Gal, 1985). In spite of a general mood of optimism regarding the direction of these efforts, some important problems have emerged.

As noted by Messier and Hansen (1987), an expert system for auditing may be developed with two different objectives. One is to develop a cognitive model of the expert auditor. Alternatively, the development of these expert systems has been motivated by the desire to elevate the performance of the practicing auditor and to realize economic benefits. The developer's goal is to produce a system that performs the audit task at least as well as an expert auditor. Such systems are sometimes developed without regard to reproducing faithfully the auditor's decision processes. Therefore, the rules represented in the knowledge base are not similar to the methods used by the expert auditor (Johnson, Jamal, & Berryman 1989).

Available audit expert systems are difficult to evaluate (Messier & Hansen, 1987). One method of evaluation is to compare the output of the expert systems with a normative solution to the problem. However, audit judgment problems are of sufficient complexity and uncertainty that there is generally no normative solution. Furthermore, "experts" often disagree about the best solution to some of these problems (Ashton, 1983; Biggs & Mock, 1983). An alternative method of evaluation is to compare the process used in the expert systems with the decision process of the expert auditor. This is tantamount to developing a cognitive model of the auditor.

Johnson et al. (1989) argued in favor of conducting research to develop a generalized cognitive model of the audit task. They contend that audit researchers have generally become preoccupied with surface rules while neglecting the operative knowledge that enables the expert auditor to perform audit judgment tasks successfully. The model they advocate explicitly defines what any cognitive processor must compute in order to perform audit tasks.

Questioning and Knowledge Acquisition

We propose a two-stage approach to knowledge acquisition for audit expert systems. The first stage would capture freely generated questions from auditors as they analyzed a series of problems. The second stage would take the symptoms identified in the first stage as a starting point. It would build on this by using question probes to gain a more detailed understanding of the relationship between the symptom and various hypotheses. The typical approach for audit knowledge acquisition has analyzed experts' protocols of their solutions to problems containing seeded errors. These studies (Biggs & Mock, 1983; Johnson et al., 1989) have yielded models that emphasized hypothesis generation and subsequent stages of diagnosis to the relative neglect of the orientation phase and symptom identification.

The two approaches stress different phases of the decision process. The question-generation process focuses on the initial acquisition of information whereas the full protocol analysis is more concerned with the subsequent evaluation of that information. From the standpoint of diagnosis, question generation yields more information about symptom identification. Full protocol analysis attempts to gain complete information about the expert's decision process once the symptom has been identified. Most often, this method examines the protocols of a small number of subjects as they examine a single problem. In contrast, because the question protocols are less dense, it is possible to analyze comparatively greater numbers of subjects and comparatively more cases (Lauer & Peacock, 1990b).

Using free generation of questions for knowledge acquisition would yield (a) information about the auditor's orientation process and the determination of appropriate normal values for the company and (b) information about symptom-hypothesis pairs. The second phase would involve asking follow-up questions to produce a more complete model of the relationship between symptoms and hypotheses. Additional insight can be obtained by asking questions to clarify the relationship between the structural, behavioral, and functional levels for specific symptoms that have been identified.

Initial follow-up questions may be used to find hypotheses that could account for the symptomatic condition on the structural level. These could ask about what specific business activities could lead to the symptomatic result. Causal antecedent questions would be used here frequently. For example, asking why inventory utilization has improved could identify the cause as the use of an improved inventory process, such as a new just-in-time inventory system. This would motivate further questions about what other activities would be affected by the new inventory system. Additional queries could ask about whether standing procedures or policies could affect the outputs or the recording of the outputs of some business process to make them symptomatic. In the same example, changing accounting procedures for recording inventory from one time period to the next could show that some of the improved inventory utilization is illusory.

A more elaborate model can be developed by examining the relationship between hypotheses at the structural level and the functional level. Further insight can be gained by asking what sorts of goals and plans are consistent with the hypothesized relationship between the symptom and the structural cause. In the preceding example, this kind of question would ask why management would want to change accounting procedures. Answers to this question should stimulate additional questions about related goals. The relationship between these newly discovered goals and work arrangements and policies at the structural level can then be explored. The inquiry process for these follow-up questions could also proceed by first examining the relationship between symptoms and goals at the functional level and then seeking elaboration at the structural level.

Symptoms and the hypotheses generated by searching for relationships between structure, behavior, and function can be further analyzed to discover their importance. This can be accomplished by asking about the import, frequency, and evoking strength of symptoms and hypotheses (Miller, Pople, & Myers, 1982). *Import* is the degree to which a diagnostician is compelled to explain the symptom when it occurs. For example, to determine the import of longer-than-average accounts receivable aging, one could ask how necessary it is to explain this symptom in any audit. Additional questions could ask about the specific factors that contribute to import for a particular symptom. In the previous example, these questions could ask about whether above-normal accounts receivable aging is more important for particular industries or firms of a certain size. The ability to use a variety of cases for generating questions makes it possible to inquire about factors that changed the import of a particular symptom from one case to another.

If hypotheses are generated to explain a particular symptom, questions can be asked to ascertain the *frequency* with which companies with the problem exhibit the symptom. For example, how often do companies without a discount policy have longer-than-average accounts receivable aging. Further questions can probe for factors that lead to increased frequency such as industry type or market conditions. Further information regarding hypothesis quality can be gained by asking about *evoking strength*. Evoking strength is determined by the strength of a particular diagnosis for explaining some finding. For auditing, evoking strength would answer the question: "Given a company with accounts receivable aging greater than the industry average, how strongly should I consider their lack of a discount policy as an explanation?"

CONCLUSION

Diagnosis has been characterized as an information gathering problem (Clancey, 1988). Information is sought to develop a mental model of the system under study. The study of auditors' questions offers a means of studying their decision processes that is consistent with this focus on information acquisition. It emphasizes their search for information to a greater extent than their subsequent evaluation of the acquired information. This contrasts with the approach taken by much of the research on audit judgment. A common research paradigm has been to present the auditor with a set of cues. This research has analyzed how these cues were used to arrive at some criterion judgment. For complex tasks such as audit diagnosis, it is likely that the skilled practitioner's active search and acquisition of information is an essential component of expertise.

Therefore, a requirement for a faithful model of the expert auditor's diagnostic processes will include the expert's inquiry during the initial stages of problem formulation. We have presented evidence and a reasoned argument that the establishment of a norm through the initial orientation and the identification of symptoms is particularly important for audit diagnosis. The use of free generation of questions and follow-up question probes when knowledge is elicited from experts is well-suited to modeling the auditor because of this emphasis on information acquisition.

REFERENCES

American Institute of Certified Public Accountants (AICPA, 1976). Using the work of a specialist, *Statement on Auditing Standards No. 11.*

American Institute of Certified Public Accountants (AICPA, 1988). Analytical procedures, *Statement on Auditing Standards No. 56.*

Ashton, R. H. (1983). *Research in audit decision making: Rationale, evidence, and implications* (Research Monograph No. 6). Canadian Certified General Accountant's Research Foundation Vancouver, B.C.

Biggs, S. F., & Mock, T. J. (1983). An investigation of auditor decision processes in the evaluation of internal controls and audit scope decisions, *Journal of Accounting Research, 21,* 234–255.

Biggs, S. F., & Selfridge M. (1986). *GC-X: A prototype expert system for the auditor's going concern judgment.* Unpublished manuscript, University of Connecticut, Storrs, CT.

Chandrasekaran, B., & Milne, R. (1985). Reasoning about structure, behavior, and function. *SIGART Newsletter, 93,* 4–59.

Clancey, W. J. (1988). Acquiring, representing, and evaluating a competence model of diagnostic strategy. In M. T. H. Chi, R. Glaser, & M. J. Farr (Eds.), *The nature of expertise* (pp. 343–418). Hillsdale, NJ: Lawrence Erlbaum Associates.

Davis, R. (1983). Diagnostic reasoning based on structure and behavior. In D. G. Bobrow (ed.), *Qualitative reasoning about physical systems* (pp. 347–410). Cambridge, MA: MIT Press.

Einhorn, H. J., & Hogarth, R. M. (1982). Prediction, diagnosis, and causal thinking in forecasting, *Journal of Forecasting, 1,* 23–36.

Felix, W. L., & Kinney, W. R. (1982). Research in the auditor's opinion formulation process: State of the art. *Accounting Review, 57,* 245–271.

Gal, G. (1985). *Using auditor knowledge to formulate data model constraints: An expert system for internal control evaluation.* Unpublished PhD dissertation, Michigan State University, East Lansing, MI.

Graesser, A. C., & Clark, L. F. (1985). *Structures and procedures of implicit knowledge,* Norwood, NJ: Ablex.

Graesser, A. C., Lang, K., & Horgan, D. (1988). A taxonomy for question generation, *Questioning Exchange, 2,* 3–15.

Graham, L. E., Damens, J., & Van Ness, G. (1990). Developing risk advisor: An expert system for risk identification, *Audit Judgment Symposium,* Center for Accounting Research, University of Southern California.

Johnson, P. E., Jamal, K., & Berryman, R. G. (1989). Audit judgment research. *Accounting, Organizations, and Society, 14,* 83–99.

Kelly, K. P., Ribar, G. S., & Willingham, J. J. (1986). Interim report on the development of an expert system for the auditor's loan loss evaluation. *Auditing Symposium VIII,* University of Kansas.

Klahr, D., & Dunbar, K. (1988). Dual space search during scientific reasoning. *Cognitive Science, 12,* 1–48.

Kuipers, B. (1987). Qualitative simulation as causal explanation. *IEEE Transactions on Systems, Man, and Cybernetics, SMC-17, 3,* 432–444.

Lauer, T. W., & Peacock, E. (1990a). An analysis of comparison questions in the context of auditing. *Discourse Processes, 13,* 349–361.

Lauer, T. W., & Peacock, E. (1990b). Questioning methodology and the study of audit judgment. *Audit Judgment Symposium,* Center for Accounting Research, University of Southern California.

Messier, W. F., & Hansen, J. V. (1987). Expert systems in auditing: The state of the art. *Auditing: A Journal of Theory & Practice, 7,* 94–105.

Miller, R. A., Pople, H. E., Jr., & Myers, J. D. (1982). INTERNIST-I, an experimental computer-based diagnostic consultant for general internal medicine. *New England Journal of Medicine, 307,* 468–476.

Milne, R. (1987). Strategies for diagnosis, *IEEE Transactions on Systems, Man, and Cybernetics, SMC-17, 3,* 333–339.

Mintzberg, H. (1979). *The structuring of organizations.* Englewood Cliffs, NJ: Prentice-Hall.

Porter, M. E. (1985). *Competitive advantage.* New York: Free Press.

Tversky, A. (1977). Features of similarity. *Psychological Review, 84,* 327–352.

Wenger, E. (1987). *Artificial intelligence and tutoring systems.* Los Altos, CA: Morgan Kaufmann.

14 The Role of Questioning in Learning from Computer-Based Decision Aids

Paul John Steinbart
Memphis State University

Researchers in the fields of accounting and information systems have long been interested in finding ways to improve decision-making quality. One approach that has received a great deal of attention involves the development of computer-based decision aids, such as decision support systems and expert systems, that are designed to complement the strengths and mitigate the cognitive limitations of human decision makers. Another intriguing possibility, however, is that use of such tools may also improve decision making by helping users better understand how to make decisions. Indeed, it has been argued that one of the primary benefits of using the simulation ("what if") features of a decision support system is that it allows the decision maker to explore how changes in various assumptions affect the ultimate decision (Courtney, Paradice, & Mohammed, 1987; Pracht & Courtney, 1988). Similar claims have been made about the explanation facilities in expert systems (Biggs, Messier, & Hansen 1987; Gal & Steinbart, 1987; Harmon & King, 1985; Waterman, 1986). Those facilities permit the user to ask the system why a particular piece of information is needed or how a specific conclusion was made. The claim is that through repeated questioning of that type users will see the entire reasoning process of the expert system and this should help them better understand the basis for making that particular decision.

The ability to learn from the use of computer-based decision aids is of special interest to researchers in applied fields of business (e.g., accounting, auditing, information systems, etc.) because expert judgment in most of those domains is developed not only through formal training, but also through on-the-job experience. The trend toward increased use of computer-based decision aids, however, may be subtly changing the nature of that practical on-the-job experience. Traditionally, whenever inexperienced decision makers were unsure of what to do next, they would seek advice from someone with experience in making that decision. Now, however, firms are beginning to store preferred judgment strategies in computer-based decision aids (e.g., expert systems). Consequently, inexperienced decision makers can now first turn to the expert system's explanation facilities for advice before directly interacting with the firm's expert. Such an approach clearly makes more efficient use of scarce resources and expertise. Nevertheless, it also raises questions about the ability of people to effectively learn in that manner.

The results of previous research do not provide any clear answers about people's ability to learn from decision aids. Studies report that users believe that decision aids help them better understand the decision process (Aldag & Power, 1986; Naylor & Schauland, 1976). Attempts to verify those perceptions experimentally, however, have produced mixed results. Some studies have reported that users of such tools can improve their understanding of the decision model (Pracht & Courtney, 1988), can adopt the decision strategy used by the system (Door, Eining, & Groff, 1988), and can apply that strategy to other similar problems (Chorba & New, 1980; Kasper, 1985). Other studies, however, have reported that users are unable to learn the decision model employed by such systems (Clancey, 1983, 1984; Dos Santos & Bariff, 1988), and do not exhibit any significant improvement in their decision-making ability (Aldag & Power, 1986; Blocher, Krull, Scalf, & Yates, 1988; Goslar, Green, & Hughes, 1986).

Those mixed results suggest that the ability to learn from the use of a decision aid is affected by other factors. It is important to remember that the advice provided by a decision aid usually is presented in the form of text. Consequently, factors that affect text comprehension may affect people's ability to learn from the advice offered by decision aids. For example, research has found that people's recall of text can be improved by asking them questions about the material that they have read (Graesser & Clark, 1985; Pressley, McDaniel, Snyder, & Turnure, 1988; Pressley, McDaniel, Turnure, Wood, & Ahmad, 1987; Shank, Myers, & Rayner, 1988). Therefore, it may be possible to improve people's ability to learn from the advice presented by a decision aid by asking them questions about that advice. In addition, research has also found that different types of questions tend to elicit different kinds of reasoning behaviors (Graesser, Lang, & Horgan, 1988). If that is so, then asking users of decision aids different types of questions about the advice being offered may affect how well that advice is understood. The remainder of this chapter explores both of those possibilities.

THE UTILITY OF QUESTIONING USERS
ABOUT AN EXPERT SYSTEM'S ADVICE

What is the best way to transfer knowledge about decision-making strategies? Perhaps the most straightforward approach is to explain directly to the learner the rationale that supports the decision currently being made. Indeed, the explanation facilities of expert systems are designed to do just that. When the user asks the system why it needs a particular piece of information, the explanation is couched in terms of how that information will be used to accomplish a step in the system's judgment strategy. For example, rule-based expert systems typically respond to questions about why some item of information is needed by displaying the rule that triggered the request for that information. The user has the option of responding to that explanation by asking why that rule was being followed; the system then displays another rule that, together with the first rule, forms part of the line of reasoning being followed. Thus, if repeated enough times, such questioning by the user will eventually reveal the entire goal hierarchy that the system is following.

As noted earlier, however, the explanations provided by expert systems appear in the form of text on the terminal screen. Graesser and Clark (1985) argued that a reader's comprehension of text includes many inferences that are made when reading the passage. If that is so, then comprehension is likely to be affected by the quality and quantity of the inferences made while reading. Indeed, there is evidence that one of the characteristics that differentiates successful from unsuccessful learners is that the former tend to generate more inferences spontaneously while reading than do the latter (Bransford et al., 1982). Moreover, successful learners' inferences also tend to include more detailed elaborations about the meaning of the material being read.

Some studies have reported that unsuccessful learners can be taught to make the kinds of inferences that improve their comprehension of written text (Franks et al., 1982; Stein, Bransford, Franks, Owings, et al., 1982; Stein, Bransford, Franks, Vye, & Perfetto, 1982). Graesser and Clark (1985) pointed out that asking people questions about text that they have read may cause them to make additional inferences about the material in that passage. Therefore, it may be possible to use questions to prompt people to generate the types of elaborative inferences that facilitate learning. Indeed, several studies have found that including questions in written text improves people's subsequent recall of that material (Pressley et al., 1987, 1988; Shank et al., 1988). The research conducted by Pressley and colleagues clearly illustrates the benefits of such questioning. Subjects were asked to study sentences that presented arbitrary facts and were later tested on their ability to recall those facts. Two types of sentences were used: (a) simple sentences, which merely stated that some action occurred (e.g., "the short man stood on a stool"), and (b) elaborated sentences, which not only presented the arbitrary fact, but also included an additional clause that explained the purpose of that action (e.g., "the short man stood on a stool to reach the cookie jar"). One half of the subjects in each condition also read a question that prompted them to think about the sentence that they had read. The question accompanying the simple sentences asked the reader to think of a reason why the action occurred; the question accompanying the elaborated sentences asked the reader to think about how the elaboration explained the reason for the action. Subjects who read the sentences that were accompanied by a question scored higher on subsequent recall tests than did subjects who read the sentences that were not accompanied by questions.

Questioning may also facilitate the learning of judgment strategies. For example, Carlson and Dulany (1985) examined people's ability to learn complex judgment rules and found that learning was greater when subjects were required to consider explicitly the rule's applicability in a given situation than when they were merely allowed to use the rule to solve a problem. Similarly, Lewis and Anderson (1985) reported that subjects who had to explain what they were doing, and why they were doing it, at each step in the decision process learned the overall strategy better than did subjects who merely practiced each step without giving such explanations.

The research reviewed in this section has significant implications for users' ability to learn from the advice provided by decision aids such as expert systems. As mentioned earlier, users can query expert systems to see the rules that are being followed. It is also possible to design the system to display automatically the rule that triggered the system's request for information. Indeed, the manuals of some of the tools used to build expert systems even suggest that the system be designed to display automatically the rules so that users will understand the decision process being followed. The results of studies such as those conducted by Pressley et al. (1987, 1988), however, suggest that users will better understand the system's explanations if they are accompanied by a question that requires users to think about the reasoning strategy implied by a particular rule. The next section discusses the results of an experiment that was designed, in part, to address that issue.

EXPERIMENT 1: EFFICACY OF SYSTEM-INITIATED QUESTIONING

This section reports the results of an experiment that examined the effects of system-initiated questioning on users' understanding of the explanations provided by an expert system. The experiment manipulated two independent variables: the design of the human-computer interface and the system's decision model. The discussion in this section is limited to the effects of alternative interface designs; the interested reader is referred to Pei, Steinbart, and Reneau (1990) for complete details of the experiment.

Subjects and Task

Undergraduate students at Memphis State and Arizona State universities participated in the experiment. Subjects were accounting majors enrolled in a required course on accounting information systems. All subjects had previously taken courses on the use of microcomputers; this was their first exposure, however, to an expert system.

The task involved the evaluation of a company's computer-based internal controls. Internal control evaluation is a major topic in the accounting information systems course. The evaluation is made by collecting evidence about the existence of specific internal control procedures. Internal control procedures are prescribed methods for performing a specific task in a manner that will reduce the likelihood of errors (either accidental or intentional) arising during the processing of data. For example, one of the objectives of any company is to prevent unauthorized transactions from being processed. An internal control procedure that can help accomplish that objective is to restrict access to source documents to only those people who are authorized to initiate that transaction.

Interface Design: System-Initiated Questioning

Subjects were randomly assigned to use one of two versions of an expert system. Both versions asked the user a series of 27 questions about the existence of specific computer-based internal controls.[1] The two versions differed from one another in the design of the human-computer interface. The basic version of the system was designed so that after the user responded to each of the system's requests for data, the rule that triggered that request was automatically displayed. Thus, the user was able to follow each step of the judgment strategy being followed by the system. In contrast, the enhanced version occasionally (four times) accompanied the display of a rule with an additional question that asked the user to think about the meaning or significance of that rule. Thus, users of the enhanced system were prompted to generate elaborative inferences about the rules that were displayed. Table 14.1 illustrates the type of interaction that occurred with each version of the expert system.

Results

Two tests were administered to assess learning: The first was given immediately after subjects had used the expert system during a 1-hour training session and the second was given 1 week later. Learning was measured as performance on a 12-question test about internal control procedures. Two types of questions from Graesser et al.'s (1988) question taxonomy were used: (a) causal antecedent questions and (b) goal-oriented questions. The causal antecedent questions asked subjects to identify the missing control procedures (cause) that allowed some stated problem to occur. The goal-oriented questions asked subjects to describe the type of problem that would be avoided by implementation of some specific

---

[1]The sequence of those questions was also varied as a result of manipulating the specific judgment model being used by the system. See Pei et al. (1990) for more complete details.

TABLE 14.1
Interaction With Basic and Enhanced Versions of Expert System

---

Basic Version

Step 1: System asks for data and user responds (bold).
Is access to source documents restricted?

YES

Step 2: After user responds, system displays current rule.

IF: Access to source documents is restricted
THEN: Unauthorized transactions may be input - probability = 1/10

Step 3: System then generates next question.
Is source document authorization verified?

Enhanced Version

[Steps 1 and 3 identical to basic version]
Step 2: After user responds, system displays current rule.

IF: Access to source documents is restricted
THEN: Unauthorized transactions may be input - probability = 1/10

NOTE: What do you think would be the effect if you had answered that the access to
source documents was NOT restricted? You may want to do a similar sensitivity analysis
on your answers to the remaining questions.

Adapted from Pei, Steinbart, and Reneau (1990).

control procedure. The test consisted of 4 goal-oriented questions, 4 causal antecedent questions in an abstract, context-free setting, and 4 context-specific causal antecedent questions. Table 14.2 presents examples of each type of question.

Table 14.3 presents the results on both the immediate and delayed performance tests. Users of the enhanced version of the system generally scored higher on the tests than did users of the basic version. Thus, it appears that asking users questions about the system's advice helps them to better understand that advice. That finding is consistent with previous research on text understanding (Pressley et al., 1987, 1988; Shank et al., 1988). The results of the current experiment, however, extend the findings of that previous research in three ways. First, the benefits of questioning readers about the meaning of text was found to hold even when the text was presented on a computer screen, rather than on paper. Second, previous research had used continuous prompting to encourage elaboration; the current experiment showed that the learning benefits can occur even with intermittent prompting. Third, Table 14.3 also shows that the benefits persisted on the delayed test, suggesting that system-initiated questioning facilitates not only the acquisition, but also the retention of knowledge.

Table 14.3 also shows that performance differed on the three types of questions that were used. Specifically, subjects did better at answering goal-oriented

TABLE 14.2
Questions Used to Measure Learning of Internal Control Knowledge

---

Goal-Oriented Questions

Output control totals are reconciled with input and processing control totals. What possible errors and irregularities could occur when this control procedure was not established and followed?

Context-Free Causal Antecedent Questions

In an EDP (electronic data processing) environment that used both batch and on-line processing for various accounting applications, what control procedures could be used to detect and correct incorrectly processed transactions?

Context-Specific Causal-Antecedent Questions

The Wilkinson company used a batch system to update its inventory record. Each day, the inventory master file was constantly updated (five to six times) by two transaction files, purchases and sales. The computer program that updates the inventory master file can also initiate purchase requisitions for inventory items that are below minimum reorder points. The company's internal control procedures on sales and purchases are very tight. Thus, it is very unlikely that any unauthorized transactions can be input to sales and purchase files.

At the year's end, the company's auditor found that some of the inventory account balances were incorrectly updated and some unnecessary purchase requisitions were issued by the computer.

What are the applicable controls that could be implemented to prevent, detect, and correct this problem?

Adapted from Pei, Steinbart, and Reneau (1990).

TABLE 14.3
Summarized Results of Experiment 1

Test Question Type	Expert System Version	
	Basic	*Enhanced*
Panel A: Immediate posttest problem solving (% correct)		
Context-free causal antecedent	40.7	40.7
Context-specific causal antecedent	33.2	42.7
Goal-oriented	53.7	62.3
Panel B: Delayed posttest (% correct)		
Context-free causal antecedent	47.4	51.4
Context-specific causal antecedent	31.9	40.4
Goal-oriented	54.0	59.6

See Pei, Steinbart, and Reneau (1990) for complete details of the analysis.

questions than the causal antecedent questions. That finding is consistent with the results of prior research (Graesser & Clark, 1985; Graesser et al., 1988) that different types of questions are not of equal difficulty and that goal-oriented questions tend to be easier to answer than are causal antecedent questions. That raises another issue concerning the ability of users to learn from decision aids. Studies have found that it is easier to transfer problem-solving skills from harder versions to easier versions of the same problem than the reverse (Hayes & Simon, 1977; Kotovsky, Hayes, & Simon, 1985). If that is true, then using more difficult (e.g., causal antecedent) types of questions to prompt users to think about the explanation offered by a decision aid may be better than using simpler (e.g., goal-oriented) types of questions. Experiment 2 was designed, in part, to investigate that possibility.

EXPERIMENT 2: EFFECT OF ALTERNATIVE QUESTION TYPES ON LEARNING

Gal and Steinbart (in press) conducted an experiment to investigate the effects of interaction style and question type on the ability to learn from a computer-assisted training program. This section presents only the results pertaining to the effect of training on different types of questions (i.e., goal-oriented or causal antecedent); the interested reader is referred to Gal and Steinbart (in press) for a complete discussion of the experiment.

Subjects and Task

Students at Memphis State and the University of Massachusetts at Amherst who were taking a required accounting information systems course participated in the experiment. As in Experiment 1, all subjects were accounting majors and had previous experience in using microcomputers.

Subjects were required to solve basic problems involving the relationship between internal control procedures and possible errors. Whereas Experiment 1 dealt with computer controls, Experiment 2 focused on manual control procedures. The following is an example of a manual control procedure: "Customers are not billed until the billing department receives documentation that the merchandise has indeed been shipped." The objective of that control procedure is to prevent the billing of a customer for merchandise that is never received.

Question Type

Subjects were randomly assigned to use one of two different versions of a computer-assisted training program. The goal-oriented version presented descriptions of a manual control procedure and asked subjects to think about the purpose of that control. Subjects then pressed a key to see the system's description of the control's objective. In contrast, the causal antecedent version presented a brief description of a problem and asked subjects to think about the likely missing control procedures that had allowed that particular error to occur. Table 14.4 presents examples of each type of training question.

Results

Subjects used one version of the tutorial program during the experimental session and were then tested during the next class session to assess how well they had learned the material. Table 14.5 presents mean scores on the performance test. The test contained questions that required subjects to identify the purpose of a given control and also questions that required subjects to identify the causes of a given problem. Thus, subjects trained on one type of problem but were tested on both.

The results indicate that there was a difference in the effectiveness of the two different types of training. Subjects who practiced reasoning about the causal antecedents of problems did better on both types of test questions than did subjects whose practice focused on thinking about the purpose of specific control procedures. The scores also show that the causal antecedent problems were more difficult than the goal-oriented problems. Thus, the results indicate that prompting people to engage in the more difficult type of reasoning about control pro-

TABLE 14.4
Question Types Used in Experiment 2

Causal Antecedent Reasoning

Statement of problem:	A customer receives a bill for an item that was ordered but was never shipped.
Question:	What do you think is the cause of the problem and an appropriate control?

[Answer: Invoices should be prepared by the billing department on receipt of documentation (such as a bill of lading) from the shipping department that the merchandise has been shipped]

Goal-Oriented Reasoning

Statement of Problem:	Customers are not billed until the billing department is notified by the shipping department that the goods have been shipped.
Question	What do you think is the purpose of this control?

[Answer: to prevent billing customers for goods they never received]

Adapted from Gal and Steinbart (in press).

TABLE 14.5
Posttest Performance Results of Experiment 2
(percentage correct)

Training Focus	Test Problem Type	
	Goal-Oriented	Causal Antecedent
Goal-oriented (n = 44)	70.6	29.4
Causal antecedent (n = 36)	81.0	34.7

cedures helps them to better understand the underlying relationships so that they can apply that knowledge to solve other types of problems.

SUMMARY AND CONCLUSIONS

This chapter described two experiments that investigated the issue of learning from computer-based decision aids. Experiment 1 investigated whether asking users questions about what the system is doing facilitates learning the judgment model embedded in the system. The results indicated that such system-initiated questioning did help users learn the rules used by an expert system. Experiment 2 investigated the effect of asking users different kinds of questions. The results indicate that two types of questions differentially affect the amount of learning that occurs.

A number of issues present themselves as candidates for future research in this area. One issue concerns the optimal timing of prompting questions. Previous research in psychology has used continuous prompts to encourage people to generate elaborations about what they are reading (Pressley et al., 1987, 1988). Experiment 1 extended that finding by showing that intermittent prompting was also effective. But how frequently should users be prompted? This is an important issue for learning from decision aids, because too frequent prompting may degrade overall system performance to the point where it is no longer efficient to use it as a decision aid.

A second area for future research concerns the use of alternative question types. In both Experiments 1 and 2 there was some evidence that different question types differ in terms of difficulty. In addition, the results of Experiment 2 indicate that training with different types of questions affected performance on subsequent performance tests. That experiment, however, only examined two of the categories (goal-oriented and causal antecedent) in Graesser et al.'s (1988) taxonomy of question types. Other types of questions are also likely to play a role in many business decisions. Therefore, the effect of training with additional question types also needs to be studied.

A third issue concerns the possibility of using system-initiated questioning to mitigate some potential long-run problems with using automated decision aids. There is abundant anecdotal evidence, for example, concerning the harmful effects of ubiquitous calculator use on people's ability to do mental arithmetic. It is possible that more complex judgment skills may similarly be affected by prolonged reliance on tools such as decision support and expert systems. Thus, a topic for future research would be to investigate whether system-initiated prompts to think about the judgment strategy being followed by a decision aid would help either to prevent or reduce atrophy of judgment skills.

Finally, it would be important and useful to test whether the results of the present experiments can be extended to practical field settings. Typically, people know that they are expected to learn how to make particular types of decisions, but they do not usually expect to be "tested" on their knowledge. Experiments 1 and 2 both took place in settings in which subjects knew that they would later be tested on their knowledge of the material. Thus future research needs to determine whether similar results would be obtained in a setting in which subjects did not anticipate such explicit testing.

In summary, one way to improve decision making is to train people to become better decision makers. Indeed, the development of expert judgment skills in business typically requires extensive on-the-job training in making decisions. The increasing use of decision aids, however, is subtly altering the role of the decision maker and, thereby, the nature of such on-the-job training. Consequently, it is important to research the factors that influence the ability of people to learn while they use decision aids. The experiments described in this chapter represent an initial attempt to address that issue.

REFERENCES

Aldag, R. J., & Power, D. J. (1986). An empirical assessment of computer-assisted decision analysis. *Decision Sciences, 17*, 572–588.

Biggs, S. F., Messier, W. F., Jr., & Hansen, J. V. (1987). A descriptive analysis of computer audit specialists' decision-making behavior in advanced computer environments. *Auditing: A Journal of Practice & Theory, 6*, 1–21.

Blocher, E. J., Krull, E. G., Jr., Scalf, K. A., & Yates, S. V. N. (1988, September). *Training and performance effects of a knowledge-base system for analytical review.* Paper presented at First International Symposium on Expert Systems in Business, Finance, and Accounting, University of Southern California, Los Angeles, CA.

Bransford, J. D., Stein, B. S., Vye, N. J., Franks, J. J., Auble, P. M., Mezynski, K. J., & Perfetto, G. A. (1982). Differences in approaches to learning: An overview. *Journal of Experimental Psychology: General, 111*, 390–398.

Carlson, R. A., & Dulany, D. E. (1985). Conscious attention and abstraction in concept learning. *Journal of Experimental Psychology: Learning, Memory, and Cognition, 11*, 45–58.

Chorba, R. W., & New, J. L. (1980). Information support for decision-maker learning in a competitive environment: An experimental study. *Decision Sciences, 11,* 603–615.

Clancey, W. J. (1983). The epistemology of a rule-based expert system—a framework for explanation. *Artificial Intelligence, 29,* 215–251.

Clancey, W. J. (1984). Methodology for building an intelligent tutoring system. In W. Kintsch, J. R. Miller, & P. G. Polson (Eds.), *Method and tactics in cognitive science* (pp. 51–83). Hillsdale, NJ: Lawrence Erlbaum Associates.

Courtney, J. F., Jr., Paradice, D. B., & Mohammed, N. H. (1987). A knowledge-based DSS for managerial problem diagnosis. *Decision Sciences, 18,* 373–399.

Door, P., Eining, M., & Groff, J. E. (1988). Developing an accounting expert system decision aid for classroom use. *Issues in Accounting Education, 3,* 27–41.

Dos Santos, B. L., & Bariff, M. L. (1988). A study of user interface aids for model-oriented decision support systems. *Management Science, 34,* 461–468.

Franks, J. J., Vye, N. J., Auble, P. M., Mezynski, K. J., Perfetto, G. A., Bransford, J. D., Stein, B. S., & Littlefield, K. (1982). Learning from explicit versus implicit texts. *Journal of Experimental Psychology: General, 111,* 414–422.

Gal, G., & Steinbart, P. (1987). Artificial intelligence and research in accounting information systems: Opportunities and issues. *Journal of Information Systems, 2,* 54–62.

Gal, G., & Steinbart, P. J. (in press). Interface style and training task difficulty as determinants of effective computer-assisted knowledge transfer. *Decision Sciences.*

Goslar, M. D., Green, G. I., & Hughes, T. H. (1986). Decision support systems: An empirical assessment for decision making. *Decision Sciences, 17,* 79–91.

Graesser, A. C., & Clark, L. F. (1985). *Structures and procedures of implicit knowledge.* Norwood, NJ: Ablex.

Graesser, A. C., Lang, K., & Horgan, D. (1988). A taxonomy for question generation. *Questioning Exchange, 2,* 3–15.

Harmon, P., & King, D. (1985). *Expert systems.* New York: Wiley.

Hayes, J. R., & Simon, H. A. (1977). Psychological differences among problem isomorphs. In N. J. Castellan, D. B. Pisoni, & G. R. Potts (Eds.), *Cognitive theory* (Vol. 2, pp. 21–41). Hillsdale, NJ: Lawrence Erlbaum Associates.

Kasper, G. M. (1985). The effect of user-developed DSS applications on forecasting decision-making performance in an experimental setting. *Journal of Management Information Systems, 2,* 26–39.

Kotovsky, K., Hayes, J. R., & Simon, H. A. (1985). Why are some problems hard? Evidence from the Tower of Hanoi. *Cognitive Psychology, 17,* 248–294.

Lewis, M. W., & Anderson, J. R. (1985). Discrimination of operator schemata in problem solving: Learning from examples. *Cognitive Psychology, 17,* 26–65.

Naylor, T. H., & Schauland, H. (1976). A survey of users of corporate planning models. *Management Science, 22,* 927–937.

Pei, B. K. W., Steinbart, P. J., & Reneau, J. H. (1990). *The effect of alternative knowledge organizations and interface style on learning from an expert system.* Unpublished manuscript, School of Accounting, Tempe, AZ, Arizona State University.

Pracht, W. E., & Courtney, J. F. (1988). The effects of an interactive graphics-based DSS to support problem structuring. *Decision Sciences, 19,* 598–621.

Pressley, M., McDaniel, M. A., Turnure, J. E., Wood, E., & Ahmad, M. (1987). Generation and precision of elaboration: Effects on intentional and incidental learning. *Journal of Experimental Psychology: Learning, Memory, and Cognition, 13,* 291–300.

Pressley, M., McDaniel, M. A., Snyder, B., & Turnure, J. E. (1988). Elaborative interrogation facilitates acquisition of confusing facts. *Journal of Educational Psychology, 80,* 268–278.

Shank, D. M., Myers, J. L., & Rayner, K. (1988). Elaborate inferences during reading: Do they occur on-line? *Journal of Experimental Psychology: Learning, Memory, and Cognition, 14,* 410–420.

Stein, B. S., Bransford, J. D., Franks, J. J., Owings, R. A., Vye, N. J., & McGraw, W. (1982). Differences in the precision of self-generated elaborations. *Journal of Experimental Psychology: General, 111,* 399–405.

Stein, B. S., Bransford, J. D., Franks, J. J., Vye, N. J., & Perfetto, G. A. (1982). Differences in judgments of learning difficulty. *Journal of Experimental Psychology: General, 111,* 406–413.

Waterman, D. A. (1986). *A guide to expert systems.* Reading, MA: Addison-Wesley.

15

A Question Theoretic Analysis of Problem Formulation: Implications for Computer-Based Support

David B. Paradice
Texas A&M University

Decision support systems (DSS) have focused much attention on decision-making activities. Only recently, however, have researchers expanded their concern to supporting the earliest stages of the decision-making process. Traditionally, DSS have focused on the design of alternative solutions and the selection of the ultimate solution approach. This orientation implicitly assumes an accurate initial problem representation, which may not actually exist.

The process of problem formulation is normally unstructured (Paradice & Courtney, 1986). Leavitt (1975) recognized the need for research on problem formulation over 15 years ago. More recently, Lyles and Mitroff (1980) and Smith (1988, 1989) have reemphasized the need for exploring the mechanisms of problem formulation. Mintzberg, Raisinghani, and Theoret (1976) noted that little is known about the problem formulation phase of the decision-making process, except that humans do not appear particularly adept at it! The complexity of problem formulation may be attributed to the possibility that there are many factors that influence the problem formulation process, including biases that stem from a person's background and training (Ackoff, 1979; Reitman, 1964), the salient impact of the first stimulus that affects a person (Judson & Cofer, 1956), the large number of alternatives in the problem space (Newell & Simon, 1972), a person's ability to decompose problem-space complexity (Newell & Simon, 1972; Reitman, 1964), and the vast and diverse experiences of particular individuals (Rowe, 1977).

Existing research has shed a modest amount of light on problem formulation *support* processes. We have learned that computer-based systems can effectively support problem formulation activities (Ata-Mohammed, Courtney, & Paradice, 1988; Paradice & Courtney, 1986, 1987). We have also learned that computer-based systems that support the development of causal models can have a positive effect on decision-making processes, especially when combined with graphics interfaces (Loy, Pracht, & Courtney 1987; Pracht & Courtney, 1988). On the other hand, much of the prior research has focused on relatively routine problem formulation activities. Although the problem situations studied have been complex, they have had a clear-cut underlying structure. For example, the work by Courtney and his colleagues has involved participation in a complicated business simulation (Jensen & Cherrington, 1977). Although complex, the simulation requires and guarantees well-formed problem structure. Therefore, the simulation behaves in precisely the manner that researchers *expect* the variables in the simulation to behave in practice.

Problem formulation processes are difficult to study, even in very simple problem situations. Often, researchers rely on verbal protocols of problem solvers working on relatively structured tasks in a laboratory setting. Much has been learned using these approaches. However, many problems that people confront are messy, ill-structured problems involving stakeholders that have vested interests in the problem situation and any potential problem solution. Some of these problems seem unsolvable, or at best will require massive amounts of resources to solve.

An important future direction for research in computer-based support for problem formulation is to expand our knowledge of difficult problem domains (Mason & Mitroff, 1973). These domains are truly unstructured. The problems are novel and complex. Alternative solutions are difficult to identify because the underlying problem structure is not easily determined. Because of this lack of structure, alternative solutions may not be backed with conviction. Moreover, since any solution to these problems frequently requires substantial resources, lack of confidence hampers the implementation of a solution.

The purpose of this study is two-fold. First, the processes that people exhibit in formulating the structure of difficult problems is examined. Second, areas in which computer-based tools might provide effective problem formulation support are identified.

PROBLEM FORMULATION
AND QUESTION PROCESS THEORIES

Many activities support problem formulation processes. This study seeks to investigate how one of those activities, question asking, relates to problem formulation. Graesser and his associates have investigated the cognitive processes that underlie question generation (Graesser, Lang, & Horgan, 1988; Graesser, Person, & Huber, chap. 9 in this volume) and question answering (Graesser & Black, 1985; Graesser & Clark, 1985). The work by Graesser and colleagues forms a basis for the analysis of questions in this chapter. Similarly, conceptual models have recently evolved that provide some insight into problem formulation. In the sections that follow, these models are first discussed, then merged to provide a framework for the study of actual problem formulation activities.

Merging Problem Formulation and Question Generation

Smith (1989) developed a model of problem definition (i.e., problem formulation) that consisted of three stages: recognition, development, and exploration. The *recognition stage* involves the identification of the gap that exists between the current and desired states. Evidence that the problem exists surfaces in this phase, as well as any challenges to the problem's existence. The *development stage* focuses on elaborating the problem situation. Individuals with a vested interest in the problem solution are identified along with their values and objectives. Competing problem perspectives emerge and relevant knowledge of the problem situation is generated. A comprehensive working definition of the problem is proposed during this stage. The *exploration stage* identifies possible directions for the analysis to follow. Problem boundaries are identified, as well as inherent constraints and difficult aspects. If possible, the problem is decomposed into subproblems. The possible causes of problems are identified during the exploration stage. Potential methods for achieving a problem solution are generated. If necessary, *problem redefinition* can occur during any of the problem definition stages previously defined. Redefinition reflects new evidence and insights into the problem.

A crucial activity during each of these stages is acquiring the knowledge used to determine problem structure. Interrogative activities performed by the problem formulator presumably drive the knowledge acquisition process. That is, the problem solver undergoes a continuous process of asking questions and attempting to answer them.

Graesser et al. (1988) developed a taxonomy for categorizing questions that adults ask in different discourse contexts. They identified three separate dimensions for question analysis: semantic, pragmatic, and communicative. The *semantic dimension* specifies the type of information being requested. The *pragmatic dimension* specifies the purpose of asking the question. The *communicative dimension* evaluates properties of communicative interaction.

Graesser et al.'s semantic dimension was borrowed from the work of Lehnert (1978). Lehnert identified a rather comprehensive set of semantic categories in a question taxonomy, which is shown in Table 15.1. The question categories were developed to recognize essential conceptual differences in questions that cannot be accounted for using other taxonomies. Lehnert (1978) claimed that other approaches, such as categorization by grammatical part of speech and the who/what/when type of taxonomy, are not comprehensive systems and are not

TABLE 15.1
Semantic Categories of Question Taxonomy

Causal antecedent	Inquires about the events or states that caused something to occur.
Causal consequent	Inquires about the effects of an event.
Comparison*	Asks how one entity, attribute, or event is different from or similar to another
Concept completion	Requests further clarification.
Disjunctive	Inquires about which of a set of alternatives is the case.
Enablement	Asks about the resources, abilities, or conditions needed by an agent to carry out an action.
Expectational	Inquires why expected events or actions failed to occur.
Feature specification	Requests a nonquantitative value for an attribute.
Goal orientation	Asks about an agent's reasons, motives, or goals that account for an action.
Instrumental/Procedural	Inquires about plans or procedures used by an agent to execute an intentional act.
Judgmental	Asks for advice, opinion, or judgment.
Quantification	Requests a quantitative value (magnitude or frequency) for an attribute.
Verification	Inquires whether a proposition is true.

*Taken from Lauer and Peacock (1990). Remaining definitions taken from Lehnert (1978).

motivated by anything beyond surface linguistic descriptions. Lehnert's approach provides a means for categorizing questions on the basis of meaning and the type of response that is appropriate. Lehnert's taxonomy provides a comprehensive but parsimonious approach to analyzing question-answering processes. More recently, Lauer and Peacock (1990) have argued that comparison questions should be added to Lehnert's taxonomy.

Graesser et al. pointed out that a single utterance may serve many pragmatic purposes. Also, the pragmatic function of a speech act is conceptually separate from its literal meaning. Although the pragmatic dimension is distinct from the semantic dimension, "there clearly are systematic relationships" between the categories (Graesser et al., 1988, p. 9). Graesser suggested these relationships are most straightforward when the pragmatic aspect of a question is a bona fide attempt to acquire information.

Graesser argued that existing models of comprehension and communication limit the ability to perform significant quantitative work along the communicative dimension. Thus, this dimension is not considered further in this chapter.

EXPECTED OBSERVATIONS
FROM THE MERGED THEORIES

These theories, when merged, can provide a framework within which one might make certain expectations. In the sections that follow, Smith's (1989) problem definition model is combined with the work on question processes (directed by Lehnert and Graesser) in order to identify those types of questions that one would expect during problem formulation processes. That is, the goal is to map the question categories on the semantic dimension to the three stages of problem formulation.

Recognition Stage. Several of the question categories described in Table 15.1 would be expected in a protocol of the recognition stage of problem formulation. Goal-oriented questions would identify the desired state. Feature specification questions describe the properties of the desired state. Comparison questions would determine how the desired state differs from the current state. Each of these question categories addresses an aspect of the gap between the existing state and the desired state.

Development Stage. The development stage should exhibit questions oriented toward establishing stakeholder positions and values. Challenges to competing problem formulations would be expected as participants dispute those problem formulations that do not match their own. The goal-oriented question category would reflect the values and objectives of the participants. Disjunctive questions identify competing alternative formulations. Comparison and feature specification questions refine the alternative problem perspectives. In some cases, quantification questions would be generated to determine precisely what the alternative formulations are.

Exploration Stage. The exploration stage investigates problem characteristics. Causal antecedent questions would be used to define the causes of problems so that reoccurrence of the problem can be avoided. Causal consequence questions would be expected to identify solutions that appear most constructive. Instrumental/procedural and enablement questions would be expected during this stage to determine the methods for moving from the problem state to the solution state. Feature specification and quantification questions determine measurement of the extent to which desired states have been achieved. Judgment questions would reflect problem boundaries.

PROTOCOL ANALYSIS OF PROBLEM FORMULATION

As a starting point for analyzing the problem formulation process for difficult problems, transcripts from 30 television broadcasts were obtained. The shows included (and number of each) in the analysis were "Donahue" (8), "Nightline" (9), "This Week with David Brinkley" (1), "20/20" (1), and "Bill Moyer's World of Ideas" (1). Those excluded contained little or no "discussion" of the problem at hand. Four problem areas were selected: (a) homelessness in America, (b) the drug problem in America, (c) nuclear power use and how to handle nuclear waste, and (d) depletion of the atmospheric ozone layer.

The transcripts include comments from academic experts, industry experts, congressmen, and workers that deal with these problem areas on a daily basis. Consequently, the analysis may provide some insight into how people structure these problem areas. These types of television broadcasts are critical in shaping how the average American obtains information used for problem formulation processes. Graesser et al. (1988) noted the questioning that occurs in these contexts has some important features in common with questioning in normal social interaction. However, some "gamesmanship" exists as a result of trying to put the best face on one's particular stance in these problem areas. One cannot ignore a politician's need to satisfy a constituency or a talk-show host's need to supply some amount of entertainment. In spite of these characteristics of the context from which the data is drawn, the underlying assumption is that the programs reflect some of the characteristics of actual problem formulation processes. More specifically, the following assumptions are made regarding the analysis:

1. Talk show hosts are neutral with regard to opinion, they seek only to arrive at the true problem structure.
2. Although participants may take a stance, their ultimate concern is in determining the correct problem structure.
3. Any transcript segments lost due to editing the show would not significantly alter the following analysis.

Problem Formulation Perspective Analysis

Table 15.2 shows an analysis of the questions asked in the 20 transcripts. Frequencies are provided for the 13 semantic question categories, segregated by Smith's problem definition stages. Because Smith's work was not developed with protocol analysis explicitly considered, there occasionally was some ambiguity or uncertainty in classifying the questions. In addition, some questions in the protocols were not relevant to the problem formulation process and were therefore unclassified. A total of 663 questions were classified in this analysis.

TABLE 15.2
Questions Asked During Problem Formulation Stages

Problem	Recognition Stage			Development Stage			Exploration Stage			
	CS	PE	PC	IS	VI	AP	BI	PD	PC	SE
Causal antecedent	2	2	2	2	3	4	1	0	22	3
Causal consequent	5	2	4	5	2	0	1	0	4	10
Comparison	1	2	0	0	0	0	0	0	0	2
Concept completion	4	18	5	11	18	14	20	2	6	22
Disjunctive	1	4	0	3	3	0	1	4	0	9
Enablement	0	2	0	0	1	0	0	0	0	3
Expectational	0	1	2	0	2	0	0	0	0	2
Feature Specific.	0	6	1	10	2	2	2	1	4	14
Goal Oriented	0	0	2	3	7	0	0	0	1	2
Instrumental/ procedural	0	3	0	7	5	4	13	4	0	61
Judgmental	2	19	6	14	26	11	8	0	5	49
Quantification	1	4	0	5	4	4	5	2	0	9
Verification	2	21	2	16	12	9	6	2	4	24
Totals	18	84	24	76	85	48	57	15	46	210

Recognition Stage: CS = current state/desired state; PE = problem evidence; PC = problem challenge
Development Stage: IS = stakeholder identification; VI = values identification; AP = alternative perspective
Exploration Stge: BI = boundary identification, PD = problem decomposition; PC = problem causes; SE = solution exploration.

Recognition Stage. There are 126 questions in the recognition stage. Very few of these questions explicitly addressed the existence of a gap between the current state of affairs and some desired state. Participants in the discussions focused almost entirely on the current state of affairs. Causal consequent and concept completion questions accounted for half of the question types in this category.

Many of the questions sought explicit evidence that the problem existed. The evidence identified the manifestations of the problem. Examples of questions that fell into this category were "On what basis did you reach this conclusion?" and "What did you find when you went into this area?". Verification questions were used most often (21 of 84 questions) to establish evidence of a problem. Experts were frequently asked for their judgments (19 of 84 questions). The number of concept completion questions (18 of 84 questions) indicates the experts were frequently asked to expand on their judgments.

There were few questions directly challenging a problem's existence. Only 24 of 126 recognition stage questions fell into this category. An example of a challenge question is: "What's the difference between this [drug use] and all those guys who drink all those martinis at lunch. . . ?" As in the problem evidence category, information in this area is obtained by asking experts for judgments (6 of 24 questions) and then asking them to expand their response (5 of 24 questions). Causal consequent questions occurred slightly more often (4 of 24 questions) than questions in other semantic categories.

In summary, these problems are generally recognized as problems. General agreement on the problem existence and evidence is acknowledged, but the desired state of existence goes unspecified. The existence of these problems was rarely challenged.

Development Stage.   There were 209 questions from the protocols that were in the development stage of problem formulation. Many development stage questions focus on stakeholder identification (76 of 209 questions). Verification questions were used frequently (16 of 76 questions) to identify participants that have first-hand knowledge of the problem at hand. These questions seek information about the person's background and experiences. For example, two questions in this category were "You're homeless, are you?" and "Have you ever been taken to lunch by Westinghouse, General Electric, or Babcock and Wilcox?"

Experts were also asked their opinions regarding stakeholder identification (14 judgment questions). Again, concept completion questions were used to "follow up" on verification and judgment type questions. For example, the question "But you don't think your homeowners policy should cover that, do you?" was followed by "Hold on a minute, what kind of risks are we talking about?" Finally, feature specification questions (10 of 76 questions) frequently elicited concerns of persons with a direct stake in the problem. For example, homeless persons were asked about conditions of their existence.

Participants also sought to determine the motives, values, and goals of other participants. These programs often attempt to bring persons together with conflicting problem views, so this activity should be expected. The process was accomplished by first asking one's judgment about some problem aspect (26 of 85 questions) and then exploring the response via a concept completion question (18 of 85 questions). An example of this occurred in the discussion of the ozone depletion problem. The expert was first asked why an energy efficient light bulb is not promoted more vigorously. The answer suggested that energy efficiency is not politically important, so the following question explored the political issues. Surprisingly, only 7 explicit goal-oriented questions were used in this aspect of the development stage.

There was a very low evidence of establishing alternative problem perspectives. As before, concept completion (14 of 48 questions), judgment (11 of 48 questions), and verification (9 of 48 questions) questions were used to acquire information on alternative perspectives. This result may be due to the fact that the individuals who were brought into the process already had conflicting problem views. Since at least two problem formulations were generally represented during these programs, little activity was spent exploring yet additional alternative formulations. One might also hypothesize that alternative development activity was difficult because the participants already had strongly held views of the problem (i.e., problem formulations).

Exploration Stage.   There were 328 questions classified into the exploration stage. Only 57 of the 328 questions attempt to define the problem boundaries. Over half of these questions occurred in the protocols addressing the homeless issue. Many of these questions sought to identify the limits to which government agencies were responsible for assisting the homeless.

The least amount of effort (15 of 328 questions) explored possible problem decomposition. This type of question is aimed at finding smaller, solvable problems. There were comparatively few questions that probed for the causes of problems (46 of 328 questions). As expected, many of the questions oriented at determining causes of problems were framed in causal antecedent questions (22 of 46 questions).

The exploration stage had many more questions that addressed possible solutions than questions that addressed the problem boundaries and causes. Exploration of the solution was pursued frequently by instrumental/procedural questions (61 of 210 questions). For example, one participant suggested the following plan for nuclear waste disposal: "Why not fly it into space, why not shoot it right into the sun?" Expert opinion was actively sought (49 judgment questions). Verification and concept completion questions (24 and 22 of 210 questions, respectively) were also used to supplement the solution information.

SUGGESTIONS ON PROBLEM
FORMULATION FACILITATION

MIS researchers seek computer-based approaches to support decision-making processes. Support may be improved by enhancing either the efficiency or the effectiveness of the decision-making process. Typically, improvements in efficiencies occur first through automation. At a minimum, a computer-based system could be designed to maintain records of important problem aspects that have been identified in earlier problem formulation sessions. The system could record assumptions made during the problem formulation process. The computer could graphically represent the problem structure (see Hodges, 1990; Loy et al., 1987; Pracht & Courtney, 1988). Being able to access and regenerate this information would prevent the need for repeatedly reconstructing the current problem formulation (Conklin & Begeman, 1988), thus increasing the efficiency of the process. Many of the characteristics of support systems for group processes would be useful here (DeSanctis & Gallup, 1987). Although *quantitative* database facilities do not appear to be warranted in supporting these processes, the evidence indicates some type of *qualitative* database capability is needed.

Deductive database capabilities, based on some inferencing capability, would manipulate the qualitative data.

Efficiency improvements alone are unlikely to have much impact on attaining a solution to the difficult problems analyzed here. Improvements in process effectiveness are required. Thus, potential improvements in effectiveness are explored next.

Recognition Stage.   The analysis revealed little activity that focused on identifying the desired state of existence during the recognition stage. Yet Bostrom (1989) noted that an ability to establish a desired outcome state is a powerful organizing device. These two observations would appear to be incompatible.

Causal modeling techniques can provide a structure needed to support knowledge organization in problem domains such as these; that is, problems that are characterized by a wide range of influencing factors that combine in complex ways. Causal models are graphic representations of a problem space in which events are believed to cause other events to occur. For example, if event A causes event B to occur, a picture containing a circle labeled "event A" with an arrow leading to a circle labeled "event B" would be a causal model of this situation. The entities in the causal model can be described further by attributes, thus supporting the feature specification questions that are asked. We have demonstrated that causal models provide a basis for explanation and advice (Paradice & Courtney, 1987).

In their simplest form, causal models contain only circles and arrows. The model can be enhanced by adding some indication to the arrows of the influence of one event on another. For example, event A might *definitely* lead to the occurrence (or nonoccurrence) of event B, or event A might be only *somewhat likely* to lead to event B. Causal models can be enhanced with mathematical approaches, such as path analysis, that can provide more problem structure as the problem-domain knowledge evolves (Paradice & Courtney, 1986). Path analysis estimates the magnitude of the linkages between components in a causal model. This analysis can provide more information about the relationships reflected in the model.

Causal modeling is an attractive approach to problem formulation because humans often seek causal explanations of events (Asher, 1983). Kasper (1985) has shown that the process of building a model of a problem situation has inherent benefits. We have shown that causal models augmented with path analysis techniques may form the basis of systems that can construct models of problem situations without human intervention (Paradice & Courtney, 1987).

By incorporating some means for the computer to construct causal models automatically, a computer-based system could begin to take an active role in the problem formulation process. Instead of simply accepting inputs that describe causal entities and their attributes, the system could request *desired* states (causal entities) and features of those states.

Few questions were found that challenged the existence of a problem. Presumably the act of challenging a problem's existence would lead to a better understanding of the problem structure. For example, the gIBIS system (Conklin & Begeman, 1988) provides a method for specifying problems, problem aspects, solutions, and arguments (for and against the problem aspects and solutions) in an unstructured problem environment. The ability to create and store the arguments about problem aspects provides one means for cultivating challenges to a problem's existence. Presumably, if no arguments arise, then there are no challenges. If there is lack of questions aimed at these challenges, a computer facility is needed for raising them.

Development Stage.   The problem formulation process for particularly difficult problems is expected to be a group process. Few humans possess the capabilities to process the many complex interactions of the factors influencing the problem. Also, a single human is unlikely to be able to implement a solution to these complex problems either because of the vast resources required for their solution or due to the conflict that may exist between various parties with a vested interest in the problem. As such, some time in each stage of the problem formulation process is likely to be devoted to socially oriented goals. This study indicated that the time during the development stage is devoted primarily to identifying the experience and expertise of the discussion participants.

A fair amount of "feeling out" can be expected whenever groups of people are brought together to structure a difficult problem situation. Certainly, whenever strong views are held about a problem formulation, the participants holding "competing" views will be curious about other participants' vested interests. This information could be available in an information system so that participants could determine various discussants' qualifications. If readily available and accurate, this information could make the problem formulation process move along more quickly.

Stakeholder analysis (Mason & Mitroff, 1981), which has been automated in other domains (McIntyre & Higgins, 1987), could be integrated at this stage. Assumption surfacing techniques (Mason & Mitroff, 1981) could be utilized here to determine the basic beliefs that individual stakeholders are using. Hidding (1988) has also noted the importance of determining assumptions while "conceptualizing" problems.

As previously noted, the present study had few questions directed toward developing alternative perspectives. Bostrom (1989) suggested the use of framing and reframing techniques to cultivate different problem perspectives. A group-oriented computer-based system could be used in this regard. Each participant would build a problem model, share it with other participants, and then emphasize the differences. These differences represent alternative perspectives of the problem structure.

Bostrom also suggested posing questions that relax problem constraints.

These questions begin with phrases such as "Can you act as if . . . ," "Imagine . . . ," "If . . . ," and "Let's suppose . . . ," "How would you . . . ." These questions could be driven by the causal model suggested earlier. The system could select model entities or attributes, challenge their accuracy, and propose a model without the entity or attribute. The system could draw on its memory of prior models to create a new perspective. The system might also test model components, perhaps using database and statistical facilities. Once an unsupported model component is found, the system would begin prompting for more information regarding the correctness of this component.

Although creating alternative perspectives is beneficial, the ultimate goal must be constructing a single comprehensive model of the problem at hand. The computer-based system will need some capability for assisting the problem formulators in determining a common problem formulation. The system could combine components of competing models to develop a synthesized model, thus providing a new perspective. Automated dialectic approaches (Hodges, 1990; Mason, 1969; Mitroff & Emshoff, 1979) could resolve this issue. The ultimate goal of computer-based support in this stage should be a single, comprehensive formulation of the problem structure to which all stakeholders are committed. Achieving this consensus is a difficult problem in its own right.

Exploration Stage.   The fixation with the current problem state was evident again in the exploration stage. The "solutions" that were examined are hypothesized to move the stakeholders *from* the problem state, rather than *toward* a desired state. This situation reflects the earlier lack of outcome orientation that has been hypothesized as critical in problem-solving tasks.

If causal modeling techniques were utilized in the recognition stage of the problem formulation process, then a computer-based system could lead discussion (based on the model) and stimulate exploration. For example, a system could identify a desired state in the causal model and then prompt the user with "How would one achieve . . ." and "What resources are needed to achieve . . . ." Submodels in the causal model could be identified that represent suitable problem decompositions. Example system-generated questions would have the form "What will be the value of ⟨state attribute⟩ when ⟨desired state⟩ is attained?"

Notably, no graphic aids were utilized during the hours of discussion that were studied. The fact that the television medium was not exploited in this manner is surprising, given that graphic approaches have been demonstrated to be very powerful devices for conveying many types of information (Jarvenpaa, 1989). Studies by Pracht (1986) and Loy et al. (1987) indicate that graphics-oriented causal modeling tools improve problem formulation processes.

Although some prior research into question-answering processes has recommended minimal responses, the transcripts indicate that questions are often asked to obtain *more* information than was given in responses to earlier questions. The following exchanges, both from transcripts dealing with the homeless issue, illustrate:

> Donahue: Why did you tear up the money, Miss Brown?
> Brown: Because I didn't want to go to sleep with money on me, and after I received my ten dollars per day, that was it. People would then come by with dollars and say, "Do you want a dollar?" I would say, "No, I don't need it." Then they would take it and ball it up and throw it at me. Now—
> Donahue: Some people did.
> Brown: No, all people—
> Donahue: You mean actually throwing money at you?
> Brown: Or lay it down.
> Donahue: You found that what, to be an indignity, is that it?
> Brown: Yes, I was insulted and degraded by it.

Or, in another exchange (here Donahue refers to living at O'Hare airport):

> Donahue: You used to live there, did you?
> Brooks: Yeah.
> Donahue: You picked a chair and then stayed there all night or—?
> Brooks: No, you don't. You stay maybe in a section for awhile, but you move on to somewhere else to another building or a different area. . . .

One reason for these "follow-up" questions must be that the participants in the discussion want to learn what they can about the other participants. Another reason could be the issues at the heart of these problems are complex and thus require detailed explanations. Additionally, these questions provide a natural means for continuing the discussion. (A theory of conversational processes would probably address this aspect.)

Experience shows systems such as Eliza (Weizenbaum, 1966) can be constructed that elicit information from individuals in a manner that is quite "humanistic." Systems that are developed to support problem formulation should elicit as much information as possible. A critical point, of course, will be knowing when to stop the elicitation process.

SUMMARY

Problem formulation processes are difficult to study, even in very simple problem situations. Often, researchers rely on verbal protocols of problem solvers working on relatively structured tasks in a laboratory setting. Much has been learned using these approaches. However, many problems that people confront are messy, ill-structured problems involving stakeholders that have vested interests in the problem situation and any potential solutions. Some of these problems seem unsolvable, or at best will require massive amounts of resources to solve.

This research has examined how individuals formulate particularly complex problem situations. An attempt has been made to achieve some external validity by examining television transcripts of actual problem discussions. A side benefit of this approach is that there is no influence of the researcher on the participants in the discussion, because they had no knowledge that their comments might be used this way.

There are some obvious limitations to this approach, however. One must assume that a certain amount of gamesmanship occurs in front of the television cameras as participants attempt to convey their views. However, it could be argued that this process also occurs in corporate conference rooms every day. The only difference may be that some of the television participants have undoubtedly received professional training on how to manipulate the medium, whereas most workers have not.

Problem formulation processes for difficult problems frequently gets mired in discussions of the current problem state. That is, considerable effort is spent identifying the expertise, values, and objectives of participants in the problem formulation process. The participants lack problem-structuring skills and aids that could facilitate the process. The participants are eager to propose and explore solutions, but less willing to identify contributing subproblems or possible problem causes. Moreover, participants in the problem formulation process seldom elaborate on their goals.

Several techniques could facilitate the problem formulation process. Outcome orientation would encourage participants to shift their focus from the current problem state to the goal state and alternative solutions. Computer-based causal modeling would provide a flexible problem representation scheme and could drive the automated knowledge acquisition processes. Graphical approaches should be considered. Over time, the computer-based approaches will provide histories of problem structures and records of proposed solutions. These records could prove extremely valuable in solving similar future problems.

The lack of a theory of conversation is a severe handicap in providing computer-based support for problem formulation in real-time. Ideally, the computer-based system could monitor the discussion of the problem, constructing the causal model as the problem is discussed, and request clarifying information as needed. In this ideal situation, the computer would also direct the discussion, as meeting facilitators do today (Bostrom, 1989). Such support depends on the computer's ability to understand the discussion. This requires the computer technology to be able to understand natural language, a capability that is not within the immediate grasp of artificial intelligence.

MIS researchers may be at a point that is similar to the phase that management scientists encountered several decades ago. The theory in management science was well on its way to being developed, but the computational complexity of significant problems precluded their solution. Computer-based systems provided a powerful method for solving these problems. Similarly, the computer may be a powerful tool that is needed to help explore the mechanism of problem formulation. As the complexity of the decision-making environment increases, computer-based systems might have the greatest payoff in improving the knowledge acquisition process as problems are formulated.

Researchers are improving the tools and the theories that could be used in this ideal setting. A challenge for researchers in this area will be to keep abreast of the work being pursued in all of the relevant fields, such as cognitive science, artificial intelligence, information systems, and group-decision support systems.

REFERENCES

Ackoff, R. L. (1979). The future of operational research is past. *Journal of the Operational Research Society, 20,* 94–104.

Asher, H. B. (1983). *Causal modeling* (2nd ed.). Beverly Hills, CA: Sage.

Ata-Mohammed, N., Courtney, J. F., & Paradice, D. B. (1988). A prototype DSS for structuring and diagnosing managerial problems. *IEEE Transactions on Systems, Man, and Cybernetics, 18,* 899–907.

Bostrom, R. P. (1989). Successful application of communication techniques to improve the systems development process. *Information and Management, 16,* 279–295.

Conklin, J., & Begeman, M. L. (1988). gIBIS: A hypertext tool for exploratory policy discussion. *ACM Transactions on Office Information Systems, 6,* 303–331.

DeSanctis, G., & Gallupe, R. B. (1987). A foundation for the study of group decision support systems. *Management Science, 33,* 589–609.

Graesser, A. C., & Black, J. B. (Eds.). (1985). *The psychology of questions.* Hillsdale, NJ: Lawrence Erlbaum Associates.

Graesser, A. C., & Clark, L. F. (1985). *Structures and procedures of implicit knowledge.* Norwood, NJ: Ablex.

Graesser, A. C., Lang, K., & Horgan, D. (1988). A Taxonomy for Question Generation. *Questioning Exchange, 2,* 3–15.

Hidding, G. J. (1988). DSS conceptualizers in O.R.: Should you apply A.I.? In G. Mitra (Ed.), *Mathematical models for decision support* (pp. 665–694). Berlin: Springer-Verlag.

Hodges, W. S. (1990). *DIALECTRON: A prototypical dialectic engine for the support of strategic planning and strategic decision making* [Computer program]. College Station, TX: Texas A&M University. (Department of Business Analysis and Research)

Jarvenpaa, S. L. (1989). The effect of task demands and graphical format on information processing strategies. *Management Science, 35,* 285–303.

Jensen, R. L., & Cherrington, M. L. (1977). *BML participant's manual* [Computer program manual]. Dallas, TX: Business Publications.

Judson, A. J., & Cofer, C. N. (1956). Reasoning as an associative process: I. Direction in a simple verbal problem. *Psychological Reports, 2,* 469–473.

Kasper, G. M. (1985). The effect of user-developed DSS applications on forecasting decision-making performance in an experimental setting. *Journal of Management Information Systems, 2,* 26–39.

Lauer, T. W., & Peacock, E. (1990). An analysis of comparison questions in the context of auditing. *Discourse Processes, 13,* 349–361.

Leavitt, H. J. (1975). Beyond the analytic manager: Parts I and II. *California Management Review, 17*(3), 5–12 and *17*(4), 11–21.

Lehnert, W. G. (1978). *The process of question answering.* Hillsdale, NJ: Lawrence Erlbaum Associates.

Loy, S. L., Pracht, W. E., & Courtney, J. F. (1987). Effects of a graphical problem structuring aid on small group decision making. In E. A. Stohr (Ed.), *Proceedings of the Twentieth Hawaii International Conference of Information Systems* (pp. 566–574). North Hollywood, CA: Western Periodicals.

Lyles, M. A., & Mitroff, I. I. (1980). Organizational problem formulation: an empirical study. *Administrative Science Quarterly, 25,* 102–119.

Mason, R. O. (1969). A dialectic approach to strategic planning *Management Science, 15,* B403–B414.

Mason, R. O., & Mitroff, I. I. (1973). A program for research on management information systems. *Management Science, 19,* 475–483.

Mason, R. O., & Mitroff, I. I. (1981). *Challenging strategic planning assumptions.* New York: Wiley.

McIntyre, S. C., & Higgins, L. F. (1987). Knowledge base partitioning for local expertise: Experience in a knowledge based marketing DSS. In E. A. Stohr (Ed.), *Proceedings of the Twentieth Annual Hawaii International Conference on System Sciences* (pp. 528–535). North Hollywood, CA: Western Periodicals.

Mintzberg, H., Raisinghani, D., & Theoret, A. (1976). The structure of 'unstructured' decision processes. *Administrative Science Quarterly, 21,* 246–275.

Mitroff, I. I., & Emshoff, J. R. (1979). On strategic assumption making: a dialectical approach to policy and planning. *Academy of Management Review, 4,* 1–12.

Newell, A., & Simon, H. A. (1972). *Human problem solving.* Englewood Cliffs, NJ: Prentice-Hall.

Paradice, D. B., & Courtney, J. F. (1986). Controlling bias in user assertions in expert decision support systems for problem formulation. *Journal of Management Information Systems, 3,* 52–63.

Paradice, D. B., & Courtney, J. F. (1987). Causal and non-causal relationships and dynamic model construction in a managerial advisory system. *Journal of Management Information Systems, 3,* 39–53.

Pracht, W. E. (1986). A graphical interactive structural modeling aid for decision support systems. *IEEE Transactions on Systems, Man and Cybernetics, 16,* 265–270.

Pracht, W. E., & Courtney, J. F. (1988). The effects of an interactive graphics-based DSS to support problem structuring. *Decision Sciences, 19,* 598–621.

Reitman, W. R. (1964). Heuristic decision procedures, open constraints, and the structure of ill-defined problems. In M. W. Shelly II & G. L. Bryan (Eds.), *Human judgments and optimality* (pp. 282–315). New York: Wiley.

Rowe, A. J. (1977). How do senior managers make decisions? *Business and Economics,* 17–20.

Smith, G. F. (1988). Towards a heuristic theory of problem structuring. *Management Science, 34,* 1489–1506.

Smith, G. F. (1989). Defining managerial problems: A framework for prescriptive theorizing. *Management Science, 35,* 963–981.

Weizenbaum, J. (1966). ELIZA—a computer program for the study of natural language communication between man and machine. *Communications of the ACM, 9,* 36–44.

16

Question Asking, Artificial Intelligence, and Human Creativity

Alex Kass
Institute for the Learning Sciences
Northwestern University

The central claim of this chapter is that the key to creativity lies in the ability to ask oneself useful questions. To support and elaborate this claim I discuss two computer programs that I have developed, which take two rather different approaches to studying the role of question asking in the creative process. The first program is an artificial intelligence (AI) system called ABE (Adaptation-Based Explainer). ABE attempts to develop creative hypotheses by adapting stored explanations to new situations. ABE's ability to tweak its stored explanations is based on a set of hypothesis-adaptation questions that the program knows how to ask itself. The second program, called Sounding Board, is a piece of educational software that attempts to teach users how to develop creative solutions to problems by teaching them to ask themselves useful questions. Sounding Board is not itself creative, but the combination of Sounding Board and a user can be more creative than the user alone. Sounding Board can help a user put the facts and rules he knows to creative use.

These two programs attack creativity from different angles. ABE asks itself questions in an attempt to be creative, whereas Sounding Board asks the user questions in an attempt to make the user more creative. These are two different ways of addressing the same fundamental research issues: What role do questions play in the creative process, how can a computer program ask useful questions (of itself or of others), and what classes of questions is it useful for a system to ask?

AI, EDUCATION, RULES, AND QUESTIONS

Albert Einstein once said, "Imagination is more important than knowledge." He was half right. The essence of his statement is that knowing a lot of facts and rules (the sort of thing generally taught in schools) is less important than an ability to use creatively the facts and rules you know. This is an important truth. Traditional education has stressed domain-dependent facts and rules, such as the temperature at which water freezes and the procedure to converting Fahrenheit to centigrade, way beyond their importance, often to virtual exclusion of teaching anything else. This approach encourages rote learning, and often produces students who are not prepared to apply what they know, or to think for themselves. Within AI the story is pretty much the same; representing knowledge, in an expert system, for instance, generally means representing facts and rules that an expert knows about a particular domain. But this approach to AI has proven quite problematic. For one thing, most experts are quite bad at articulating a set of rules that guide their behavior. This makes it difficult to build rule bases that reproduce expert behavior, and it calls into question the assumption that rules are central to what makes an expert good at what he or she does. Furthermore, a narrow focus on domain rules tends to result in brittle computer systems whose behavior does not degrade gracefully in novel situations, and which are utterly unable to transfer knowledge between domains.

So if Einstein had said that imagination was more important than knowing many domain rules, he would have been right on target. But the research described in this chapter suggests that he was wrong to contrapose imagination and knowledge because imagination *depends* on a kind of knowledge, although not the kind of knowledge typically taught in schools. What imagination depends on is knowing good questions to ask. Some of these questions are domain-dependent, but many are quite general. Solving new problems and developing new theories depends on knowing to ask questions like the following:

- What solved problem does this unsolved problem remind me of?
- Which of the standard assumptions might be wrong?
- What can replace a missing ingredient of the old solution?
- What are the standard causes of things like the thing I'm trying to explain?
- Who might be able to perform an action like the one I am considering?

In addition to these general questions, each domain has many domain-dependent questions. For instance, some questions that might be relevant to ask when trying to come up with creative marketing ideas are as follows:

- What do we offer that our competitors do not?
- What are our customer's needs?
- What success stories can we tell our customers?

304

The domain-dependent knowledge necessary to answer these questions is important, but it is even more important to know the questions themselves; knowing the questions to ask at least tells what facts and rules you need to find out, but knowing the rules does not tell you what questions to ask. Furthermore, the same expert who has trouble telling a system designer what rules govern his or her behavior may have less trouble telling the system designer what questions arise when confronted with a problem.

Although this emphasis on question asking is still not practiced by the majority of researchers, it is not exactly a new idea either, especially in education. Most smart teachers quickly come to realize that it is more important to turn students into intellectually curious question-askers than to stuff them full of facts. Knowing facts does not necessarily lead to being able to put those facts to good use, but if the child's question-asking propensities are well-developed then the child will seek out the relevant facts and rules by him or herself.

The problem is that even when educators realize that they want to teach question-asking skills it is not clear how to do so. The failure is a theoretical one. What does it mean to teach someone to ask themselves useful questions? What does it mean for an intelligent system to ask itself questions? Abstract statements such as, "Imagination is more important than knowledge," or (more accurately) "Teaching someone to ask good questions is more important than teaching correct answers," are a long way from concrete educational, or system-building suggestions. Concreteness is where computers can really help. In our work we attempt to address the issues of what it means for an intelligent system to ask itself questions, and what it means to teach people to ask themselves creativity-enhancing questions. Specific computational models help us put our suggestions in concrete terms.

QUESTIONS AND CREATIVE EXPLANATION

Overview of This Section

This section illustrates how a system that knows how to ask itself a useful set of questions can develop novel hypotheses. It describes the question-asking behavior investigated in the adaption-based explanation project. We begin with a description of the problem that adaptation-based explanation attempts to address, and a comparison of the adaptation-based approach to other approaches to the explanation problem. The basic approach is described and motivated in the main text, and a set of 21 hypothesis-adaptation questions is enumerated in an appendix at the end of the chapter. Each question is accompanied by an example showing when asking the question would be useful, along with a sketch of the algorithm employed to ask it.

The Problem: Developing Creative Hypotheses

When someone understands a boring story, most of the work has been completed once he or she has figured out what the words mean. But when someone understands an interesting story, the real work begins after the language has been parsed. Understanding interesting stories is not a language issue, it's an explanation issue. The difficult part of understanding such stories is developing creative hypotheses about *why* the events that the story describes took place. For example, consider the following:

The Swale Story
   Swale was a star three-year-old racehorse. Swale won the Belmont Stakes. A few days later, he died.

This story is only three sentences long. There is nothing very tricky about the language in it. Nonetheless, it's the kind of story that an intelligent, curious reader may find quite interesting. It's difficult to *really* understand, because it may cause him to start wondering about what might have happened to Swale.

The ability to come up with hypotheses about what is really going on in a story is a hallmark of human intelligence. The biggest difference between truly intelligent readers and less intelligent ones (*especially* including less intelligent computer programs) is the extent to which the reader can go beyond merely understanding the explicit statements being communicated. It's not hard to build a computer program that can read the Swale story and can then tell you who died, and what he did before he died. A program with a little inferential capability could also answer questions about how fast Swale probably was, what his life was probably like before he died, and so forth. The ability to perform simple inference is often required to do text-level tasks, such as lexical disambiguation and resolving pronoun references. But the ability to perform text-level tasks does not constitute evidence of much human-level intelligence; in particular, there is not much creativity involved. Smart readers do something that is actually rather creative when they read: They dig for explanations. This means more than just inferring those things that the author intended to communicate implicitly; even the author of the Swale story might not know why Swale died. Achieving a creative level of understanding means developing hypotheses about questions for which there may be no conclusively correct answer at all.

The Adaptation-Based Approach

My colleagues and I have written a program that exemplifies a particular method of developing creative hypotheses called *adaptation-based explanation*. (Kass et al.) An adaptation-based explainer generates new explanations by retrieving stored explanations from memory and adapting them to new situations. In other words, it applies case-based reasoning to the task of constructing explanations.

(For some examples of previous work on case-based reasoning see Hammond, 1986; Kolodner et al., 1985; Schank, 1983; Simpson, 1985; Sycara, 1987). How would an adaptation-based explainer develop hypotheses about events such as Swale's death? The answer depends on what kinds of explanations it had already built to understand previous events; an adaptation-based explainer is very dependent on the library of stored explanations it has to work with. The system might be an expert on racehorse death in the sense of having many explanations of previous racehorse deaths stored in its memory. For instance, a veterinarian who specialized in racehorses would be expected to have many such explanations. For such an expert, understanding a story about racehorse deaths is just like understanding stories about going to restaurants for the rest of us. It's done by rote application of a structure in memory. The expert requires no creativity to understand racehorse deaths, and it learns little from them.

It is relatively easy to design a system that can handle stories that exhibit no substantial difference from stories that have been understood before. All that is required is to recognize the similarity. The interesting cases are the novel ones. Does that mean that previous explanations are of no use at all? It does not. Even explanations that are not completely applicable may have subparts that can be usefully employed to explain the racehorse's death. Even if a system cannot use the entire explanation it gets reminded of, why shouldn't it use as much as possible? When an adaptation-based explainer is not reminded of any explanations that can be applied directly to a particular situation, it attempts to modify any explanations of which it does get reminded. It builds new variations that do apply. For example, when hearing about Swale, someone might be reminded of a man who killed his wealthy wife in order to collect the life insurance money. The explanation based directly on this reminding is not applicable to Swale, since, among other things, horses do not have spouses. Nevertheless, this failed explanation can serve as a good starting point for developing the rather interesting idea that perhaps Swale's owner killed him for the property insurance money[1] *if the program knows to ask itself a question such as the following: "Since Swale didn't have a spouse, is there someone else who might have killed him for insurance money?"* An adaptation-based explainer is one that knows how to ask these sorts of questions.

Schema Application, Causal Reasoning, and Story Understanding

Adaptation-based explanation is a schema-based theory of story understanding. As such, it owes a great deal to previous schema-based theories, particularly script/frame theory (see Minsky, 1975; Schank & Abelson, 1977). It should

---

[1]To satisfy the reader's idle curiosity I should point out that Swale was under-insured, although this fact was not mentioned in the early newspaper accounts. That would make this explanation seem rather implausible.

serve as a useful introduction to adaptation-based explanation to review the purpose, as well as the limitations of script/frame theory.

The simplest theory of inference is one in which a system has a large corpus of inference rules that it chains together to create explanations. There are many problems with this theory, but the most important is that it is too inefficient. It is reasonable for a completely novel inference chain to take a long time to build; complete novelty is difficult for people. But inference-chaining systems treat *every* problem as if it were completely novel. The idea of storing frozen inference chains, such as scripts, in memory is a response to that problem.

Scripts do not make thinking easier—they make thinking unnecessary. That's the wonderful thing about scripts. Causal reasoning is a lot of work, so if you know a script that applies to a situation, you do not have to do much causal reasoning. To the extent that a script represents an explanation at all, it is an explanation of the following simple form: Event X occurred because script S applied in the situation, and one of the events predicted by S is X. There is nothing in the script that represents the causal relations between the various events.

For example, if you have a suitable restaurant script, you do not need to think about why the waitress brings a menu every time a customer is seated in the restaurant. Thinking through routine events like that every time is a waste of cognitive resources. If we had to do this all the time, we would never have the time to think any more important thoughts. By freezing expectations in a knowledge structure, the inferencing needed to understand a phenomenon the first time it was experienced can be avoided during subsequent iterations. When actions go as expected, all you need to do is follow the script. Furthermore, the kind of information that the script needs to contain in order for you to apply it is very limited. All you need to know is what to expect and when to expect it. You specifically do not need to know *why*.

Things get more interesting when unforeseen deviations from the script occur. What happens when you go to a new restaurant, and the waitress does not bring a menu? How do you adjust? Can you just skip over this line in the script as if it were just ceremonial, or is it crucial? Can another action substitute, and if so what? The restaurant script (e.g,. as formulated in Schank & Abelson, 1977) supplies no clues because the restaurant script does not tell you why the menu-bringing line appeared in the script in the first place. Usually you do not need to know, but when things do not go as expected, you do. The fact that scripts lack this kind of information makes them brittle knowledge structures that are not adaptable.

When a story does not quite match a script, it is difficult to formulate a question that will lead to a new variation on the script, because the script does not provide the causal clues to lead the question asker in the right direction. For instance, one might want to ask what other action might the waitress be performing to satisfy the goal that bringing a menu usually satisfies. The problem is that the standard restaurant script does not say what that goal is. The script just tells what to expect, not why. Therefore, it is not possible to formulate that question at a functional level of specificity. That is why a system whose knowledge is represented in script form is not good at asking hypothesis-adaptation questions. If a system is to be equipped to do anything other than abandon a script that does not exactly match the current situation, it needs a richer representation of the causal underpinnings of observed events.

Adding Adaptation to Script/Frame Theory

Adaptation-based explanation is an extension of script/frame theory for handling input that is atypical enough to raise explanation questions. Instead, one must assume that schemas will often be retrieved in situations that are only *sort of* like those they were originally built to handle.

Broadening the range of situations in which a schema will be applied introduces the need to evaluate the newly produced explanations for problems, and to do some creative adaptation to fix any problems that are found. In an adaptation-based theory of explanation, much of the burden of producing an appropriate explanation is moved out of the schema-retrieval module into the adaptation module (which we call the *tweaker*). The emphasis is shifted from pulling a perfectly appropriate structure out of memory, to being able to work with whatever the best structure pulled out of memory happens to be. Because this adaptation process is more time-consuming than simply applying structures straight out of the schema library, it makes sense to add a storage module as well, allowing the system to save and reuse the new variations of its structures that the adaptation module produces.

In the augmented theory, *retrieve and apply* evolves into *retrieve, apply, evaluate, adapt, and store*. Actually, the application, evaluation, and adaptation steps are contained in a loop; when a new variation is produced, that new variation is instantiated and evaluated again. If there are still problems with the explanation it can be further adapted. The augmented theory is essentially an application of the case-based methodology to the problem of constructing explanations. (Other case-based reasoning work on adaptation work that has influenced my thinking includes Hammond [1986] and Kolodner et al. [1985]. Some other work that specifically focuses on adapting explanations includes Koton [1988] and Simmons [1988].)

Explanation Patterns Are Adaptable Knowledge Structures.   Understanding stories that raise open-ended explanation questions requires knowledge structures that are specifically designed to encode causal explanations. In order to adapt an old knowledge structure to a new situation, rather than just applying it, the system has to have explanations for why the elements of the structure are as they are. Explanation Patterns (or XPs for short) are structures that explicitly encode causal coherence. This causal annotation is what makes explanatory memory structures adaptable, whereas those that do not encode causal reasoning are brittle.

XPs are explanation structures that are stored in memory. They contain variables so that they can be instantiated to explain new cases. In some ways, XPs are a lot like scripts and their more general successors, called Memory Organization Patterns (MOPS; Schank, 1982). But XPs serve a different function from scripts and MOPs. The central organizing principle underlying scripts is a temporal sequence of scenes. MOPs add the abstraction and subpart hierarchies, but are still essentially temporally ordered expectations. XPs, on the other hand, are intended to help process surprising events by giving a causal explanation of the event. (We will use the term *explanation* to refer to an XP that has been instantiated for a specific case.) The central organizing principle is the inference chain rather than temporal sequencing. The causal network leads from a set of explanatory premises through some intermediate beliefs to an explanatory conclusion, which is what the XP explains. The explanatory premises are those beliefs for which no further explanation is given within the XP, although there may be other XPs which can be used to explain them.

For example, the JOPLIN XP explains the death of a famous young rock star in terms of a drug overdose. The essential idea of that XP is as follows:

- Success leads to both stress and wealth;
- being a rock star leads to having many drug-using friends;
- having wealth and having drug-using friends leads to easy access to drugs.
- Stress leads to a desire for stress reduction;
- access to drugs combined with desire for stress reduction leads to drug use;
- drug use leads to drug overdose; overdose leads to death.

Computer output of the JOPLIN XP, which more closely resembles the internal representation of that knowledge structure, appears in Table 16.1.

Because XPs contain an explicit representation of the causal relationships between their components, they are very adaptable knowledge structures. If some component of an XP is inappropriate when the XP is applied in a new context, the system has a relatively easy time determining which parts of the XP must be fixed in order to repair the problem, and which other parts of the XP are affected by the potential repair. This makes it possible to know what questions to ask and how to search for answers.

A Creative Explainer That can Adapt XPs

An adaptation-based explainer consists of (a) a knowledge base containing domain-dependent facts and rules, (b) a corpus of hypothesis-adaptation questions

TABLE 16.1
Computer Output Describing the JOPLIN XP

Assumptions

> ?X? was A ROCK STAR.
> ?X? was young.

Chain or reasoning

> ?X? has a HIGH drgree of WEALTH LEVEL BECAUSE
>   ?X? was A ROCK STAR [SOCIAL-CAUSE].
> ?X? had a VERY HIGH degree of STRESS LEVEL BECAUSE
>   ?X? was A ROCK STAR [SOCIAL-CAUSE].
> ?X? had a HIGH degree of INFLUENCEABILITY BECAUSE
>   ?X? was young [SOCIAL-CAUSE].
> ?X? had access to RECREATIONAL- DRUGS BECAUSE
>   ?X? had a HIGH degree of WEALTH LEVEL [PRECONDITION-SATISFACTION].
> ?X? desired that: ?X? was drugged out BECAUSE
>   ?X? had a HIGH degree of INFLUENCEABILITY [SOCIAL-CAUSE] AND
>   ?X? had a VERY HIGH degree of STRESS LEVEL [MENTAL-CAUSE].
> ?X? TOOK DRUGS BECAUSE
>   ?X? desired that: ?X? was drugged out [GOAL-SAT] AND
>   ?X? had access to RECREATIONAL-DRUGS [PRECONDITION-SATISFACTION].
> ?X? had a drug overdose BECAUSE
>   ?X? TOOK DRUGS [PHYSICAL-CAUSE].
> ?X? died BECAUSE
>   ?X? had a drug overdose [PHYSICAL-CAUSE].

(or adaptation strategies, as we sometimes refer to them), and (c) a set of five main program modules, the tasks of which I describe in this section.

The explanation process is triggered when an understanding system recognizes an anomaly of the sort raised by the Swale story. The specifics of how anomalies are detected depend greatly on what sort of task the understander is engaged in. This detection process is discussed in Leake (1990), and is really beyond the scope of this chapter. To understand the context in which an adaptation-based explainer works, it is merely necessary to assume that an anomaly has been detected. In other words, assume that some event that is not predicted by any currently active memory structure has occurred, that this anomaly has somehow caught the attention of the system, and that the understander has invoked the explainer in order to figure out what might have caused the event.

Retrieval and Application.   The first two steps in developing an explanation are called *XP retrieval* and *XP application.* They involve extracting an appropriate XP from the system's large library and instantiating it with the variable bindings generated by the current situation. These first two steps in the explanation process are analogous to the structure retrieval and application phases performed by script-based story understanders, such as SAM (Cullingford, 1978) and FRUMP (DeJong, 1977). The structures are different and the retrieval criteria are different, but otherwise, the XPs are treated like scripts during these initial two steps.

If the anomalous event is well-explained by the retrieved XP, creative explanation is not really required. In situations such as this the explanation process is pretty much reduced to script application. But since the needs of a more flexible understanding system require that we assume that many experiences will not completely match any structure retrieved from memory, it is crucial that the explanation process include a postapplication step in which the system identifies any weakness that the explanation may have.

Evaluation.   The process of *explanation evaluation* is a complex one. Explanations can fail in many different ways: they can be inconsistent, incomplete, based on invalid assumptions, or can simply contain the wrong type of knowledge for the system's current purposes. Leake (1990) discussed the process of evaluating explanations in great detail. For our purposes, merely assume that the process can be performed. Our only real concern with regard to evaluation is what the output of an evaluator would look like. It is the description of how the XP is inadequate that drives the **XP adaptation** phase.

Adaptation.   *XP adaptation* (or *tweaking* for short) is where the real creativity comes in. The tweaker addresses the problems found during evaluation by producing a new variation on the retrieved XP that does not suffer from the problem that the evaluator identified. There are many different tweaking strategies, each appropriate to a particular class of XP failures. Each strategy corresponds to a different question that it may be useful to ask about the failed explanation. For any given failure, the tweaker may know a number of relevant question, and it may have to try asking itself more than one question before producing a variation that satisfies the evaluator.

Actually, the interaction between the evaluator and the tweaker is an iterative one. When the tweaker is done performing an adaptation, the resulting XP must be reapplied and then reevaluated. The system must ensure that the problem that originally caused the evaluator to call for tweaking has been addressed satisfactorily, and to check that no other problems of importance to the evaluator have been introduced. After each step of tweaking the evaluator has three choices:

- It can decide that the new variation is satisfactory, and should be adopted;
- it can decide that the system should give up on building a variation on the retrieved XP that fits the current case;
- or it can request further tweaking.

Storage.   Finally, when the tweaker succeeds in creating an acceptable explanation, a module responsible for *XP storage* is employed to index the new variant in memory so the results of the tweaker's labor will be available for building new explanations in the future. Script appliers did not need storage routines because they never changed their structures, but the existence of an adaptation step makes a storage step necessary as well.

The Pseudo-code in Table 16.2 summarizes the high-level adaptation-based explanation algorithm that we have implemented.

ABE's Questions

In general, the algorithms that a system must employ to ask itself hypothesis-adaptation questions can be quite complex. A typical strategy involves four main stages: First, the system must isolate the part of the XP to be altered; then it must search its knowledge base for possible answers to its question; next it must check each potential answer to see if it makes sense in the context of the XP; and finally, if it succeeds in answering the question, it must build a new explanation based on the answer. The search method checks make up the main portions of the question-asking algorithms.

In my doctoral dissertation (Kass, 1990), I proposed 21 adaptation questions, and described the algorithms required to ask them in great detail. Those 21 questions are enumerated in Table 16.3. They are discussed somewhat more extensively, with examples illustrating where they are appropriate, and how they operate, in the appendix.

There are surely more strategies than this waiting to be discovered by future researchers. The point of the project was not to enumerate every possible question that a system might want to ask itself when attempting to adapt an explanation to a new context. Rather, the point was to demonstrate the utility of developing such questions, and to provide enough examples, in enough detail, to make it clear what it is involved when a computer asks itself this type of question.

TABLE 16.2
High-Level Description of Adaption-Based Explanation Algorithm

```
LOOP1
      RETRIEVE XP
      LOOP2
            APPLYXP
            EVALUATE  EXPLANATION
            TWEAK XP
      END LOOP2
END LOOP1
STORE NEW XP
```

The outer loop involves retreiving an XP from the system's library and then running the inner loop on that retreived XP. This outer loop iterates until a satisfactory explanation has been produced or until the retreiver cannot find any more relevant XPs.

The inner loop (i.e., the apply, evaluate, tweak cycle) iterates until the evaluator decides either that a satisfactory explanation has been produced, or that is isn't worth trying to further tweak the current XP.

TABLE 16.3
Twenty-One Hypothesis-Adaptation Questions

1. What other actions are sort of like action Y?
2. What other actions does X (or agents like X) typically perform?
3. What other actions typically cause events like Z?
4. Who would have wanted to bring about one of the consequences of the action?
5. What types of agents typically perform this action?
6. Who could the agent that was originally proposed have caused to perform the action of his behalf?
7. What implements are commonly used to perform this action?
8. What type of implements would this agent typically be expected to have available to him?
9. What implements are typically available in the location where the action took place?
10. Why would the negative effects of the action be particularly unimportant to the agent involved?
11. Why would the positive effects of the action be particularly important to one agent involved?
12. Which of the negative effects of his decision might the agent not have known about, and why?
13. Are there positive effects of the action that might have motivated the agent, but were not mentioned by the original explanation?
14. Do I know an explanation that could provide a subexplanation relevant to this premise? If not can I build the subexplanation on the fly?
15. Do I know an explanation that could explain how event A might have caused event B? If not can I build the subexplanation linking the two on the fly?
16. Is it possible that one of the beliefs in the knowledge base that led to contradiction with the XP might be inaccurate for some reason?
17. Which members of the original agent category would have desired one of the goal states achieved by the action in question?
18. Which members of the original action category typically involve an implement that is observable in the current situation, or that is related to the agent in question?
19. Can the constraint be generalized to make it compatible with the current slot-filler while still maintaining the causal coherence of the explanation?
20. What generalization of slot-filler A would be compatible with B while still maintaining the causal coherence of the explanation?
21. Can the problematic belief be removed while still maintaining the causal coherence of the explanation?

Sample Adaptations

I developed the adaptation-based theory of explanation by analyzing a set of sample anomalies and associated explanations. Most of the examples you will see in this chapter revolve around unexpected deaths and disasters. I choose this domain principally because it shows up in the news often, so that it is easy to gather data. It also has the advantage that many of the informal subjects found death-and-destruction events sufficiently interesting and straightforward that they could recall stored explanations and could produce new ones.

In order to make the operation of the adaptation-based explanation process clear in a concrete way I present here a high-level description of five sample adaptations that were performed by the ABE program. Each example presented here consists of a story that the system attempts to process, an XP that is in some way relevant, a failure that occurs when applying the retrieved XP to the current story, and a variation of the XP that the adapter could produce.

The Len Bias Story

College basketball star, Len Bias, died one day after being drafted by the Boston Celtics. He was the first pick in the NBA draft.

An XP that might be relevant—The Jim Fixx XP:

Someone who regularly engages in recreational jogging also has a hereditary heart defect. The stress on the heart from exertion caused by jogging combines with the defect to cause that person to have a heart attack and die.

A failure that occurs when applying The Jim Fixx XP to the Len Bias Story: Len Bias wasn't known as a recreational jogger.

The type of failure this is: An agent of some action in the explanation is not known to perform that action.

A question that is appropriate to that failure: What other actions does the agent typically perform, that could have caused whatever the original action caused in the XP?

A result of asking that question about this example: By substituting playing basketball for recreational jogging, the adapter can build an excellent explanation based on this XP that is appropriate for Bias. A defective heart combined with the exertion from playing basketball, caused a fatal heart attack in Len Bias.

One of the strategy-types available to the adapter involves replacing a single slot-filler within a belief in the XP with an alternate slot-filler. The replacement must be more appropriate to the given situation and should also preserve most of the causal relationships that the original slot-filler participated in. In this example, the tweaker is faced with a situation in which an agent is hypothesized to have performed an action that is not stereotypically associated with him. The tweaker addresses the situation by executing a strategy that replaces the original action with one that is stereotypically associated with the agent.

The Swale Story

Swale was a star three-year-old racehorse.
Swale won the Belmont Stakes.
A few days later, he died.

An XP that might be relevant—Spouse insurance XP: Some agent is greedy and is married. The agent does not love his or her spouse. The spouse has a lot of life insurance. The agent is the beneficiary of the life insurance because spouses are generally the beneficiary of life insurance. Because the spouse has life insurance the agent knows that he or she will get money if spouse dies. Because of greed and lack of love, agent kills spouse.

A failure that occurs when applying the spouse insurance XP to Swale's death: Swale lacks a spouse.

The type of failure this is: An object slot (spouse) referenced in the XP does not in reality exist.

A question that is appropriate to this type of failure: Who would have wanted to bring about the effects of the action?

A result of asking that question about this example: By searching for other agents with similar motivations, the adapter can build from this explanation the reasonable hypothesis that Swale's owner got greedy and killed him to collect the property insurance.

This example is included to illustrate the point that just as it sometimes helps to replace the filler of an action slot, at other times, the action should be kept as is, and instead it may help to replace the filler of the agent slot.

The SPOUSE INSURANCE XP does not quite make sense when applied to Swale because racehorses do not have spouses. But when a strategy is invoked that considers who it would make sense to conjecture in the role of killing a racehorse for the insurance money, a plausible explanation is the result.

Another XP Relevant to Bias—The Janis Joplin XP

A young rock star is very successful. Success leads to wealth and stress. Being a rock star leads to having lots of drug-using friends. Stress leads to a desire for lowering stress. Drug-using friends and wealth leads to access to drugs. Access to drugs and desire for lowering stress leads to taking drugs. Taking drugs leads to a drug overdose. Drug overdose leads to death.

A failure that occurs when applying the Janis Joplin XP to the Len Bias story: Len Bias was not a rock star.

The type of failure this is: A slot-filler does not fit one of the packaging descriptions (i.e., constraints) that the XP specifies.

A question that's appropriate to that failure: What generalization of the original slot-filler might be more appropriate?

A result of asking that question about this example: Generalize the Joplin XP to apply to any star performer. This example is included for two reasons: First, to emphasize the point that there is often more than one XP that can produce reasonable explanations for a given example; and second, to illustrate a case in which generalization is an appropriate course of action.

The previous example, in which the FIXX XP was invoked to explain Len Bias's death, resulted in an explanation that would be plausible if it were not discovered that drugs were involved. But in light of that knowledge, another XP—the JOPLIN XP—suggests itself as more appropriate. Much of this explanation applies well to a famous basketball player, but it was originally encoded as applying to rock stars. A tweaking strategy that generalizes the rock star constraint to make the XP applicable to any star performer can be invoked to fix the situation.

The Pan Am Story

Pan Am flight 103 exploded in mid-air, killing all aboard.
It was en route to NYC from Frankfurt, West Germany, via London, England.

An XP that might be relevant—The terrorist bombing XP:

Someone who is engaged in intense political conflict with the people of a particular nation may kill citizens of that nation by planting bombs in crowded areas in that nation.

A failure that occurs when applying the terrorist bombing XP to the Pan Am crash: Does not specify enough about who did the bombing. Note that this might not be a problem if the understander were a Pan Am engineer who just wants to know whether it was a design flaw that caused the crash, but it would be a problem if the understander were the government agency responsible for retaliating against the perpetrators.

The type of failure this is: A slot-filler is insufficiently specified to satisfy the goals of the understander.

A question that is appropriate for this type of failure: What members of the agent category specified in the original XP are known to have an effect of the action as a goal.

A result of asking that question about this example: By searching for a more specific description of someone who might have had appropriate motivation to perform the action, the adapter can conjecture that perhaps an Iranian terrorist planted the bomb on the American Pan Am jet in order to retaliate for America's destroying an Iranian airliner.

Some adaptation strategies serve the function of making an explanation more specific. For instance, in this example, a generic terrorism XP is applied to explain a plane crash; the explanation that results, that a bomb set off by a terrorist caused the crash, is perfectly reasonable, but it does not say much about who the terrorist was. In some situations this might not matter, but in others it would (for instance, the "who" question is crucially important to those responsible for bringing the perpetrators to justice).

Developing variations of the stored explanation that can satisfy the system's need for a conjecture that is less vague requires a set of strategies whose job it is to turn vague slot-filler descriptions into more specific ones.

A Suicide Bomber Story

A teenage girl exploded a car bomb at a joint post of Israeli troops and pro-Israeli militiamen in southern Lebanon.
The bomber and a number of Israeli soldiers were killed by the blast.

An XP that might be relevant:

The terrorist bombing XP: Someone who is engaged in intense political conflict with the people of a particular nation may kill citizens of that nation by planting bombs in crowded areas in that nation.

A failure that occurs when applying the terrorist bombing to XP to this car-bombing: This does not explain an important part of the anomaly—why someone would do something that resulted in her own death.

The type of failure this is: An action that the explanation claims occurred is not sufficiently motivated by the XP. The explanation seems to claim that a more important goal was sacrificed in order to achieve a less important one.

A question that is appropriate for this type of failure: Why might the negative side effects of the action be less important than expected to the agent involved?

A result of asking the question about this example: By employing this strategy the adapter can hypothesize that besides having the above political conflict motivation, the bomber was terminally ill, and therefore did not value her own life as highly as most people would.

This example points out that sometimes a failed explanation does not have any contradiction that needs to be fixed, but instead is incomplete and needs to be reinforced with subexplanations. These subexplanations can strengthen the explanation by providing causal support for a belief that was unexplained by the original XP.

An Annotated Example of ABE in Action

This section presents an annotated transcript of the ABE computer program processing a particular story. The objective is to clarify through example some of the details that the program goes through. The point of ABE is to exercise the hypothesis-adaptation questions and their associated strategies. Therefore, other interesting issues, such as XP selection and evaluation of explanations, are glossed over. In fact, evaluation is not performed by the program itself at all. Instead, the user is asked to evaluate the high-level outline of what happens in this run of ABE is as follows:

- The program is fed an anomaly to explain—in this case it is asked to explain the unexpected death of college basketball star, Hank Gathers.
- It retrieves a set of XPs relevant to explaining deaths and disasters.
- It applies the highest-ranking of the retrieved XPs to the particulars of the Gathers case.
- It presents the explanation to the human evaluator, who decides that the explanation requires tweaking.
- The program queries the human evaluator about just what is wrong with the explanation.
- The system then retrieves hypothesis-adaptation questions that might be applicable to the problem the user has identified.
- The retrieved questions are ranked, and the highest-ranking question is asked. Its associated strategy is queued for execution.
- After the strategy is executed, the resulting explanation is resubmitted to the human evaluator. This version of the explanation is accepted by the evaluator.
- The system updates the knowledge base and adds the XP to the XP library.

In the transcript that follows, the actual computer output is in `small, fixed-width type`, and the comments are in normal type.

To start the ABE program running, the user calls the EXPLAIN function, passing it anomaly structure, which represents the anomaly for which the user wants an explanation:

```
→ (explain gathers-anom)

Explainer: The anomaly being processed is:
        HANK GATHERS was in EXCELLENT physical
        condition.
        HANK GATHERS died.
```

```
) was a star basketball player at the Loyola
Marymount University.
) He died suddenly while playing in an important
college basketball game.
```

In this example, the user requested an explanation of the predefined anomaly, named the GATHERS-ANOM, about the sudden death of a college basketball player. The anomaly itself is represented as two beliefs. The system prints out its paraphrases of those beliefs, along with the text of the story associated with that anomaly. Internally the beliefs are represented in an abstract, conceptual representation from which the program produces crude, English-like paraphrases to help the user follow the system's progress, and evaluate its explanations.

The first step the system performs is to see if it has explanation patterns with indices that match any part of the anomaly. It then ranks those that do match according to how many constants within the anomaly description are specifically matched by the index pattern associated with each tweak.

```
XP-Retriever: Found 7 XPs to consider for this
     anomaly:
     [5]   FIXX-XP
     [4]   JOPLIN-XP
     [4]   MAFIA-REVENGE-XP
     [4]   KAMIKAZE-XP
     [4]   KILL-FOR-INSURANCE-XP
     [4]   SEX-XP
     [4]   TERRORIST-BOMBING-XP
```

In this case, the retriever extracts 7 XPs as potentially relevant. The FIXX XP is ranked highest because it is a more specific match with the anomaly. The other XPs are indexed as general explanations for death, whereas the FIXX XP is indexed as an explanation for the death of someone who appears to be in superior physical condition.

The next step after XP retrieval is to apply the highest ranking XP to see what sort of explanation it produces in the context of the new anomaly. This involves instantiating the XP's variables by matching beliefs in the XP against beliefs in the anomaly and, if necessary, other beliefs culled from the story. Once an explanation is produced it is displayed for the user to evaluate.

```
Applier:  Attempting to apply FIXX-XP to GATHERS-ANOM
          Found a match for:
          (from xp) ?X? died
          (from story) HANK GATHERS died
```

```
    Evaluator: Evaluating explanation: FIXX-
    XP.EXPL-1
```

```
FIXX-XP.EXPL-1
Premise: HANK GATHERS DID RECREATIONAL JOGGING
Premise: THE HEART OF HANK GATHERS is in category
HEREDITARY DEFECTIVE HEARTS
THE HEART OF HANK GATHERS was weak BECAUSE
  THE HEART OF HANK GATHERS is in category HEREDITARY
DEFECTIVE HEARTS.
HANK GATHERS ran BECAUSE
  HANK GATHERS DID RECREATIONAL JOGGING.
HANK GATHERS had a heart-attack BECAUSE
  THE HEART OF HANK GATHERS was weak AND
  HANK GATHERS had a VERY HIGH degree of EXERTION
LEVEL.
HANK GATHERS had a VERY HIGH degree of EXERTION
LEVEL BECAUSE
  HANK GATHERS ran.
HANK GATHERS had a VERY HIGH degree of PHYSICAL
CONDITIONING BECAUSE
  HANK GATHERS had a VERY HIGH degree of EXERTION
LEVEL.
HANK GATHERS died BECAUSE
  HANK GATHERS had a heart-attack.
```

In this case, the FIXX XP has only one variable, which represents the deceased. This variable is bound by matching the variablized portion of the XP (which mentions a dying action) against the unvariablized portion of the anomaly (which mentions the same action).

Next, the user is allowed to evaluate the explanation that is generated by applying the system's chosen XP to the new situation. The user communicates his or her evaluation to the system through a series of menu choices.

```
- Please choose one of the following:
  1) Adopt this hypothesis.
     Install XP in memory + record entailed beliefs.
  2) Tweak this XP.
  3) Abandon this hypothesis for now.
  4) Abort the explainer.
```

```
Enter Choice → 2
```

The user has indicated here that he or she wants the system to try to tweak the XP. Therefore, the system presents a couple more menus that allow the user to identify what type of problem he or she wishes to identify, and which of the beliefs within the XP the problem applies to.

```
What failure type?
- Please choose one of the following:
      1) Agent-action-mismatch : physical-disability
      2) Agent-action-mismatch : stereotype-
      violation
      3) Agent-action-mismatch : mental-disability
      4) object-action-mismatch : physical-
      disability
      5) object-action-mismatch : stereotype-
      violation
      6) implement-action-mismatch : physical-
      disability
      7) implement-action-mismatch : stereotype-
      violation
      8) incomplete-explanation : covers-part-of-
      anomaly
      9) incomplete-explanation : unmotivated-action

Enter Choice → 2

Identify the belief that is a problem
- Please choose one of the following:
      1) HANK GATHERS DID RECREATIONAL JOGGING
      2) THE HEART OF HANK GATHERS is in category
      HEREDITARY DEFECTIVE HEARTS
      3) HANK GATHERS died
      4) THE HEART OF HANK GATHERS was weak
      5) HANK GATHERS had a heart-attack
      6) HANK GATHERS had a VERY HIGH degree of
      EXERTION LEVEL
      7) HANK GATHERS had a VERY HIGH degree of
      PHYSICAL CONDITIONING
      8) HANK GATHERS ran

      Enter Choice → 1
```

The user indicates that the problem is a stereotype violation involving a mismatch between an agent and an action. In particular, the part of the explanation that proposes that Hank Gathers did recreational jogging is objected to because Gathers was not known as a recreational jogger.

Once the problem is identified, the tweaking process begins. The first step within the tweak process is to retrieve all the tweaks relevant to this type of stereotype violation.

```
Tweaker:  Attempting to adapt FIXX-XP.EXPL-1
Tweaker:  Failure is: XP Failure:
          Agent-action-mismatch : stereotype-
          violation
Retriever:  Retrieving XPs indexed under failure:
Retriever:   found - SUBSTITUTE-AGENT:MENTIONED-IN-XP
  DELETE-BELIEF
  SUBSTITUTE-AGENT:MENTIONED-IN-STORY
  SUBSTITUTE-AGENT:STEREOTYPICAL-AGENT
  SUBSTITUTE-ACTION:CAUSAL-INDEX
  SUBSTITUTE-ACTION:AGENT-THEME
  SUBSTITUTE-ACTION:RELATED-ACTION ; . . .
```

The system knows quite a few questions to ask about a stereotype violation involving a mismatch between an agent and an action. Note that the names assigned to the questions by the program are slightly different than the names in this chapter, but the mappings should be sufficiently clear.

After retrieval the next step is to filter out any strategies whose tweak input filters are not satisfied, and then to rank the rest according to how specifically they match the failure that is the cause for tweaking. (The specifics of the scoring method are beyond the scope of this chapter. See Kass [1990] for details.)

```
Filter:  SUBSTITUTE-AGENT:MENTIONED-IN-XP is filtered
         out
         because only one agent is mentioned in the
         xp. ; . . .

Ranker:  Ranking remaining strategies.

Current ranking priorities:
CW = 1.0   HW = 1.0   SW = 1.0

TCE THR TMS
 0   0   3  Score: 3.0 - SUBSTITUTE-ACTION:AGENT-
THEME
 0   0   2  Score: 2.0 - SUBSTITUTE-ACTION:RELATED-
ACTION
```

```
 0   0   1 Score: 1.0 - DELETE-BELIEF
Choice point reached: 3 choices available.
Each choice involves: Trying another tweak on FIXX-
XP.EXPL-1
```

After the remaining questions are ranked, the highest ranking is executed while the other are kept in reserve in case the first one does not pan out. The program decides to begin by asking whether there is an action that is typically associated with the agent that could have caused the effects of the implausible action.

```
==== Running a tweak:
            Substitute a theme that is associated with
            the agent
            XP being tweaked:   FIXX-XP
            Anomaly to be explained:
              HANK GATHERS died
            Bindings: X is bound to HANK GATHERS.
            Explanation Failure being fixed: XP
            Failure:
              Agent-action-mismatch : stereotype-
              violation
====
Tweaker: Problems is with HANK GATHERS as the AGENT
              of
              DID RECREATIONAL JOGGING
```

The first step in executing this tweaking strategy is to collect the arguments that the tweak's search-and-inference routine will need. In this case, that means simply determining which agent node (the HANK GATHERS node) will be the starting point for the search for stereotypically associated actions.

The next step is to search for actions associated with Gathers.

```
Tweaker: 5 actions associated with HANK GATHERS are
being considered:

-

Premise: HANK GATHERS had theme WON ATHLETIC AWARDS
-
 HANK GATHERS PLAYED BASKETBALL BECAUSE
 HANK GATHERS is in category COLLEGE BASKETBALL STAR
 AND
 COLLEGE BASKETBALL STAR is in category BASKETBALL
 PLAYERS AND
 BASKETBALL PLAYERS had theme PLAYED BASKETBALL.
```

```
Premise: HANK GATHERS is in category COLLEGE
BASKETBALL STAR
Premise: COLLEGE BASKETBALL STAR is in category
BASKETBALL PLAYERS
Premise: BASKETBALL PLAYERS had theme PLAYED
BASKETBALL
-

HANK GATHERS PRACTICED BASKETBALL SHOTS BECAUSE
  HANK GATHERS is in category COLLEGE BASKETBALL STAR
  AND
  COLLEGE BASKETBALL STAR is in category BASKETBALL
  PLAYERS AND
  BASKETBALL PLAYERS had theme PRACTICED BASKETBALL
  SHOTS.
Premise: HANK GATHERS is in category COLLEGE
BASKETBALL STAR
Premise: COLLEGE BASKETBALL STAR is in category
BASKETBALL PLAYERS
Premise: BASKETBALL PLAYERS had theme PRACTICED
BASKETBALL SHOTS
-

HANK GATHERS TOOK PERFORMANCE DRUGS BECAUSE ; . . .
-

HANK GATHERS LIFTED WEIGHTS BECAUSE ; . .
```

The system comes up with five actions that it can associate with Gathers. One of these is directly indexed as associated with the GATHERS node (winning awards) whereas the others are the result of inference chains, involving the hierarchy of categories that Gathers is in.

After the set of prospective replacement actions is collected, the system checks to see which might actually make appropriate substitutions by seeing whether any of the actions can form inference chains linking to aspects of the original XP that the original action linked to.

```
Checking a candidate Replacement: HANK GATHERS WON
ATHLETIC AWARDS
  Trying to link up to: (''HANK GATHERS ran'')
  Does NOT link up with the rest of the XP.
  Cannot create a tweaked explanation based on HANK
  GATHERS WON ATHLETIC AWARDS
Checking a candidate Replacement: HANK GATHERS
PLAYED BASKETBALL
  Trying to link up to: (''HANK GATHERS ran'')
```

```
This chain DOES link up with the rest of the xp:
   Inference: HANK GATHERS PLAYED BASKETBALL →
HANK GATHERS ran ; . . .
```

In this example, the relevant aspect of the original action (recreational jogging) is that it led to running, which led to exertion. The exertion combined with the heart defect led to a heart attack, which led to death. So the system checks to see if the replacements lead to any of these effects. Most of them do not. For example, winning awards does not cause running, physical exertion, heart attacks, or death, at least not by any short casual chain that the system could discover. However, playing basketball does, so it can form the basis of a tweak.

Once a suitable replacement action is found, the system builds a new variation on the FIXX XP in which playing basketball replaces recreational jogging.

```
Creating a new tweaked explanation.

   Adding an index to FIXX-XP-1:
      ?X? PLAYED BASKETBALL
   Adding: ?X? ran BECAUSE
            ?X? PLAYED BASKETBALL.
   Adding: ?X? PLAYED BASKETBALL BECAUSE
            ?X? had theme PLAYED BASKETBALL.
   Adding: ?X? had theme PLAYED BASKETBALL BECAUSE
            ?X? is in category COLLEGE BASKETBALL
            STAR AND
            COLLEGE BASKETBALL STAR had theme
            PLAYED BASKETBALL.
   Adding: Premise: ?X? is in category COLLEGE
BASKETBALL STAR
   Adding: COLLEGE BASKETBALL STAR had theme PLAYED
            BASKETBALL BECAUSE
            COLLEGE BASKETBALL STAR is in category
            BASKETBALL PLAYERS AND
            BASKETBALL PLAYERS had theme PLAYED
            BASKETBALL.
   Adding: Premise: COLLEGE BASKETBALL STAR is in
category BASKETBALL PLAYERS
   Adding: Premise: BASKETBALL PLAYERS had theme
PLAYED BASKETBALL

   Deleting a belief: ?X? DID RECREATIONAL JOGGING
   Deleting supporter inference:
      Premise: ?X? DID RECREATIONAL JOGGING
```

```
      Deleting supported inference:
      ?X? ran BECAUSE
        ?X? DID RECREATIONAL JOGGING.
Deleting orphaned beliefs.
```

Making the replacement involves (a) adding in the new belief, along with the inference chain that causes the system to believe it, (b) adding the inferences that link the new belief to its implications in the XP, and then, (c) deleting the old belief from the XP, along with any other beliefs that were around solely to support the belief being deleted.

Once the new XP is built, the next step is to repeat the evaluation procedure, allowing the user to see the new explanation and to decide whether it needs any more tweaking.

```
      Evaluator: Evaluating explanation: FIXX-
XP-1.EXPL-1


FIXX-XP-1.EXPL-1
Premise: HANK GATHERS is in category COLLEGE
BASKETBALL STAR
Premise: THE HEART OF HANK GATHERS is in category
HEREDITARY DEFECTIVE HEARTS
Premise: COLLEGE BASKETBALL STAR is in category
BASKETBALL PLAYERS
HANK GATHERS had theme PLAYED BASKETBALL BECAUSE
  HANK GATHERS is in category COLLEGE BASKETBALL
STAR AND
  COLLEGE BASKETBALL STAR had theme PLAYED
BASKETBALL.
HANK GATHERS had theme PLAYED BASKETBALL BECAUSE
  COLLEGE BASKETBALL STAR is in category BASKETBALL
PLAYERS AND
  BASKETBALL PLAYERS had theme PLAYED BASKETBALL.
HANK GATHERS PLAYED BASKETBALL BECAUSE
  HANK GATHERS had theme PLAYED BASKETBALL.
HANK GATHERS ran BECAUSE HANK GATHERS PLAYED
BASKETBALL.
THE HEART OF HANK GATHERS was weak BECAUSE
  THE HEART OF HANK GATHERS is in category
HEREDITARY DEFECTIVE HEARTS.
HANK GATHERS had a heart-attack BECAUSE
  THE HEART OF HANK GATHERS was weak AND
```

    HANK GATHERS had a VERY HIGH degree of EXERTION
LEVEL.
HANK GATHERS had a VERY HIGH degree of EXERTION
LEVEL BECAUSE HANK GATHERS ran.
HANK GATHERS had a VERY HIGH degree of PHYSICAL
CONDITIONING BECAUSE
    HANK GATHERS had a VERY HIGH degree of EXERTION
LEVEL.
HANK GATHERS died BECAUSE HANK GATHERS had a heart-
attack.

- Please choose one of the following:
        1) Adopt this hypothesis. Install XP in memory
        + record entailed beliefs.
        2) Tweak this XP.
        3) Abandon this hypothesis for now.
        4) Abort the explainer.

Enter choice → 1

This time around the user finds the explanation satisfactory and requests that it be adopted.

    When an explanation is adopted, it is added to the XP library. Since the distinction between the new variation and the original was that the new one applies to people who play basketball, playing basketball is added as an index for the new XP. That way, the next time a basketball player dies unexpectedly, this new variation will be preferred over the one that involves recreational jogging. In addition, some new hypotheses are added to the knowledge base, such as the belief that Gathers had a weak heart.

Explainer: Explanation process successful. Storing
FIXX-XP-1.EXPL-1
    Adding #{XP 20 FIXX-XP-1} to the XP library.
    Indices: ?X? PLAYED BASKETBALL -   ?AGENT?
    died
    Adding new hypotheses to the knowledge base:
THE HEART OF HANK GATHERS is in category HEREDITARY
DEFECTIVE HEARTS
THE HEART OF HANK GATHERS was weak
    HANK GATHERS had a heart-attack
Explainer: Explanation process complete.

Educational Software as a Means
of Studying Cognitive Issues

In this section I present a different kind of question-asking program. This one aims its questions at a user rather than at itself. The program's goal is to teach the user to solve problems more creatively rather than to be creative itself.

Education is a promising application area for computational theories of cognitive theories (and particularly for computational theories of question asking), but education can be more than that as well. Educational software *of a certain type* can serve as an important alternative methodology to AI software for developing and testing cognitive theories. The Sounding Board program is a program of that type. It is intended to serve the twin goals of demonstrating a useful, innovative approach to educational software, and of developing an alternative computational paradigm for studying the role of question asking in the reasoning process.

The reason that a computational alternative to the AI methodology is desirable is that some of the strengths of the AI methodology also lead to difficult limitations. AI has been successful as a methodology for studying issues in cognitive science for three main reasons:

1. The task of developing computer algorithms places the focus on *process models* rather than on descriptive models, and provides a perspicuous language for describing and comparing such models.

2. The *discipline of developing implementable algorithms*—specific enough to be implemented on a computer—forces the researcher to examine many details that might otherwise be overlooked. (Many nontrivial processing details *seem* trivial when introspecting because they require little *conscious* thought. Only when one is actually pushed to specify how a computer will perform the process does the complexity of the task become apparent);

3. The *running computer program* one has built allows one, at least occasionally, to observe surprising behavior that points out strengths and weaknesses of the theory, which would be difficult to envision before the program was built.

However, the requirement for detailed specification that provides much of the strength of the AI methodology also limits it. The limitations become more and more acute as AI theories become more complex and more knowledge-intensive. In particular, the third advantage, the use of the working program to demonstrate the strengths and weaknesses of the theory is more difficult to achieve in practice, particularly for intensively knowledge-based theories such as the adaptation-based theory of explanation that was discussed in the previous section.

There are really two relevant problems. First, getting a knowledge-based program to perform intelligently on an open-ended set of examples requires more than an adequate theory; *a knowledge-based theory of cognition requires a very big knowledge base* as well. Consider the adaptation-based theory of explanation: Each question that an adaptation-based explainer knows corresponds to a method it can use to search its knowledge base for the domain knowledge necessary to perform an adaptation.

The domain knowledge is not what the theory is about, but the system needs to have an awful lot of it in order to work robustly. Achieving human-level abilities requires thousands upon thousands of uninteresting facts and rules. So when the program fails to perform at a human level of performance, it is not clear why. Is it because of a flaw in the theory or a gap in domain knowledge?

Furthermore, because the theory of how the knowledge is used will have a big effect on the theory of knowledge representation, the knowledge-base must be a custom-built one. It is unlikely, at least for quite some time, that a new AI theory will be able to run with an off-the-shelf knowledge base. Each new theory generally implies something new about how the knowledge base should be represented; therefore, a new knowledge-base is required for most new theories. For these reasons, it is very rare that a knowledge-based AI program ever works on more than a few examples. It is not uncommon for doctoral dissertations to be published based on programs that worked on as few as one or two. The ABE program performed only the five samples discussed in the paper and trivial variations. Even though we believe the theory to be much more general, we do not have the knowledge base to prove it.

Another relevant problem is that *a theory of cognition is never a theory of all cognition, but rather a theory of a few component processes.* For every issue that a researcher addresses he must leave many unaddressed. For every process that the researcher implements fully, he must leave others unimplemented. But how then to test the program? The typical strategy is to *kludge* the components that are not the current focus of theoretical attention; in other words, to implement them in a way that is not general—a way that works for the examples the researcher has in mind, but for those only. But this also limits the generality of the overall program. Even if the components that are fully implemented are general, there is no way to run them on an open-ended set of examples because the weak links in the chain, the kludged sections about which theoretical claims are not even being made, will trip the program up.

So we see that when viewed as a method for studying cognition AI offers at least three significant advantages, but also runs into at least two roadblocks. The obvious question is how one might maintain the significant advantages without having to rely on an inadequate knowledge base, and without having to include kludged modules in the system.

The solution I propose here is to get a human being into the loop. In the standard AI paradigm, the idea is that the system is supposed to operate on its own, as an intelligent system. Human intervention is considered cheating. However, inasmuch as this approach becomes less practical as the problems being addressed become more difficult and knowledge-intensive, it might make more sense to consider computational models that include interaction with a human user. The idea is to consider the human and the program together as an intelligent system, with the user and the program each making a well-circumscribed contribution to the overall task. The program can structure the overall problem-solving process and provide some of the knowledge (such as the questions to ask), whereas the user can perform the parts of the processing that are not part of the theory and can supply much of the domain-specific knowledge.

This notion of dividing the labor between a program and a user also suggests an approach to education. This approach is different from the standard conception of education in which the student is required to rediscover solutions that the teacher already knows. In this alternative conception of teaching, the student and teacher each play a role in solving problems better than either could have solved individually; the teacher suggests questions that might allow the user to put his or her domain knowledge to use effectively.

In the following section I discuss a program, called Sounding Board, which implements this user/computer team-up in a very simple fashion. Despite its simplicity, the Sounding Board effectively shows the ways in which the approach can be useful educationally, and suggests how such programs can serve as an alternative way to implement computational models of cognition. After describing the Sounding Board Program I discuss a somewhat more ambitious program, which I am starting to implement now: a case-adaptation coach that teaches the student to perform the sort of case-adaptation that ABE performed.

Coaxing Versus Tutoring

A central assumption underlying the traditional model of a tutor's job is that the tutor is more knowledgeable about the subject than the student. One implication of this assumption is that the tutor naturally comes to view his or her role to be one of knowledge transmission. Because the assumption is that the tutor knows the answers whereas the student does not, it follows that the tutor's job is to increase the proportion of the answers that the student does know. The tutor would consider him or herself supremely successful if the student eventually came to know as much as the tutor.

Bringing the student up to the teacher's level of ability through knowledge transfer is not the only role that a teacher can play. Indeed, it may not be the most useful role, especially for computer-based teaching. For example, a coach's role often needs to be quite different from that, for the simple reason that the coach my be working with someone whose abilities at the performance task already equal or even exceed his or her own. The coach's principal value is not that he or she is better than the student (the coach may in fact be better, but this is neither necessary nor sufficient). The coach's value derives from knowing ways to help any student improve his or her own abilities. Roger Bannister's track coach never ran a 4-minute mile, and Mike Tyson's boxing coach probably holds no illusions about being able to take Tyson's title away, yet these coaches still have something important to offer. Rather than adopting the goal of bringing the pupil up to the coach's level of ability, the coach adopts the goal of extending the abilities that the student already has. Part of the coach's job may involve transferring knowledge the way a tutor does, but much of the coach's job looks more like coaxing than like tutoring. The coach helps by prompting the student at an appropriate moment to think about what he or she is doing somewhat differently.

Classroom teaching tends to be more like tutoring than it is like coaxing. This is, perhaps, because the coaxing model is thought to be appropriate only for developing physical, as opposed to intellectual, skills. Alternatively, it may be because teachers believe that when a pupil actually is less able than the teacher, the tutoring mode is more appropriate. But my claim here is that neither of these arguments is correct. Education might be a lot more effective if teachers thought less in terms of transferring knowledge and more about coaxing the student to use a certain kind of thought process. Toward that end we are designing computer-based teachers that focus on coaxing rather than tutoring.

Goldstein (1977) introduced, and John Brown and his associates (Burton & Brown, 1982) have adopted, the useful idea of "coaching" as a model of computer-based education. Although Sounding Board follows their notion of a subtler, less intrusive form of intervention, we wish, in advocating the "coaxing" aspect of coaching, to suggest something more radically different from the traditional model of tutoring. Coaxing means asking students the kinds of questions that will cause them to apply *their own* mental abilities in a new way, rather than concentrating on transferring specific knowledge. It is not just the style of intervention, but the purpose of the intervention, that we have in mind. Graduate advisors are good examples of intellectual coaches. Two aspects of advanced research force the advisor to concentrate on coaxing rather than tutoring. First of all, advising a dissertation project involves helping a student solve a problem for which the answer is currently unknown. Furthermore, by the time the student becomes advanced, he or she will know more about the specifics of his or her little corner of the problem than anyone else, including the advisor. The advisor's main role, therefore, cannot be to supply answers. Rather, the advisor must act as a problem-solving catalyst. The second reason that graduate advisors do not act like tutors is that the goal of graduate training is not merely to teach the student the answers to specific questions; it is much more important to teach the general skills of asking and answering the types of questions that are important in the particular field of research. The advisor can coax the student to try a different path. The advisor can offer questions that might be fruitful to think about; and he or she can suggest broad problem-solving strategies that worked in the past, but actually implementing the strategies and formulating the answers must remain the student's responsibility.

Coaxing is clearly more appropriate than tutoring when the "answers" are not known and when the student may have as much domain knowledge as the teacher, but most educational computers will not be training PhD students. However, even in settings where tutoring is viable, such as grade schools, high schools, and professional training settings, coaxing still has much to recommend it, particularly for computer-based teaching. The realization of computer programs that are as intelligent, or even as knowledgeable, as a reasonable school teacher is still a long way off. The tutor model depends on the tutor being a lot smarter than the student; and although this may be true of human teachers, we would be a lot better off not having to count on it for computer-based teachers.

But even if we imagine for a moment that we could build programs with sophisticated student and domain models, there are still pedagogical motives for preferring coaches. The coaxing model makes the student, rather than teacher, the central participant in the educational experience. The student is encouraged to be more active, and therefore, is likely to be more committed to the experience. Also, coaxing places emphasis on teaching a methodology for skill improvement, as opposed to teaching specific domain knowledge. In the long term, telling students something they do not know is less useful than teaching them to ask the kind of question that will cause them to search for the answer themselves.

Note that the shift of emphasis away from merely transferring domain knowledge toward teaching a method of thinking about problems does *not* imply that one cannot find a way to transmit specific domain knowledge through coaxing; it just takes a somewhat more creative teacher to do so in that mode. For example, a program could coax a student to search for information in an on-line library of case studies—and it could do so without knowing the details of the cases' contents. The rest of this chapter is devoted to describing two different coaxing programs. This is the idea behind the case-adaptation coach. But let us start with a program that does not teach domain specific knowledge at all, but just concentrates on teaching good questions to ask.

The Sounding Board

The Sounding Board implements a theory of creativity enhancement put forth by Roger Schank in his book, *The Creative Attitude* (Schank, 1988). The basic premise behind both the theory and the program is that creative problem solving depends on the ability to have one's mind "systematically wander" over aspects of the problem, and that asking oneself a standard set of questions can enhance one's ability to do this. (This is a simpler, less structured model than the one underlying ABE.)

In his book, Schank identifies and categorizes approximately 45 questions along the following lines:

Question: about objects:
Where does one usually find itens like X?

Who usually uses items like X usually used for?
What are items like X usually used for?
What problems do items like X cause?
Why do people want items like X?

Questions about actions and events:
What usually causes X to occur?
What does X usually cause?
Who performs actions like X?

Questions about Agents:
What motivates X to act as he does?
How does X get the resources to act as he does?
Why didn't do action Y instead of action Z?

The current version of the Sounding Board program knows approximately 700 questions. We started with questions like those suggested by Schank. The question set then evolved, with many new questions added, and some deleted, as we tested the program on sample problems. Some of the questions are very general, such as those above, whereas others are specific to a particular problem type. The program instantiates a variablized question such as those above in order to ask a question that is specifically tailored to the student's current problem. The goal of the program is simply to ask a question that will get the student thinking in an interesting direction.

An excerpt from a typical Q/A dialog with the program looks as follows. The program is asking the questions, the user providing the reponses, and noting any additional ideas that occur to him as a result of thinking about the questions and responses:

Problem Identification

Question: What problem are you working on?
Response: I'm trying to land the Motorola account.
—

Question: What larger objectives would getting Motorola's business help achieve?
Response: It would get our foot in the door of the IC industry.
—

Question: Should we start by focusing the SPECIFIC problem you've identified or the more GENERAL one?
Response: Getting Motorola's business.
—

Question: Is getting Motorola's business a matter of maintaining the status quo, or of achieving something new?
Response: Achieving something new.

Idea Generation

Question: How would you categorize the goal of getting Motorola's business? (For instance, selling, managing, organizing, designing, fixing)
Response: Selling professional services.

—

Question: Who is currently doing the business with Motorola that Alex wants to be doing?
Response: An internal shop.
Response: SciTech.
Response: Some of it isn't getting done at all.

—

Question: Why should Motorola do business with Alex rather than SciTech?
Response: We have more experience in the industry.
Response: We have more general business sense.
Note: I better make sure that I read up on all the latest innovations in chip manufacture before I make my presentation.

—

Question: How can you impress upon Motorola that your advantages are important?
Response: Tell them stories of less experienced competitors.

—

Question: What success stories could Alex tell Motorola?
Response: None.

—

Question: What success stories could you MAKE relevant?
Response: There was the time we reduced Apple's inventory needs by 20%.
Note: Be sure to have Joe get me the writeup of the Apple engagement.

—

Question: Who is really great at solving problems like getting Motorola's business?
Response: John Smith—the boss where I used to work.

—

Question: How could Alex get John Smith's help?
[Skipping inappropriate question.]

—

Question: What would John Smith do in this situation that Alex could do?
Response: Tell a lot of good success stories.

—

Question: What might keep Motorola from appreciating the advantages Alex offers?
Response: Our staff is young.
Response: They might think that we are too expensive.
Response: The MIS manager there is kind of threatened by me.
Note: Make sure they realize that our solution is less expensive in the long run.

—

Question: Who else within Motorola might be better to deal with?
Response: Maybe the operations manager.
Note: Make sure the operations manager is contacted about the presentation.

—

Question: What recreational activities is Alex really good at?
Response: I'm really good at chess.

—

Question: How could you apply the skills that make you good at chess to getting Motorola's business?
Response: Maybe I should do more complex strategic planning.

—

Question: What sets this client apart from others who Alex has done business with?
Response: They're bigger.
Response: They do most of their business with the government.

—

Question: How should Alex adapt strategy to take the special qualities of Motorola into account?
Response: We might want to especially emphasize that the firm has experience with large clients.

Second Example

—

Question: What problem are you working on?
Response: I'm having a lot of trouble with Bill.

—

Question: Would you describe this issue as a personal problem or an interpersonal problem?
Response: Interpersonal problem.

—

Question: What about Bill causes problems for Alex?
Response: He never does his status reports on time and they are usually incomplete.

—

Question: What reasons does Bill give for not doing status reports adequately?
Response: He says he has higher priorities.

—

Question: Why do you think Bill is not doing status reports adequately?
Response: I think he hates paperwork.

—

Question: What skills or knowledge does Bill lack which are required to do status reports adequately?
Response: He doesn't write well.

—

[Jumping to a previous question.]

—

Question: Why do you think Bill is not doing status reports adequately?
Response: Lacks motivation.

—

Question: What unintentional rewards are there for not doing status reports?
Response: People meddle in your work less.
Response: You can leave for home earlier in the day.

—

Question: What can be done to stop associating people not meddling in your work with not doing status reports?
Response: I could scrutinize his work especially carefully when I don't get reports.

—

Question: What unintentional punishment is there for doing status reports?
Response: It consumes time.

—

Question: What can be done to stop associating it consumes time with doing status reports?
Response: I could make it clear what I do and don't really need to know.

—

Question: What does Bill value?
Response: Autonomy.
Response: Recognition.

—

Question: What other situation does this problem remind you of?
Response: It reminds me of when I kept trying to get my girlfriend to go to a movie she didn't really want to see.

—

Question: How was that situation resolved?
Response: I never wound up seeing that movie and we eventually broke up.
Note: Make sure not to push Bill too hard on this. Use subtle persuasion and keep things in perspective.

Many of the questions that the Sounding Board asks are rather obvious. That does not mean that the user would necessarily have thought to ask the questions without the program's prompting. Perhaps *because* they are so obvious users often fail to ask themselves such questions *explicitly*. As a result, the ideas that can be sparked by asking the questions do not occur. As the preceding sample dialogue exemplifies, the answers to obvious questions can lead in interesting directions.

Coming Up With the Next Question

Sounding Board does not use much domain knowledge to perform its task. All of the knowledge is encoded in the questions. Behind-the-scenes inferences are not performed. The basic mode of interaction with the program is not unlike Weizenbaum's Eliza (Weizenbaum, 1966). The program asks a natural-language question, and the user gives a natural-language answer. But the similarity ends there because the objectives of the two programs—and, therefore, the types of questions and the criteria and mechanisms used for question selection—are very different.

Eliza was trying to mimic intelligence, whereas Sounding Board is trying to encourage intelligence. Since imitating a psychotherapist was Eliza's goal, its main task was to find a key word in the input for which it knew something therapist-like to say. For instance, if the user types any sentence containing the word *computer* the program might respond with, "Do computers make you uncomfortable?" On the other hand, Sounding Board's objective is to make the user consider the problem from a useful angle rather than to ask whatever question makes the program appear to know something about a word the user has mentioned. Therefore Sounding Board must respond to user input according to the *type* of problem to which the user's input refers. For example, suppose the user indicates that he or she is trying to become more productive. When the program asks, "What is the cause of your productivity problem?", the user answers, "I don't have the computer I need to get my job done." Because the program characterizes this as a missing resource problem, it will go on to ask resource-related questions (e.g., what the user needs the computer for, how one usually gets a computer, etc.). On the other hand, suppose the user instead answered, "My boss keeps making me switch to a new kind of computer." This is not a resource problem, it is a case of an agent performing an unhelpful action. Therefore the program would proceed in a different direction; it would start asking about the boss's motivations.

To summarize the comparison: Eliza embodied a rather simplistic theory of how to simulate intelligence by indexing the program's questions by key words that could be expected in the user's input. Sounding Board proposes a slightly more complex mechanism: indexing the program's questions by the categories of answers that the user might give to the program's previous question, to achieve the simpler task of encouraging creative thinking.

The major technical issue not faced when designing AI systems, which must be faced when building educational software, is user interface design. For Sounding Board the main issue was how to allow the user to answer the program's questions. A multiple-choice interface would not allow the user to think in the open-ended way that is required to develop creative solutions. A natural-language interface would allow for open-ended input, but is not realizable because robust natural language process requires a great deal of domain knowledge, and the whole premise is that the domain knowledge resides in the user, whereas the program knows only the questions to ask.

Luckily, the program does not really have to understand the implications of an answer. It just has to categorize it. If the user mentions a resource program, for example, the program does not have to infer the implications of missing the resource—that's the user's job. All the program has to do is categorize the problem as a resource problem and extract what the missing resource is.

About one third of the time, categorization task can be accomplished by associating a set of simple response patterns with each question, and seeing if any of the response patterns match the user's answer. The program only relies on this method when the user's response is simple enough that a conclusive interpretation can be made. Most of the user's answers are too unpredictable to be reliably handled by pattern matching.

To handle the majority of cases, in which the program either cannot find a match or has an uncertain match, the system asks the user how to interpret the answer. It presents a categorization/confirmation screen, which allows the user to help the Sounding Board interpret the answer. First the program presents the various answer types that it recognizes for the question (e.g., when the program asks what the problem is, it then wants to identify whether the answer indicates a resource problem, an interpersonal problem, or an unachieved goal problem, etc.). Then, once the user indicates the category that his or her answer fits into, the program allows the user to specify the slot-fillers that are relevant to that answer type. For example, if the user specifies that his or her answer is about an unhelpful agent, then the program will request that the user specify who the agent is and what problematic action he or she is performing. In addition to making the answer understandable to the program, this process forces the user to rethink the answer and to internalize the categorization scheme.

Types of Questions

The main theoretical issue we have faced while building Sounding Board concerns the content of the question theory: What categories of answers should the program recognize for each question that it asks, and what question should the program ask after getting a certain category of response to the previous question? That theory is still very much in flux. Our method for developing it is largely empirical. As we get subjects to use the program, certain questions that the program should have asked become obvious, so we add them. After doing this for a while we began to see patterns develop. At this point we are aware of seven categories of questions that it is useful to have the Sounding Board ask. Codifying these categories helps us develop the question-base further. For instance, we can now develop new follow-ups by running through the set of categories, and asking ourselves if there are any questions of that type that would make good follow-ups. As the theory of question categories matures we hope to write software tools that will make use of that theory to help question writers develop the question base further.

The categories of questions we have identified thus far are as follows:

Questions for Internal Use. Some of the questions the program asks are pretty dull for the user to answer, but the answers are important because they allow the program to follow up with more interesting questions. A challenge to the question writer is to strike a balance, limiting the number of dull questions as much as possible, and never stringing too many together in a row. There are two main question types in this category:

1. **Problem-classification questions.** Example: "What problem are you working on?" These help the program figure out what kinds of questions are appropriate.
2. **Slot-filler identification questions.** Example: "Who are your competitors?" These help the program instantiate the follow-up questions with specifics appropriate to the user's problem.

Thought-Provoking Questions. Most of the questions the program asks are intended primarily to make the user think about the answers, rather than to get the answers that the program will use. The following are the categories of such questions that have been identified thus far:

3. **Attention-focusing questions.** Example: "What do you offer that your competitors do not?" These focus the user's attention on parts of the problem he or she may have been taking for granted.
4. **Barrier-busting questions.** Example: "What computer would you get if price were no object?" The idea of these questions is to eliminate some barriers from consideration long enough for the user to realize what he or she really wants.
5. **Reminding-facilitating questions.** Examples: "Who would be really good at solving problems like getting Motorola's business?" "How have others solved this problem?" These questions get the student to think about solutions he or she may already know.
6. **Context-switching questions.** Example: "What recreational activities are you good at?" Sometimes it is helpful to completely forget about the specific problem-at-hand for a moment, and then to follow up by bringing the new context to bear on the old by asking a question about how they relate, such as, "How could you use your chess skills to help you land the Motorola account?"
7. **Domain-level problem-solving questions.** Example: "Is there some way that parallel processing could help here?" If the program knows questions that are specific to the domain of the problem (as identified by problem-classification questions), then these can also sometimes be helpful.

User Control

The basic premise underlying Sounding Board is that the student will know more about the problem that he or she is working on than the electronic teacher. This implies that the student/user should maintain as much control over the direction that questioning will take as possible. The philosophy we have adopted is that the program should supply *initiative,* while the user maintains *control.* Thus, a passive user will be asked what the program believes are the most appropriate questions at any point, while the interface to the program allows several different avenues for a more active user to change the course of the questioning at any point. The following facilities help the user exercise this control.

An *inappropriate question* button tells the program to go down a track that is slightly different from the one it is currently pursuing. This is important because sometimes a question that makes sense in most contexts does not make sense in the user's specific context. For instance, in the transcript presented earlier, the program started one line of questioning by asking who would be good at solving the user's problem. The user responded by naming a competitor, and the program followed up by asking how the user could get the person to help him. Had the user identified a friend or colleague, this line of question might have been useful, but in the current context it might prove annoying. By telling the program that the question is inappropriate, the user can get to change tracks. In this example, it instead asks how the user could become more like the person who is good at solving the problem.

A *history button* allows the user to examine all the questions and answers that have been given so far and to go back to them and reconsider them, in order to add, change, or recategorize answers.

A *redirect menu* allows the user to jump to a very different kind of question at any point. For instance, if the user gets bored with specific questions about sales techniques, he or she could choose to switch to questions about the big picture, or about decision making, or other situations that this one reminds him or her of.

FUTURE WORK: A CASE-ADAPTATION COACH

ABE explored the role of question asking in the context of a rather structured, case-based theory of hypothesis formation. In contrast, the question-asking theory explored by the Sounding Board project is much less structured. It is more free-form, brain-storming kind of theory, rather than a case-based one. However, the educational mode is not, in theory, limited to such free-form theories. For instance, it can be used to explore the case-adaptation theory as well. We have just begun to design such a program, called the Case-Adaptation Coach. In this section, we describe the outlines of this new project.

The goal of the Case-Adaptation Coach is to teach the student to think creatively about business problems, using Case-Based Reasoning. Three major skills that a student must learn in order to reason based on cases are as follows:

1. To change contexts and apply stored experiences in novel ways.
2. To suspend judgment about solutions that do not quite work in their initial form.
3. To realize that sometimes a bit of creative tweaking is better than either abandoning an old solution altogether or ignoring the potential problems with applying an old solution in a new situation.

The basic steps that a session with the program would include are as follows:

1. Present typical textbook problems along with the textbook solutions.
2. Present a difficult problem that is in some way related to at least one of the textbook problems, but for which no textbook solution will work without modification.
3. Coax the student to select one of the textbook cases presented in Step 1 to use as a starting point in building a solution.
4. Coax the student to identify concerns with the solution he or she has chosen.
5. Coax the student to identify ways of building a new variation on the old solution that solves the new problem.

The preparatory steps, 1, and 2, are fairly straightforward, and noninteractive. But Steps 3–5 each involve an interesting coaxing module. Each step requires a different kind of skill and calls for different kinds of coaching.

Coaxing Case Selection

The idea is to coach the student to remind himself intentionally. This phase begins with the program asking a very broad question, "Does this new case remind you of any of the cases we've discussed?" If the user is not reminded immediately, the program would coach the user to remind him or herself by asking, "What features characterize the current problem?" and then, for each feature that the student mentions, asking if any of the textbook cases shared any of those features. This should generally be enough to help the student notice similarities between the new case and one or more textbook cases. If it is not, the program can attack the problem from the other direction. It can run down the list of textbook cases, ask the student to verbalize the key features of each, and then ask if the current case shares any of those features.

Coaxing Problem Detection

Here again, the idea is to start with rather broad questions, and to become more specific only if necessary. The program would begin by asking a question like, "Do you have any concerns about applying the solution that worked for the 123 Company to the case of the XYZ Company?" If the student voices no concern, the program could push a little harder by asking, "Aren't there any differences between the companies that might be relevant?" If a question at this level prompts a concern (e.g., the student might indicate that the companies are in different industries), then the program would try to elicit possible implications of the differences with questions along the following lines: "How might the fact that the companies are in different industries be relevant to the proposed solution?" The idea is to force the student to identify explicitly a problem he or she can then fix in the modification phase.

Coaxing Solution Modification

Once the student identifies a potential problem with the case-based solution (e.g., "Perhaps the textbook solution would be too expensive in XYZ's industry"), the coach attempts to suggest very general modification strategies that the student might try in order to fix the solution. A number of researchers have identified domain-independent case-adaptation strategies (see, e.g., Carbonell, 1986; Collins, 1977; Hammond, 1989; Kass, 1990). The strategies are of the following sort:

- Reorder the steps of a plan to eliminate a bad interaction between plan steps.
- Find an alternate method of achieving one of the goals that does not cause a negative side effect.
- Combine the current plan with another known plan that achieves whatever goals the current plan does not.
- Replace an action that one of the agents could not perform with another action that he or she typically does perform, and which could cause same effects as the original action.
- Provide additional motivation to an agent who might not otherwise do the job required.

Case-adaptation programs have typically tried to select the best strategy and implement it all on their own. This is a difficult, knowledge-intensive task for a program to perform. But it would be neither necessary nor desirable for a case-adaptation coach to do all that. The coach would just be responsible for suggesting some relevant strategies. It is the student's job to make the final selection and to actually decide what it means to apply a particular strategy to a particular problem. A coach needs only a high-level understanding of its own case library to coax the student toward a creative solution by suggesting a few broad adaptation strategies that might be useful to apply.

SUMMARY: USING COMPUTERS
TO STUDY CREATIVITY

This chapter has addressed two major issues: The role of question asking in creativity and the ways that computers can be used to study that role.

The central point is that although researchers in both AI and education have traditionally given primary importance to domain-level facts and rules, there is a kind of knowledge that is even more important. The most important thing that a person or system aspiring to creativity needs to know is how to ask useful questions. Knowing how to ask oneself a question means knowing how to put one's knowledge to use. Sounding Board demonstrates that even a simple program, with very little domain knowledge, can help a user put his or her knowledge to use, thereby facilitating the creative process by asking useful questions at the right time.

Among other things, ABE and Sounding Board demonstrate that there are really two parts to knowing how to ask oneself questions: One is knowing *what* questions to ask, and the other is knowing *how* to ask oneself those questions. Sounding Board addresses the "what to ask" part but not the "how to ask" part. Sounding Board merely suggests the questions to ask, leaving all the issues related to how to ask those questions to the user. This approach makes it easy to explore many different question types quickly and easily. Adding new questions to the Sounding Board system is a relatively simple task compared to adding new questions to ABE's library. For that reason, it has been possible to equip Sounding Board with hundreds of questions in less time than it took to develop a set of 21 question-asking strategies for ABE.

Since each question in ABE's library corresponds to a detailed memory-search and inference algorithm, ABE is not quite as facile a vehicle for exploring the space of possible questions. But what ABE lacks in breadth it makes up in depth. ABE specifies a detailed theory of what it actually means to ask oneself a question. It also specifies in precise terms the types of facts and rules (and the structure of that knowledge) needed to answer the questions that it specifies.

ABE and Sounding Board thus have rather complementary strengths as cognitive science research tools. This illustrates a more general methodological point we have tried to make in this chapter. AI software and educational software provide two complementary methodologies for using computers to study cognition. Each provides the core advantages inherent in the computational approach, including highlighting process models and enforcing the discipline of producing implementable algorithms. Building an intellectual coach has the additional advantage of allowing a theory to be tested even while parts of the process model remain unspecified (since the student can fill the gap). On the other hand, developing AI programs forces the researcher to be even more precise about the process models being proposed, thus facilitating a deeper, more detailed analysis of the individual components.

In practice, the mode of inquiry chosen to attack a particular problem is generally a function of how a particular researcher was trained, rather than being based on a conscious decision about what sort of tool will best address the questions that the researcher wants to answer. This has usually been particularly true about AI versus educational software; researchers trained in AI build AI systems whereas those trained in computer education build educational software. This is unfortunate. In the future, researchers interested in using computers to study cognition should be prepared to use whichever tool is best suited to the problem they are currently working on. If the goal is to develop a broad theory and to test it with a very large amount of domain knowledge, then the researcher should consider the approach of building a piece of educational software to get a human (and his knowledge-base) into the loop. On the other hand, if the research goal is to do a somewhat narrower but deeper study of a particular component of cognition, and the ability to have the program be tested in many different domains is not as crucial, then a stand-alone AI system may be more appropriate. The two system types we have identified are unlikely to exhaust all the possibilities. For instance, the case-adaptation coach we are currently building is a coach of a more knowledge-intensive type, placing it somewhere between the Sounding Board's simplicity, and ABE's complexity. Computers will contribute to cognitive science best if researchers consider the entire array of computational approaches that can be applied to the problem, so that they can choose the right tool for each job.

APPENDIX: ABE'S 21 QUESTION-ASKING STRATEGIES

There is not enough room here to give the detailed kind of description of the question-asking algorithms presented in Kass (1990). This section contains only a very abbreviated description of each question-asking strategy, concentrating on what the questions are and when they might be asked, rather than on how exactly the system asks them of itself. Each of the 21 questions is presented along with a description of the situations in which it applies, an example of how it works, and a very high-level description of the algorithm involved in asking it.

Replace an Action : Use Action Hierarchy

Question: A very common reason for invoking the tweaker is that an explanation makes a claim of the form, "agent X performed action Y," that the system does not believe. This first strategy addresses such situations by asking the question:

"What other actions are sort of like action *Y*?" This raises a couple of important questions: What does "sort of like" mean in this context, and what is involved in finding a reasonable substitution in memory? Those are among the topics addressed in this tweak description. In addition, because this is the first tweak described, some of the issues relevant to all substitutions will be touched on here, using this specific strategy as an example of how those issues arise.

Description: Replace an action found in the original XP with an alternative action. Search by finding an action that is closely related to the original action in the action hierarchy. Check proposed replacements to be sure they are compatible with the original agent and are capable of being involved in some of the same causal relations as the original action.

Applicable to: This tweak is applicable to any incompatibility problem that involves an action, such as an agent-action mismatch, an object-action mismatch, or an implement-action mismatch.

Example: Applying the JOPLIN XP to the case of Swale's death generates an explanation that includes the implausible hypothesis that Swale took recreational drugs. Recreational drug-taking is represented in the system's knowledge base as both a kind of drug taking and a kind of recreational activity. So, when recreational drug-taking shows up somewhere that it is not appropriate, this strategy brings other kinds of drug-taking actions (such as the taking of medicinal, or performance-enhancing drugs) and other kinds of recreational activities (such as playing at sports, reading books, and going to the movies) into consideration. Some of these related actions can form the basis of plausible explanations in the context of a JOPLIN-based explanation of Swale's death.

Replace an Action : Use Agent-Theme Links

Question: This strategy is an alternate method for dealing with a situation in which the system does not believe that agent *X* performed action *Y*. It asks a slightly different question: **"What other actions does *X* (or agents like *X*) typically perform?"**

Description: Replace an action found in the original XP with an alternative action. Search by finding an agent that is stereotypically associated with one of the categories that the agent of the original XP is in. Check prospective replacements to be sure they are capable of causing some of the same effects as the original action.

Applicable to: The domain of applicability for this strategy is the same as for the previous strategy. Any plausibility problem involving an action, such as an agent-action mismatch, implement-action mismatch, or object-action mismatch.

Example: Applying the FIXX XP to the Bias story yields an explanation that claims that Bias suffered a heart attack as a result of the exertion from recreational jogging. This explanation is not completely implausible, but Bias was not known as a recreational jogger. Even less appropriate would be to apply the FIXX XP to Swale's death, because racehorses are certainly not typical recreational joggers. Although recreational jogging is not stereotypically associated with Bias or Swale, it is pretty clear that some of the actions that are associated with each of these agents could serve just as well in the explanation. Playing basketball is associated with Bias, and running in races is associated with Swale, and each of those actions could have caused the same type of exertion that jogging caused in Fixx. This strategy brings actions that are stereotypically associated with a category the agent is in—the way playing basketball is associated with being a basketball player, and running in races is associated with race horses—into consideration.

Replace Action : Use Stereotypical-Cause Links

Question: This strategy is a third method for discovering an action to replace one suggested in the original explanation in order to deal with a situation in which the system does not believe that a particular action in the explanation, Y, actually occurred. This strategy does so by selecting an event, Z, that the original explanation claimed was a result of Y, and asking the question: **"What other actions typically cause events like Z?"**

Description: Replace an action found in the original XP with an alternative action. Search by finding an action that is indexed as a typical cause of one of the events in the XP. Check that the proposed replacement is compatible with the original agent and the original object.

Applicable to: Any plausibility failure involving an action, such as agent-action-mismatch and Implement-action-mismatch.

Example: Suppose that the MAFIA REVENGE XP is applied to explain a certain death. That XP predicts that X was killed by Y in retaliation for X having killed a mob-brother of Y. But suppose that the evaluator does not believe that X would have killed someone. The action of killing someone would have to be replaced by the tweaker. Inasmuch as the relevant consequence of the hypothesis that X killed Y's friend is that Y becomes very angry at X, employing this strategy in this context would mean searching for a replacement action by seeking out actions that stereotypically make people seek revenge. Actions indexed as having such consequences include cheating someone at business, having an affair with someone's spouse, and injuring someone's friend. Each of these would be brought into consideration by this strategy.

Replace Agent : Use Goal-Satisfaction Links

Question: This strategy begins a second major subcategory of slot-replacing strategies. The first set all represented methods of replacing an action with another, equivalent action. The members of this second set are applicable to many of the same explanation failures, but they deal with them differently. Rather than replace the action, they attempt to replace the agent. This strategy does so by asking the question: **"Who would have wanted to bring about one of the consequences of the action?"**

Description: Replace the original agent of one of the actions in the XP. Find another agent who is known to have one of the consequences of the action as a goal. Check that the new agent is capable of performing the action.

Applicable to: Any agent-action mismatch or agent-object mismatch.

Example: Because the JOPLIN XP requires the victim to inject itself with drugs, it is not applicable to a horse, such as Swale. Even when drugs are replaced with performance-enhancing drugs to account for the fact that recreational drugs are not administered to horses, the system is left with an implausible explanation suggesting that Swale gave himself performance-enhancing drugs. The system would modify this variation of the JOPLIN XP again, however. Using this strategy, the system would search the knowledge base for another agent who would have been motivated to give Swale drugs. Inasmuch as trainers are indexed as having the goal of making horses run faster, which is a direct consequence of administering performance-enhancing drugs, the system could develop the very plausible hypothesis that Swale's trainer might have given him drugs to make him run faster.

Example: The SPOUSE INSURANCE XP fails when applied to Swale because Swale did not have a spouse. But if the system searches for another agent who could have been motivated to kill Swale in order to collect insurance money, it can develop the hypothesis that perhaps his owner might have acted out of such a motivation.

Replace Agent : Use Stereotypical-Agent Links

Question: This strategy involves replacing the agent of one of the action descriptions within an XP. It does so by asking the following question: **"What types of agents typically perform this action?"**

Description: Replace the agent of one of the actions found in the original XP. Search for an agent who stereotypically performs that action. Check that the agent could have performed the action in the current context and that he or she had some possible motivation to do so.

Applicable to: This strategy applies to any XP failure that involves an agent. These include mismatches between the agent and an action, and those between an agent and an object.

Example: Applying the JOPLIN XP to explain Swale's death generates a hypothesis that includes the claim that Swale administered drugs to himself. Taken literally, this is implausible because (among other things) Swale, by virtue of being a horse, was physically incapable of administering drugs. Swale was not a suitable agent for the action, M-ADMINISTER-RECREATIONAL-DRUGS. However, veterinarians typically do administer drugs to horses, and while a variation of the JOPLIN XP in which a veterinarian gave Swale recreational drugs still has some problems, it is closer to an explanation that could be quite interesting. In particular, this strategy can be chained together with the strategy that replaces an action with an alternative that is a neighbor in the action hierarchy. In that case, it could replace the action of administering recreational drugs with the action of administering medicinal or performance-enhancing drugs. The result would be a plausible explanation that closely matches the hypotheses put forth by human subjects when we asked them what they thought might have happened to Swale.

Replace Agent : Use Delta-Agency Inferences

Question: A third question the system can ask in an effort to find an alternative agent it can substitute into an XP is as follows: **"Who could the agent that was originally proposed have caused to perform the action on his behalf?"**

Description: Replace the original agent of one of the actions in the XP. Find an agent who the original agent could have caused to perform the action in his stead. Check that the agent could have performed the action in the current context.

Applicable to: This strategy addresses the specific subclass of agent mismatches in which the agent who was originally proposed by the XP would have been motivated to perform the action, but would have been unable to do so. This strategy has a slightly more narrow domain of applicability than the other strategies for replacing an agent. It only applies to those agent-related mismatches in which the agent, although unable to perform the action in question, was believed to have the goal of doing so. The other strategies for replacing agents that we have discussed eliminate the original agent from the explanation altogether. With this strategy, however, the original agent plays an important role in the output explanation. Although no longer assumed to have performed the action in question, the original agent will be assumed to have persuaded the alternate to convince the new agent to perform the action. (Those other two strategies leave open the possibility that the original agent will play a role somewhere else in the XP, but they do not *require it*, as this strategy does.)

Example: After tweaking the SPOUSE INSURANCE XP a bit, the system might propose an explanation that suggests that Swale's owner killed him in order to collect the insurance money. This could be a very interesting, plausible explanation, unless the system knew that Swale's owner had an alibi. If Swale's owner was known to be elsewhere at the time that Swale was killed, then he clearly could not have performed the killing himself. In that case, this strategy could be invoked to come up with someone, such as one of the owner's employees, who Swale's owner could have forced or persuaded to perform the killing.

Replace Implement : Use Action-Implement Links

Question: This begins the third set of slot-replacement strategies—those that replace the filler of the implement slot in an action description. All of the strategies in this category address plausibility failures in which one of the tools that an XP suggests were used to perform some action is inappropriate in the current context. This strategy addresses such problems by asking the following question: **"What implements are commonly used to perform this action?"**

Description: Replace an implement used in one of the actions in the original XP. Search for one that is typically used to perform the action in question. Check that the original agent is capable of using the implement and that the action, when performed by the agent with the new implement, could have caused some of the effects that the original explanation called for.

Applicable to: This strategy is applicable to any plausibility problem involving the implement used to carry out an action. Typically this is either an implement-inadequacy mismatch, where the action, if performed with the suggested implement could not have had the proposed effect, or an agent-implement mismatch, in which the proposed agent of some action would have been unable to use the proposed implement.

Example: Suppose that the system developed an explanation, based on what it believed about CIA plots against Fidel Castro, that claimed that the CIA attempted to kill Khomeni by planting an exploding cigar in his collection. The evaluator could object to this explanation on the basis that Khomeni, by virtue of being a devout Moslem, would not be expected to smoke cigars. The implement, an exploding cigar, would be inadequate for the task. This strategy would attempt to adapt the explanation by replacing the exploding cigar with a tool typically used to perform political assassinations. Using this method the system could hypothesize that they tried to kill him with a car bomb or with gunfire.

Replace Implement : Use Agent-Implement Links

Question: This strategy attempts to find a replacement for an implement mentioned in the original XP by asking the straightforward question: **"What type of implements would this agent typically be expected to have available to him?"**

Description: Replace an implement used in one of the actions in the original XP. Search for an implement that is typically used by the agent of that action. Check that the original agent is capable of using the implement and that the action, when performed by the agent with the new implement, could have caused some of the effects that the original explanation called for.

Applicable to: This strategy is applicable to the same set of failures as the previous one—any plausibility problem related to an implement mentioned in the XP.

Example: Suppose that the system finds out that someone was killed, and thus invokes the TERRORIST BOMBING XP to explain why someone was killed, but evidence turns up that the deceased did not die in an explosion. The implement proposed by the XP for carrying out the killing is a bomb, but that is not a possibility in the current context. If information is known about the suspected killer, then this may provide clues about plausible implements. For instance, if the suspected killer is a prize-winning marksman, then a rifle is a reasonable guess. If the killer is a pharmacist, then the system will consider the use of poison.

Example: Applying the MAFIA REVENGE XP to the Pan Am disaster yields an explanation that an enemy of the U.S. shot down the airliner with a gun in retaliation for a killing performed by an American. The gun is clearly not the appropriate weapon. The most obvious implement of destruction with which to replace the gun depends on who the hypothesized enemy is. If the enemy was a major military power, such as the Soviet Union, then an air-launched missile would be a likely weapon, because they have been used to destroy airliners before. On the other hand, if the hypothesis was that a terrorist organization committed the act, then an on-board bomb would be hypothesized because that is the weapon typically associated with such agents.

Replace Implement : Use Location-Implement Links

Question: This strategy attempts to find a new implement that could have been used to perform an action by asking: **"What implements are typically available in the location where the action took place?"**

Description: Replace an implement used in an action in the original XP. Search for one that is typically found at the location where the action was performed. Check that the new implement could have been used by the original agent to perform the original action, with at least some of the original causal consequences.

Example: Suppose that a stabbing takes place inside a hospital that has a metal-detector at the door, so that the killer could not have brought any weapon in. It is reasonable to guess that the killer used a scalpel to do the stabbing because scalpels are items found in hospitals.

Elaborate Motivation : Downplay Negative

Question: This strategy remedies a vagueness problem involving an anomalous intentional action by asking the question: **"Why would the negative effects of the action be particularly unimportant to the agent involved?"**

Description: Elaborate an explanation by explaining one of the decisions made by one of the agents in the original XP. Augment the explanation with a hypothesis about why a bad effect on the decision would be less important to the agent than one would typically expect.

Applicable to: This strategy applies to the subclass of vagueness failures that result when an explanation posits that an agent performed an action that he or she would not normally be expected to perform, without providing a sufficient explanation of what might have motivated the agent to perform that action.

Example: This strategy searches for rules that indicate reasons why one of the bad side effects of a problematic action might have been given less weight by the agent than the evaluator would have expected. In the suicide-bombing example, dying might have been less important to the suicide bomber if she were convinced that she were terminally ill and knew she would die soon anyway, or if she were depressed enough to have decided that it was not particularly important to go on living.

Example: If terrorists perform a killing at an airport, the system may replace the standard tool for escaping from the scene of the crime—via an automobile—with an airplane. It may hypothesize that because the terrorists were at an airport, where airplanes are available, that they planned to escape via an airplane.

Elaborate Motivation : Amplify Positive

Question: This strategy remedies problems related to unmotivated intentional actions by asking the question: **"Why would the positive effects of the action be particularly important to the agent involved?"**

Description: Elaborate an explanation by explaining one of the decisions made by one of the agents in the original XP. Augment the explanation by constructing a hypothesis about why a positive effect of the decision would be exceptionally important to the agent.

Applicable to: The same as for the previous strategy: unmotivated intentional action problems.

Example: This strategy is like the last one in that it also looks for value-system adjustment rules that might be relevant to the story at hand, but this strategy looks for a different kind of rule. Whereas the previous strategy looks for a rule indicating why a bad side effect could have been less important than normally expected, this one assumes that the negative side effects have their normal value and instead searches for a reason to believe that one of the positive effects might have been *more* important than expected.

For example, the TERRORIST BOMBING XP could be made suitable to the suicide bombing story if it were elaborated to include a subexplanation that showed why the death of the Israeli soldiers was especially important to the bomber; so important that it outweighed the negative effect of the bomber's own death. For instance, inasmuch as the system knows that the importance of killing an enemy will increase for an agent if the enemy kills a member of the agent's family or a close friend, and it knows that many Palestinians have had family and friends killed by Israeli soldiers, it could hypothesize that one of the soldiers might have killed a friend or family member of the bomber.

Elaborate Motivation : Identify Knowledge Gap

Question: The third method for dealing with anomalous actions is to ask the following question: **"Which of the negative effects of his decision might the agent not have known about, and why?"**

Description: Elaborate an explanation by explaining one of the decisions made by one of the agents in the original XP. Augment the explanation with a hypothesis about why the agent involved might not have expected one of the bad effects of the decision.

Application to: The same as for the last two strategies: Vagueness failures involving insufficient motivation for performing a hypothesized action.

Example: This strategy can be applied to suicide bombing example to give a different sort of answer than that given by the previous two strategies. Instead of looking for reasons why she would not have cared about dying, or reasons why she would have been especially anxious to kill the Israeli soldiers, this strategy would elaborate the TERRORIST BOMBING XP by identifying possible reasons that the bomber would have failed to predict one of the negative effects of the action and therefore would not have brought its negative value into the equation at all. For instance, by using this strategy the system could hypothesize that perhaps the bomber did not predict that she would die because she did not realize that she would be inside the car at the moment of the explosion. Perhaps the people who convinced her to perform the bombing had not told her that the car would explode while she was inside.

Elaborate Motivation : Add Positive Effect

Question: The fourth method we present for remedying problems related to anomalous intentional actions does so by asking: **"Are there positive effects of the action that might have motivated the agent but that were not mentioned by the original explanation?"**

Description: Elaborate an explanation by explaining one of the decisions made by one of the agents in the original XP. Augment the explanation to include an extended projection of the positive implications of the action, which may have motivated the agent.

Applicable to: This strategy, like the previous three, is applicable to vagueness failures involving insufficient motivation for a hypothesized decision.

Example: As an example, we once again consider a way that the TERRORIST BOMBING XP can be elaborated to explain the suicide bombing story. The relevant question is: Is there something positive that the agent knew or believed would result from her action, which the evaluator may have overlooked in its initial projection? For instance, if the agent held the belief that she would be rewarded after death if she died in this way, this additional benefit could shift the balance in favor of performing the action.

Elaborate Explanation : Explain Premise

Question: Addresses a situation in which some premise P is unconvincing, by asking the following question: **"Do I know an explanation that could provide a subexplanation relevant to this premise? If not, can I build the subexplanation on the fly?"**

Description: Elaborate an explanation by explaining a belief that was a premise in the original XP. If possible, do so by retrieving another XP that explains the premise. Otherwise, build the explanation by backward chaining.

Applicable to: Whereas the previous four strategies were specific to explanations of intentional behavior, this strategy is a less constrained, domain-independent strategy relevant to any vagueness problems involving unconvincing premises. It is common for explanations to be free of contradiction and produce reasonable causal chains, yet be unconvincing because one of the causal chains terminates with a premise that is not believable without further explanation. This type of problem is particularly common in the XPs that are output by other tweaking strategies; changing an XP to address one kind of problem often involves introducing new premises to the XP that may not stand on their own.

Example: When the JOPLIN XP is applied to Swale's death, the resulting explanation needs to be adapted to account for the fact that Swale could not have injected himself with drugs. Several substituters address problems like this by searching for an alternate agent who could have performed the action. In this example, let us assume that a strategy is invoked that develops the hypothesis that Swale's owner gave him drugs in order to kill him. The explanation is free of contradictions in the way that the original was not, because humans are capable of administering drugs. But this explanation would not be particularly convincing in the absence of an explanation of the premise that Swale's owner wanted to kill Swale. This strategy can address situations such as this by building subexplanations for arbitrary premises. In this example, the premise could be addressed by invoking other XPs that the system knows. For instance, a tweaked version of the SPOUSE INSURANCE XP could be appended to the tweaked version of the JOPLIN XP to produce a new explanation that concatenates them in an interesting way: Perhaps racehorse owners sometimes kill them by administering an overdose of recreational drugs in order to collect on the insurance policies they have taken out on their horses.

Explanation patterns will not be available to address every subexplanation that this strategy might ever be called on to build. For instance, suppose that the FIXX XP is applied to a racehorse who comes from a family known to be free of hereditary heart defects. In that case, after a strategy is invoked to substitute running in races for recreational jogging, the system will be left with an explanation that is free from contradiction, but that simply assumes that the horse's heart was weak. If the evaluator called on the adapter to support this premise with a subexplanation, the adapter would not (given its current XP library) have any relevant XPs so it would have to resort to backward chaining to build an inference chain that would explain the premise.

Elaborate Explanation : Connect Events

Question: Remedies an explanation that does not tie events *A* and *B* together by asking the question: **"Do I know an explanation that could explain how event *A* might have caused event *B*? If not, can I build the subexplanation linking the two on the fly?"**

Description: Elaborate an explanation by building a causal chain between two events of the events mentioned in the original XP. If possible, retrieve a secondary XP that can be used to explain the consequent in terms of the antecedent. Otherwise, employ bidirectional search, forward chaining from the antecedent event and backward chaining from the consequent, to build a chain between the two.

Applicable to: Vagueness failures related to insufficiently strong causal links.

Example: An XP based on the folk wisdom that too much sex leads to death will not convince an evaluator that is looking for a serious explanation, because it contains no inference chain between sex and death. However, one could splice in a variation of the FIXX XP, which relates the physical exertion involved with sex to death. This would result in an explanation that hypothesizes that too much sex leads to stress on the heart, which, combined with a weak heart, leads to a fatal heart attack.

Elaborate Explanation : Question Prior Belief

Question: Remedies a conflict between the knowledge base and the original XP by asking the question: **"Is it possible that one of the beliefs in the knowledge base that led to contradiction with the XP might be inaccurate for some reason?"**

Description: Elaborate the explanation with a reason that a belief in the knowledge base should be revised. Consider negating one of the beliefs that causes a contradiction with the claims of the XP.

Applicable to: Any plausibility failure.

Example: If the system attempted to apply the FIXX XP to particular person, X, who died a day after having had a medical exam in which he or she was given a clean bill-of-health, the evaluator would be likely to object to the resulting explanation because of the following chain of reasoning:

- If someone with a heart problem of even minor severity has a medical exam, the heart problem will be detected during the exam.
- Heart problems take more than a day to develop from a point at which they are not detectable in an exam to the point where they are life threatening.
- X had a medical exam the day before X died and no heart problem was detected.
- Therefore, X did not have a detectable heart problem the day before X died.
- Therefore X could not have had a critical heart problem on the day X died.
- The FIXX XP could not apply to X because it only applies to people who have severe heart problems.

If an XP suggests that a victim had a heart problem, this strategy would consider the hypothesis that perhaps the victim actually *did* have a heart problem, even if the knowledge base states otherwise. In order to support such a hypothesis, the system would attempt to augment the explanation to explain away the contradiction. The beliefs involved in the inference chain just described can be called contradiction-creating beliefs because the conclusion that there is a contradiction depends on each of those beliefs. The job of this strategy is to undermine the contradiction by negating one of the contradiction-creating beliefs. Perhaps heart problems can develop in a single day. Perhaps medical exams do not always detect heart problems. Or perhaps the victim did not actually have a medical exam on the day before he or she died. Sometimes a creative system must, in service of entertaining an interesting new hypothesis, question the facts it has come to believe.

This strategy considers each of the contradiction-creating beliefs in search of one it can call into question. It augments its input explanation with additional explanatory structure that indicates why the original conclusion (in this case, the belief that X lacked a heart problem) was incorrect. The strategy attempts to locate the weakest link in the inference chain that originally led to that contradiction. It builds an explanation suggesting that the inference chain should be negated or at least qualified so that it no longer contradicts the explanation. For instance, if X were a competitive athlete, the system might support the hypothesis that X did not really have a medical exam with the explanation that X did not want to have his medical problems discovered for fear that he would be disqualified from competition. Because of this, he lied about having had an exam. Or the system might qualify the belief that medical exams detect heart problems with the proviso that this is true only if the doctor performing the exam is competent. It then adds to the XP the hypothesis that the doctor was not competent in this case.

Refine Agent Description : Use Goal Filter

Question: Attempts to make a vague agent description more specific by asking the following: **"Which members of the original agent category would have desired one of the goal states achieved by the action in question?"**

Description: Refine an agent description. Search under the category originally specified for an agent who was known to have one of the consequences of the original action mentioned in the XP as a goal. Check that the new, specific agent is compatible with the action, object, and implement involved in the original action, and that he would have had the goal of performing the action.

Applicable to: Vagueness failure that involves an agent description.

Example: When a generalized version of the MAFIA REVENGE XP is applied to explain the Pan Am 103 disaster, the resulting explanation (that terrorists destroyed the jet in order to extract revenge against the U.S.) is plausible but vague. It is vague with regard to which terrorists might have been involved.

This strategy addresses problems like this by searching for a more specific category that has the following two properties:

1. The new category must be a subcategory of the category put forth by the original XP.

2. The members of the subcategory must be known to have a goal that might motivate them to perform the action.

In this example, the original category is ENEMY OF US. The motivation proposed by the XP is to take revenge against the U.S. in retaliation for an unspecified wrong (of roughly the same severity as destroying a passenger airliner) that the U.S. perpetrated against this enemy. This strategy searches for subcategories of EN-EMIES-OF-US (which include the categories SOVIET-ALLIES and EXTREMIST-ARAB-COUNTRIES, as well as the subcategories of these categories, and so forth, until the system's representation bottoms out at specific individuals, governments, or other organizations). Each of these categories is searched for members who are known to have the stated motivation. Since one of the members of the extremist

Arab nations is Iran, the system checks its knowledge base to see if Iran had a goal that would motivate it to destroy an American plan. As it turns out, Iran did profess to have the goal of destroying an American passenger jet in retaliation for the American shoot-down of one of its planes. Therefore, this strategy puts forward the hypothesis that Iranian terrorists performed this sabotage.

Refine Action Description : Use Implement Filter

Question: Attempts to make vague action descriptions more specific by asking the question: **"Which members of the original action category typically involve an implement that is observable in the current situation or that is related to the agent in question?"**

Description: Refine an action description. Make the original, vague action description less vague by hypothesizing that the specific method used to perform the action was one that involves an implement that either is mentioned in the current story, or is associated with the agent who performed the action. Check that the action is plausible in the current context.

Applicable to: Vagueness failures that involve an action description.

Example: Consider a situation in which a physician's wealthy wife dies unexpectedly. If an explanation-building system applied the SPOUSE INSURANCE XP to this situation, it would produce an explanation hypothesizing that the doctor killed his wife in order to collect life insurance money. Such an explanation contains much useful content but it is silent on the issue of *how* the killing was performed. There are many types of killing actions, such as stabbing, hanging, electrocuting, exploding, poisoning, and shooting. If a more specific description of the killing is required, the system would need to invoke a strategy such as this one to make a conjecture about which killing method is used.

What is reasonable conjecture about the method of killing involved in a murder where the murder suspect is a doctor? The following is one plausible line of reasoning: doctors typically administer drugs; drugs can be used as the implement in a poisoning action; poisoning is a standard method of killing someone; therefore, it is reasonable to conjecture that poisoning was the method of killing used.

Generalize Constraint : Reconcile With Slot-Filler

Question: This tweak addresses a situation in which one of the constraints that the XP places on one of the slots does not match the slot-filler provided by the current situation. It does so by asking the question: **"Can the constraint be generalized to make it compatible with the current slot-filler while still maintaining the causal coherence of the explanation?"**

Description: Generalize a constraint to make it compatible with the current story. Check that the causal links in the explanation still make sense after the generalization.

Applicable to: Plausibility failures in which a slot-filler provided by the current context does not meet one of the constraints posted by the XP.

Example: If the system has a SUICIDE BOMBING XP that calls for a Moslem religious fanatic, and it tries to use that XP to explain a killing in which the killer is
a Christian zealot, the explanation will fail to apply. The system can generalize
the explanation by generalizing the constraint that requires a Moslem religious
fanatic to one that allows for any religious fanatic.

Generalize Slot-Filler : Reconcile With Other Slots

Question: Address a failure in which two slot-fillers, A and B, are incompatible
with each other by asking the following question: **"What generalization of slot-
filler A would be compatible with B while still maintaining the causal coherence of the explanation?"**
Description: Generalize one of the slot-fillers within one of the XP's beliefs to
make it compatible with the other slot-fillers in the belief. Find the least general
node that is compatible with the other slot-fillers in the belief.
Applicable to: Any slot-filler incompatibility problem.
Example: If the FIXX XP is applied to Swale it will fail because Swale does not fit
the stereotype for recreational jogging, which is one of the actions that the
resulting explanation will conjecture that he performed. However, if this action
is generalized from M-RECREATIONAL-JOGGING to M-PHYSICAL-EXERCISE, the
more general version of the explanation is still causally coherent, and makes
sense when applied to Swale.

Delete Problematic Belief

Question: Handles any plausibility within a belief by asking: **"Can the problematic belief be removed while still maintaining the causal coherence of the
explanation?"**
Description: Delete a problematic belief from the XP. Delete the causal links in
which the belief participates. Delete any beliefs that are no longer connected to
the anomaly once the first anomaly is deleted.
Applicable to: Any plausibility problem.
Example: The JOPLIN XP has a number of causal strands that come together to
form an explanation of why rock stars die of drug overdoses. One strand involves
stress leading to a desire for stress-reducing activities, of which drug-taking is
one. Another strand involves a connection between being a rock star and having
drug-using friends. this, in turn, has two implications: access to drugs and peer
pressure to take drugs. A final thread involves the wealth that comes from being
a rock star, which makes it easy to afford drugs.
Although each strand in the JOPLIN XP makes the explanation stronger, that does not
mean that each strand is strictly necessary. If the strand involving wealth were
removed, so that the explanation could apply to rock performers who were not
rich, the explanation would still supply a useful explanation involving the stress
of performing and the influence of drug-taking friends. Alternatively, one of the
other strands could be removed instead, to produce an explanation that applied,

say, to rock performers who were not rich, or star performers who were not rock artists. All that is really needed to build a variation of the XP that applies to these other cases is to prune away the parts of the explanation that do not apply and to check that what is left is still coherent.

ACKNOWLEDGMENTS

Many people have contributed to the design and implementation of the systems described in this chapter. ABE is a descendent of the SWALE system, which was designed by David Leake, Chris Owens, and the author, under the direction of Roger Schank. Louis Pryor helped to implement some of ABE's adaptation strategies. Sounding Board has been worked on by a large group of people. Beth Beyer, Rob Campbell, John Regalis, and the author designed the initial versions of the system and developed the initial question bases, again under Schank's direction. Mike Engber and Pete Welter have made many important improvements to the system. Kerim Fidel has greatly extended the question base.

I would also like to thank Robin Burke, Yehiel Hayon, Tom Lauer, and Art Graesser for very helpful editorial comments.

REFERENCES

Burton, R. R., & Brown, J. S. (1982). Investigation of computer coaching for informal learning activities. In D. Sleeman and J. S. Brown (Eds.), *Intelligent tutoring systems* (pp. 79–97). London: Academic Press.

Carbonell, J. G. (1986). Derivational analogy: A theory of reconstructive problem solving and expertise acquisition. In R. S. Michalski, J. G. Carbonell, and T. M. Mitchell (Eds.), *Machine learning: An artificial intelligence approach* (vol. 2, pp. 371–392). Los Altos, CA: Morgan Kaufmann.

Collins, G. (1977). *Plan creation: Using strategies as blueprints* (Tech. Rep. No. 599). Yale University, Department of Computer Science, New Haven, CT.

Cullingford, R. (1978). *Script application: Computer understanding of newspaper stories* (Tech. Rep. No. 116). PhD dissertation, Yale University.

DeJong, G. F. (1977). *Skimming newspaper stories by computer* (Tech. Rep. No. 104). Yale University, Department of Computer Science, New Haven, CT.

Goldstein, I. P. (1977). *The computer as coach: An athletic paradigm for intellectual education* (Tech. Rep. AI memo 389). Massachusetts Institute of Technology, Cambridge, MA.

Hammond, K. J. (1986). *Case-based planning: An integrated theory of planning, learning and memory* (Tech. Rep. No. 488). PhD dissertation, Yale University, New Haven, CT.

Hammond, K. J. (1989). *Proceedings of the 1989 Workshop on Case-Based Reasoning*. San Mateo, CA: Morgan Kaufmann.

Kass, A. M. (1990). *Developing creative hypotheses by adapting explanations*. PhD dissertation, Yale University, New Haven, CT. [Published as ILS Tech. Rep. No. 6, Northwestern University, Evanston, IL.]

Kolodner, J., Simpson, R., & Sycara, K. (1985). A process model of case-based reasoning in problem solving. In A. Joshi (Ed.), *Proceedings of the Ninth International Joint Conference on Artificial Intelligence* (pp. 284–290). Los Angeles, CA: IJCAI.

Koton, P. (1988). Reasoning about evidence in causal explanations. In J. Kolodner (Ed.), *Proceedings of a Workshop on Case-Based Reasoning* (pp. 260–270). Palo Alto: Morgan Kaufmann.

Leake, D. B. (1990). *Evaluating explanations.* PhD dissertation, Yale University, New Haven, CT.

Minsky, M. (1975). A framework for representing knowledge. In P. Winston (Ed.), *The psychology of computer vision* (pp. 211–277). New York: McGraw-Hill.

Schank, R. C., & Abelson, R. (1977). *Scripts, plans, goals and understanding.* Hillsdale, NJ: Lawrence Erlbaum Associates.

Schank, R. C. (1982). *Dynamic memory: A theory of learning in computers and people.* Cambridge, England: Cambridge University Press.

Schank, R. C. (1983). The current state of AI: One man's opinion. *AI Magazine, 4,* 3–8.

Schank, R. C. (1988). *The creative attitude.* New York: Macmillan.

Simmons, R. G. (1988). A theory of debugging plans and interpretations. In *Proceedings of the Seventh Annual National Conference on Artificial Intelligence* (pp. 388–424). Palo Alto, CA: Morgan Kaufmann.

Simpson, R. L. (1985). *A computer model of case-based reasoning in problem-solving: An investigation in the domain of dispute mediation.* PhD dissertation, School of Information and Computer Science, Georgia Institute of Technology, Atlanta, GA.

Sycara, E. P. (1987). *Resolving adversarial conflicts: An approach integrating case-based and analytic methods.* PhD dissertation, School of Information and Computer Science, Georgia Institute of Technology, Atlanta, GA.

Weizenbaum, J. (1966). Eliza—A computer program for the study of natural language communication between man and machine. *Communications of the Association for Computing Machinery,* 36–45.

Author Index

Printed and bound by CPI Group (UK) Ltd, Croydon, CR0 4YY

17/10/2024

01775685-0010

Subject Index

A

Accounting control procedures, 277, 280
Adaption-based explanation, 306-307, 309-310
  example, 314-328
Anaphora resolution, 193, 206-207
Arc search procedures, 151, 242-245
Artificial intelligence, 304, 329-331
Assumption surfacing, 297
Auditing, 254

B

Boolean queries, 190

C

Case-based reasoning, 307, 342
Causal principles, 262
Causal structures, 32, 35, 153, 237, 296
Cognitive models of language, 191, 194
Command-based interfaces, 134
Common ground, 177-180, 247
Comparisons, 262
Complexity, 257
Computer-assisted software engineering (CASE), 123
Concept clustering, 208
Concepts, 196
Conceptual graphs, 31, 49, 132, 236
  advantages of using, 43
  nodes and question probes, 39

Convergernce mechanisms (to narrow search space for answers), 241-246
Conversation monitoring, 181
Creativity, 344
  creative hypotheses, 306
Critical dates, 224

D

Data models, 51
Databases, 231
  relational, 132, 193
Data-flow diagrams, 52
Decision aids, 273-274, 283
Decision support systems, 287
Designs
  and satisficing, 104
  as inquiry, 104-105, 120-121
  boundary conditions for, 116
  of query capabilities, 144
  relationship to evaluation, 122
  questions as guides for, 90-95, 112-117
Design objectives, 109, 121
Design techniques, 110
Diagnosis, 255-259
Direct manipulation user interface, 125
Discourse Representation Structure (DRS), 193, 199
Discourse Representation Theory (DRT), 193

E

Ease of learning, 106, 108